An Instance of Treason

An Instance of Treason

Ozaki Hotsumi and the Sorge Spy Ring

CHALMERS JOHNSON

Stanford University Press
Stanford, California
1964

To Sheila

Acknowledgments

This book could not have been written without the assistance of several good friends in Tokyo and Berkeley. Masumi Junnosuke of Tokyo Metropolitan University often discussed the Ozaki-Sorge case with me in 1961 and 1962 and helped me obtain materials and photographs in Japan. We traveled together to pay our respects at Ozaki's grave in Tama cemetery on June 3, 1962. Masumi Hisako often helped her husband and answered many of my inquiries by mail. Ozaki Hotsuki generously made available to me several photographs of his elder brother and family. Murata Shirō, the proprietor of Murata Bookstore, Meguro, Tokyo, performed miracles in obtaining out-of-print books, and he brought to my attention several rare items concerning the Sorge case. Muraoka Yoshio, my language tutor in Tokyo, offered many helpful suggestions in my search for materials. Kim Yong-mok, a graduate student in political science at the University of California, Berkeley, worked diligently and creatively as my research assistant during 1963.

I would also like to thank Professor Robert A. Scalapino, Chairman, Department of Political Science, University of California, Berkeley, who supported this study both professionally and with funds. The book was completed with additional funds made available by the Institute of International Studies, University of California, Berkeley.

I am especially grateful to J. G. Bell of Stanford University Press for his encouragement and enthusiasm, and to Gene Tanke for his competent editorial assistance. My wife, Sheila K. Johnson, read and typed the entire manuscript and offered valuable suggestions for its improvement. I am, of course, solely responsible for the material and the interpretations contained herein.

C. J.

Contents

❧❧

Chapter One	THE POLITICS OF ESPIONAGE	1
Chapter Two	INFLUENCES	21
Chapter Three	SHANGHAI	41
Chapter Four	SMEDLEY AND SORGE	60
Chapter Five	THE ORGANIZATION OF THE RING	84
Chapter Six	SPY AND SCHOLAR	114
Chapter Seven	THE FRUITS OF ESPIONAGE	140
Chapter Eight	ARREST, TRIAL, AND EXECUTION	169
Chapter Nine	A HERO OF OUR TIME	200
Appendix: Was Itō a Judas?		217
Notes		227
Glossary		257
Bibliography		259
Index		271

Eight pages of photographs follow p. 182

An Instance of Treason

Cruel are the times, when we are traitors
And do not know ourselves; when we hold rumour
From what we fear, yet know not what we fear,
But float upon a wild and violent sea
Each way and none.
                                              Macbeth

Destiny stands by sarcastic with our *dramatis personae* folded in her hand.
                    GEORGE ELIOT, *Middlemarch*

Chapter One

The Politics of Espionage

※‡‡※

Ozaki Hotsumi (1901–1944) combined in his short life two careers. He was known to the Japanese public as the most influential semi-official expert on China during the first four years of the Sino-Japanese war (1937–41); as the writer of numerous books and articles, and later as a consultant on China to the first Konoye cabinet and the research departments of the South Manchurian Railroad, he proved that he was both better informed and more outspoken on the "China Problem" than any other individual Japanese. But he was also a Comintern spy, a man often called the greatest traitor in Japanese history; and he was hanged by the Japanese government on November 7, 1944. During the time he was advising and criticizing the Japanese government on its actions in China—and also contributing to the general fund of scholarly knowledge on Chinese politics, economics, and social history—he was the leading Japanese member of the Sorge spy ring. From 1930 until three days before the apprehension of Dr. Richard Sorge, special agent of the Soviet Union in Japan, on October 18, 1941, he worked with Sorge and provided him with the most secret information from the highest executive circles of the Japanese government.

Ozaki was never a member of any Communist Party, but he was intellectually a very special kind of Communist. "To be a Communist" has meant something different in every decade since the founding of the First International, and being a Communist in Japan in the nineteen-thirties was quite different from being a Communist in the period of postwar Stalinism or in the contemporary milieu of the "multi-centered bloc." To understand Ozaki's willingness to cooperate with Sorge, we must try to re-enter his intellectual and social environment, try to understand the police state, militarism, fascism, the

Comintern, imperialism, and the nature of all the other forces that assailed the minds of Japanese intellectuals. Even with that sort of understanding it is hard to label Ozaki. He was a crypto-Communist, but he often acted and wrote in a way quite divorced from any Party line. He was completely isolated from the Japanese proletariat, and indeed from any mass movement; and although Sorge reminded him that a Japanese mistake in China would serve the general Communist cause, he often advised the Japanese government against a full-scale invasion of China. Ozaki was a Communist, but one with a private vision; and an attempt to reconstruct that vision should provide insights into the intellectual life of prewar Japan, and perhaps into the problem of political action by committed intellectuals everywhere.

In postwar Japan the case of Ozaki Hotsumi has assumed the proportions of an ideological Dreyfus affair. In 1962 a play entitled "A Japanese Called Otto" ("Otto" was his Comintern code name) was being performed in Japan, and at least one biography and countless reminiscences of him have been published. He has been lionized by an element of the leftist intelligentsia and damned with faint praise by the Japanese Communist Party. Men as different as Saionji Kinkazu, the grandson of the late *genrō*, Kazami Akira, Chief Cabinet Secretary in the first Konoye cabinet and Minister of Justice in the second, and Inukai Ken, son of the murdered last party premier and postwar leader of the Democratic Party, have come together to praise him and his works, and they have been joined by Hosokawa Karoku, Nakanishi Ko, and Horie Yūichi, all prominent prewar liberals and postwar Communists. The letters Ozaki wrote from prison to his wife Eiko were published in 1946 and became the leading best seller of that year; since then they have been issued and reissued by at least seven different publishers, and well over 100,000 copies had been sold by 1962. It is perhaps more illustrative of the significance placed on the Ozaki-Sorge case by Japanese intellectuals that the first three volumes in the series *Gendai-shi shiryō* (*Materials on Modern History*), which began appearing in 1962 under the imprint of the outstanding publishing house Misuzu Shobō, are devoted entirely to the police and court records of the Sorge case.[1]

Although the Sorge case and Ozaki's position in it have been recognized in Japan as important to any understanding of the transformation of Far Eastern society since 1937, the same has not been true abroad. When the case was made public to the world in 1949, in the report released by the Supreme Commander for the Allied Powers (SCAP),[2] Ozaki was gratuitously characterized as a traitor; the U.S. Army had not raised the questions of traitor to whom and from what viewpoint, and had apparently taken no interest in the fact that Ozaki's writings had predicted with startling accuracy the future of Chinese politics. Again, in 1952, in General Willoughby's sensational account of the Sorge case, the real Ozaki was buried in a mass of misinformation and maligned out of flagrant political bias. Willoughby, the former head of SCAP intelligence, wrote of Ozaki, "It is amazing that a man could feel so deeply on the subjects of China, Japanese militarism, and communism, could write so much and so widely, and yet never betray himself to the vigilant Japanese censors and Thought Police."[3] Indeed, it is so amazing that one ignores it only at the expense of not understanding Ozaki Hotsumi, his role in the Sorge ring, the intellectuals who unknowingly aided him before the war and have since become more leftist than he was, and the forces that made the same man a Japanese nationalist and a Comintern spy.

Was Ozaki Hotsumi a traitor? The question is fundamental, but the answer can only be paradoxical: he was a traitor for the most patriotic reasons. First of all, it must be understood that Ozaki was no mere spy; he pursued two careers at once, both of them superficially antagonistic but both actually resolved in his own mind. He was, on the one hand, a gatherer of information useful to the Soviet Union— information that he believed was being transmitted to the Communist International in Moscow, but which was really being sent to Department Four (Intelligence) of the Red Army. On the other hand, he was a highly respected journalist for one of Japan's great dailies, the *Asahi shimbun,* and his journalism was not just a cover for his espionage; he was as liberal as an informed critic could be in the Japan of the nineteen-thirties. After he left China in 1932, hardly a month passed in which he did not publish an article warning the Japanese government of the rising head of Chinese nationalism being provoked by the Japanese Army, and he did not hesitate to point out that this nationalism was serving the interests of the Chinese Communist Party. In addition to his many articles, Ozaki published six books in the critical years between 1937 and 1940, and two of them are of such value to an understanding of the Chinese revolution that they can be read with profit today. Both of these works—*Gendai Shina ron* (*On Modern China*) published in May 1939, and *Shina shakai keizai ron (On Chinese Society and Economy)* published in June 1940—have been reprinted in postwar Japan.[4]

Considered simply as spies, Ozaki and his partner, Richard Sorge (Ph.D., Political Science, University of Hamburg, August 8, 1920), were possibly the most intellectually overqualified spies in modern history. Neither was a spy for financial gain; their motivations were political, and of the two, Ozaki's were the more sophisticated and the more daring. Ozaki became a traitor to Japan because Japan failed to fulfill its self-proclaimed destiny in East Asia. He was an intellectual whose background, experiences, and knowledge compelled him to political action, and the problem he faced is one that everyone in the world confronts today—how his own nation should react to the national unification and awakening of the Chinese people. We shall return to this problem often, so let us pause briefly to outline its dimensions.

In relations between nation-states, all nations are legally equal according to the doctrine of sovereignty, but mutual recognition of sovereign independence is not enough to bring "great power" status. Since the mid-nineteenth century any nation pretending to exercise true sovereignty must possess military power. The indispensable foundation for military power is industrial capacity, and until now only two states have industrialized independently, without being controlled in some fashion by the original beneficiaries of the industrial revolution: these two states are the Soviet Union and Japan. Japan was the only industrialized state in the Far East, the only prewar military power in the Orient, and therefore the only "great power" in Asia.

The emergence of Japan as a truly sovereign state influenced the development of Asian nationalism as profoundly as did the Bolshevik revolution. Particularly in China, Japan was the tutor and exemplar for the earliest Chinese nationalist revolutionaries, as Soviet Russia came to be for their successors. The significance of the Japanese achievement for Chinese nationalists lay in the fact that Japan had successfully forestalled pressures from the European imperialists, and had gained, by hard work and sacrifice, the power to deal with them as equals. Moreover, Japan was prepared to help its Chinese brothers expel foreign imperialists from China, and Japanese nationalists actively aided many Chinese revolutionaries in the years just before the

First World War.[5] But the puzzle about Japan as an Asian nation is that it betrayed the confidence that so many Asian modernizers had placed in it.

Japan became more imperialist than the imperialists — first in Korea, then in Manchuria, and most disastrously in China itself. It was Japan that was responsible for providing the final aggregate of foreign pressure on Chinese society that led to the radical nationalist awakening, under Communist auspices, of World War II.[6] So far from leading an Asian revival, Japan became its most dangerous foe, and opposition to Japan was the rallying cry under which the Chinese people finally threw off foreign influence. Ozaki Hotsumi, as a Japanese intellectual and an acute observer of Chinese politics, sympathized with the anti-imperialist roots of the Chinese revolution. More important, he was intellectually and emotionally appalled to discover—at the age of 27, while stationed in Shanghai as an *Asahi shimbun* correspondent—that Japan not only stood aloof from mass social action in China but also was attempting to reverse its course. After 1937 he knew that Japanese military intrusion on the continent was radicalizing the Chinese revolution and driving it into the hands of the Communists. One Japanese student of Ozaki's career summarizes his dilemma as follows: "Why should the success of the Chinese revolution be to Japan's disadvantage? Ozaki's thought returned again and again to that question. The attempt to solve it became the greatest concern of his later life."[7]

Ozaki knew that the China Incident, as the Japanese euphemistically called their aggression in China, would lead to World War II; he predicted it as early as 1935.[8] He also knew that World War II would provide the crucible within which the conditions for a Chinese social revolution would be forged, and he thought that the war would similarly lead to great changes in Japan. Before 1937 he opposed the war; but when the war itself expanded, he came to support it for his own reasons. If Japanese militarism should cause a Communist revolution in China and at the same time so bleed Japan as to bring about a Communist revolution at home, Ozaki believed that a genuine Greater East Asia Co-Prosperity Sphere might then come into existence. In his mind, this new alliance would be based on the cooperation of a Communist Japan, China, and Russia, and he worked passionately for its realization.

It was within this context that Ozaki reconciled his espionage activities for the Communist International and his service as an adviser to the Japanese government. He believed that his assistance to the Comintern not only protected the homeland of Communism—he was a committed supporter of Japan's "southern advance" against the colonies of Great Britain, France, the United States, and Holland rather than against the Soviet Union—but also established his personal claim with the leaders of the Soviet Union.* At the same time, he supported, after 1937, two Japanese policies that reflect his simultaneous commitment to Asian nationalism. These two policies were the New Structure Movement (Shin Taisei Undō) and the movement for a Greater East Asia Co-Prosperity Sphere (Dai Tōa Kyōei Ken).

The New Structure Movement, which flourished between 1938 and 1940, was an attempt by the liberal intellectuals around Premier Konoye to launch a non-party political movement, a movement that would create a political instrument which could serve as a counterfoil to the military's hegemony in Japan. Because it eventually produced the Imperial Rule Assistance Association (Taisei Yokusan Kai)—the only real expression of Japanese totalitarianism — the movement's original left-wing, anti-militarist inspiration has been largely ignored abroad. Ozaki, who strongly supported the efforts of the Konoye group, believed that the New Structure Movement would prepare the way for an elitist revolutionary regime in Japan, and he actually did some of the organizational planning for this future regime while serving as a cabinet consultant. In the autumn of 1939, he told Kawai Teikichi, one of the subordinate members of the Sorge ring:

"The military is the almighty one in Japan today. However, the army places too much confidence in its own strength; it rushes along in a high-handed manner, but it faces eventual political bankruptcy because of the paucity of its political ideas. The last ace will be Konoye. By advancing him, we can switch the so-called New Order in East Asia into socialism on the basis of close cooperation with the Communist Parties of the Soviet Union and China. However, I do not think that Konoye's strength alone can see it through to the finish. Konoye is a

* According to Aochi Shin, one of Ozaki's former editors, Ozaki told the attorney for his second trial, Takeuchi Kintarō, that he had hoped to meet Stalin personally through Sorge; his idea was to bring about a Konoye-Stalin meeting and to end the Pacific War on a basis favorable to both the U.S.S.R. and Japan. Aochi Shin, former assistant editor of *Chūō kōron* and editor of *Nihon hyōron*, in *Gendai-shi no magarikado (Turning Points in Modern History)* (Tokyo, 1959), p. 191.

Kerensky; he is a bridge to the next political power. I am not now a member of Konoye's five-man brain trust, but I am supporting him for the time being in order to prepare the way for the true revolutionary regime."[9]

Farfetched as these boasts may sound today, many liberal intellectuals, of whom Ozaki was representative, supported Prince Konoye for reasons hardly less utopian.[10] Ozaki's involvement in the Shōwa Research Association (Shōwa Kenkyū Kai), the formal organization of the intellectuals in the Konoye circle, was the obverse of his espionage activities in the Sorge ring, but both activities were related in his own mind. Even after the militarists and their bureaucratic allies subverted the New Structure Movement for their own purposes, Ozaki continued to believe that the pressure of war on Japanese society would lead to a socialist revolution.[11]

At the time he first gained some recognition in Japanese political circles, Ozaki's chief political concern was the avoidance of war: localization and settlement of the China Incident, peace with the Soviet Union, and prevention of a war in the Pacific. But this concern was always tempered by his Asian nationalism—he hated British imperialism and wanted to see the liberation of all Asian nations from colonialism. As the war continued to develop in spite of the efforts of Japanese liberals to wrest control from the military, Ozaki's attitude toward it underwent a slow but perceptible change. Like most intellectuals, he was at first quite skeptical of the New Order in East Asia. But when Wang Ching-wei, one of Sun Yat-sen's closest associates, began to collaborate with the Japanese in China, Ozaki became one of the most outspoken champions of the East Asian Cooperative Body and of the Japanese military advance southward. There is considerable irony in this. The intellectuals of the Konoye group provided the ideological cover for Japanese aggression in Asia—liberation from Western imperialism and the construction of a new East Asia on the basis of independence and equality—and they did it for left-wing purposes. Eventually, both the New Structure Movement and the New Order in East Asia movement (Tōa Shinchitsujo) were taken over by the ultra-nationalists. European imperialism was replaced by the more predatory Japanese variety; and after the Imperial Rule Assistance Association was established, the intellectuals who had originally conceived the movement were arrested as Communist sympathizers.[12] Nevertheless, Ozaki, like many of his associates, had a private reason for supporting the New Order: the vision of eventual unity between a Communist China, Russia, and Japan. Aochi Shin recalls: "When I once asked Ozaki if this [unity] was not the real intention behind his theory of the East Asian Cooperative Body, I remember that he affirmed it with a grim smile."[13]

Because he was in the mainstream of the liberal intellectual movement around Prince Konoye, Ozaki's loyalties were apparently never questioned by his associates. In fact, after he was arrested, Konoye and many others were convinced that the charges were a frame-up by the Kempei or the Tokkō,* an attempt to help eliminate the ostensibly liberal Prince from political life.[14] As an intellectual in politics, Ozaki fought for sanity against mysticism, for international cooperation against national aggression, and for liberalism against fascism, as did many of his non-Communist associates. To judge from this alone, Ozaki was a martyr rather than a traitor. But he was also a Communist and a spy, a Japanese nationalist and a Communist internationalist at the same time.

Ozaki Hotsumi was certainly a Marxist or a Communist, but not in the sense that those terms are generally understood in the West. Virtually all intellectuals and academicians in prewar Japan were thoroughly familiar with Marxism, and anyone educated at a Japanese university in the nineteen-twenties had been exposed to Marxist ideas. Nevertheless, only a few intellectuals actually became Communists. Those who did were a special breed, and one that became temporarily extinct in the nineteen-thirties. Partly for sociological rea-

---

* The Kempei were the military police, created as a branch of the army in 1881. They dealt with military offenses generally, but often saw their function as extending beyond strictly military confines. The Tokkō, or Tokubetsu Kōtō Keisatsu (Special Higher Police, often known in translation as the Thought Police), were created in 1911 as a special agency within the Home Ministry, Police Bureau (Naimushō Keihokyoku), and were specially charged with repressing the left-wing social-reform movement. Tokkō were established in all prefectural governments in 1928, and in 1932 they were divided into six departments: special police work (section one for left-wing activities, section two for right-wing activities), foreign nationals in Japan, labor relations, Koreans in Japan, censorship, and arbitration. The Tokkō had offices in Shanghai, London, and Berlin. They enforced the many security laws, notably the National Defense Security Law (Statute 49, March 6, 1941) and the New Peace Preservation Law (Statute 54, March 8, 1941), under which both Ozaki and Sorge were tried and executed. For a study basically friendly to the Tokkō, see Kobayashi Gorō, *Tokkō keisatsu hiroku* (*Secret Record of the Special Higher Police*) (Tokyo, 1952).

sons, and partly because of fierce police repression, Japan never experienced a Communist movement comparable to those that flourished in Germany before Hitler or in postwar Italy.[15]

Like most educated Japanese, it was as a student—between 1919 and 1925, at Tokyo Imperial University—that Ozaki discovered in Marxism a powerful instrument of social analysis and criticism. At Teidai,* he became a member of the Shinjinkai (New Man's Association), a social science study group of the sort that appeared in all universities during Japan's liberal twenties, but he never joined the Communist Party. Several of his friends encouraged him to do so, but he was scornful of the Party's extremism and factional disputes, and in any case his jovial habits and independent personality would have made Party membership unattractive.

It was not college life but the Chinese revolution—and the place of imperialism in it—that accelerated Ozaki's interest in Marxism. As he later wrote from prison, "Grasping the China problem from a leftist point of view completely fascinated me. It was not that the study of Marxism stimulated my interest in China; it was rather that the unfolding of events in China sharpened my interest in Marxist theory."[16] Ozaki went to Shanghai in 1928 and did not return to Japan until 1932. It was in Shanghai, which he once described as "a huge tubercular nodule of imperialist contradictions,"[17] that he came to know the revolutionary Chinese literati of the Creation Society (Ch'uang-tsao She). Here he met the most famous literary figure of modern China, Lu Hsün, and helped translate Lu's *The True Story of Ah Q* into Japanese.[18] Here, too, he met the foreign Communists who frequented the Zeitgeist Bookstore—including the journalists Agnes Smedley and a man called "Johnson" (alias Richard Sorge), who both shared his disgust with foreign imperialism in China.

In 1930 Ozaki agreed to help Sorge compile information on internal Chinese politics, Japanese intentions in Manchuria, and other data that both men could acquire as practicing journalists. Ozaki knew, or thought he knew, that Sorge was an "official" of the Communist International, and he believed that he was aiding the anti-imperialist cause of the Chinese revolution by assisting the Comin-

* Teidai is an acronym for Teikoku Daigaku (Imperial University); today the former Tokyo Imperial University is known as Tokyo University, and is called Tōdai.

tern. Only after his arrest in 1941 did he learn that Sorge had been an agent for Department Four of the Red Army since 1929.* It is well known today that by 1930 the Comintern was a subordinate arm of Russian foreign policy, but it would be wrong to ignore the emotional appeal that the Communist International had for great numbers of anti-fascist and anti-imperialist activists, even after Stalin consolidated his personal dictatorship. In Shanghai in 1930, as in Spain six years later, many intelligent liberals still believed that the Comintern stood for practical political action against fascism and imperialism.

Events in Shanghai offered Ozaki even more palpable reasons for helping Sorge. Throughout the turbulent years between 1928 and 1932, Ozaki was an eyewitness to the White Terror, the anti-Japanese boycotts, the efforts of foreigners to manipulate factions in the new Nationalist Government, and the Japanese military reinforcement of its imperialist demands. Perhaps the most shattering influence on him, as a Japanese, was the Battle of Shanghai, which took place January 30–31, 1932. On the afternoon of the 31st and again the next day, Ozaki, as the *Asahi* correspondent, visited beleaguered North Station, where the Chinese Nineteenth Route Army, reinforced by Chinese students, was fighting desperately against the Japanese landing force. He saw Japanese soldiers execute bound and blindfolded Chinese prisoners, and he saw the bodies of young Chinese men and women whose positions had been overrun. Henceforth, Japanese aggression in China could never be an abstraction for him.[19]

Even so, Ozaki broke off all contact with Sorge between 1932 and 1934. He returned to the Osaka office of the *Asahi* and enjoyed a quiet life with his wife and daughter, Yōko. (Yōko was born in Shanghai on November 17, 1929; her name uses the first character for the Yangtze River.) He knew many Japanese progressives and Communists during this period, but he still refused to join the Party. He concentrated on advancing his already considerable reputation as a journalist, and he translated into Japanese Agnes Smedley's fictionalized autobiography, *Daughter of Earth*.[20] But this tranquil period was

---

* As Ozaki said in 1942: "Strictly speaking, I have not been able to determine the exact department to which I belonged. This is the first time I have heard that I belonged to Department Four of the Red Army. During my Shanghai period, I generally believed that I was working for the Comintern, and I did not know exactly that I was working for an espionage section." Interrogation of Ozaki by Preliminary Judge Nakamura Mitsuzō, June 16, 1942, *Gendai-shi shiryō*, II, 307.

soon interrupted. On May 15, 1932, Naval Academy cadets assassinated the last party premier of Japan; on February 20, 1933, the famous proletarian novelist, Kobayashi Takiji, was arrested and murdered at the Tsukiji police station in Tokyo; and on February 27 of the same year in Germany, the Nazis burned the Reichstag. These, and many other events that touched him more personally, struck hard at Ozaki's equanimity. In the next year, on a May Sunday in Nara's deer park, he again met Richard Sorge; Sorge asked him to aid the Comintern, and he agreed.

That meeting launched the most fantastically successful espionage operation of World War II. Espionage in Japan carried with it far greater risks than providing assistance to Communists in Shanghai, for nothing less than the respective futures of China, Japan, and Russia were at stake. In 1934, neither Ozaki nor Sorge could have imagined that in 1941 they would report by radio to "Wiesbaden," the code name of their receiving station in Siberia, the approximate date of the German attack on the U.S.S.R. and the result of the July 2 Council in the Imperial Presence (*gozen kaigi*), at which Japan decided to maintain the Russo-Japanese Non-Aggression Pact. By 1941 Sorge would be a confidant of the German Ambassador, a respected Far Eastern expert for the *Frankfurter Zeitung,* and a one-time nominee of the Nazi Party to lead Nazis residing in Japan; Ozaki would be at the height of his influence as Japan's leading authority on China and the war that Japan was fighting there. Before 1941 was out, both would be facing the gallows—but with their mission accomplished.

But what was their mission? One of the most fascinating aspects of the Sorge case is that the obvious answer—defense of the Soviet Union—does not comprehend all the known information on the ring's activities. Ozaki's involvement with the Konoye intellectuals in an effort to stem the tide of fascism in Japan is but one of several activities that lead one to wonder whether he gave first priority to his espionage or whether he merely played at being a spy. Turning briefly to Sorge, we encounter an entirely different dimension of ambiguity.*

Richard Sorge, a German national, was born in Baku, southern

---

* On June 4, 1962, while discussing the Ozaki case with Matsumoto Shigeharu (a member of the Konoye circle), I suggested that Ozaki was a much more complex man than Richard Sorge. Matsumoto, who had met Sorge at the German Embassy in Tokyo, disagreed and asserted that he, too, was unquestionably a brilliant and complex man.

Russia, on October 4, 1895; his paternal grandfather, Friedrich Albert Sorge, had been a Secretary General of the First International and a close friend of Marx and Engels. Sorge joined the Hamburg branch of the German Communist Party in 1920 and went to Moscow in 1924. He worked for the Comintern until 1929, when he was transferred to the intelligence section (Department Four) of the Red Army. Beyond these details, Sorge was radically different from most spies who have served the Soviet Union since 1917. None were ever given the free hand that he had, and the U.S.S.R. never tolerated another man so notorious for his heavy drinking, his extravagant relations with women (including the mistresses of his own espionage agents), and his apparently flagrant indifference to the dangers of his position. On May 13, 1938, for instance, he was speeding through Tokyo on his newly purchased motorbike; having had too much to drink, he ran it into a stone wall and had to be hospitalized for severe hemorrhaging. Except for the alertness of another member of the ring, who reached the hospital ahead of the police and removed various incriminating reports from his clothing, Sorge's spying activities would have ended then and there.[21]

Sorge was different from the usual Soviet spy in still other ways. Like Ozaki, he wrote more on political problems than was strictly necessary to maintain his cover as a journalist. The list of Ozaki's works published between the years 1935 and 1941 (censored by the Japanese government and including only works published under his true name) runs to more than sixty items, or almost a major article or a book per month; similarly, Sorge was a regular contributor to Karl Haushofer's influential *Zeitschrift für Geopolitik* (including Haushofer's seventieth birthday festschrift issue). Moreover, Sorge had influential Nazi connections, in addition to his own Nazi Party membership, and he made a habit of intimidating lesser figures in the German Embassy in Tokyo with his Nazi mannerisms.[22]

What is perhaps most intriguing is that Sorge supplied Berlin with information at the same time he was transmitting his coded messages to Moscow. If we can trust the memoirs of Walter Schellenberg (chief of German foreign intelligence in Himmler's organization), Sorge's reports were highly regarded in Berlin even though it was suspected that he might also be aiding the Soviet Union.[23] It seems most likely that Sorge was sending information to Berlin chiefly in order to maintain his cover as a Nazi; for several years he feared a security check by the Gestapo, never knowing that one had already been made.

Both Sorge and Ozaki used their political connections to obtain the information they sent to "Wiesbaden," but they regularly published the same information in various journals. They were not specialists in technological intelligence, but compilers of political data on the trend of events. Occasionally, like all good journalists, they got big stories that they had to hold back for a while, and they did sometimes send these stories to Russia before breaking into print with them. This is not to deny that they were spies, but rather to draw attention to the nature of their spying and to the paranoid atmosphere in which they operated. The Japanese police, for instance, charged Sorge in 1942 with reporting to Moscow on the February 26 Incident of 1936 and on the agrarian backgrounds of the young officers involved in it.[24] They could have read Sorge's report on the Incident and his heavily researched three-part article on Japanese agriculture in *Geopolitik* years before they arrested him.[25]

Ozaki was a leading scholar on China; Sorge had an authoritative knowledge of Japanese history, folklore, and economics. Sorge often used members of the spy ring as researchers on his own projects, and the Japanese police, upon searching his home, were amazed to discover a library of over a thousand volumes on Asia. From the material compiled about them, both Ozaki and Sorge emerge most clearly as intellectual adventurers (a comparison between Sorge and T. E. Lawrence would not be farfetched); they contradict every stereotype of the typical Communist. Sorge was an idealist who had virtually become a nihilist by the time World War II broke out; his intelligence and his eccentricity have been commented upon by everyone who ever met him.[26] Ozaki's strongest left-wing admirers concede that he had a "feudal" attitude toward women, no experience in the struggles of the proletariat, and a typically Japanese "elitist" attitude toward the masses; he is said to have had both a warm, sociable personality and a somewhat egotistical sense of his personal involvement with the destiny of Japan.[27] Yet while neither Ozaki nor Sorge was a typical Communist spy, each was unquestionably committed to the overthrow of fascism in the name of Communism.

Thousands of pages have been written about the Sorge case in Japan, but nothing resembling a consensus on its meaning has yet emerged. One view is that Sorge was a Nazi agent sacrificed by the Germans in order to indict Konoye—through Ozaki (and Saionji and Inukai)—as a Communist sympathizer. The purpose of such a move, it is argued, would have been to force out the third Konoye cabinet and to bring in a Japanese government that would have declared war on Russia.[28] Powerful arguments support this view, as do the circumstances surrounding the discovery of the ring by the Tokkō and the fact that the only two Russians who ever discussed it, the councilor and the first secretary of the Russian Embassy in Tokyo, denied Russian implication and said that the whole incident was something cooked up by the Nazi SS.[29] There is also the problem of the ring's radio transmitter. When the Japanese police experimented with it, their messages were received in Nagoya, Osaka, and Sapporo, but not in Seoul or Hsinking, and the spies were supposed to have been able to reach Vladivostok or Khabarovsk. However, most of these problems can be resolved. Authorities now agree that the ring was exposed not by radio direction finding, which Sorge always outwitted, but by the Tokkō's breaking down (or bribing) of Itō Ritsu. Moreover, no German sources support the theory that Sorge was first of all a German agent, and Schellenberg denies it.

There are many other theories: that it was all a police frame-up; that Sorge was not executed but traded to Russia for a Japanese spy (which has been refuted by Miyake Hanako, Sorge's mistress, who moved his body from the Sugamo prison potter's field at Zōshigaya to Tama Cemetery after the war);[30] and that the extensive confessions and memoranda written by Ozaki and Sorge in prison would not have been written by real spies. But from the full police and court records it now seems clear that the Sorge group was nothing more nor less than one of the most successful organizations in the history of Soviet espionage. The Russians must be given credit for boldness in making use of so unusual and iconoclastic a man as Sorge.

However, even among those Japanese who agree on the essential nature of the ring, judgments on Ozaki's role in it differ according to political predilections. Former Foreign Minister Shigemitsu Mamoru, not unexpectedly, has argued that Ozaki was a super-traitor who successfully duped the Japanese government into attacking the United States and Great Britain when its real enemy was Russia.[31] On the other hand, Horie Yūichi, a prewar associate of Ozaki's and a Communist since the war, once wrote: "We can never think of him as a spy or a traitor. He gave his life to oppose war and to prevent our country from falling into its present miserable condition. We believe that his activities in the anti-war, anti-imperialism struggle were no different in intent from those of Nosaka Sanzō [present Secretary General of the Japanese Communist Party], who fought the Japanese militarists in north China."[32] Horie changed his opinion, however, after the SCAP report pointed to Itō Ritsu, one of the top figures of the Japanese Communist Party, as Ozaki's betrayer.

In the minds of his closest prewar associates, Ozaki remains an intellectual, a patriot, and an idealist, a man who found a personal answer to the painful question asked so often after the war: "Why didn't somebody do something to stop the growth of fascism?"[33] Most of these men have had long experience in China, and for them the ultimate justification for Ozaki's spying is his acute understanding of the Chinese revolution and his anguish at witnessing Japan's behavior in China. At least two of them, both prominent prewar politicians and friends of Ozaki's, have spent the postwar period attempting to atone for their involvement in Japan's China policy by becoming champions of Communist China: Saionji Kinkazu became a trustee of the Sino-Japanese Cultural Exchange Association; and Kazami Akira, who traveled to Communist China in the mission of the Socialist Diet members in 1959, was an influential supporter of Sino-Japanese rapprochement until his death in 1961.[34] The example set by Ozaki during the war has also influenced many postwar liberals for whom the total rupture between China and Japan is a continuing disaster; they feel that Japan, with her historic position as the first industrialized state in Asia, should be assisting the revolution on the mainland.

Independent researchers have been more skeptical about contributing to the apotheosis of Ozaki. They agree that he was a liberal intellectual with strong Marxist leanings and a genuine authority on China, but they cannot believe that he first decided to help Sorge because he seriously thought it would further his plan for a Communist New Order in East Asia. Certainly, such a motive would have been unrealistic in the extreme. Ozaki was a political unknown when he agreed to assist Sorge, and the later success of the ring's operations depended as much on luck as on the initial commitment of the participants. Ozaki first came into real prominence in December 1936, when Chiang Kai-shek was kidnapped by Manchurian troops at Sian;

as the price for Chiang's release, the troops demanded that he give first priority to a national front against the Japanese and discontinue the civil war against the Communists. With no more information than a dispatch stating that Chiang had been seized, Ozaki wrote an article predicting the outcome of the Sian Incident: the creation of the second Kuomintang–Chinese Communist Party United Front against Japanese aggression.[35] The article made him famous. In the spring of 1937 he was asked to become a member of the Shōwa Research Association. Two months after the Marco Polo Bridge clash, he published his famous *Arashi ni tatsu Shina* (*China Facing the Storm*), and he found his words being taken seriously by the many Japanese now forced to deal with Chinese problems. Even so, it was almost too much for Sorge to believe when Ozaki told him, in July 1938, that he had been appointed a consultant to the Konoye cabinet. Sorge had certainly made one of the luckiest choices in the history of espionage.

Sorge, too, rose to prominence through circumstances he could neither control nor predict. After establishing himself in Tokyo, he cultivated the friendship of the Military Attaché at the German Embassy, General Eugen Ott. Their World War I experiences established a close bond of companionship between them, and the attaché found the Far Eastern correspondent for the *Frankfurter Zeitung* and *Amsterdam Handelsblad* a valuable source of information on Japanese political and military developments. Like Ozaki, Sorge made it a practice never to seek information directly from his contacts; both concentrated on making themselves such important sources of information that their informants would volunteer policy information in order to gain their opinions. Sorge could hardly have guessed in 1935 how handsomely his friendship with Ott would pay off. In February 1938 Ambassador von Dirksen was transferred to London and General Ott became the Ambassador to Tokyo. Sorge continued as Ott's personal friend and indispensable adviser, and he was soon given virtual run of the Embassy. On occasion, he even carried his microfilm reels to Soviet agents in Shanghai in sealed German diplomatic pouches. In 1941, when Japanese police informed Ott that they suspected a security leak in the German Embassy, the only two persons he took into his confidence and asked to assist him in his investigation were his Gestapo officer and the ranking Nazi journalist, Richard Sorge.[36]

These startling developments must be understood in their proper sequence. It took no special brand of courage for Ozaki to join Sorge in 1934. It was not unusual then, nor is it today, for a Japanese intellectual to flirt with the extreme left, particularly if he happens to be a China specialist with considerable continental experience. Ozaki was not the only Japanese "China hand" who sympathized with the anti-imperialist revolution in China; many well-known prewar Japanese students of contemporary China—notably Tachibana Shiraki, Hosokawa Karoku, Hirano Yoshitarō, and Nakanishi Ko—managed to hold positions in the wartime Japanese government (particularly in the research departments of the South Manchurian Railroad) while holding proto-Communist views. Often they had been educated in Shanghai at the East Asia Common Script University (Tōa Dōbun Shoin Daigaku),* and Ozaki knew several Japanese leftist students there during his Shanghai days. Tōa Dōbun was an institutional survival from the days when Japanese nationalists were committed to aiding rather than crippling the Chinese revolution, and it is erroneous to suggest (as Willoughby does) that it was a leftist institution.[37] At the time of the Great Revolution (1927 and after), many of its present and former students supported the anti-imperialist struggle in Shanghai as Asian nationalists. Ozaki was in this tradition.

Ozaki agreed to aid Sorge at a time when almost any other similarly placed Japanese intellectual might have done the same. Then events took over. By 1938 Ozaki and Sorge were no longer merely reporting developments; they were helping to make the very decisions their espionage was supposed to uncover. Even so, it must have been difficult for them to see themselves as spies. They had little reason to fear personal danger. If caught, they would have faced no more than a light sentence under the pre-1941 Peace Preservation Law, and a prison term for violating that capricious act was regarded as a virtual badge of distinction among prewar leftists. The law under which they were executed was enacted only six months before their arrest, and by then it was too late for them to quit.

Of greater significance is the fact that Ozaki and Sorge were jour-

---

* Tōa Dōbun was a large, well-endowed Japanese university established by the Tōa Dōbun Kai (East Asia Common Script Society) in 1901. The founder of the parent organization was Prince Konoye Atsumaro (1863–1904), the father of Premier Konoye and an early advocate of Asian unity. The university specialized in training Japanese scholars in Chinese studies. See *Tōa dōbun shoin daigaku shi* (Tokyo, 1955).

nalists. News-gathering in militarist Japan was not a straightforward occupation. All the best reporters, foreign and domestic, cultivated contacts, for the "leak" was the only source of hard news in Tokyo. It would have been difficult to find a competent newsman in Japan on the eve of Pearl Harbor who had not been accused by the police of being a spy.[38] Sorge himself included in his defense the statement that he had never had to steal information; it was, he said, supplied to him.[39] There was no such thing as a political "secret" in Tokyo journalistic circles, and many (although not all) of the facts that the Tokkō accused the ring of transmitting to Moscow (the capital of a nation with which Japan was not at war) were common, published information.

In the light of these considerations, some postwar analysts have argued that Ozaki's involvement with Sorge was something less than an act of conscious commitment. Kaji Ryūichi, former chief editorial writer for the *Asahi* and one of Ozaki's fellow employees, has stated that "those who knew Ozaki well and knew his case thoroughly considered him to be a victim of the times, an inquisitive intellectual who was unfortunate."[40] This view is in conformity with a different approach—one that places Ozaki squarely in the midst of all the other liberal intellectuals who had their backs to the wall after the failure of parliamentarism in Japan. Members of the intelligentsia in the period of the military cliques (*gumbatsu*) were characterized, as they still are today, as converts or recanters (*tenkōsha*), because in order to survive during the nineteen-thirties they had to subscribe publicly to the prevailing national myths of Japan. Since none of them had been supporters during the nineteen-twenties of the inflated myth of the organic unity of the state (*kokutai*) or of Japan's special role among nations, those who went through the required motions of public life in the succeeding decade must have been "converts." Among such intellectuals, as well as among left-wingers, some made "disguised conversions" (*gisō tenkō*); the members of the Shōwa Research Association, and Ozaki in particular, are considered today the most representative members of this group.[41] As disguised converts (*gisō tenkōsha*) few of those who survived the war have had difficulties living down their wartime affiliations; among them are Rōyama Masamichi, Taira Teizō, Ryū Shintarō, Ushiba Tomohiko, Matsumoto Shigeharu, and many other Japanese intellectuals and politicians of liberal views. The intellectual who towered above these men and influenced all of them, Miki Kiyoshi (1897–1945), did not himself survive the war.[42]

Ozaki was also a *gisō tenkōsha* who ostensibly supported ultra-nationalist policies of aggression, but he did so for liberal, and even Communist, reasons. He thus went further than most, but the distinction is still one of degree. Because he combined the roles of government adviser and spy, his case has had great fascination for postwar intellectuals who have tried to assess Japan's recent history and attempted to assign responsibility for the war. In the face of fascism, was the role of *gisō tenkōsha* an appropriate response for a "humanist" (the universal term in postwar Japan for a member of the non-Communist left)? Is treason a meaningful concept when the leadership of a nation has fallen into the hands of men who are driving it toward its own destruction? (Wasn't General Willoughby forgetting, in his fulminations against the "grimacing face of the Red Medusa" and the "twilight zone of fellow-traveling dupes and befuddled liberals,"[43] that the traitor to Japanese militarism could be considered his wartime ally?) On the other hand, is the specific content of Ozaki's synthesis between his governmental activities and his spying for Russia supportable? Did Ozaki even believe in it himself, or was it something that occurred to him only in prison, when he wondered whether his double life might not have been schizophrenic? From Ozaki's prison letters we occasionally gain the impression that his own heroism frightened him in retrospect: "I literally risked my life for my beliefs and ideology. Thinking this over again now is difficult—like dying once and coming back to life. One may dream that he passed the night on an overhanging cliff and then was miraculously saved, but the torment until he reaches safety is truly indescribable. However, I have now reached a point where all is calm. Only someone who has risked his life for his beliefs can understand this."[44]

The Sorge-Ozaki case is one of the great spy stories, filled with unforgettable details. In order to avoid drawing attention to themselves, the ring's five members would gather at Sorge's Azabu house as guests at one of his prodigious drinking parties; then, after the Nazis and the Japanese army officers had left, these five—notorious as late carousers—would hold their meetings. But theirs is much more than a spy story; it is a piece of history within a fabric of historical events that is still profoundly significant. The Sino-Japanese war became the vehicle for the social mobilization of the Chinese people, and it placed the leadership of that movement in the hands of the Chinese Communist Party. While Ozaki understood the dynamic forces involved in the Chinese revolution, his belief that the Comintern might provide a framework for international cooperation was utopian. A Communist community of nations now seems laughable in the light of the Sino-Soviet split, but the appeal of the Comintern to men like Ozaki in the nineteen-thirties was an important element in promoting the Chinese Communist revolution. Ozaki may never have understood that the secrets he sent to the "Comintern" were not likely to help the Chinese masses; but he understood the fundamental strength of those masses in a way that his militarized countrymen never grasped and that the Soviet Union is only now beginning to comprehend.

Men will continue to differ in their judgments of Ozaki. For some he will be a tragic figure, for others a contemptible traitor, and for a few an object of pity. But all will agree that the roots of his behavior rest in a genuine tragedy—the fact that Asia's one industrialized nation so confounded the Chinese revolution that at last only an anti-Japanese totalitarian dictatorship in China could hope to overcome the chaos brought on by the war. Irrespective of personal praise or blame, Ozaki's life offers us a microcosm of the tragedy of Far Eastern politics in the twentieth century.

Chapter Two

Influences

✿✿✿

Ozaki Hotsumi's only connections with the working class were symbolic: he was born on May Day and hanged on the twenty-seventh anniversary of the Bolshevik revolution. Although his parents were of humble, even poor, background, none of his ancestors has the slightest claim to proletarian status. Ozaki had been an honored name among the rural samurai (*gōshi*) in Gifu prefecture from the time of Kusunoki Masanori, in the fourteenth century; and until 1929, Ozaki's permanent registered domicile (*honseki*) still read "West Shirakawa village, Kamo district, Gifu prefecture"—names that evoke the traditions of the Taira and Japan's military past. But Ozaki never lived in Gifu (although he did borrow the name Shirakawa, or "white river," for his most famous pseudonym, Shirakawa Jirō); he was born on May 1, 1901, in the Shiba (now Minato) ward of Tokyo. When he was six months old his parents took him to the new Japanese colony of Taiwan, and he did not return to the capital until he was eighteen.

At the time Hotsumi was born, his father, Ozaki Hotsuma (he had changed his given name, Hotarō, while a student in Tokyo), was a poorly paid journalist. He had come to the city at the age of nineteen intending to study medicine, but he soon abandoned the idea of becoming a physician and devoted himself entirely to poetry and Chinese (*Kambun*), an avocation he had learned from his father. In the eighteen-nineties Hotsuma held various magazine editorial positions, wrote poems, and married Nomura Kita, a young widow and the daughter of a minor ex-samurai (a man who had been the secretary in Edo of Doi Ōinokami, one of the Tokugawa vassals). He was soon in need of a more secure position in order to support his growing family (his first son, Honami, was born in 1898), and immediately after Hotsumi was born, he left Tokyo for Taiwan, where he had accepted a post on the colony's only newspaper.

Taiwan in 1901 had been a Japanese possession for only six years, and the natives were still waging guerrilla warfare against their new rulers. The Governor-General at that time was General Kodama Gentarō* and the Chief of the Civil Affairs Department was Gotō Shimpei.† These two men were to restore order on the island and transform it into a profit-making Japanese colony. Gotō, in particular, was charged with devising policies that would quell the civil disturbances, and in 1898 he placed Taiwan under emergency law and promulgated his "bandit punishment order," which specified severe penalties for any kind of anti-Japanese activity. He also enforced the *pao chia* system of neighborhood collective responsibility in order to break communication between the "bandits" and the civilian population, and he offered clemency to partisans who would surrender. In 1900, despite some Japanese success in suppressing the resistance, the Boxer Rebellion in China spurred the Taiwanese into renewed activity. According to official estimates, between 1897 and the virtual extermination of the partisans in the summer of 1902, over 7,500 persons were killed and 8,700 were arrested. Even after that, Taiwanese rebellions occurred with great frequency.[1]

Ozaki's father was indirectly employed by Gotō Shimpei. Before Hotsuma's arrival, there had been two newspapers in Taiwan: the *Taiwan shimpō,* which began publication on June 17, 1896, and the *Taiwan nippō,* which brought out its first issue on May 8, 1897. Both were sensation-mongering papers of the worst Meiji sort, and they were an annoyance to the Civil Administrator because they ran exposés of the colonial government's shortcomings. Moreover, one paper was affiliated with the Chōshū clan and the other with Satsuma —the two principal competing factions among Meiji leaders. In 1898, to put an end to their sniping at the colonial government and at each other, Gotō ordered the two papers to combine into one, the *Taiwan*

---

* General Kodama (1852–1906) served on the General Staff during the Sino-Japanese War of 1894–95, which resulted in Japan's acquisition of Taiwan. Later he was Chief of Staff to Marshal Ōyama Iwao in Manchuria during the Russo-Japanese War, and he became Chief of the General Staff in 1906. He and Gotō are known today as the pacifiers of Taiwan.

† Gotō Shimpei (1857–1929) was one of the most famous Japanese politicians and bureaucrats of the early twentieth century. He served as Civil Administrator of Taiwan from 1898 to 1906, and then became head of the new South Manchurian Railroad. He held innumerable cabinet posts, notably as Foreign Minister during the Siberian Expedition; he negotiated with A. A. Joffe in 1923 concerning the Soviet-Japanese dispute; and he is known as the rebuilder of Tokyo after the earthquake.

nichi-nichi shimpō. He also insisted that the new journal include a Chinese-language section, which was designed to win support among educated Taiwanese for the government's anti-resistance campaign. Because of his knowledge and ability in Chinese, Ozaki's father was hired in 1901 as a journalist for the Chinese section of the *Taiwan nichi-nichi shimpō*.

In 1899 Governor-General Kodama had established in the suburbs of Taihoku (the Japanese reading for T'aipei) a special compound for Japanese residents called Nants'aiyüan, and it was here that the Ozaki family came to live. Ozaki Hotsumi was raised and educated in Taiwan, and he did not leave the island until he went to Tokyo to enter the Imperial University. The importance of this upbringing for Ozaki cannot be overstated; in later years he experienced an acute sense of guilt when he recalled his childhood—a feeling shared by many Westerners who have witnessed the humiliations of colonialism as young members of the ruling class.[2] In his first *tenkōsho* (conversion statement), completed in Sugamo prison, June 8, 1943, Ozaki recalled: "One experience of my youth which was different from that of most persons is that in my contacts with the people of Taiwan, even in quarrels with my boyhood companions, my connection with the controlling and governing classes was revealed to me as a concrete fact of daily life. This experience later aroused in me an extraordinary interest in the problem of national liberation, and it also gave me an insight into the China problem."[3]

Ozaki's father had been an almost penniless journalist in Tokyo, but in Taiwan he and his family were members of the ruling elite. His son Hotsumi attended special schools established by the colonial government for the children of Japanese, and he was brought home from school in a ricksha. Even the education he received was different from that offered in Japan. After completing elementary school (1908–13), Ozaki enrolled in Section One of the Taihoku Japanese Middle School (equivalent to a high school), an institution patterned after the English system. Gotō Shimpei, who established the school in 1899 with only 26 students, had ideas of training a colonial elite, and he employed an English headmistress to teach deportment and "self-reliance" to the dependents of his administrators. In middle school, where all the students were boarders, Ozaki received a cosmopolitan basic education; he made the English language his best subject.

This was not the life to which Ozaki's parents had been accustomed, and his father reacted to it by becoming a strong Japanese nationalist.

Ozaki Hotsuma has been described as a "fierce advocate of the Imperial Way" (*kōdōshugisha*)—that is, a believer in the unique qualities and mission of the Japanese race to lead the peoples of East Asia —and he attempted to justify the policies of colonialism to his son in these terms.[4] During Ozaki's school days, there was a lot for his father to explain. Gotō Shimpei had consolidated Japanese rule by 1902 and had begun constructing railroads, introducing hygiene, and improving the harbors; but the Taiwanese, influenced by the Wuch'ang Rebellion in China, resumed armed resistance to the Japanese in 1911. Ozaki's younger half-brother estimates that three to four thousand persons were killed in the rebellion between 1911 and 1915.[5] Also, the Japanese initiated in 1910 their *riban seisaku,* the policy of subjugating and forcibly assimilating the aboriginal Kao-sha, a racial minority living in the mountains of Taiwan. Ozaki's father participated in some of the operations against these Malay-derived peoples, operations that lasted until at least 1933 and produced the Kao-sha uprising of 1930.

Ozaki Hotsuma's belief in Japan's civilizing mission was not significantly different from that of several other Meiji leaders (Konoye Atsumaro, Prince Konoye's father, for example), but he had encountered Japanese nationalist ideology earlier than most. His father (Ozaki's grandfather), Ozaki Matsutarō, had been a follower of Hirata Atsutane (1776–1843), one of the first advocates of the "divinity" of the Japanese people. As a youth in Gifu, Ozaki Hotsuma had studied Shintō and the Japanese classics (*kokugaku*) well before his position in Taiwan made such an ideological rationale useful, and well before it became the national cult of Japan.[6] Moreover, his interest in and knowledge of the Chinese classics complemented his belief in a twentieth-century Asian renaissance. Hotsuma sought to transmit these facts and ideas to his son. During Hotsumi's vacations from middle school, his father taught him Chinese and gave him a foundation in Sinology. Hotsuma had Ozaki reading in Confucianism and the dynastic histories while he was a high school student, and he recited to him stories and maxims from the classical Chou period. It was a foundation that Ozaki made good use of later, although it was a use undreamed of by his father.

Ozaki's mother was a very different sort of person. Ozaki Kita was thirteen years older than her husband and had been previously married to a police official named Kurogawa, to whom she had borne five children. Following Kurogawa's premature death after a long illness, she left these children with his brother (who had been supporting them all after Kurogawa's death) and married Ozaki Hotsuma. In her new life, Kita gave birth to three more boys, Honami, Hotsumi, and Hotsuka. (Hotsuka succumbed to an illness while a prep school student in Kōchi, Shikoku.)* Little is known about Kita, but we may infer from the circumstances of her second marriage that she possessed an independent mind in the face of Japanese family customs. It may be that Kita transmitted some of her independent character traits to her seventh child, as Ozaki himself believed. In one of his prison letters to Eiko, he wrote: "I believe that the main distinguishing characteristic of my personality is an open-mindedness—at present, to a fault! Partly this is inherited from my mother, and partly it is due to the southern climate of Taiwan, where I spent my childhood and youth."[7] There is no doubt that Ozaki possessed an open, "Mediterranean" personality of the sort unusual among Japanese; all of his associates have commented upon it. Moriyama Takashi of the *Asahi*, a close friend from the time he met Ozaki in Shanghai in 1928, describes him as cheerful, rash, quick to jump to conclusions, sociable, and something of a dandy.[8]

Despite the unrest of the colony in which Ozaki was raised, he seems to have had a happy childhood; his letters from prison were filled with fond recollections of the mountains and the climate of Taiwan. Such features of his environment as the police station directly opposite the Japanese civilians' compound, its stone exterior pierced with rifle embrasures, stuck in his memory, but they influenced him only retrospectively.[9] Ozaki was not an opponent of imperialism, nor was he even aware that there were two sides to the issue, when he graduated from Taihoku Middle School in 1918. His ambitious parents knew that he had a greater potential for advancement than their other sons, and they accordingly sought for him the kind of education that would admit him to the highest circles of Japanese life.

As World War I was drawing to a close, Ozaki applied for admission to the Tokyo Dai-Ichi Kōtō Gakkō (First Higher School, abbre-

---

* Kita herself died long before her husband (in December 1933), and Hotsuma took a second wife, Yoshida Kimi. Kimi, however, had long been Hotsuma's mistress and had already had two children by him—a boy, Hotsuki, and a girl, Hotsue. Ozaki Hotsuki, Hotsumi's younger half-brother by more than twenty years, never knew his famous relative; but his interest in Shōwa history has led him to become the leading writer on the Sorge case in postwar Japan. His sensational book *Ikite iru yuda (The Living Judas)*, published in 1959, is the most serious attack on Itō Ritsu as the betrayer of the Sorge ring to be written from a basically left-wing point of view.

viated Ichikō), graduation from which was the initial step toward a degree from Tokyo Imperial University. Ichikō was one of several preparatory colleges established after the Meiji Restoration to train students for entrance to the Imperial Universities. Admission was by three-day formal examination and was highly restricted; as a consequence, a close *esprit de corps* developed among the chosen students that often lasted throughout their adult lives. Ozaki was admitted to Ichikō (located at Hongō, which is today the site of Tokyo University) in September 1919, when he registered in the Department of Literature, Second Form (foreign languages, emphasizing German). Two other young men who figure prominently in the Sorge case were among the select forty beginning the study of German with Ozaki in 1919. One of them, Ushiba Tomohiko, became one of the private secretaries to the Premier in the first Konoye cabinet, and was to invite Ozaki into the innermost Konoye brain trust, the Asameshi Kai (Breakfast Society); the other, Matsumoto Shin'ichi, became a journalist and a China specialist, and was the closest adviser to the Ozaki family during Hotsumi's treason trials.

In one sense, Ozaki was better prepared than most of his classmates to profit from the education he was about to receive; his life in Taiwan had given him a perspective on the world outside of Japan that other students did not enjoy. However, no young man of eighteen from a good family and intending to pursue a bureaucratic career could be fully alerted to the challenges that he would encounter at the university. The end of the First World War ushered in a period of intellectual and social iconoclasm in Japan that was unmatched until the American occupation after World War II. In their prep school days, Ozaki and his classmates heard of the controversies that were beginning to assail the Imperial University (such as the Morito Incident), but they were mainly engrossed by neo-Kantianism. The only foreign authors that Ozaki recalled having read during this period were Wilhelm Windelband and Heinrich Rickert. In Japanese, he was introduced to the works of the German-trained economic philosopher Sōda Kiichirō.

When Ozaki graduated from Ichikō and entered Tokyo Imperial University in March 1922, he began to respond to the social pressures erupting in Japan after the war. It was then five years after the Russian revolution, and the Japanese intervention in Siberia, which was to discredit the army for almost a decade, was just coming to a close.

Nishida Kitarō, representing a new wave of idealism in philosophy, was lecturing at Kyoto University; and the principles of democracy and socialism, stimulated by Allied propaganda during the war and then brought into question at Versailles, were being closely debated in educated circles. Unrest among industrial workers and farmers was becoming conspicuous. In 1922, peasant associations were organized and tenant demonstrations took place in Hokkaidō and Hyōgo prefectures; and on July 25, some 1,500 workers struck the Noda Shōyu works. Later in the same year, on November 25, seven to nine thousand women workers walked out of the Kishiwada, Izumi, and Terada spinning mills in Osaka, thereby threatening to cut off production of Japan's basic export, textiles. As Ozaki took up his studies in the Political Science Department of the Law School at Teidai, the Women's League to Obtain Political Rights was formed; and on July 25, 1922, the famous Communists Sakai Toshihiko, Yamakawa Hitoshi, Arahata Kanson, Kondō Eizō, and Tokuda Kyūichi established a committee for organizing a Japanese Communist Party.[10]

In the years that followed, Ozaki heard many conflicting views of Japan's future and an intellectual's proper role in it. At the university he attended the lectures of Minobe Tatsukichi, the liberal legal specialist who advocated *tennō kikansetsu,* an interpretation of the Meiji Constitution that would have moved Japan further along the road toward genuine parliamentary government. He also heard the lectures of Professor Uesugi Shinkichi, an archconservative who propounded a theory of the absolute sovereignty of the emperor (*tennō shukensetsu*)—the view that ultimately prevailed and made possible the independence of the military from the powerless Japanese Diet. Ozaki not only studied Japanese political and legal philosophy; he became sensitive to social issues simply by reaching political consciousness in this particular period of his nation's history.

Japan was ripe for labor organization, and both Communists and right-wingers worked to manipulate it. With the slackening of the war boom that had brought Japan into the first rank among industrial nations, popular discontent swelled to major proportions. Japanese workers and farmers began to listen sympathetically to anti-capitalist propaganda at home and to agitation for expansion abroad. Moreover, the success of the Anglo-Saxon nations at Versailles in defeating the racial equality clause in the peace treaty and the passage of the Oriental exclusion act of 1924 in the United States encouraged a sense of chauvinism among all Japanese. In the late Taishō period, while the Communists and the ultra-nationalists vied for control of the maturing Japanese nation, the mass of the population progressively lost faith in the ability of its parliament or its politicians to do anything at all. It was commonly believed, and not without reason, that the Diet was controlled by the capitalists. Whether or not most Japanese genuinely desired a "national renovation," it is certain that they were discontented, and extremist organizations of both the left and the right went well beyond the law in trying to capitalize on this discontent.[11]

There were many specific incidents that influenced Ozaki at this time. He later recalled, in his first tenkōsho from Sugamo prison: "When I entered the Law School of Tokyo Imperial University (1922), I began little by little to experience doubts about the course that I ought to pursue. The cause of these doubts, of course, was the indefinable sense of insecurity that had seized Japanese society. It was in this context that 1923 became the first major turning point of my life. In the summer of that year the first wave of arrests of Communists took place;* and many of those arrested—including Sano Manabu and Inomata Tsunao—were affiliated with Waseda University. I was living near Waseda at that time, and these arrests made a particularly deep impression on me."[12] Ozaki mentions several other incidents that led him to take a greater interest in politics. The most important among these was the Kantō earthquake of September 1, 1923, and the man-made tragedy that accompanied that greatest of natural disasters.

The Kantō earthquake destroyed much of Tokyo and all of Yokohama, killing some 132,807 people. In its immediate aftermath there were several incidents of blind and wanton murder involving members of outcast and left-wing groups. The most widespread attacks were on Koreans; violent mobs seized, tortured, and killed Koreans in the frantic belief that they were using the disaster as an opportunity for rebellion. As Noel Busch has written: "Wars arouse patriotic fervor and a sense of purpose, but earthquakes are more likely to produce gloom, despair, and inertia. They generate resentment, but this is not directed toward anyone in particular; it is a rage completely

---

* On June 5, 1923, the Tokyo police arrested more than a hundred leftist sympathizers under the Radical Social Movements Control Law of 1922. They took virtually no action against radical right-wing organizations.

at loose ends and one which seeks a target."[13] The Koreans, a despised and outcast group, became the object of the wrath of many dazed survivors of September 1, 1923. Busch estimates that between 500 and 1,000 Koreans were killed; Korean estimates, perhaps reflecting an understandable sense of outrage, run to over 6,000.[14] By the third day after the earthquake, the attacks stopped as suddenly as they had begun.

More difficult to understand is the calculated killing of Communists and labor leaders by the police. Immediately after the earthquake, Kawai Yoshitora and eight other leaders of the Nankatsu Labor Union were taken to the Kameido police station and killed.* Even more appalling was the arrest of Ōsugi Sakae, a leader of the labor movement since the late Meiji period and the best-known Japanese anarchist. He and his family were seized by the Kempei and then killed in their cells by Captain Amakusa Masahiko (who, after serving a ten-year sentence, played an active role in the government of Manchukuo). Whatever caused these incidents, they had a profound effect on Ozaki. In his *tenkōsho,* he wrote that the fate of the Koreans, the Nankatsu union leaders, and Ōsugi produced in him an urgent desire to learn more about the relationship between politics and the treatment of minorities. It is not known whether Ozaki had yet even heard of Marx, but he does date his intention to study "social problems" from the time of the Great Earthquake.

Shortly after these events took place, Ozaki became a member of the Shinjinkai (New Man's Association) at Teidai. The Shinjinkai, founded on December 23, 1918, was the first and most famous of the social science study groups created by students at Japanese universities after the First World War. Another equally well-known organization, the Kensetsusha Dōmei (League of Builders), was organized at Waseda University in the same period. Both of these associations had students who were Communists—the most famous being the Shinjinkai leaders Shiga Yoshio and Itō Yoshimichi, who later attained commanding positions in the Japanese Communist Party—but few of their members had Communist affiliations. The typical member of the Shinjinkai was a liberal student, like Ozaki, who adopted this

---

* Nankatsu is an area of Katsushika ward, Tokyo. The union, founded by Watanabe Masanosuke in November 1922, held an extremely left-wing and militant position within the labor movement. See Langer and Swearingen, *Red Flag in Japan* (1952), p. 22 (in which the name of the union is romanized as Nankan).

socially tolerated method of student protest but took care not to go so far to the left as to endanger his chances for bureaucratic employment. For sound sociological reasons, the period just before graduation from the university was one of strong rebellion for many Japanese students—and this remains true in the sixties. The college years are the last time in a normal life that Japanese society will forgive real independence and nonconformity; and often we find that the more radical a man was as a student, the more conservative he is in later life.* Ozaki was part of this general pattern. By 1923 he had acquired an interest in social problems, which had led him to begin participating in meetings and lectures sponsored by the Shinjinkai. But this was not yet a commitment; it was only an awakening. If he had not gone to Shanghai in 1928, he could probably be seen today among the chauffeur-driven figures who come and go at the *Asahi* building in Yūrakuchō—those successful men whose pseudo-Marxist vocabulary camouflages a hard core of conservatism.

The first person to introduce Ozaki to various Marxist works was the well-known postwar philosopher Yamasaki Ken, himself a student at Meiji University in 1924.† Yamasaki and Ozaki were introduced to each other by mutual acquaintances in the autumn of 1924; they became close friends, and Yamasaki lent Ozaki several books in German, including the *Communist Manifesto* and Bernstein's life of Ferdinand Lassalle.[15] During the following year, Ozaki and Yama-

---

* An extreme example of this phenomenon is Mizuno Shigeo, who had a peripheral involvement with Ozaki in 1941. (This is not the Mizuno who was a key figure in the Sorge case and died in Miyagi prison in 1945.) As a student (one class ahead of Ozaki at Ichikō), he was an extreme radical; he became a member of the Communist Party and was seized in the mass arrests of March 15, 1928. (As a young man he also produced excellent Japanese translations of Anatole France and André Maurois.) Later, he made a true *tenkō*, and today he is one of Japan's leading industrialists: he owns or controls Kokusaku Pulp Company, Educational Radio, the *Sankei shimbun* (Japan's *Wall Street Journal*), and Fuji Television. See Shimano Kiyoshi, "Mizuno Shigeo," in *Tenkō*, I, 150–63.

† Yamasaki (b. 1903) graduated from Waseda University in 1930 and received his doctorate there in 1933. He specialized in the philosophy of Hegel and Marx, and became well known after World War II for his materialistic critique of Nishida's idealism, and for his many books, which include *Mujun no ronrigaku* (*The Logic of Contradictions*) and *Benshō-hō nyūmon* (*Introduction to Dialectics*). Ozaki read Yamasaki's books even in prison; in his letter of May 31, 1944, he wrote that he had just finished reading Yamasaki Ken's *Kagakusha no tame no tetsugaku* (*Philosophy for Scientists*) with "deep interest." (*Aijō*, p. 211.) Yamasaki was among the thirty or so friends who gathered at Ozaki's graveside on November 7, 1946 (the second anniversary of his execution), and who formed the Ozaki Hotsumi Biography Compilation Committee.

saki had many free-ranging conversations on philosophy and politics, particularly concerning Kant and Hegel, whom Yamasaki had studied closely. In 1925, Yamasaki enrolled at Waseda University and became a student of the famous left-wing publicist Ōyama Ikuo.* Under the influence of Ōyama's lectures, Yamasaki transmitted to Ozaki his own increasing acceptance of Marxist categories and assumptions.[16] Ozaki, however, remained only a student of Marxism, and he held strong reservations about both the theory and practice of Communism in Japan. His oldest personal friend, Matsumoto Shin'ichi, has said: "Ozaki was a patriot pure and simple until the end of his university period," although "his faith in the 'national essence' had been wounded."[17] Another old associate and one of his biographers, Kazama Michitarō, states that after reading the *Communist Manifesto* Ozaki said to Yamasaki, "Marx is interesting reading, but he is frighteningly dogmatic."[18] Ozaki remained aloof from the Communist movement until he reached Shanghai in 1928.

One particular occurrence of this period had an immediate impact on Ozaki's future; it made him decide to spend a year in graduate school studying sociology and economics before entering upon a permanent career. The cause of this decision was the Morito Lecture Meeting, sponsored by the Shinjinkai at Teidai in January 1925, two months before Ozaki's graduation. Morito Tatsuo, Minister of Education in the post–World War II Katayama and Ashida cabinets and former President of Hiroshima University, was in 1920 an assistant professor at Tokyo University. In January of that year, he had published an article entitled "A Study of the Social Thought of Kropotkin" in the journal *Keizaigaku kenkyū (Economic Research)*. The government charged that this article contained "dangerous thoughts" and forced the publisher to withdraw the magazine. Morito and the editor, Ōuchi Hyōe (a famous economist in his own right), were then indicted for violating the Newspaper Act of 1909; Morito received a

---

* Ōyama Ikuo (1880–1955) was a teacher at Waseda, his alma mater, from 1912 to 1915, when he accepted employment with the *Asahi*. As an *Asahi* editorial writer, he was in the vanguard of the movement to democratize Japan after the First World War. Forced to resign in 1918 because of censorship, he guided the so-called "student thought movement" as editor of its journal *Warera (We)* until 1921, when he was rehired by Waseda University. In 1926 he became chairman of the central committee of the new Workers' and Peasants' Party (Rōdō Nōmin-tō). In 1931 he and his wife fled to the United States, and he did not return to Japan until after the war, when he devoted himself to the Communist-promoted "peace movement." He received the Stalin Prize in 1951, and died in November 1955.

three-month jail term and a fine of 70 yen ($35), and Ōuchi spent thirty days in prison and paid 20 yen ($10). Tokyo Imperial University's ultra-conservative professor Uesugi had labeled Morito's article a "criminal offense," but the great majority of intellectuals had seen its suppression as a violation of freedom of inquiry.[19] Five years after this incident, Morito was asked by the Shinjinkai to speak at the University from which he had been driven, and Ozaki was in the audience. Morito's lecture, entitled "Thought and Struggle," ended with this statement: "To think in this age necessarily means to struggle. Thought must be supported by struggle, and only that thought which is accompanied by struggle will flourish." These words so impressed Ozaki that he could repeat them almost verbatim eighteen years later, in his first *tenkōsho* from prison.[20]

Ozaki graduated from the Political Science Department of the Law School at Teidai in March 1925, and when he entered the graduate school in May he needed money at once for tuition fees and living expenses. He had written to his father but had received no response, and so he called upon the former Civil Administrator of Taiwan, Gotō Shimpei, then recently retired as head of the post-earthquake Tokyo Rebuilding Board. Ozaki's plan to study sociology and economics did not impress Gotō at first; but when asked who his professors were, Ozaki tactfully mentioned having heard Uesugi's lectures, at which Gotō mellowed and agreed to help him. Gotō offered to support Ozaki for one year of graduate school at the then comfortable rate of 50 yen (about $25) per month, and Ozaki gratefully accepted.[21]

Ozaki's formal objective in graduate school was the study of labor law, but he spent most of his time reading in his rooms or talking with Yamasaki. His classwork was restricted to participating in a new seminar on "the theory of historical materialism," established by Assistant Professor Ōmori Yoshitarō of the Department of Economics in the spring of 1925. In this seminar Ozaki read the basic Marxist and Soviet texts, including Marx's *Capital,* Lenin's *Imperialism* and *State and Revolution,* and Bukharin's latest rationalization of Soviet policy.[22] Such books were not readily available in Japan in 1925 and certainly not in Japanese. Ozaki bought his copies at the International Bookstore in Kyōbashi, and he must have spent a large part of every day patiently translating the German editions. By this time, however, another subject was becoming more important to him than either the theory of Marxism or the practice of Communism; it was during this year as a graduate student that he began to study "the China problem."

In 1925 the Chinese revolution was beginning to gain momentum with the anti-Japanese strikes in Shanghai (the May 30 Movement) and anti-British strikes and boycotts in Canton and Hong Kong. Ozaki saw in China an extreme example of the confrontation between imperialism and nationalism, categories he had studied at the university and in which his life in Taiwan and his early Chinese studies had given him a personal interest. Moreover, the Chinese revolution of 1924–27 was a struggle that many persons, including Westerners and Chinese nationalists, interpreted primarily in economic, Marxist-derived terms; it was considered proper that anyone investigating the Chinese revolution should also study Marxism and the pronouncements of the Comintern (whose party was then allied with the Kuomintang).* Ozaki's study of Marxism and his deepening interest in China were thus closely related.

In September 1924, before entering graduate school, Ozaki had taken and failed the Higher Civil Service Entrance Examination. He explained his failure to his friends and parents by saying that he had not yet learned enough about society and politics. But as May 1926 and the end of his studies approached, Ozaki had to think hard about his future. He was so advanced a student by then that he no longer found a bureaucratic career attractive; in fact, he had decided shortly after the Morito lecture not to sit for the civil service examination again. Instead he made up his mind to become a journalist—and for a rather unusual reason. "I selected the newspaper field," he later said, "because it afforded me a kind of neutral observation zone from which I could study the Far Eastern situation."[23]

In an interesting article written on February 7, 1927, for the Ichikō Alumni Association journal, Ozaki argued that a newspaper career should be attractive to men "who are aware of the sickness of capitalist society and have doubts about the existing social system and who therefore do not like the idea of occupying positions as govern-

---

* Under Tokkō interrogation in 1941, Ozaki answered a question about the history of his Communist beliefs by saying that Karl Wittfogel's Das erwachende China (Awakened China), which he read as a graduate student in 1926, had made a "deep impression" on him. Gendai-shi shiryō, II, 100. See also Ozaki Hotsuki, Zoruge jiken, p. 27. Ironically enough, Ralph de Toledano, in his apoplectically McCarthyite survey of the Sorge case, also acknowledges the assistance he received in preparing his book from Dr. Karl August Wittfogel. Spies, Dupes, and Diplomats (New York, 1952), p. x. For Ozaki's opinion of Wittfogel's "hydraulic theory" of Oriental society, see Aijō, letter of March 15, 1943, pp. 55–56.

ment officials or company employees." At the same time, however, he already believed that non-partisan, critical newspaper editorializing was in rapid decline and that news companies were beginning to "sell a commodity" like any other commercial enterprise.[24]

In May 1926 Ozaki reported for work in the city editor's department of the Tokyo *Asahi shimbun*. As a reporter, Ozaki was a flop; his first supervisor, city editor Suzuki Bunshirō,* remembers: "Ozaki came to us with a good record . . . but as a city desk reporter, both his news sense and his writing style were completely hopeless. . . . He was affable and unpretentious, but what he wrote as newspaper copy was uniformly mediocre. He did not stand out."[25] If we judge Ozaki strictly as a newsman, Suzuki's recollection is probably accurate. In his February 1927 article for the Ichikō alumni journal Ozaki wrote disparagingly of the "aggressiveness" required of a good reporter—a quality that he personally lacked. In later years Ozaki's entire journalistic reputation rested on his analytical and interpretive writings; after his return from China in 1932, he wrote only background and feature stories. It did not take the *Asahi* long to discover that Ozaki was not cut out for the city desk. In early 1927 he was transferred to the magazine department; and in October 1927 his personal request was granted and he was attached to the China section of the *Asahi*'s Osaka office.

During his sixteen months of employment in Tokyo, Ozaki continued to study Marxism. He met another reporter at the *Asahi*, one Kiyonoya Toshisumi, who shared his interest in left-wing thought, and the two of them organized a private seminar to investigate Stalin's recently published book, *Problems of Leninism*. Reading such things was dangerous, but it was not yet illegal in Japan. Much more dangerous was Ozaki's decision to become a member of the Kantō Publishing Workers Union, which Kiyonoya had invited him to join. This union was affiliated with the Rōdō Hyōgikai (Labor Council), the left splinter federation of the Japanese labor movement, and was itself a target of Communist infiltration. Ozaki joined under the alias of Kusano Genkichi, but he attended only two or three meetings.[26] As a member of this union, he might well have been seized in the mass arrests of Communists on March 15, 1928; but he had cut off all contact with Kiyonoya and the union when he departed for Osaka in October

---

* Years later Suzuki became editor-in-chief of the Japanese edition of the *Reader's Digest* and also acquired a minor reputation as a literary critic.

1927. Ozaki continued moving leftward during this period, but his flirtation with the union may have had a sobering effect. Later in Osaka when a close friend urged him to join the Communist Party, he refused, giving as his reasons the factionalism and extreme leftist position of the Party.[27] Also, whatever his attitude toward the Japanese Communist Party at this time, his attention was increasingly diverted from domestic politics by his new commitments: in 1927 he began investigating the "China problem" professionally, and a month after his transfer to Osaka he was married.

Ozaki's marriage would have been unusual in any culture, but in Japan it was extraordinary: he married his sister-in-law. At the time Ozaki entered Ichikō (September 1919), his elder brother, Honami, married Hirose Eiko of Ōtsu city, Shiga prefecture. The Hiroses of Ōtsu and the Ozakis of Shirakawa, Gifu, were acquainted; and it was the Gifu grandparents' idea that their eldest grandson should marry Judge Hirose's daughter. Eiko visited the Ozaki family in Taiwan in 1917; and Honami and Eiko were married in 1919 in Tokyo, where the groom was a student at Meiji University. It was not a love marriage, and the two young people had almost nothing in common: Honami was an ordinary student in the business administration department, Eiko was a poet by inclination and training. Not long after their marriage, the couple took a two-story house near Waseda University and made the upper floor available to Honami's younger brother, Hotsumi, who was also a student in the capital. Eiko thus knew Ozaki and his classmates throughout their university days, and they all constituted a circle of friends. But Ozaki did not steal his brother's wife. Honami and Eiko became estranged in the years 1925–27, while Honami was serving a period of compulsory military duty and Eiko was living at home in Gifu. After Honami's release from the army, they both returned to Tokyo but found life with each other impossible; they separated early in 1927, and Eiko became a bookstore clerk in order to support herself. During the spring and summer of 1927, Ozaki visited Eiko often, and they soon ceased to regard each other merely as relatives. During the same summer Honami took a new wife (recommended to him by his mother's relatives, the Nomuras), thereby legally freeing Eiko to remarry.* When Ozaki

---

* Honami went to work as an administrative employee for one of the Sumitomo-owned mining corporations and spent his entire career with the one firm. He eventually retired to live in the country. See Kazama, *Aru hangyaku,* p. 13.

went to Osaka in October 1927, Eiko followed him in November, and they were married almost at once after she arrived.[28]

Ozaki later claimed to have had a premonition at the time of his marriage that he and Eiko were beginning a radically new life in Osaka. He wrote to her in 1943: "Do you remember the words of our vow when I married you? They did not mean merely that we would face ordinary difficulties together. Rather, I had a feeling at that time that my life was taking a new direction; and I tried to imply in our pledges that my future would be full of extreme hardships which you would have to face with me. I held my own view of the trend of the times and I decided my own fate in relation to this trend. You must understand that this is why I did not want to have children even though I am fond of them."[29] This particular passage, which has often been quoted in Japan for its maudlin content,[30] is partly Ozaki's self-justification to his wife and partly an accurate commentary on how he felt when he left his apprenticeship behind. The Ozakis did have one child, but they were never particularly close in their marriage. Eiko was as surprised as any politician in the Konoye circle to discover in 1941 that her husband was an international espionage agent, and how he became a spy is one thing that Ozaki tried over and over again to explain to her in his letters from prison.

Moreover, despite his feeling that they were "destined" to face difficulties together, Ozaki made no effort to be faithful to Eiko. Kawai, Matsumoto, Kazama, and others all state that Ozaki had many mistresses and that he loved to regale his associates with tales of his adventures. Even his postwar apologists concede that he had a "feudal" attitude toward women and that he considered the idea of the emancipation of women bizarre; as Matsumoto Shin'ichi put it, "Every inch of him was not a revolutionary."[31] Probably the only woman that Ozaki ever met on the basis of equality was Agnes Smedley. This being the case, one of the real mysteries of his personality is how he could have written such extraordinarily sensitive and learned letters to a wife who was never his intellectual companion. In a later chapter, we must explore that justly popular volume *Love Is Like a Falling Star*—which, incidentally, made Ozaki's widow a relatively wealthy woman.

The events that Ozaki saw his own fate bound up with were great events indeed for a man just assigned to cover the Chinese revolution. The year 1927 was one of the most exciting in Chinese history. The country appeared to have united behind the armies of Chiang Kai-shek; at the same time, Chiang's police were killing revolutionary workers by the thousands in the cities. Japanese armies were intervening against Chiang in Shantung, and the nucleus of the Red Army was gathering on the Hunan-Kiangsi border under Mao Tse-tung. Ozaki did not yet know of or understand all these events, but he was already emotionally involved with them. To leftist revolutionaries, idealists, and intellectuals everywhere, the Chinese revolution of the late twenties was the greatest single movement of the Comintern period until the Spanish Civil War. In 1927–28, Ozaki did more than edit and rewrite the China copy that came into the *Asahi's* Osaka office; like many others, he began to study the events taking place in China with fervor.

Shortly after setting up housekeeping in Osaka, Ozaki paid a visit to Hosokawa Karoku, a staff researcher at the Ōhara Social Problems Research Institute (Ōhara Shakai Mondai Kenkyū-jo), to seek assistance in furthering his private studies on the Chinese revolution. Thus began the lifelong relationship between Ozaki on the one hand and Hosokawa and the Ōhara Institute on the other. (Neither Hosokawa nor his employer was ever aware of Ozaki's later spying operations.) The Ōhara Institute, where several members of the Sorge ring found work, was one of Japan's most famous private social science research organizations; it was founded and endowed by Ōhara Magosaburō (1880–1943), the philanthropist owner of Kurashiki Rayon. Ōhara was an exceptional person. The scion of an immensely wealthy landed family in Kurashiki, Okayama prefecture, he expanded his fortune by successful investments in many diverse fields. After the First World War, as a Christian, a reformer, and one of the richest cotton-spinning capitalists, he endowed hospitals, agricultural research stations, art museums, and the Ōhara Social Problems Research Institute.

The Institute opened its offices in Osaka on February 9, 1919. Its purpose was to study industrial relations, domestic economics, and social welfare problems; and its publications, *Nihon rōdō nenkan* (*Japan Labor Yearbook,* 1920–55), *Nihon shakai jigyō nenkan* (*Japan Social Work Yearbook,* 1920–26), and the journal of the Ōhara Institute (1923–36), contain some of the very best prewar Japanese social research. The director of the Institute from its founding until his death in 1949 was Takano Iwasaburō, a professor at Teidai until 1919, when he resigned in protest over the Morito incident.* Besides hiring the incident's two chief participants, Morito and Ōuchi Hyōe, Takano brought with him a group of young economists and social scientists who had also quit their jobs over the Morito case. Other top figures at the Ōhara Institute over the years included Kushida Tamizō (a Marxist economist), Ryū Shintarō (later an associate of Ozaki's in the Konoye brain trust, and today editor-in-chief of the *Asahi*), Gonda Yasunosuke (the author of Gonda's German-Japanese Dictionary), Kuruma Samezō (an economist and the Institute's director after Takano), and Hosokawa Karoku.[32]

Hosokawa was ten years older than Ozaki; like him, he was a graduate of Ichikō and Teidai (in political science), and he was interested in modern Chinese politics. He and Ozaki became close friends in 1927, and they cooperated on many Chinese research projects until Ozaki's arrest in 1941.† In 1927, after meeting Ozaki and hearing of his interests, Hosokawa organized an informal "Chinese revolution research seminar" that met once or twice a month at the Ōhara Institute. At these meetings, Ozaki met several other China

---

* Takano was not solely an academic or a researcher. He became president of the state-owned Japanese Broadcasting Corporation (NHK) after 1945. Before heading the Ōhara Institute in 1919, he was a vociferous supporter of Japan's pioneer labor union, the Yūaikai.

† Hosokawa is well known to Japanese intellectuals today, but for reasons wholly unconnected with the Sorge case. He became a Communist Party member of the House of Councilors after the war and was at one time leader of the Communist Diet members. But his chief prominence came as the central figure in the famous Yokohama Incident (1942–45), when the militarists arrested the editors of *Chūō kōron, Kaizō, Nihon hyōron*, and the Iwanami publishing house. It was Hosokawa's article "Sekai-shi no dōkō to Nihon" ("Trends in World History and Japan"), published in the August and September 1942 issues of *Kaizō*, that caused the entire repression. Although the article had passed the civilian censor, the Chief of the Army Information Bureau declared that it was Communist propaganda; he arrested Hosokawa on September 14, 1942, and ordered *Kaizō* closed for being Communist-inclined. The investigation of Hosokawa and his acquaintances finally led to the arrest of virtually every editor of an intellectual magazine in Japan during 1944. On July 10, 1944, further publication of *Chūō kōron* and *Kaizō* (both magazines represent middle-of-the-road opinion comparable to that of *The Atlantic Monthly* in America, which they resemble) was prohibited under the Peace Preservation Law; and their cases were in the courts when the war ended. See Hosokawa Karoku, "Shosai no omoide" ("Memories from My Study"), *Shisō*, March 1954, pp. 105–14; Aochi Shin, "Janarizumu to kyōfu, aru sōgō zasshi henshūsha no omoide" ("Journalism and Terror, Memoirs of a General Magazine Editor"), *Shisō*, June 1954, pp. 67–71; *Ōhara shakai mondai kenkyū-jo sanjūnen shi* (*Thirty-Year History of the Ōhara Social Problems Research Institute*), prepared by the Ōhara Institute (Tokyo, 1954).

specialists in the Kansai (central Japan) area, and he furthered his own knowledge of Chinese economics. One product of the seminar was Hosokawa's pamphlet *Shina kakumei to sekai no myōnichi (The Chinese Revolution and the World of Tomorrow)*, which Ozaki later had translated into Chinese when he was in Shanghai. Ozaki and his seminar associates were certainly Communist-inclined in this period, but, like many Japanese intellectuals then and now, they never stepped beyond the bounds of legality. Marxism was to them a new, all-embracing economic and social science; none of them thought of "making" a revolution (as the right-wing products of this same age thought and did). When the second major series of arrests of Communists occurred on March 15, 1928, the "Chinese revolution research seminar" quickly went out of business; but Ozaki had made a close friend in Hosokawa, and they would meet again.

The March 15 Incident—the arrest of over 1,000 persons allegedly affiliated with the Communist Party—was the first in a series of events that drove Ozaki further to the left and eventually into partnership with Sorge. Ozaki himself was never arrested before 1941, but many of his friends were arrested, tortured, beaten, and otherwise intimidated in the years after 1928. In each case, Ozaki tried to be of assistance to his friends even though he endangered himself and, later, the security of the spy ring. The first case was that of Fuyuno Takeo, a friend of Ozaki's at Teidai and a member of the Japanese Communist Party (JCP). Fuyuno had been expelled from the university for participating in the left-wing student and labor movements; he had then become an organizer for the extreme left labor federation, Rōdō Hyōgikai. He had tried to recruit Ozaki into the Party in Tokyo, but Ozaki refused. Shortly after Ozaki had come to Osaka, the penniless Fuyuno appeared at his *Asahi* office and asked for aid. Ozaki was supporting him with dinners and small amounts of money in early 1928. Fuyuno continued to suggest that Ozaki join the Communist Party, but Ozaki was still digesting Marxism at this time and had no interest in becoming a labor organizer.

Fuyuno was arrested March 15, 1928, in Osaka. On the morning of the eighteenth, he called the newspaper offices and asked Ozaki for help: he had been moved from one police station to another all over the city, and he had received several severe beatings. Ozaki brought him some clothes and food but could do nothing more. Fuyuno was sentenced to seven years for violating the Peace Preservation Law and died in prison before half his sentence was served.[33] This incident, and several others that occurred after Ozaki's return to Japan in 1932, made Ozaki recall Morito's remark about the connection between thought and struggle. As Japanese society became increasingly dominated by the army and the police, Ozaki became increasingly willing to aid the Comintern and Sorge; it was this sort of incident that finally led Ozaki to "betray" the society that was forcing him into rebellion.

The arrests of March 15 inaugurated an era of police pressure on left-wing and labor-farmer political activities that did not end until September 1945. Ozaki was out of the country when the hardest waves hit, and he thereby avoided making either an ultra-nationalist *tenkō* or a false move that would have resulted in his own imprisonment. In November 1928 the Osaka *Asahi shimbun* sent Ozaki to Shanghai as its special correspondent. Ozaki's prison recollection of the three-day voyage from Kobe to Shanghai suggests the great meaning that his first trip to the continent had for him:

"[Miyazaki] Tōten* has written that when he first started up the Yangtze on his way to Shanghai, he was moved to tears without knowing why. Similarly, the emotion I experienced during my own first entrance into Shanghai was one of the most powerful of my entire life. Yōko, your father and your mother departed from Kobe on a big ship, not just a ferryboat. We traveled only second class. Eiko was seasick, but as for me, I was sometimes delighted to be on the voyage and at other times I was so tense I could not do anything."[34]

---

* Miyazaki Tōten (Torazō) (1871–1922) was one of the early twentieth-century Japanese supporters of Dr. Sun Yat-sen and the Chinese revolution. A passionate Asian nationalist, he was a close associate of Sun in China and of Aguinaldo in the Philippines. For a description of his career, see Jansen, *The Japanese and Sun Yat-sen* (1954). Miyazaki's book, referred to by Ozaki, is *Sanjūsan nen no yume (The Dream of Thirty-Three Years)* (Tokyo, 1926).

Chapter Three

Shanghai

In November 1928 Ozaki and Eiko rented a house on Woosung Road in the Japanese section of the Shanghai International Settlement, and Ozaki began his work at the *Asahi shimbun*'s Shanghai office on north Szechwan Road. Shanghai, with a population of approximately three million in 1928, was one of the world's largest cities, and it owed all of its growth, wealth, poverty, diversity, and special legal status to imperialism. A village had existed at the confluence of Soochow Creek and the Whangpoo River at least since the late Sung dynasty, but the modern city dates only from the Treaty of Nanking (1842), which ended the Opium War. Within the International Settlement and the French Concession (the foreign-controlled portions of greater Shanghai), residents were subject to European law, paid taxes to Europeans, and were beyond Chinese police jurisdiction—which was the greatest attraction of the place for revolutionaries in 1928.

Ozaki arrived in Shanghai at a confusing period in the development of the Chinese revolution. Looking back, we know that Shanghai was just then beginning to lose its prominence in the revolution; but in 1928 it still seemed likely that the factory proletariat of Shanghai—the largest group of industrial workers in China—would again become the chief instrument for a nationalist victory. The May 30 Movement of 1925, which originated in Shanghai, had been the first real mass political demonstration of the Chinese revolution, and its influence was still felt in the city three years later.* In order to under-

* The May Fourth Movement of 1919 initiated the popular anti-imperialist movement, but it was more the work of the intelligentsia than of the working class. The treaty-port workers were first mobilized by the May Fourth Movement, but they did not make a show of strength until 1925.

stand Ozaki's involvement with Chinese revolutionaries in Shanghai, as well as with international revolutionaries from Moscow, we must recount briefly the events that preceded his arrival.

The May 30 Movement, a series of anti-foreign general strikes and boycotts in Shanghai between 1925 and 1927, was the popular counterpart of the military revolution that brought Chiang Kai-shek to power in 1928. In 1925 Chiang already viewed himself as the successor to Sun Yat-sen, and he was organizing in Canton the armies with which he intended to unify the country by force. His enemies were the provincial warlords (and their foreign backers), who had misruled China since the collapse of the dynasty in 1912. His allies were the Chinese Communist Party (CCP) and the Soviet Union. The Soviet Union was an indispensable partner, for after the Sun-Joffe agreement of 1923 it provided Chiang with the military and technical assistance that made his Northern Expedition possible. The CCP's contribution to the revolutionary effort was manpower—chiefly the workers of the treaty ports, who had been organized by the Party into fighting trade unions.

The Kuomintang–Communist Party alliance was a Machiavellian arrangement from the beginning; the allies intended to cooperate only until a national revolutionary government could be installed, at which time each would fight for control of it. The Communists needed Chiang's armies in order to defeat the warlords, but after that had been accomplished they hoped to dispose of Chiang and his clique. Similarly, Chiang required the support of the nationalistically aroused workers of the cities, whom the Communists controlled, but he planned to purge the leftist unions upon gaining power. Although it was Chiang who managed to execute his plan in 1927, the May 30 Movement—the spark that brought the Communist-organized unions to political life—had a significance transcending the CCP's defeat. It provided the Party with its first substantial cadre of members, including several of today's highest-ranking leaders, and it stimulated a period of rapid growth. At its Fourth Congress, in January 1925, the CCP had only 994 regular members; at the Fifth Congress, in April 1927, it had 57,957.[1]

The course of events leading to the May 30 Movement began on February 9, 1925. On that day, Chinese textile workers struck the No. 5 mill of the huge Japanese spinning concern, the Naigai Wata

Kaisha (Foreign and Domestic Cotton Company).* The Naigai workers charged that they were being brutally mistreated by company foremen and that their low wages were exploitative. Within less than a week the strike had spread to six other Japanese mills and involved more than 30,000 Chinese employees. The Japanese denied that the Chinese workers had a right to strike, and the Chinese looked on their Japanese masters as imperialist exploiters. There were fierce clashes between plant guards and strikers, and in one of them a Japanese plant manager at the Toyoda spinning mill was beaten to death. In early May the Japanese responded by locking out workers at the un-struck mills, thereby further provoking the workers' fury. On May 15 the strikers smashed their way into one of Naigai's plants and de-stroyed some $40,000 worth of equipment. Japanese managers and Sikh constables drove them from the plant with gunfire, and killed one man—Ku Cheng-hung—who is now honored in Communist China as a national martyr.[2]

Word of Ku's death spread rapidly, and on May 21, five thousand people gathered in Chapei, the Chinese city north of the Interna-tional Settlement, for his funeral. The date fittingly coincided with National Humiliation Day, the anniversary of Yüan Shih-k'ai's ac-ceptance of Japan's Twenty-One Demands on China (May 21, 1915). The Kuomintang and the Communist Party both called for a cam-paign of open defiance to obtain compensation for Ku's death and to protest the "unequal treaties" under which the foreigners remained in China. Demonstrations were continuous, and by the end of the month some sixteen leaders—mostly students—had been arrested by the foreign police for passing out leaflets and engaging in political agitation. In order to continue their campaign and to protest these latest arrests, the workers and students decided to hold a mass demon-stration in the International Settlement itself. On Saturday afternoon,

---

* Naigai was the largest operator of cotton cloth spinning mills in China; it con-trolled a total of fifteen plants. The company was founded by Japanese merchants in Kobe in 1887. Between 1909 and 1924 it obtained control of 17 spinning instal-lations, only two of which were in Japan. Eleven were located in Shanghai, three in Tsingtao, and one in Mukden. The company employed 460 Japanese in China and 15,400 Chinese (6,600 men and 8,800 women). Its working day was 21 hours, consisting of two shifts of ten-and-a-half hours each, for 300 days per year. S. T. King and D. K. Lieu, *China's Cotton Industry* (Shanghai, 1929), p. 22; and *Nihon kindai-shi jiten*, p. 213.

May 30, 1925, about two thousand men and women gathered in front of the Louza Police Station on Nanking Road. It was a hostile, milling mob, and as it began to advance on the station, the English policeman in charge, Inspector Everson, ordered his force of eleven Sikhs and eleven Chinese to fire directly into the crowd. At least eleven people were killed instantly or died soon afterward.

These eleven deaths provoked the greatest sense of national grievance in China since 1919. Everson had fired into the crowd without a warning shot, Asians had killed Asians at the command of a foreigner, and the slaughter took place on Chinese territory which had been wrested from China by military force. Photographs of the victims were published in all major Chinese cities, and nationalists and Communists alike urged that nationwide anti-foreign demonstrations be staged. In Tientsin a group of distinguished conservative intellectuals (including Liang Ch'i-ch'ao) signed the Tientsin Manifesto denouncing the use of force by the imperialists. On June 1, students, workers, and—most significant of all—Chinese businessmen of the General Chamber of Commerce declared a general strike and boycott against all foreign enterprises in Shanghai. Later in June the general strike spread to Canton and Hong Kong, where Chinese seamen and dock employees walked out, forcing foreign businesses to suspend operations.

The strikes in Kwangtung led to the most serious incident involving foreigners during the national revolutionary period, and it produced a rupture between China and Britain that was not healed until Chiang Kai-shek's rapprochement with Anglo-American interests in 1927. On June 23, 1925, students, workers, and some of Chiang's military cadets were holding a demonstration of sympathy for Chinese workers in front of the Canton foreign concession area, Shameen. As they marched past the Shakee Road Bridge leading into the concession, French sailors on the gunboat *Altair* (moored at the concession wharf) and British soldiers inside the foreigners' area opened fire with machine guns. Fifty-two Chinese were killed and 117 wounded. This was the Shakee-Shameen Massacre that led to the great Canton general strike described in Malraux's novel *The Conquerors*.

In Shanghai itself, the Municipal Council (the foreign government of the International Settlement, known as the Kung-pu-chü) took steps to halt the movement by breaking the alliance between the workers and the bourgeoisie. Chinese businessmen had supported the nationalistic goals of the May 30 Movement, but they had had an ulterior motive: so long as the general strike was directed at foreign-owned mills, the Chinese mills stood to gain. During June the Chinese middle classes supplied the funds needed to support the men on strike and to keep up the pressure on the foreigners. But on July 6 the Municipal Council retaliated by cutting off the supply of electricity (the only publicly owned utility in Shanghai) to the non-struck Chinese mills, thus forcing them to shut down. By this move the middle classes were not only deprived of their favored position, but given an additional 40,000 workers to support. At the end of July they capitulated. Chinese police closed the headquarters of the General Labor Union in the Chinese sector, and on August 12 the Japanese contributed to the restoration of business by settling their strike. The Japanese mills raised wages slightly and decreed that "no arms are to be carried by foremen in the mills under ordinary conditions."[3] On September 9 the British-dominated Shanghai Municipal Council again turned on the electricity to the Chinese mills.

The May 30 demonstrations in Shanghai thus ended with the workers returning to their factories, but the emotional force behind the movement remained. An international board of inquiry (United States, Great Britain, and Japan) exonerated the foreign police, but the Municipal Council was sufficiently troubled to retire both Inspector Everson and the Police Commissioner on pensions effective December 1, 1925. The Council also forwarded a check for $75,000 to the Chinese Commissioner for Foreign Affairs "as a mark of sympathy for the wounded and the relatives of those who were killed,"[4] but the check was returned by the Chinese. Although their general strike had failed, the workers of Shanghai remained the most highly organized and politically conscious group in China. Less than two years after May 30, 1925, they delivered the largest city in China to the Kuomintang armies, who entered without firing a shot.

In April of 1927 Chiang's Northern Expedition armies were marching down the Yangtze toward Shanghai. Before Chiang reached the gates of Shanghai, workers had seized the Chinese sector to welcome his entrance. But by then Chiang had allied himself with the middle classes of the treaty ports and with British and American commercial interests; and their price for recognizing him and supplying him with credits was that he break with the Communists. This he was prepared to do, and after occupying Shanghai, his police proceeded to liquidate the Communist-dominated unions in what leftists came to call the White Terror. As the *China Weekly Review* reported on August 20:

"For four months a systematized massacre has been going on in the territory controlled by Chiang Kai-shek. It has resulted in the smashing of the people's organizations in Kiangsu, Chekiang, Fukien, and Kwangtung, so that in these provinces one finds Kuomintang headquarters, and labor, peasant, and women's unions transformed from forceful, determined organs into docile, spineless organizations, so effectively 'reorganized' that they will carry out the will of their reactionary masters."[5]

The Communist Party was virtually destroyed, and it remained defunct until 1928, when Mao Tse-tung began to rebuild it along entirely different lines, giving it a new revolutionary strategy based on peasant armies capable of fighting a guerrilla war. Those few Communists, mostly writers and intellectuals, who were not captured by Chiang's police either fled into exile abroad or took refuge in the Shanghai International Settlement.

Ozaki came to Shanghai just after Chiang Kai-shek had formally established the National Government at Nanking (October 1928). He had followed the May 30 Movement and the revolution closely from Japan, and he sympathized with the anti-imperialist, anti-capitalist motives of the Communists and radical nationalists. Like them, Ozaki deplored the fact that the revolution had come under the control of Chiang Kai-shek; and, as a Japanese and an Asian nationalist, he was profoundly disturbed by the new Nanking government's close ties with Great Britain and the United States—ties symbolized by Chiang's marriage, on December 1, 1927, to Sung Mei-ling, a Wellesley graduate and the daughter of a Christian, middle-class, Shanghai family. But Ozaki did not realize until after he came to China how severely compromised his own nation was with respect to the goals of the Chinese revolution.

While in Japan, Ozaki had reasoned that Britain, as the foreign power that had been in China the longest, and the one that had the greatest investment and the largest profits, was therefore the most culpable of the imperialists. But when he arrived in Shanghai, the slogans he heard from Chinese demonstrators were "Expel Japan!" and "Boycott Japanese goods!"[6] For the first time he began to explore the realities of Japan's position in China, and his researches revealed to him a picture very different from the one he had been building up in his own mind.

Britain, he discovered, had not held a dominant economic position in China since the First World War. Before 1914, British cotton-spinning mills employed more workers than all other spinning enterprises combined, but the war had cut back British overseas investment and drawn British cotton goods produced in Shanghai to the European market. In order to meet the Chinese demand no longer filled by Britain, Chinese and Japanese industrialists greatly expanded their productive capacities. Japan had originally gained the right to establish factories in China under the Sino-Japanese commercial treaty of 1896, and this right was extended automatically to all other foreign states via the "most-favored-nation" principle. However, the boom in cotton textile mills, which were the most common kind of foreign factories built in China and the biggest foreign employers in Shanghai, began in 1918. In that year the Shanghai Tariff Commission adopted new tariff rates on different grades of imported cotton yarn. The Japanese found that their yarn manufactured in Japan and sent to China was now unfavorably priced, and this encouraged them to establish mills within China's borders, where the tariff did not apply. In 1918 Japan's cotton yarn production in China was 290,000 spindles;* by 1921 it had increased to 867,000.[7] In 1928, the year Ozaki arrived in Shanghai, there were 59 mills in the city. Of these, 24 were Chinese, 32 were Japanese (but worth four times as much as the Chinese mills), and only three—the Ewo mills of Jardine, Matheson and Company—were British.[8]

Japan's position as the chief imperialist in China was not based wholly on its investment position. The old nineteenth-century tradition of a united front among foreigners against the Chinese was beginning to break down. In part this was because Japan had taken advantage of the First World War to replace Britain as the leading trader in China, and in part it was a matter of prejudice—white men could not treat the Japanese wholly as equals because the Japanese were of a different race. The last attempt to create unity among the imperialists came in 1922, with the Nine-Power Treaty of Washington.† The treaty stipulated that "the contracting powers, other than China, agree to refrain from taking advantage of conditions in China in order to seek special rights or privileges which would abridge the rights of subjects or citizens of friendly states, and from countenancing action inimical to the security of such states."[9] In practice,

* A spindle is a measure of yarn equal, in the case of cotton yarn, to 15,120 yards.

† Probably the only time that all the imperialists were truly united against the Chinese was during the Boxer Rebellion, when they created the International Force to relieve the embassies in Peking.

however, both the Anglo-American powers and the Japanese made commitments and took actions that abridged the rights of their treaty partners.

After the First World War and particularly after the May 30 Movement, Chinese anti-foreign, nationalist propaganda began to single out the Japanese for special disapprobation, and the Europeans did not rally to Japan's defense. In the past, whenever Britain had been the object of nationalist attacks, it had always insisted that it was only one of the several treaty powers and that the Chinese ought not to criticize Englishmen alone.[10] The English were generally supported in this claim by the other imperialist powers—notably, by their Japanese allies between 1902 and 1922. By the late nineteen-twenties, however, Japan considered its economic interests in China too important to be threatened by the emergence of an anti-foreign nationalist movement; the European and American powers, on the other hand, had grown much less hostile to the national unification of China. Among the major Western exports to China had been Bibles and missionaries, and missionaries had long felt an interest—never articulated in meaningful political terms, but an interest nevertheless—in national unification and reform of the "unequal treaties" in China.[11] The Japanese did not receive the wholehearted support of the other foreign powers in China partly because many Westerners had begun to sympathize with the Chinese.

It would be unfair to state these differences among the imperialists in black-and-white terms. In many ways the British were simply more sophisticated than the Japanese in "handling" Chinese nationalism: they opposed it until it became unopposable and then shifted their support to the most malleable leader among the nationalists. European businessmen in the treaty ports had traditionally viewed Chinese revolutions with about the same attitude as their Japanese counterparts: "The Taipans [heads of firms] had come to think that the chaos backstage was not such a bad thing after all. Foreigners were killed in the course of military operations inland once in a while. . . . But the complete absence of unified control and authority precluded a concentrated push against the Settlement. As long as Chinamen kept fighting Chinamen, they had no time to fight their foreign guests."[12] This was the way things had been in China for seventy-five years, and the British businessmen in Shanghai were not breaking with tradition when they agreed to support Chiang Kai-shek; they did so only to avoid provoking the formation of a new Communist-Nationalist front directed against them. Besides, it wouldn't hurt British business if the Japanese took the blame for imperialism in China.

The Japanese position was more difficult. As latecomers to China, and as Orientals besides, they were never fully accepted into the imperialist club. Most serious for them, however, was that they failed to understand the emergence of Chinese nationalism even to the limited extent that the Anglo-American powers did. In 1925 the Japanese government was pursuing the Shidehara, or "soft" China policy, the essence of which was to avoid antagonizing the Chinese by unilateral Japanese action (as they had with the Twenty-One Demands) and to rely upon joint action by all the foreign powers to force the Chinese to honor the unequal treaties. But as some imperialists began to sympathize with the Chinese against the Japanese, new political groups in Japan began demanding an independent Japanese policy on the continent. This new attitude was greatly accelerated by the worldwide depression, but the first signs of Japan's hostility to Chinese nationalism began appearing in the same year Ozaki arrived in Shanghai. In May of 1928 Chiang's armies and Japanese troops fought at Tsinan, in Shantung, and on June 4 the Japanese Kwantung Army engineered the blowing up of Chang Tso-lin's special train in Mukden. In 1931 the Japanese seized all of Manchuria before the nationalist virus could infect it, and on January 24, 1932—just before Ozaki left China—Japan virtually annexed the Hongkew and Yangtzepoo districts of Shanghai. These were the first shots in the Sino-Japanese struggle that led, in 1937, to the full-scale Japanese invasion of China.

As a member of the *Asahi* staff in Shanghai, Ozaki became a good news analyst; more than that, he made himself a first-rate scholar on Chinese sociology and economics. He combed through Chinese regional newspapers for information on conditions in the interior.[13] He studied languages with a passion. He was already proficient in English and German, and could read French; he knew a smattering of Latin, Esperanto, and Malay; and he had studied Russian while working in Osaka (although he states in his prison letters that he needed a dictionary to read Russian and that his facility with the language was not great).[14] His ability to read Chinese was perfect, thanks to his father's early instruction, but his command of spoken Chinese—like that of many Japanese "China hands"—was imperfect. He employed three tutors while he was in Shanghai, and he worked with them often; as a result, he developed a good Shanghai dialect, and although he never learned to speak Mandarin, he did learn enough spoken Chinese to travel.

During his first year in China, Ozaki covered several big stories. The first was the Shanghai May Day demonstration of 1929, which was severely repressed by the International Settlement Police. Ozaki walked down Nanking Road early on the morning of May 1 and talked to Chinese store owners as they put up heavy louvered shutters over their shop windows. It was illegal for the workers to hold celebrations in the Settlement, but they intended to do so anyway. After the shops were closed up, the people poured into the streets lighting firecrackers and shouting anti-foreign slogans. The foreign police—composed of English, Japanese, and Americans (the French concession in Shanghai was independent of the International Settlement)—soon arrived, flying their national flags on their motorcycles. They drove the motorcycles directly into the Chinese crowd, and Ozaki was appalled to see Japanese flags in the melee and to see Japanese policemen beating Chinese.[15]

Ozaki's next major story took him to Nanking. In June of 1929 he attended the reinterment of Sun Yat-sen at the spectacular mausoleum built on Purple Mountain outside the capital. Chiang Kai-shek had constructed the memorial to reinforce his claim as Sun's rightful successor and to secure his dictatorship over the Kuomintang; nevertheless, Sun's reburial was the first occasion since Chiang's accession to power for honoring the famous dead revolutionary, and it brought many Chinese and Japanese nationalists to Nanking.* Among the Japanese visitors was Inukai Ki, destined to be Premier of Japan within eighteen months and to be assassinated, after only five months in office, by extreme right-wing militarists. With him was his son, Inukai Ken (1896–1960), whom Ozaki met there for the first time; it was the beginning of an acquaintance that would later bring them to work closely together in the Breakfast Society and the Shōwa Research Association.[16]

During 1929 Ozaki's researches into Chinese politics carried him beyond private reading and covering important news stories for the

---

* Regardless of the ulterior motives of the Kuomintang in 1929, this memorial (called Chung-shan-ling) is still maintained in good condition today by the Chinese Communists. Nozawa Yutaka, *Son Bun, kakumei imada narazu* (*Sun Yat-sen and the Revolution That Never Succeeded*) (Tokyo, 1962), p. 240.

Asahi. Except for the period between August and mid-October, when he was hospitalized with typhoid fever, he entered into extensive semi-professional associations with left-wing revolutionaries living in Shanghai, associations that would eventually lead him to Richard Sorge. Kazama Michitarō contends that Ozaki made these personal contacts not in order to participate actively in the Chinese revolution but only in order to understand it better, and to promote favorable relations between Chinese leftists and Japan.[17] But although it is true that he had a strong scholarly interest in the Chinese revolution, and never took part personally in the sort of overt left-wing activities for which he might have been arrested, there is no doubt that he was emotionally involved in Chinese politics. In 1942 he replied to a police questioner: "At that time [1928–32], I was young and I saw the effects of the Chinese revolution everywhere; I believed that Shanghai itself was the crucible of the revolution. Attempting to grasp the actual state of colonialism and semi-colonialism in China, I delved freely into all kinds of left-wing literature. It was fascinating, but it was also habit-forming. I really thought that I had the formula for the course of world revolution laid out before my very eyes."[18]

Ozaki got to know many people in Shanghai, and through them he met many more. Naturally enough, his earliest friends were other Japanese interested in China: journalists for the *Asahi*, the Rengō Tsūshin (United Press in Japan), and other agencies; employees and researchers at the Shanghai office of the South Manchurian Railroad; and advanced students at the Japanese university, Tōa Dōbun. Some of these men were more strongly committed to Marxism than he was; others, like his close friend Miyazaki Seiryū (a cousin of Torazō and a member of the staff at the *Asahi*), were anti-Marxist but more devoted to a popular Chinese revolution than many Communists. One of Ozaki's first contacts in Shanghai was Yamakami Masayoshi, Chief of the China Section of Rengō Tsūshin, a man who was to play an indirect role in the Sorge ring in 1932. Yamakami had been implicated in the Dawn People's Communist Party Incident of 1921 and had served a short jail sentence then. In December of 1928 Yamakami took Ozaki to a two-story building (a bookstore below and a tea shop upstairs) located in the same neighborhood as the *Asahi shimbun*. There he introduced Ozaki to several comrades of the almost defunct Creation Society, one of the most famous associations of Chinese revolutionary writers and intellectuals.[19]

It was logical that leftist Japanese should befriend members of the Creation Society, for all of its members could converse easily in Japanese. The Society was founded in the summer of 1921 by Chinese students educated in Japan; and its leaders—Kuo Mo-jo, Yü Ta-fu, Chang Tzu-p'ing, and Ch'eng Fang-wu—were all strongly influenced at the time by trends in Japanese literature.[*]

In its early years the Creation Society introduced to China the highly emotional, romantic novel then in vogue in Japan. However, after the May 30 Movement, the Society abruptly shifted its interests and frankly advocated literary propaganda for the Communist cause. (Its famous slogan, taken from the title of one of Ch'eng Fang-wu's works, was "From literary revolution to revolutionary literature.") Even in making this switch, the Society revealed its Japanese affiliations: Kuo claims to have been converted to Marxism by his reading of Kawakami Hajime's *Social Organization and Social Revolution* (*Shakai soshiki to shakai kakumei*).[†]

When Ozaki first came to the offices of the Creation Society, Kuo Mo-jo had already fled to Japan to avoid Chiang's police, but many well-known leftist intellectuals were still living in the relative safety of the International Settlement. Those whom Ozaki recalled most clearly in later years were Yü Ta-fu, the minor novelists Feng Nai-ch'ao and P'eng K'ang, the physician and dramatist T'ao Ching-sun, and the Communist playwright Shen Tuan-hsien (better known under his pen name, Hsia Yen).[20] The Creation Society itself was disbanded as an organization in February 1929, but Ozaki remained a personal friend of many of its former members throughout his stay in Shanghai. During 1929 Yü Ta-fu and T'ao Ching-sun edited a left-wing journal called *Mass Literature* (*Ta-chung wen-i*), and they asked Ozaki to contribute to it.[21] He wrote two articles for them, one

---

[*] Kuo and Yü became outstanding figures in modern Chinese literature. Chang dissociated himself from the Society after it adopted Marxist principles in 1925, and went on to collaborate during the Sino-Japanese war with that other returned student from Japan, Wang Ching-wei. Ch'eng and Kuo remained faithful to Communism throughout the revolutionary period and became leading spokesmen on literary policy in Communist China. Yü Ta-fu was killed by the Japanese in 1945 in southeast Asia.

[†] Kawakami (1879–1946) was a prominent Japanese Marxist economist and the translator of *Das Kapital*. On Kuo's conversion, see C. T. Hsia, *A History of Modern Chinese Fiction 1917–1957* (New Haven, 1961), p. 97. Hsia's work contains the best study of the Creation Society available in English (Chapter 4, pp. 93–111). See also *Gendai Chūgoku jiten*, pp. 397–98.

entitled "Trends in Japanese Proletarian Literature" ("Nihon puro-retaria bungaku no dōkō") and the other on the weakness of the Communist movement in Great Britain. In all of his left-wing publishing, Ozaki used one of two pen names, Shirakawa Jirō or Ou Tso-ch'i. The characters of the latter, a Chinese-style name, are pronounced "Ō-sa-ki" in Japanese.

Although Ozaki was only 28 years old and lacked any practical revolutionary experience, his opinions were of interest to the Creation group. He told Japanese police in 1942: "I attended a discussion meeting of the Creation group in late 1929 during which I was asked to explain how the left-wing literature movement was carried out in Japan among young people. I quoted to them examples from our *Shōnen senki* [*Youth Battle Flag*]."[22] *Youth Battle Flag* was the junior edition of *Senki* (*Battle Flag*), the prominent journal of Nappu (Nippon Proleta Federatio), a league of left-wing writers.[23]

Ozaki's association with Creation Society members was apparently not so close as to draw him into the feuds of the Chinese left literati and make him unwelcome in other groups. In 1928 the Creation Society and another association of proletarian writers, the Sun Society (T'ai-yang She, founded by Chiang Kuang-tz'u and Ch'ien Hsing-ts'un), launched a violent attack on Lu Hsün, the most famous figure in twentieth-century Chinese fiction. Lu had often ridiculed the work of self-styled proletarian writers, although he himself supported revolutionary fiction and is today idolized by the Chinese Communists. In summarizing his position on proletarian literature in an essay entitled "Literature and Revolution" (April 4, 1928), Lu agreed with Upton Sinclair that all literature is propaganda but that "not all propaganda is literature."[24] Convinced that the Creationists wrote mere propaganda, he dismissed them as beneath contempt. This feud divided Lu Hsün and the Creation Society group until the founding of the League of Left-Wing Writers on March 2, 1930, and even after that date it continued on a personal basis.

Despite his connections with the Creation Society, Ozaki was introduced to Lu by T'ao Ching-sun in early 1930, and he seems to have made a favorable impression on the famous writer. According to Masuda Wataru (the translator of Lu Hsün into Japanese and one of Japan's leading authorities on modern Chinese literature), Lu once told him that Ozaki was "a man of broad learning and reliable character."[25] Ozaki saw Lu Hsün often; and although he was not a member of the League of Left-Wing Writers, he was invited to attend its gathering in honor of Lu Hsün on his fiftieth birthday, September 17, 1930. Ozaki brought Agnes Smedley to the party with him, and he translated while she talked with Lu.[26]

T'ao Ching-sun, who had made this meeting possible, was Ozaki's closest literary associate during this period. T'ao had been in Japan with his father from 1907 until 1929 and had received his education entirely in Japanese schools; he was a graduate of Kyushu University Medical School and had completed some post-graduate research at Tōhoku University. After returning to China in May of 1929, he succeeded Yü Ta-fu as editor of *Mass Literature*.[27] The incident that brought Ozaki and T'ao Ching-sun into literary collaboration occurred early in 1931. Twenty-three alleged Communists, including five members of the League of Left-Wing Writers, were seized by the International Settlement police and turned over to the Kuomintang. On February 7, 1931, all twenty-three were tortured and killed; only six of them were ever identified. It was one of the most brutal incidents of the White Terror.[28]

This massacre prompted Ozaki and T'ao to publish a collection of Chinese articles in Japanese in order to expose the White Terror to Japanese intellectuals. Their efforts were comparable to the publicity given the incident in English in the magazine *New Masses*. The book that resulted from their joint translation was entitled *Hōki* (Chinese *Feng-ch'i*, or *Insurrection*), and it included articles by Yeh Ch'en, T'ien Han, Feng Nai-ch'ao, Cheng Po-chu, and T'ao Ching-sun; the registered translator was "Ou Tso-ch'i"—Ozaki.[29] In 1931 Ozaki contributed to another Japanese edition of Chinese literary propaganda, this time without the collaboration of T'ao. He added an introduction to a volume of translations by Shen Tuan-hsien (Hsia Yen) and Lin Shou-jen. The book bore the title of its most famous piece, Lu Hsün's *The True Story of Ah Q*, but it also included stories by Hu Yeh-p'in, Jou Shih, and Feng K'eng—all martyrs of the February 7 massacre. Ozaki's introduction, signed "Shirakawa Jirō," was entitled "The Present State of the Chinese Left-Wing Literary Front." The registered translator for the entire volume was Lin Shou-jen—a pseudonym for Yamakami Masayoshi, the man who had first introduced Ozaki to the Creation Society.[30]

Ozaki's acquaintances in Shanghai included not only Chinese leftists but a number of Marxist students at the Japanese university, Tōa

Dōbun, and these were the more dangerous connections. Had he been any more active among these Japanese leftists he would probably have become known as a Communist to the Japanese consul in Shanghai; he might then have been deported to Japan, as were several of his Japanese student friends, and placed under arrest. Ironically enough, had he become known as a Communist he would have been useless to Sorge, and he would probably be alive today.

In late 1929 the Kiangsu Provincial Committee of the Chinese Communist Party was directing much of its attention to establishing front organizations in Shanghai. These fronts played upon the theme of "resisting imperialism," and their activities included boycotts of foreign goods, propaganda among foreign soldiers and sailors in Shanghai, and financial support for the International Red Relief (MOPR).[31] The membership of these organizations—the most important for our purposes being the Japan-China Struggle League (Nisshi Tōsō Dōmei)—included Chinese, Koreans, Europeans, and Japanese. Tōa Dōbun was a major recruiting ground for Japanese members, and by late 1930 what amounted to a Japanese cell of the Chinese Communist Youth League had been established there. It was with these young men that Ozaki began to associate in 1930. He became their adviser and supporter, but he never implicated himself beyond extrication; when the Japanese consul arrested and deported some of the students in 1931, Ozaki's name was not mentioned.

Ozaki's Marxist-inclined friends at Tōa Dōbun were Anzai Kuraji and Katō Eitarō of class 27 (enrolled in April 1927 and graduated in March 1931) and Mizuno Shigeru, Nakanishi Ko, and Kawamura Yoshio of class 29 (April 1929 to March 1933). Twelve years later all but Katō had been arrested in connection with the Sorge case, although only Mizuno had actually played a role in the ring. Mizuno, regarded by Ozaki as a sensitive and personable young man, collaborated with him until both of them were arrested in 1941. He became the secretary of the China Research Office (Shina Kenkyū Shitsu) in 1938, and he translated Sun Yat-sen's *San-min chu-i* (*Three Principles of the People*), under Inukai Ken's supervision, for the Konoye circle.[32] He died in Miyagi prison on March 22, 1945.

Of the other four students, only Anzai and Nakanishi became involved in postwar Japanese politics. Anzai is today a member of the Central Committee of the Japanese Communist Party.[33] He was expelled from Tōa Dōbun in 1931, and was in prison between 1934 and

1937. After his release he worked as a researcher for the South Manchurian Railroad, first in Dairen and then in Kalgan; he was arrested again in connection with the Sorge incident in June 1942, but was released in January 1943 for lack of evidence. Nakanishi Ko was also expelled from Tōa Dōbun in 1931. After leaving Shanghai in 1932, he worked as a researcher for the South Manchurian Railroad at the Dairen office from May 1934 until his arrest for connections with the Sorge ring in June 1942. He was held by the Japanese police without trial until September 11, 1945; he was then tried, and although he was not a member of the ring, he was sentenced to life imprisonment on September 28, 1945. Not quite two weeks later he was released in the general amnesty for political prisoners decreed by the Allied command. In the postwar period he edited the Communist journal *Mimpō,* became a director of the leftist China Research Institute, and was elected to the upper house of the Diet as a Communist. His *History of the Chinese Communist Party,* published in 1949, is dedicated to Ozaki Hotsumi, Mizuno Shigeru, Kawamura Yoshio, and others.[34]

Little is known of Kawamura and Katō. Kawamura became chief correspondent in the Shanghai office of the *Manchukuo Daily News* (*Manshū nichi-nichi shimbun*) during the nineteen-thirties, and he supplied Ozaki with information in the first years of the latter's association with Sorge. Kawamura was arrested on March 31, 1942, and he died (or was killed) in prison shortly thereafter. The only information I have found on Katō Eitarō is one line in the history of class 27 at Tōa Dōbun, written some 25 years after the class graduated, in which Katō is described as a man of "prodigious intelligence."[35]

In late 1929, Anzai, Katō, and Mizuno called on Ozaki at the *Asahi shimbun* offices. They admired Ozaki as a leftist reporter for Japan's most distinguished newspaper, but they could also feel comfortable with him because he was only a few years older than they were. They asked if he would help them edit a student newspaper and invited him to join a social science research association (comparable to the study societies in Tokyo, where Ozaki had read Stalin and Bukharin). Ozaki agreed to both proposals. Under his guidance, the students brought out one issue of the newspaper, called the *Kiangnan Student News* (*Kōnan gakuhō*), but it was promptly banned by the university's censors. The research association, which often met at Ozaki's home, had a somewhat longer existence; it soon became the student nucleus of the Japan-China Struggle League.

The Japan-China Struggle League was an anti-imperialist, Communist-front organization created in December 1930 by two members of the Chinese Communist Youth League. The two Chinese were Wang Hsüeh-wen and Yang Liu-ch'ing, both of whom spoke Japanese. Wang, who is today a leading Chinese Communist intellectual, was educated at Kyoto Imperial University, where he studied under the Marxist economist Kawakami Hajime. During the war he was a deputy director of the Marx-Lenin Institute in Yenan (Mao was director); after 1949 he became editor of the important Communist theoretical journal, *Hsüeh-hsi (Study)*; and he was a delegate from Kiangsu province to the first National People's Congress in 1954.[36] Yang, a labor agitator rather than an intellectual, was born in Taiwan and had known the Japanese Communist labor leaders Yamamoto Kenzō and Watanabe Masanosuke there; during the mid-nineteen-thirties he was arrested in Shanghai and deported to Taiwan, where he died in prison at T'aichung. The two men worked together in creating various left-wing fronts, but the Japan-China Struggle League was the first of their projects to provoke police retaliation.

In September of 1930 Wang, Yang, and a student leader at Tōa Dōbun named Nishizato Tatsuo created the China Problems Research Association at the university, and this new Marxist study group absorbed the students whom Ozaki had been meeting at his home. It is unclear today whether Ozaki's student friends introduced him to Wang and Yang, or whether he met Wang as a member of the League of Left-Wing Writers. In any case, Ozaki later testified to the police that he knew both of them and that he admired Wang's intellectual abilities.[37] Nishizato is listed along with Wang in a contemporary Japanese government intelligence study as one of the two leaders of the Japan-China Struggle League.[38] Ozaki never mentioned Nishizato's name, but he probably knew him as a graduate of Tōa Dōbun's class 26 (graduated March 1930) and as a newsman on the *Shanghai nippō*, a Japanese-language daily.[39] Ozaki, Anzai, Nakanishi, and the others all participated in the enlarged seminar; and Ozaki must have known and probably approved when the seminar transformed itself into the Japan-China Struggle League in December of 1930. The League was intended to be an action group in the struggle against imperialism.

The Struggle League's accomplishments before the Japanese consul put it out of business were slight. The members called a student strike to protest certain changes in university administration, and they held a memorial meeting to commemorate the third anniversary of the Canton Commune (December 11, 1927). Their third project was their last. On December 16, 1930, when the Imperial Japanese Navy's training ship called at Shanghai, members of the League passed out "souvenir" matchboxes to the cadets and sailors as they came off the ship.[40] Inside the boxes were notes that read: "Down with Japanese imperialism. Support the Chinese Soviets. Turn your guns around and overthrow the capitalist-landlord state. The Chinese Communist Party—Banzai! Soldiers, workers, peasants—Banzai!"[41]

That evening Japanese consular police called at Tōa Dōbun and found some of the matchbox propaganda in the dormitories; for this "insult" to the Japanese Navy, they arrested about fifty students, including Ozaki's friends. Mizuno was expelled from Tōa Dōbun in January and deported to Japan in August 1931. Nakanishi was expelled at the same time, but he did not return to Japan until February 1932. Anzai returned to Tokyo at once, and in October 1931 he became a member of the Tokyo section of the Communist Youth League; he was arrested again under the Peace Preservation Law in March 1934 and given a four-year sentence, but he was released early in 1937. Nishizato left Shanghai before he could be arrested, but he was apprehended in June 1931 in the Tokyo offices of the *Proletarian Youth News (Musan seinen shimbun)*, the organ of the Japanese Communist Youth League.[42] Ozaki was neither arrested nor implicated; in fact, he probably covered the arrests for the *Asahi*. But he certainly knew the inside details of the incident and may even have helped plan it. It may be that his successful precautions against having his name linked with such events reflected, even then, a concern for more significant activities.

Despite his liaisons with the Creation Society and Tōa Dōbun, Ozaki's more important contacts were with Japanese journalists of his own age, notably Yamakami of Rengō Tsūshin, Kawai Teikichi of the *Shanghai Weekly News,* and Funakoshi Hisao of the *Shanghai Daily News*. These and other leftist Japanese, particularly certain employees in the Shanghai office of the South Manchurian Railroad, were also non-student members of the Struggle League, but they had no intention of allowing themselves to be arrested for pranks. Kawai, for example, fled to Peking in December 1930 to avoid a charge of distributing Communist propaganda. By the summer of 1931, he and most of the other members of the Japanese-national front groups not yet known to the police had returned to Shanghai, but they were no longer interested in risking arrest. At the same time, events in Manchuria were beginning to portend the eruption of a much more serious type of Japanese imperialism than they had known in Shanghai. Before the year was out, their friend, colleague, and fellow thinker, Ozaki Hotsumi, would be approaching them with a novel proposal for helping the liberal cause. For by the time the Tōa Dōbun students were arrested, Ozaki had already met Miss Agnes Smedley and Dr. Richard Sorge.

Chapter Four

Smedley and Sorge

During 1929 and 1930, Ozaki and his associates began to frequent the Zeitgeist Bookstore near Soochow Creek in Shanghai.[1] The Shanghai Zeitgeist, a branch of the Zeitgeist Buchhandlung of Berlin, was one of the Comintern's outlets for Soviet materials and for books of general interest to intellectuals. The financial backing for the Zeitgeist shops came from the International Union of Revolutionary Writers in Moscow, which was in turn part of the mosaic of left-wing intellectuals' organizations created by that impresario of the Communist front, Willi Münzenberg. (Until Münzenberg's expulsion from the Comintern in 1937, his activities ranged from creating the League to Struggle Against Imperialism and Colonial Oppression—whose members included Nehru, U Nu, Albert Einstein, James Ford, and Ozaki's friends Kawai and Funakoshi—to popularizing Eisenstein's *Potemkin* and Pudovkin's *Storm Over Asia* around the world.)[2]

The managers of the Shanghai Zeitgeist were Mrs. Irene Wiedemeyer and her younger sister, whose name is not known. Irene Wiedemeyer was married to a Chinese Communist named Wu Shao-kuo, whom she had met in Germany in 1925, and she had studied briefly at Sun Yat-sen University in Moscow. Her bookshop remained a popular center for left-wing intellectuals in Shanghai until 1933, when the Nazis cut off her contacts with the German Communist Party and her suppliers. She traveled to Europe in the fall of 1933, and when she returned to Shanghai the following year she reopened her shop in a different location—this time as the Shanghai representative of International Publishers of New York, an organizational affiliate of the U.S. Communist Party. Mrs. Wiedemeyer's bookstore was intended to provide a meeting place for traveling Communists, and it served this purpose well. Sorge and Smedley met there, and in late

1929 Irene Wiedemeyer introduced Agnes Smedley to one of her Japanese customers, Ozaki Hotsumi. As Ozaki recalled this meeting for the police in 1942: "One day when I was reading at the Zeitgeist Bookstore, Mrs. Wiedemeyer introduced me to the well-known American writer and contributor to the *New Masses,* Miss Agnes Smedley. She was in Shanghai as the correspondent for the *Frankfurter Zeitung.* After that I contacted Smedley at her apartment in the French Concession, and we once had tea together in the lobby of the Palace Hotel."[3]

Late in 1929 Smedley moved from the French Concession to the European section of the International Settlement, and Ozaki visited her often at her apartment there, first as a journalist and later as a co-worker for the Comintern. In describing some of their conversations, he said: "We talked about the problems of opium and hygiene, and of the peasants and workers. She asked me what I thought about the internal disputes within the Kuomintang. At this time Smedley was working on behalf of the International Red Aid and devoting a great deal of time to the Noulens Incident.* She was also particularly interested in organizing a worldwide protest to the White Terror.

* On June 15, 1931, the Shanghai Municipal Police arrested Mr. and Mrs. Hilaire Noulens (whose real names were Paul and Gertrude Ruegg), as representatives of the Far Eastern Bureau of the Comintern. This was the first indication that the Comintern had an office in Shanghai after the Kuomintang-CCP split. Noulens had numerous aliases, including the name W. Almas, under which he appeared at the Second Pan-Pacific Workers Conference. Mr. and Mrs. Noulens were turned over to Chinese authorities and were tried by court-martial at Nanking during October 1931; Noulens was sentenced to death and his wife to life imprisonment. But both were released and deported in June 1932, after the Soviet Union intervened (the U.S.S.R. and Nanking did not reestablish diplomatic relations until December 1932). The Noulens Defense Committee, for which Smedley worked, was a worldwide Comintern organization to obtain their release. See Robert Magnenoz (pseud. for Robert Jobez, former Deputy Commissioner of Intelligence, French Concession Police, Shanghai), *De Confucius à Lenine, La Montée au pouvoir du Parti communiste chinois* (Saigon: Editions France-Asie, 1951), pp. 113–19 [Hoover Institution]. Willoughby mistakenly contends that the Noulens were both imprisoned by the Nanking government: "Despite MOPR [International Red Aid] efforts, the Rueggs were found guilty of seditious activities and imprisoned in Nanking. With the release of many political prisoners, when Nanking fell to the Japanese, the pair were liberated in September 1937 and have since disappeared." *A Partial Documentation of the Sorge Espionage Case,* p. 44. Willoughby's history is also imprecise; Nanking fell on December 13, 1937. Jobez, incidentally, was one of the former European police officials in China who assisted in Willoughby's investigation of the Sorge case. Cf. Robert Magnenoz (Robert Jobez), *L'Expérience communiste en Chine* (Paris: Les Iles d'Or, 1954). See also Gunther Nollau, *International Communism and World Revolution,* p. 142.

Because of these concerns, I introduced her to Lu Hsün and translated for her."[4]

Agnes Smedley (1894–1950) was one of the most famous pro-Communist publicists of the Chinese revolution and an important contributor to the American proletarian literature movement in the thirties and forties.* Like Ozaki, she was never a member of a Communist party, but she came to be eulogized by such eminent Communist leaders as Mao Tun, Ting Ling, Lao She, Hung Shen, Madame Lu Hsün, General Hsiao Hua, and Madame K'ang K'o-ch'ing (the wife of Chu Teh, the Red Army commander whom she helped to make famous throughout the world). After her death in London, her ashes were taken to Peking and placed in the cemetery for revolutionaries at Papaoshan on May 6, 1951. Agnes Smedley's role in the Sorge ring's operations was minor and confined to its Shanghai phase, but she became a close friend of Ozaki's. In one of his letters from prison he recalled: "I have translated a book written by an outstanding woman. It concerns a young girl who, while fighting against poverty and adversity, cuts her own path through the world. It is a unique work, and one already world-famous. My own translation may not be very good, but it gives me great pleasure to think that someday Yōko might retranslate this book."[5]

The book to which Ozaki was referring was Agnes Smedley's fictionalized autobiography, Daughter of Earth (1929). He had completed his translation in 1934 and published the work under a new title, Onna hitori daichi o yuku (A Woman Walks the Earth Alone). The first Japanese edition, which appeared in August 1934, listing the translator's name as Shirakawa Jirō, was filled with blank circles (maru-maru) indicating the censor's deletions. After the war, Ozaki's Onna was reissued in two more editions (1951 and 1958), unexpurgated and under his own name.[6] In his introduction to this book, Ozaki gives a livelier description of his meeting with Smedley at the Palace Hotel: "Once in Shanghai someone said to me jokingly, 'There is an extremely unusual woman reporter here whom you must meet. However, I suggest that you call on her not because she's a woman reporter, but only to satisfy your own curiosity. She's not much to look at.' The woman I met was Agnes Smedley. I was waiting for her

---

* Her books on China include Chinese Destinies (1933); China's Red Army Marches (1934); China Fights Back, An American Woman with the Eighth Route Army (1938); Battle Hymn of China (1943); and The Great Road, The Life and Times of Chu Teh (1956).

in the lobby of the Palace Hotel, when she dashed in, wearing a bright red suit. She sat down opposite me, completely ignoring all formal greetings, and started talking. She pulled out a cigarette and smoked during our conversation. Although I do not remember it too well, I think we talked about the state of Japanese research on Chinese agriculture."[7] This singular woman from a farm near Osgood, Missouri, was to make many contributions to the history of modern Asia, and not the least important of them was introducing Ozaki to Richard Sorge.

Agnes Smedley was educated in the original school of hard knocks. After a brutalized childhood, and with virtually no formal elementary education, she worked at various menial jobs across the country in order to attend classes at Tempe Normal School in Arizona, New York University night school, and summer school at the University of California at Berkeley. During the First World War she became interested in the movement for colonial liberation through her acquaintance with several Indian exiles in the United States. She helped them in their attempts to persuade President Wilson to bring the Indian case before the peace conference; but because they had accepted money contributed by a German society, she and the Indians were arrested and imprisoned for a short time on a charge of having aided German espionage.[8] After the war she signed on as a stewardess on a Polish ship bound for Europe, jumped ship in Danzig, and went to Berlin. Between 1920 and 1928 her home base was Berlin, where she was active in the Indian nationalist movement in exile and lived with Virendranath Chattopadhyaya, an Indian revolutionary who later joined the Communist Party. Her intense desire for personal independence made her suspicious of both marriage and motherhood (she had two abortions during a brief early marriage to Ernest Brundin), and in Berlin she worked to establish one of the world's first birth-control clinics. In June of 1921 she made her first trip to Moscow, accompanying Chattopadhyaya and an Indian delegation to the Third Congress of the Comintern.[9] After returning to Germany she taught an English seminar at the University of Berlin and studied and wrote on Indian history.[10] In 1927 she attended a meeting of the League Against Imperialism in Brussels and met the Indian delegate, Jawaharlal Nehru.

In 1928 Smedley was hired as a correspondent for the *Frankfurter Zeitung* and departed for the Far East. En route, she stopped in Moscow to attend the Sixth Congress of the Comintern (July 17 to September 1, 1928) and then traveled across Siberia. After spending a few months in Harbin, Tientsin, Peking, and Nanking, she arrived in Shanghai in May of 1929. As a well-known supporter of Indian independence and a champion of various leftist causes, she attracted the immediate attention of the British police. The records of the Shanghai Municipal Police list her as a member of the Friends of the Soviet Union, the Hindustan Association in Berlin, the Berlin Indian Revolutionary Society, the Noulens Defense Committee, the All-China Labor Federation, and the China League for Civil Rights.[11] Between 1929 and 1933 she lived for short periods in Canton and Nanking and made a brief trip to the Philippines in 1930. Although she was harassed by the police throughout this period on the technicality of having two passports (one from the United States and one from Germany), Smedley was never secretive about her political activities, and in numerous articles for both Comintern-supported and independent left-wing journals around the world, she openly popularized and defended the revolutionary cause in China.

On May 17, 1933, Smedley left Shanghai by rail for Peking, and from there she continued on to the Soviet Union, where she entered a rest sanitarium and wrote her book *China's Red Army Marches.* After regaining her health, she worked briefly on the staff of the International Union of Revolutionary Writers. She returned to the United States in 1934, visited her family, and then sailed for Shanghai in October aboard the *President Cleveland.* On October 19, 1934, during the ship's stopover in Yokohama, she spent the day with Ozaki. It was the last time they saw each other; after that, Sorge forbade Ozaki to contact her because she was a known Communist sympathizer. Her connections with Sorge had ceased when she left China in 1933; and even when she had been collaborating with him (1930–33) she believed, like Ozaki, that he was a Comintern functionary.[12]

In the fall of 1936, Agnes Smedley began to travel in north China. She was in Sian in December when Chang Hsüeh-liang carried out his coup against Chiang Kai-shek; and in August of 1937, following the outbreak of the Sino-Japanese war and the establishment of the second united front of the Kuomintang and the Chinese Communist Party, she went to the Eighth Route Army's base at Yenan. From Yenan she became the first Western journalist to visit the Communist army's field headquarters in Shansi, and for the rest of the year she marched with the troops of P'eng Te-huai and Lin Piao in the Communist battle zones in north China. In 1938 she became the accredited correspondent of the *Manchester Guardian* and worked at the Chinese Red Cross office in Hankow. After the fall of Hankow she traveled through Ch'angsha, Chungking, and the Communist and Nationalist guerrilla areas in central China, reporting on military conditions. She spent 1940 lecturing in Chungking, but chronic illness led her to return to the United States in the summer of 1941. She had spent roughly twenty years abroad. Between 1941 and 1949 in the United States, she wrote her influential *Battle Hymn of China* (1943), lectured at Skidmore College, and contributed articles to many national magazines in support of the Communist forces in China.

Agnes Smedley had been a consistent propagandist for the Chinese Communists, a supporter of the Comintern in the twenties and early thirties, and a friend to Sorge and Ozaki in Shanghai. But she was not a part of the Sorge espionage group in Tokyo, and, as we shall see, Sorge's operations in Japan were radically different from his essentially journalistic information gathering in Shanghai between 1930 and 1933. Thus, in February of 1949, when General Charles Willoughby accused Agnes Smedley of being a member of the Sorge Soviet spy ring, he accused her of the one service she had not rendered to the international Communist movement. The Department of the Army publicly repudiated the SCAP report (February 20, 1949), and Agnes Smedley served notice that she would sue General MacArthur for libel if he would accept responsibility for Willoughby's work.[13] Willoughby defied the Department of the Army by becoming a friendly witness for the House Committee on Un-American Activities.[14] From then on, the American "exposé" of the Sorge case descended into a morass of McCarthyite charges and countercharges, and the meaning of one of the most interesting cases of Soviet espionage was completely obscured.*

Smedley responded to General Willoughby with her customary

* Willoughby never seemed to understand that he and his report had to be repudiated not because Sorge's espionage was a fiction, but because it was an embarrassment to the United States for him to be trying to interpret it. His talent for historical generalization may be inferred from the following samples: "In Shanghai, in the early thirties, we are not dealing with the period of our uneasy alliance with the Soviets (1941–45), but with the prewar years of 1930–39, in the heyday of the Third International, prelude to the infamous Stalin-Hitler Pact, sole factor that made World War II at all possible." *Shanghai Conspiracy*, p. 274. "Shanghai was the vineyard of Communism. Here were sown the dragon's teeth that have ripened into the Red harvest of today and the farm labor was done by men and women of many nationalities who had no personal stakes in China other than an inexplicable fanaticism for an alien cause, the 'jehad' of Pan-Slavism for the subjugation of the Western World." *A Partial Documentation of the Sorge Espionage Case*, p. v.

candor. "There has been no secrecy," she said, "about my knowing Ozaki. He was a noted writer and a correspondent in China for many years, and it was as such that I knew him. He was bitterly opposed to Japanese imperialism. He gave his life in the fight against its criminal war, for his own people and all peoples."[15] In 1946, Smedley had written to Ozaki Eiko offering condolences to the family and suggesting that Yōko might retranslate *Daughter of Earth* and take any profits from it. She did not sue General MacArthur (the Army would not allow him to be sued), and in 1950 further investigation of the "American aspects of the Richard Sorge spy case" became academic: on May 8 of that year Agnes Smedley died suddenly in London, following surgery for stomach ulcers. The Sorge case continued to excite McCarthyite interest for a short time, but there were no other Americans to implicate in it, and the fact that Sorge and Ozaki had been spies against American enemies during wartime tended to compromise its value as a cold war issue.[16]

We can never know Smedley's own reasons for helping Sorge in Shanghai in 1930, but her interests seem to have been like Ozaki's and Kawai's: internationalist, idealistic, and not at all Stalinist. She herself wrote: "For years I listened to Communists with sympathy and in later years in China I gave them my active support, but I could never place my mind and life unquestioningly at the disposal of their leaders. I never believed that I myself was especially wise, but I could not become a mere instrument in the hands of men who believed that they held the one and only key to truth."[17]

Richard Sorge arrived in Shanghai in January 1930 as the correspondent of the *Soziologische Magazin* of Berlin.* He had traveled to Shanghai from Berlin via Paris and Marseille. It is not known what name he had given his employers (who had hired him as a correspondent just two months earlier), but he introduced himself in Shanghai as an American journalist named "Johnson." He stayed at the Anchor Hotel and the YMCA before renting a permanent apartment, but once settled he began to establish his "group." For this purpose he went first to the Zeitgeist Bookstore to locate Smedley. As he put it: "The only person living in China known to me as a possible contact was Agnes Smedley. I had heard about her when I was in Europe.

* For a description of the materials written by Sorge while in prison, upon which the following discussion is based, see the Bibliography.

I requested her assistance in setting up my group in Shanghai, particularly in helping me to select Chinese associates."[18] Smedley cooperated willingly and introduced him to various Chinese who had pro-Communist sympathies but who were not members of the Chinese Communist Party. The most important of these, a man who became Sorge's first confidant and source of information in China, was identified by Sorge in 1941 simply as "Wang." During the summer Sorge traveled to Canton for two or three months and recruited other Chinese there as suppliers of information. In October or November of 1930 he met Ozaki Hotsumi.

Sorge himself was reasonably certain that it was Smedley who introduced the two of them, and Sorge's later meetings with Ozaki usually took place at Smedley's apartment. It was difficult for Sorge to take Ozaki to a Chinese restaurant in the International Settlement because Japanese were unwelcome in Chinese establishments; and Sorge rarely met anyone in Hongkew, the Japanese area of the International Settlement, because of the danger of Japanese police surveillance. Similarly, he almost never invited Chinese or Japanese to his own apartment in Shanghai in order to avoid attracting police attention. Ozaki claimed that his first knowledge of "the American named Johnson" came from a certain Kitō Gin'ichi, a member of the U.S. Communist Party who had come to Shanghai via French Indo-China and had been introduced to Ozaki by a student at Tōa Dōbun. Kitō asked Ozaki to meet "Johnson," but Ozaki distrusted Kitō personally and made inquiries to Smedley about the American journalist. Smedley told Ozaki that he should say nothing to anyone about "Johnson," and later she herself introduced Ozaki to Sorge. Sorge affirms that he hardly knew Kitō and that Kitō was never one of his aides.

Sorge and Ozaki appear to have taken an instant liking to each other. In 1941 Sorge wrote of Ozaki: "He was my first and most important real confederate. . . . Our relationship, both business and personal, was perfect. The information he collected was the most accurate and the best that I ever obtained from any Japanese source, and I formed a close personal friendship with him at once. . . . He had direct access to members of the Chinese Communist Party [in the Creation group], but at the time I knew almost nothing—actually nothing at all—about this."[19] But if there were things that Sorge did not know about Ozaki, there were a great many more things that Ozaki did not know about his new friend.

Exactly one year before his meeting with Ozaki, Sorge had been sitting in the Moscow office of General Ian Antonovich ("Ya") Berzin, chief of Department Four, Intelligence, Soviet Red Army General Staff.* Sorge and Berzin were talking about Sorge's assignment to Department Four, his deliberate severing of all contacts with the Communist International, and his forthcoming trip to the Far East. Sorge explained to Berzin his views on the need for collecting comprehensive political intelligence and the necessity of divorcing this kind of activity from relations with local Communist parties. Berzin —who had already heard about the new project from Sorge's friends in the Comintern, O. A. Piatnitskii, D. Z. Manuilskii, and O. Kuusinen—agreed with Sorge but stressed the need to gather military information as well. Sorge received a briefing from the Eastern Section of Department Four, and just before leaving for China he held last-minute discussions with the Eastern Section, the Political Section, and the Code Section.[20] He then set off on his first assignment within the

* Berzin (1881–1937), an old military associate of Voroshilov, was the chief of Department Four between approximately 1926 and 1935. He was succeeded by General M. S. Uritskii, whom we will encounter later. Berzin was Military Attaché and Chief of Military Mission in Spain during the Civil War. He arrived in Madrid on August 27, 1936, and returned to Moscow in late 1937, where he was killed in the purges.

Oddly enough, General Willoughby, the former chief of SCAP intelligence, had apparently never heard of General Berzin, the chief of Soviet military intelligence. The Japanese translator of Sorge's prison memoirs (written in German) approximated the sound of "Berzin" as "Berudein," and Willoughby's translator of the Japanese text into English then turned "Berudein" into "Beldin." To indicate that this was an approximation, Willoughby's translator put "Beldin" in quotation marks (e.g., *A Partial Documentation of the Sorge Espionage Case*, Appendix, p. 26). But Willoughby did not verify any proper nouns, and the name "General Beldin" appears throughout his book *Shanghai Conspiracy* without the quotation marks (e.g., p. 166). Since the German original of Sorge's memoirs was destroyed in the bombing of Tokyo (see the Bibliography), we cannot check that version; however, for Department Four of the Red Army General Staff and General Berzin, see John Erickson, *The Soviet High Command* (1962), pp. 357, 429–30, 502, 794; and D. J. Dallin, *Soviet Espionage* (1955), pp. 4–5. For Berzin in Spain, see Hugh Thomas, *The Spanish Civil War* (1961), pp. 262, 621. Willoughby's error has been repeated by various other writers following him, e.g., Meissner, *The Man With Three Faces* (1955), p. 19. There is no "General Beldin."

Errors comparable to the misspelling of Berzin's name appearing in *Shanghai Conspiracy* include the following: "Richterfelder" for Lichterfelde, a district of Berlin (p. 134); "van Glieber" for Lieutenant Colonel Hermann von Kriebel (p. 180); and "Olitsky" (p. 74) or "Ulitsky" (p. 169) for General M. S. Uritskii. An error concerning Max Clausen, one of the members of the Sorge ring itself, is mentioned in the note on page 102, in Chapter Five.

Soviet Union's new intelligence program—an assignment that ultimately led him to fame and to the gallows.

Sorge's participation in the Communist movement, like Ozaki's,
was not prompted by any proletarian experience. Basically, Richard
Sorge was a bourgeois idealist who turned to the German Communist
Party during World War I as a practical way of preventing further
"imperialist wars." He was born October 4, 1895, in Baku, on the
Caspian Sea in Russia. His father, a German, was the senior petro-
leum engineer for the Caucasus Oil Company; his mother was the
daughter of a Russian capitalist in the city of Kiev. Richard was the
second son of a family that later included seven children. Sorge's
father, a prosperous German nationalist and a supporter of imperialism, held views on social questions that were diametrically opposed
to those of his own father, Friedrich Albert Sorge. Richard's grandfather Friedrich, who knew Marx and Engels, had fought in the Baden
War of 1848 at the age of 22 and as a result had been forced to seek
exile in America in 1852. When the headquarters of the First International were moved to New York City in 1872, Sorge became its Secretary General for about two years. After the dissolution of the International, he retired from socialist activities and became a music
teacher, but he had a later influence on the American labor movement
through his close friendship with Samuel Gompers. Friedrich Sorge
died in 1906, when Richard was eleven years old.

By that time Richard's parents had moved to Berlin. He had the
comforts that a wealthy middle-class family could provide, and in
school he did well in history, literature, philosophy, and athletics. It
was 1914 that changed everything: "The World War of 1914–1918,"
he said, "had the most profound influence on my entire life. Even if I
had never been motivated by other considerations, the World War
alone would have been enough to make me a Communist. I was eigh-
teen-and-a-half years old when the war broke out, a high school student living in the Lichterfelde district of Berlin."[21]

Sorge's father had died in 1911, and in 1914, without consulting his
mother, Richard volunteered for the army. He was given six weeks
of training on a drill field outside Berlin and then sent to Belgium,
where he fought in the battle on the banks of the Yser. It was a
progress, as he called it, "from the school chair to the slaughtering
block."[22] In Belgium his excitement about the war soon gave way to
revulsion, confusion, and emptiness. Sorge writes that none of his fel-

low soldiers knew what the war was about and that his own adolescent knowledge of history soon convinced him that he had simply been ensnared in another one of Europe's countless, meaningless wars. The first pacifist he ever met was a soldier from Hamburg; they became close friends, but the soldier was killed in early 1915. Shortly after his friend's death, Sorge himself was wounded and sent back to Germany to recuperate. He was appalled by what he saw on the home front: the rich lived well from the black market, and the poor were desperate; profiteering and material objectives had replaced the ostensibly idealistic purposes of the war that had been taught in the army. He volunteered for service again and was sent to the Eastern front. There he was wounded a second time, and during 1916 he made a difficult passage home through Russia. Of that period, he said: "I reached the conclusion that Germany could make no further contribution to the world—in terms of ideas or otherwise—and that England and France were equally incapable of helping Germany or the other nations. No fatuous declamations on spirituality or high ideals could shake this conviction of mine. Since that time I have never been able to tolerate protestations of idealism or high purpose by leaders of a nation at war, regardless of the people on behalf of whom they espouse them."[23]

Nevertheless, Sorge chose to return to the front rather than remain in Germany, and there he received a third wound, this one serious. In the field hospital where he spent several months, he met a doctor and his daughter, who was a nurse. Both of them were members of the radical faction of the Social Democratic Party, and they gave Sorge his first concrete knowledge of the German revolutionary movement. They provided him with books and told him of Lenin, who was then living in Switzerland. He began to study socialist theory seriously. As soon as he was barely able to move, he returned to Germany and enrolled at the University of Berlin. After reading Marx and Engels, and particularly after hearing of the Bolshevik revolution, he decided that Communism was the political expression of justice in his age and that he must join the movement. He said: "All of the particular solutions to problems of my personal and material existence since that time have followed from that decision. With World War II now entering its third year, and particularly with the outbreak of the German-Soviet war, I believe even more strongly that my decision of twenty-five years ago was correct."[24] Sorge wrote that testament in 1941; he did not live to witness Korea, Hungary, or de-Stalinization.

Sorge was officially released from further military service in January 1918, and he became a student at the University of Kiel. There he joined the Independent Social Democratic Party, and he contributed to the Kiel Mutiny (November 3, 1918) by delivering secret lectures to the sailors in their barracks. At the end of 1918 he returned with some friends to Berlin to work at the Party's headquarters; but he arrived in the midst of the Spartacist rebellion, and after being detained for a few days at the railroad station he was sent back to Kiel. In 1919 he moved to Hamburg, where he continued his studies to prepare himself for the Ph.D. examinations in political science. He received his degree from the University of Hamburg in 1920. During the same year, at the time of the Kapp Putsch, the Independent Social Democratic Party, along with the Spartacus League and other radical groups, merged to form the German Communist Party (KPD). Sorge, now a Communist, continued to serve the Hamburg branch of the KPD in the capacity of local training chief.

Between 1920 and 1922, Sorge held his first job—as a teacher in an Aachen preparatory school. He was dismissed at the end of 1922 for engaging in "heated political controversy."[25] In order to support himself and serve the Party, he became a miner in the Aachen coal fields. The work was strenuous, and it was harder for Sorge because of his war injuries, but he stuck with it; he organized a Communist cell among the workers at the first mine where he was employed, and he moved on to two other mines during 1923. He tried to do the same thing in Holland late in 1923, but he was discovered and deported. By then he was unable to return to Aachen; he was known there, and the mine authorities had threatened to turn him over to the Allied military forces occupying the Rhineland. And so, with the approval of the Party Central Committee in Berlin, he became an assistant in the social science department of the University of Frankfurt.

In Frankfurt Sorge gave as much of his time to Party work as he did to the University. As in Hamburg, he headed Party training activities, and he also was adviser to the local Communist newspaper. In the winter of 1923–24, the KPD was banned from political life for a few months; but Sorge, not being well known in Frankfurt, was able to keep the local branch going underground by personally maintaining the membership register and the Party's funds, and by serving as liaison officer with the Party Central Committee in Berlin. As a result of his efforts, the ban against the KPD had almost no effect on the Party's functioning in Frankfurt. Holding this key position in the

Frankfurt Communist Party led to one of the major turning points in Sorge's life.

The German Communist Party, in a seriously weakened condition after its abortive attempts to generate Communist revolutions in various parts of the country in 1923, held a clandestine Congress (its ninth) in Frankfurt in April of 1924. In order to attend this Congress and bring the KPD more firmly under Soviet control, the Comintern illegally sent into Germany several high-ranking delegates—including Piatnitskii, Manuilskii, Kuusinen, and S. A. Losovskii (the head of Profintern, the Red Trade Union International).* Sorge was assigned the delicate task of protecting the Comintern representatives and deciding what activities they might safely undertake. He himself was also a delegate to the Ninth Congress. During their stay in Germany, the Comintern leaders became good friends with Sorge, and because his personal prospects did not look much better than those of the KPD, they invited him to come to Moscow to work at Comintern headquarters. After obtaining the approval of the Party leaders in Berlin, Sorge left for Moscow at the end of 1924. His new job was to assist the ECCI in setting up an intelligence bureau for the Comintern. He went to work in January 1925.

Sorge had been a member of the KPD and its predecessors between 1918 and 1924, but when he was transferred to Moscow Piatnitskii switched his name from the rolls of the German Communist Party to those of the Communist Party of the Soviet Union. He was admitted to the CPSU in March 1925 and assigned to a Comintern cell in the Moscow district. Sorge became a worker for what he later called the "Comintern Intelligence Division, one of three major sections that formed the basis for concrete organizational and political leadership of the Communist International."[26] Presumably, this intelligence division was part of the ECCI's Org-Bureau, headed by Piatnitskii, which also included the International Relations Section, the Finance Section, and the Administration and Correspondence Section.† The

---

* Kuusinen and Piatnitskii were members of the four-man Secretariat of the Communist International from the Fourth World Congress (1922). Manuilskii (1883–1959) was, from 1925 on, a member of the Executive Committee of the Communist International (ECCI) and permanent Comintern representative to the German Communist Party.

† Details of the internal organization of Communist International headquarters are by no means clear even today. The most recent study on this subject is Nollau, *International Communism*, Chapter 4, "The Organization and Methods of the Communist International."

Intelligence Division was probably created within one of these sections in early 1925, when the Stalinist leaders Manuilskii and Piatnitskii obtained control of key positions in the ECCI. Sorge said that Kuusinen was head of the division at one time, and he explained its functions as follows: "It was the long-established practice of the Org-Bureau of Comintern headquarters to send special representatives to the various Communist parties in order to assist them with organizational problems. It was decided to expand the work of these emissaries to include intelligence activities."[27] The objects of this intelligence work included collecting data on labor movements, on factions in local parties, and on general political and economic conditions. It did not yet include political and military information of the type later required by the Soviet state.

Sorge became one of these special emissaries, and during 1927 he went to Denmark and then to Sweden. He attempted to gather basic political and economic information on these trips, but he found that he was hamstrung by having to work with local Communist parties. Domestic Party leaders referred internal squabbles to the "man from Moscow," and occasionally one side would try to use him against the other. Working under such conditions, he was continually exposed to the threat of discovery by the police, which would have ruined his future usefulness. But he avoided discovery, and by July of 1928, when he returned to Moscow to attend the Sixth World Congress of the Comintern as a delegate from the Scandinavian countries, he had apparently become a relatively influential minor bureaucrat in the Soviet-Comintern machinery. According to the Japanese police, he was vice-chief of the Intelligence Division and a secretary to Bukharin, in which capacity he helped draft the theses of the Congress.[28] After the Congress he returned to Norway and his usual work. From there he went to England and traveled throughout the Midlands, using his knowledge of coal mining to investigate political conditions among the miners; he also stopped briefly in Scotland.

Back in Moscow in early 1929, Sorge reported to his superiors on Scandinavia and Britain and was congratulated on his work. On this last trip he had refrained from contacting local Party leaders and had been able to gather much more valuable information than in 1927. Still, he had found the lack of direct communication channels with Moscow a difficulty; if he wanted to send a report from the field, for instance, he had to use local Party organs or go through the Comintern "letter-drop" in Berlin. It was decided, therefore, that on his next trip—to China—an entirely new procedure would be followed. Sorge would be separated from the Comintern and attached as an individual operative to Red Army intelligence; he would travel under a completely legal cover and would be forbidden to contact local Communist parties or to help them in any way. In short, he was to become a spy for the Soviet government rather than for the international Communist movement.

Like the basically sound Soviet functionary he had become, Sorge believed that this was a distinction without a difference. However, as we shall see, the distinction posed a problem of immense complexity for the Japanese government after his arrest. If Sorge was an agent for the Soviet Union, there was nothing technically illegal about his being in Japan in 1941—at least not under the Peace Preservation Law that he was charged with violating. The Japanese thus persisted in referring to him as a Comintern spy, a man working for a party whose object was the eventual overthrow of the Japanese government. (He was also charged with violating the National Defense Security Law, despite the fact that his personal collecting of information took place within the German Embassy rather than within an organ of the Japanese government. Ozaki was the only important member of the ring clearly guilty of violating the Defense Security Law.) There were other complications—including rivalry between the Tokkō and the Kempei (who should have dealt with a military spy)—but all of these difficulties derived in part from Sorge's own inability to say exactly whom he was spying for. "On the point of my organizational affiliation with Moscow," he said, "I did not receive a specific explanation before I left, and I am not exactly sure what organization I belong to. Naturally, I did not ask questions on this subject. To this day I cannot say precisely whether I am attached to Comintern headquarters or to the so-called Department Four or to some other agency—like the People's Commissariat for Foreign Affairs of the U.S.S.R."[29]

Students of Soviet foreign affairs will recognize, of course, that Sorge was not really indulging in obscurantism, because after 1929 the distinction between the Soviet state and the Comintern was, in fact, of little importance. Sorge went to great lengths in his prison memoirs trying to explain to his captors the theory of "capitalist encirclement" and the Stalinist dogma that in an age of fascism and ultra-nationalism the first duty of all "international" Communists is defense of the Soviet Union. Sorge concluded: "The change in my activities from Comintern to Red Army included new tasks intended to advance Soviet foreign policy and to strengthen the defenses of the Soviet Union against attack from abroad. These activities are important and universal expressions of Communist principles, and they are no different from my Comintern activities on behalf of individual Communist parties."[30]

For Ozaki, Kawai, and the other non-Soviet Communists around the world, this became a real dilemma in the nineteen-thirties: promoting international anti-fascist solidarity often seemed to require giving treasonable assistance to the Stalinist state; at the same time the belief that one had to contribute to the anti-fascist struggle precisely by serving Soviet interests was more intense in the Far East than elsewhere because of the continuous and palpable danger of Japanese militarism. Sorge solved this dilemma in his own mind by accepting Stalin's rationalization of socialism in one country. In practical terms, this meant that he had become a spy for the Soviet Union.

In 1929, Sorge was attached to the Red Army's Department Four for administrative and technical purposes. (His own reports detailing the difficulties of intelligence collecting in conjunction with local parties may have been instrumental in bringing about this transfer.) At the same time, his new position reflected the gradual transformation of the Soviet Union and the international Communist movement under Stalin. It was now the chief of Department Four from whom he received traveling orders, requested technical assistance (e.g., his radio expert in Japan), and to whom he sent his reports; and, although he was not told and probably could not have discovered for certain, the ultimate destination of his reports was the Central Committee of the Soviet Communist Party. There are indications later, after the Moscow purges and after his arrest, that Sorge had come to understand this and to see the possible contradictions in his activities. His motivations were not the same as Ozaki's, but they were even more unlike those of the typical postwar Stalinist.

In Moscow during his Comintern period, Richard Sorge—known to his friends as "Ika" (perhaps from the verb *ikat'*, "to hiccup")—was a tall, handsome man with a slight limp. He drank rather heavily but never became obnoxious. His wife Christiane, a former librarian at the University of Frankfurt, was with him then; she was called "Ikaret," and the Sorges were welcome companions among the international Communists in Moscow.[31] (Sorge divorced Christiane a few years later, and she emigrated to America.) Sorge did some writing during his Moscow period, and his best-known book, *Der Neue Deutsche Imperialismus* (1927 or 1928), was translated into Russian and even into Japanese.[32] He wrote another book in Moscow entitled *The Economic Provisions of the Versailles Peace Treaty and the International Working Class,* but it has disappeared. Both of these volumes, of which Sorge was rather proud, were written under the name "R. Sonter," the Comintern pseudonym he had employed since 1925.[33] Sorge wrote one other early work, "The Accumulation of Capital and Rosa Luxemburg" (1922), but he later decided that it was immature and superficial. "I would not mind," he said, "if the Nazis burned every copy of that pamphlet."[34]

Sorge was a man of considerable learning, and in Japan he delighted in making the extensive researches into Asian history and art that served as a foundation for his political analyses. He later said: "Had I lived under peaceful social conditions or in a peaceful political environment, I would have liked to have been a scholar."[35] Moreover, his assignment to the Far East was not the result of a perfunctory decision made in Moscow; it was a choice he had made himself. Sorge writes that he was asked in 1929 whether he preferred to continue working in Europe or to go elsewhere, and that he answered that he wanted to go to the Far East because he was fascinated by the possible consequences of a Chinese revolution for the world Communist movement. It was only after he had worked in Shanghai for a year that he turned his attention to Japan.

During his first year in China, Sorge concentrated on organizing his informants—who were not told of his exact Moscow affiliation—and investigating the subjects on which he was to gather information. These subjects, which General Berzin had listed for him in Moscow, were the following: (1) the social and political characteristics of the Nanking government; (2) its military strength; (3) its foreign policies; (4) its domestic policies; (5) the social and political characteristics of factions opposed to the Nanking government; (6) British and American China policy; (7) the military strength of foreign powers in China; (8) the problem of "extraterritoriality" (i.e., foreign consular jurisdiction); and (9) the development of Chinese agriculture and industry. In compiling data on these topics Sorge relied upon "Wang" to gather material from Chinese informants located in

Nanking, Canton, and Peking as well as in Shanghai. At the same time, Sorge himself began to cultivate the acquaintance of certain Germans living in China.

Since the triple intervention of 1896, and particularly after the Anglo-Japanese alliance of 1902, German Far Eastern policy had tended to be Sinophile; and the First World War, when Japan acquired Germany's colonies and spheres of influence in the Far East, did nothing to change this orientation.[36] In 1927 the traditional German preference was greatly stimulated when Chiang Kai-shek appointed Germans as military advisers to his Nanking government. The Kuomintang's Soviet military aides had left after the KMT-CCP split, and Chiang hired a German ex-colonel, Dr. Max Bauer, as his chief military adviser. Bauer became an immediate favorite of Chiang's, and he established a web of close relations between German officers and the Nanking government that lasted until after the outbreak of the Sino-Japanese war. When Bauer died in 1929, his position as principal military adviser was filled by Lieutenant Colonel Hermann von Kriebel. It was Colonel von Kriebel and his associates whom Sorge quickly made his personal friends. As he described it later:

"I became well known in German social circles revolving around the Consul General's office, and I did many favors for these people. My companions included merchants, scholars, and military instructors, among whom the most important were members of the German Military Advisory Group to the Nanking government. I sought out not only persons engaged in military activities in Nanking but also persons concerned with political problems. One of these was Colonel von Kriebel, senior military adviser and later Shanghai Consul General [after April 1934]. I was often invited to Nanking by members of the Advisory Group, and they called on me in Shanghai. I also made a trip with them to Chiahsing and Hangchow [in Chekiang province]. They supplied me with a great deal of information on the inner workings of the Nanking government, its plans for subjugating the warlords, and its political and economic policies. In 1932, at the time of the Shanghai Incident, they were invaluable in providing me with accurate data on Japanese operational plans and troop strength."[37]

Obviously, Sorge was no amateur in his chosen line of work; it is doubtful whether "Wang" or any of Sorge's leftist Chinese informants had contacts closer to Chiang Kai-shek during this period than von

Kriebel and his staff. Nevertheless, Sorge was not yet an expert on the Far East; he badly needed advice on Japanese policies in China, and that is where Ozaki came in. After their initial meeting at Smedley's apartment in the late autumn of 1930, Ozaki began to supply Sorge with analytical information on Japan's China policy, the role of the Army in the Japanese government, and Japan's special interest in Manchuria. Probably more important to Sorge than these pieces of specific information were Ozaki's explanations of the basic elements of Far Eastern politics. Sorge said: "Ozaki was my teacher [concerning Japanese intentions in China], and the subjects he treated covered a very broad range. He explained to me Japan's Manchuria policy for the previous several years and her probable plans for the future."[38] The little bit that Ozaki was able to tell Sorge about the Manchurian situation shocked the Soviet agent; Manchuria was on the Soviet Union's borders, and Japan's well-known antagonism toward Russia antedated the Bolshevik revolution. In addition to his formally assigned tasks, Sorge at once began a personal investigation of Japanese foreign policy and of conditions in Manchuria. It was none too soon.

On September 18, 1931, acting on secret orders received from Colonels Itagaki Seishirō and Ishihara Kanji of the Kwantung Army General Staff, Captain Imada Shintarō and several other officers attached to the Kwantung Army destroyed the South Manchurian Railroad tracks at Liut'iaokou, outside Mukden. The Kwantung Army then charged that Chinese had sabotaged the railroad, and it used this incident as a pretext for driving the Chinese armies from Manchuria. The Manchurian Incident, as this action was called, was the opening scene in the Sino-Japanese war of 1937–45. It took the civilian Japanese government in Tokyo by surprise, and made it clear for the first time that the Japanese Army had passed beyond formal governmental control and intended to become a prime formulator, rather than an instrument, of Japanese foreign and domestic policy. It surprised Sorge and Ozaki, too. Their attention had already been drawn to Manchuria by several incidents, notably the serious clash at Wanpaoshan (near Ch'angch'un) in July 1931, when Chinese peasants battled Koreans, who had been moved to Manchuria as foils for Japanese penetration. At that time Ozaki had even told Sorge that the Japanese militarists would seize control of Manchuria before they would let it fall to the Chinese Nationalists. But this sudden provocation by the Japanese Army was worse than anything they had foreseen, and it led them to revise their primary subjects of intelligence collecting. Japan and Japanese continental policy henceforth became uppermost in the minds of both men.

The first thing that Sorge asked Ozaki to do was to help him recruit other Japanese informants, particularly someone who could go to Manchuria for an on-the-spot investigation. Ozaki consulted Yang Liu-ch'ing, one of the Chinese Communist organizers of the Struggle League, and Yang recommended Kawai Teikichi.[39] Kawai (born in 1901) has the unique distinction of being the only person alive who was involved in all phases of the Sorge-Ozaki case, including the SCAP investigation. (Willoughby had him arrested in 1949 in order to secure affidavits that could be used by the House Committee on Un-American Activities.)[40] From the historical point of view, however, Kawai is not the best possible survivor; even Willoughby went so far as to call him "a sort of Whittaker Chambers of Japan."[41] The problem is not simply that he renounced Communism after the war, but that he seems personally unstable and occasionally given to exaggerating his own role in the ring. Kawai was a *Shina rōnin*, a Japanese adventurer who drifted from job to job in China.* He was often unemployed, led a scandalous private life, and in the Japan years of the ring he was virtually Ozaki's ward. Nevertheless, he joined the Communist movement primarily for idealistic and pacifist reasons, and he aided Ozaki and Sorge to the best of his ability.

After graduating from Meiji University in 1925, Kawai worked briefly as a journalist in Tokyo and then went to China. He held various jobs in Peking between 1928 and 1930, and in August of 1930 he found work as a reporter for the *Shanghai Weekly News* (*Shanghai shūhō*). He also became one of the first members of the Japan-China Struggle League, and as such he was singled out and instructed by Yang Liu-ch'ing in the methods of clandestine activity. It was because of this special training that Yang recommended Kawai to Ozaki. According to Kawai's memoirs, he met Ozaki at Yang's house in early October of 1931. Kawai recognized Ozaki as the *Asahi*'s correspondent, but he had also been informed by Yang that Ozaki carried orders for him "in the service of the cause." Ozaki spoke briefly, asking Kawai to meet him the following day on a certain street corner in Shanghai. Kawai complied, and they were soon joined by a "foreign

* *Rōnin* were unemployed samurai who made their living as mercenaries. Kazama refers to Kawai as a *fūunji*, or soldier of fortune. *Aru hangyaku*, p. 111. Details on Kawai's limitations as a reliable source of information will be introduced later.

woman" with an automobile. She drove them to a Chinese restaurant in Nanking Road, where Kawai was introduced to a "foreign man." The two foreigners spoke German with each other, and the man spoke to Kawai in English with Ozaki translating.[42]

Richard Sorge asked Kawai, "Can you depart at once for north China and Manchuria?" After Kawai assented, Sorge continued: "The information we need is of a general coverage nature, similar to that gathered by a journalist. In particular, you must pay strict attention to the possibility of an invasion of Siberia by the Japanese Army."[43] Kawai left immediately for the north; he visited Peking and Mukden and reported back to Ozaki in January 1932 on what he had been able to learn about the Kwantung Army. He was sent to Manchuria again during 1932, and in 1933 Ozaki and Smedley helped him set up a permanent listening post in Peking (see Chapter Five). It is doubtful whether Kawai provided any intelligence that Sorge could not have read in the Shanghai newspapers, but Sorge nevertheless described him in his prison memoirs as "constantly in touch with conditions in north China" and "very anxious to work."[44] After Ozaki returned to Japan in February 1932, Sorge himself made little further use of Kawai because the latter spoke none of the languages that Sorge knew. When the ring was reestablished in Japan, Kawai was always a satellite member under Ozaki, who remained a friend even after it was dangerous because of Kawai's police record.

The attention of Ozaki and Sorge was permanently shifted from the Nanking government to Japanese imperialism when the Sino-Japanese crisis that had begun in Manchuria spread to Shanghai itself. Throughout the fall and winter of 1931, anti-Japanese demonstrations and boycotts of Japanese goods took place in the Chinese sections of Shanghai, particularly in Chapei—across the tracks of the Shanghai-Woosung railroad, on the Chinese territory around North Station. The Japanese consul protested to the Chinese mayor, and the mayor made efforts to control the situation and to disband some of the anti-Japanese societies. But on January 28, 1932, the Shanghai Municipal Council declared a state of emergency, and foreign troops of the various powers represented in China began to take up defensive positions within their assigned sectors of the International Settlement. The Japanese put marines into Hongkew, the area of the International Settlement where Japanese residents and businesses were concentrated; but they also decided to try to oust the Chinese from Chapei.

Although it came to be known simply as the Shanghai Incident, the fighting that erupted after January 30 between the Japanese naval landing party and the Chinese Nineteenth Route Army (reinforced by divisions from Nanking and Chinese students) had all the characteristics of war. The Nineteenth Route Army's stubborn resistance came as a surprise to the Japanese forces, and in China the very name of the Nineteenth Army became synonymous with the upsurge of nationalism that began in the nineteen-thirties. The Chinese soldiers and students held out through a week of bloody fighting, and then, their forces virtually annihilated, withdrew to form a new defensive perimeter around Shanghai. This position was not seriously contested, and a truce was negotiated on May 5, 1932. The truce was basically a Japanese victory, for it created a large demilitarized zone in the Shanghai area into which no Chinese troops were allowed.[45] Sorge and Ozaki had put themselves in the midst of the fighting, visiting battle positions, reporting to their papers (and to Moscow) on the abilities and weaknesses of both sides, and reinforcing their private conclusion that Japan had become the number one object for Communist espionage in Asia.

In the midst of the Shanghai Incident, Sorge's smoothly running operations were struck a blow: Ozaki's newspaper recalled him to the Osaka office. Sorge asked Ozaki to resign and remain with him, but Ozaki recognized that his usefulness would be greatly restricted without his journalistic position, and he already had premonitions of a full-scale Sino-Japanese war and of the role he might play in Japan as a recognized expert on China. He declined Sorge's request but offered to help him secure a Japanese replacement. He introduced Sorge to his old companion Yamakami Masayoshi of Rengō Tsūshin (the United Press in Japan). Yamakami met Sorge twice and assisted him, but he had to terminate the relationship because he was too busy, having recently been appointed chief of Rengō's Shanghai bureau. Yamakami then introduced Sorge to Funakoshi Hisao, also of the Shanghai Rengō office, and Funakoshi became Ozaki's replacement.

In 1932, Funakoshi was a thirty-year-old journalist educated at Waseda University and its graduate school, from which he had withdrawn in 1925. He came to China—to Tsingtao—in October 1925 to work for a Japanese business firm, and then he moved to Shanghai, where he was employed as a reporter for the *Mainichi shimbun*. In Shanghai he associated with Japanese students and journalists like Kawai, and he became a member of the left-wing study group that met at Ozaki's home during 1929. In May of 1931 Funakoshi left the *Mainichi* to join Yamakami at Rengō Tsūshin, and between 1931 and 1935 he headed first the Hankow and then the Tientsin offices. In 1935 he became chief of the *Yomiuri shimbun*'s Tientsin office. (The *Yomiuri* is one of the big three of Japanese newspapers, the other two being the *Asahi* and the *Mainichi*.) In 1936, in Tientsin, he established the China Problems Research Institute, whose members included Nakanishi Ko and the left-wing postwar China specialist Ozaki Shōtarō.*

Funakoshi's most important affiliation, however, developed after the outbreak of the Sino-Japanese war. Because of his long experience in China, he was hired as a special adviser to the Japanese Eleventh Army's Special Affairs Department in Hankow (which was charged with relations with Chinese civilians). Between the time of the capture of Hankow (October 1938) and May 1941, he worked for the Japanese Army and continued to collect intelligence for the Soviet Union. In his capacity as a spy, he reported to Sorge's successor in Shanghai, and his work was unknown to Sorge and his group in Japan. Funakoshi was arrested in Peking in connection with the Sorge case on January 4, 1942, and sentenced to ten years in prison. He died in prison on February 27, 1945.[46]

Sorge worked with Funakoshi until he left Shanghai, but this collaboration was not as satisfying as the first one. Sorge wrote: "I met Funakoshi often, and our contacts continued until my departure from China. Upon being relieved of my duties by 'Paul,' I introduced the latter to Funakoshi, and the two of them worked together from then on. My relationship with Funakoshi was not as positive as it had been with Ozaki, and he did not bring in as much intelligence."[47] Sorge was undoubtedly sorry to see Ozaki leave Shanghai, but the de-

---

* No relation to Ozaki Hotsumi. Ozaki Shōtarō, an employee of the South Manchurian Railroad Investigation Bureau during the war, is the Japanese translator of Hu Ch'iao-mu's official Communist history of the Chinese Communist Party: *Chung-kuo kung-ch'an-tang ti san-shih-nien* (*Thirty Years of the Chinese Communist Party*) (Peking, 1951; Tokyo, 1953). He is also a director of the pro-Communist Chūgoku Kenkyū-sho (China Research Institute).

parture may have given him the idea that his own next assignment might profitably be Japan. Ozaki and Eiko sailed for Kobe with their young daughter early in February of 1932. Sorge remained in Shanghai until January of 1933, when he returned to Moscow to receive warm congratulations on his success and to make a reappraisal of future needs.

Although Sorge identified his replacement in the Shanghai group only as "Paul," Willoughby presumed that this man was the American Communist Eugene Dennis, alias "Paul Walsh," who arrived in Shanghai in 1933.[48] This may well have been the case, even though Dennis was a known Communist and associated with the Comintern, which would have broken the precedent established by Sorge. But whoever "Paul" was, the men with whom we are concerned had left Shanghai by 1933. Subsequent Soviet espionage in Shanghai might fill a book, but another book awaits us in Tokyo.

Chapter Five

The Organization of the Ring

SMEDLEY: I always knew you would have to return to Japan someday, but I didn't think it would be so soon.

OZAKI: It was very sudden for me, too. But I have made my decision,
and it is my own. Yesterday I saw three Chinese boys shot down at
the Japanese military camp. Their hands were bound behind their
backs, and three machine guns were pointed at them. . . . Agnes,
at that moment I made up my mind to go back to Japan. I'm not
really sure why. Until then I never intended to leave Shanghai.
I didn't want to leave you. . . . Johnson insists that my severing
relations with him is a serious mistake, but I don't understand his
reasons.

SMEDLEY: The German who calls himself "Johnson" has no fatherland. That makes him radically different from you.

OZAKI: But Johnson's fatherland is the only socialist nation in the
world today.

SMEDLEY: It is ours, too, but it is an ideological fatherland. . . .
Japan holds a very different meaning for you.

These lines are set in the year 1932 in Shanghai, but they were first
uttered in Japanese on June 5, 1962, in Kinoshita Junji's play, "A
Japanese Called Otto." If we make allowances for the requirements
of dramatic interpretation, Kinoshita communicates in this passage,
and throughout his play, the crisis of patriotism that Ozaki experienced in working for Sorge while trying to remain loyal to his own
country.[1]

This particular crisis became acute for Ozaki only after he returned
to Japan in February of 1932. In a sense, his Shanghai experience was
a separate and distinct phase of his career. For all of his intrigues with

foreign Communists on the mainland, he had not yet made a firm political commitment. When his newspaper ordered him to return to Japan, he did so at once, and he did not see his friend "Johnson" again for over two years. Kinoshita's play seems to assume that Smedley was Ozaki's mistress; this may or may not have been true—the evidence is conflicting—but if Smedley was not, Irene Wiedemeyer's sister probably was.* But whatever Ozaki's liaisons, it is clear that he did not experience in Shanghai the sort of deep personal involvement he later found in Tokyo. He cultivated Chinese revolutionaries, Comintern agents, and radical students—and even helped Sorge gather information about China for the Comintern—for reasons quite different from those that led him to supply Sorge with information from within the Konoye cabinet.

It was perfectly possible for Ozaki to have Communist mistresses and Comintern friends without becoming deeply committed. Shanghai was one of the freer "international cities" of the period, a place where one could feel liberated from the constraints and responsibilities of his own society. Moreover, it would have been natural for any ambitious young newsman reporting on the Chinese revolution to want to know more about the Comintern. Ozaki welcomed the opportunity to gather new information from Sorge and Smedley, for what he learned could be put to good use in the background and analytical reports he was writing for the *Asahi*; Miyazaki Seiryū says that he often saw Ozaki sitting in his office reading copies of the *Daily Worker* given to him by Smedley.[2] Personal affinities were important, too. Ozaki admired both of his new friends: "Sorge and Smedley," he said, "had the greatest loyalty to their beliefs and were very talented in their work."[3] Furthermore, Ozaki was gregarious and probably found it easier than many Japanese of his time to associate comfortably with foreigners. Both Kawai and Mizuno Shigeru were struck by his cosmopolitan tastes in food and liquor; and Kawai's recollection of his first meeting with the joking, flannel-clad Ozaki smoking English cigarettes is explicitly incorporated in the stage directions to Kinoshita's play.[4] Given Ozaki's personality, it appears likely that to some extent

* Miyazaki Seiryū recalls going to Smedley's apartment with Ozaki and noting that Ozaki had a personal key and that many of his private belongings were there; and later, in Japan, Ozaki spoke to Yamasaki Ken of an "international love affair" in Shanghai. (Kazama, *Aru hangyaku*, p. 94.) On the other hand, Kawai suggests that Ozaki's Shanghai mistress was the German girl at the Zeitgeist Bookstore. (*Aru kakumeika no kaisō*, p. 21.) Neither story, however, can be proved accurate.

he saw his relationships of the 1928–32 period as permissible Shanghai adventures.

At the root of Ozaki's decision to cooperate with Sorge in Shanghai, however, was his political perspective on the international situation. As he explained it: "The special characteristics of my ideological position in later years derived from my observations in Shanghai. First, [from studying] China's so-called semi-colonial position, I acquired a deep interest in [seeing] the national liberation and national unification of China. Second, I explored the reality of England's commanding position in China and soon came to the conclusion that England was the common enemy of China and of all the oppressed peoples of the world. . . . Then came the Manchurian Incident, the signal bell announcing the opening of a new century in East Asia. . . . The Chinese were unaware of the Japanese internal situation— that anxiety had existed in Japan for several years, chiefly because of the economic depression, and that for the Japanese there seemed to be no escape from these difficulties. They spoke with one resounding voice in denouncing Japanese imperialist aggression."[5]

Ozaki reasoned that Japan's stepped-up policy of imperialism would bring her into conflict with other imperialist powers and that Japan could never really defeat China. The war that was likely to come, he argued, would be disastrous for his country. In his opinion, Japan's salvation lay in bringing to power, preferably through an elitist domestic revolution, leaders who would pursue neutrality vis-à-vis the European powers and friendship toward the Chinese revolution, which he believed to be both inevitable and justified. Moreover, he thought that close relations with Soviet Russia, a country about which he knew almost nothing, but which he supposed was firmly committed to a policy of peace, would help Japan maintain neutrality. These opinions formed the basis of his belief that he was serving a just and realistic cause by aiding "Johnson." There was as yet no question of his conducting espionage against Japan; on the contrary, with the outbreak of the Manchurian and Shanghai Incidents, he was anxious to return home in order to familiarize himself with the changes that had occurred in his absence. He retained his close friendship with Smedley and met her again in Peking at the end of 1932, but he saw no more of Sorge for two years. In his first *tenkōsho,* Ozaki wrote of the 1932–34 period: "I enjoyed a quiet life with my wife and daughter living in Inanomura, an Osaka suburb on the Hankyū line. During these few years we had an ordinary family existence, compared to which my Shanghai activities were like a dream. Only a few days ago I received a letter from my wife saying, 'I believe that Yōko and I were happiest in the Osaka days.' I had completely cut my ties with the left wing in Shanghai."[6]

Two other points about Ozaki's Shanghai activities should be stressed. First, although Ozaki was not completely unaware of the growing identity between the policies of the international Communist movement and the interests of the Soviet Union, he believed until after his arrest that he was assisting the Communist International. Sorge never told Ozaki or any of the other members of the ring, including Smedley,[7] that he was an agent of Department Four. Second, although Sorge and Ozaki enjoyed a degree of personal camaraderie, Sorge did not tell Ozaki about his own past or even reveal his true identity. He did admit sometime in 1935 that he was of German-Russian, not American, parentage; but Ozaki discovered his real name by accident. In September of 1936, while attending a reception in the Imperial Hotel for the delegates returning from the Yosemite Conference of the Institute of Pacific Relations (where he had delivered a paper), Ozaki was introduced by a Dutchman to the German foreign correspondent, "Doctor Sorge." It was the same man he had known since 1930 in Shanghai as "Johnson."[8]

Ozaki's reestablishment of contacts with Sorge occurred at Sorge's initiative, and Ozaki's willingness to collaborate with him in Japan sprang from more acute political motives than his long-standing leftist ideological inclinations. Ozaki's quiet life in the countryside of Hyōgo prefecture near Osaka did not last long. He writes that upon his return he began to hear "much shouting about crises" and that he began to "conceal his thoughts."[9] Nor was it all shouting. Less than a week after he was home, on February 9, 1932, a member of the ultra-rightist Ketsumeidan (The Blood Brotherhood) assassinated the former Minister of Finance, Inouye Junnosuke. On March 5, the Ketsumeidan struck again, killing Dan Takuma, Chairman of the Board of Mitsui Gōmeikaisha, in a fascist attack on unrestricted capitalism. These assaults culminated in the May 15 Incident of 1932: the assassination by Naval Academy cadets of the Prime Minister, Inukai Ki. It is alleged that when the cadets burst into his office Inukai said, "We can clarify these matters by discussion" (hanaseba wakaru), and that the assassins replied, "Discussion is useless" (mondō muyō).[10]

It is significant that this phrase, *mondō muyō*, has been used to characterize the style of politics that developed in Japan during the nineteen-thirties; for a political order that proclaims discussion to be useless is one that invites treason or, conversely, one that makes the very concept of treason unintelligible.

Assassinations were only the most obvious signs of Japan's new course. Arrests occurred on a massive scale; and on February 24, 1933, Japan isolated herself from the rest of the world by withdrawing from the League of Nations. It goes without saying that the Communist Party became extinct in Japan. Aside from arresting Party leaders, the police raided the Japanese headquarters of MOPR (International Red Relief) on July 25, 1933; and in October about 2,500 persons who were affiliated with or had contributed to MOPR were arrested. Pressures on intellectuals and academicians greatly increased. In January 1933, Professors Ōtsuka Kinnosuke and Kawakami Hajime, two of Japan's most distinguished economists, were arrested and charged with reformist thought.* On February 20, 1933, the proletarian novelist Kobayashi Takiji was arrested and killed by the police; and on November 28, the Communist theorist Noro Eitarō was also arrested and later died in police custody.

The Takikawa Incident at Kyoto University was the most publicized manifestation of pressure on the intellectuals during 1933. Professor Takikawa Yukitoshi of Kyoto Imperial University's Law School had displayed an interest in Soviet criminal law, and he held the then unorthodox view that adultery was a crime. As a consequence, the Education Ministry, without warning, banned the use of his standard works, *Lectures on Criminal Law* (*Keihō kōgi*, 1930) and *Criminal Law Reader* (*Keihō tokuhon*, 1932), and ordered the University's President Konishi to fire him. When law professors Suekawa Hiroshi (today the President of Ritsumeikan University), Tsunedō Kiyō (now the President of Osaka Metropolitan University), and four others organized a protest group, they were also fired (May 1933). After the war, Professor Takikawa was reinstated and made President of Kyoto University.

There were several other incidents that affected Ozaki more personally. After his return from Shanghai he had joined the *Asahi*'s foreign

* Kawakami died in 1946. Ōtsuka was rehired by Hitotsubashi University after the war and became one of its most famous professors; he was honored with membership in the Royal Economic Society of London.

bureau as a respected authority on continental problems. Kazama remarks that Ozaki's personal confidence and ability had grown so remarkably that it was hard to recognize him as the young man who had gone to Shanghai in 1928.[11] Hosokawa Karoku of Osaka's Ōhara Institute warmly welcomed his friend back to Japan, and Ozaki became a frequent caller and lecturer at that organization. He introduced Mizuno Shigeru, who had been expelled from Tōa Dōbun in 1931, to Hosokawa, who hired him as an Ōhara researcher on Chinese problems. Hosokawa in turn introduced Ozaki to Horie Yūichi, a teacher at Takamatsu Higher Commercial School (Kagawa Prefecture) and a student of Marxist economics. Horie was greatly interested in China, and Ozaki urged him to go to the continent. In early 1933 Horie obtained an Education Ministry scholarship for a year's study at Tōa Dōbun, but in August 1933, after only five months in Shanghai, he was arrested on charges of having furthered the student movement at Takamatsu Higher Commercial School. The Japanese consul returned him to Japan, and he spent almost a year in Takamatsu prison (until May 1934). During this time Ozaki made frequent trips from Osaka to Takamatsu to inquire about Horie's well-being. It was typical of Ozaki, as we shall often note later, that he showed extreme loyalty to his personal friends regardless of their predicaments or of the danger to himself.

On February 20, 1933, the police set to work to extinguish what was left of the Japanese Communist Party. The leadership had been arrested in 1928, but in 1933 virtually the entire rank and file were seized. In March the police charged Ozaki's friend Hosokawa with being a Communist sympathizer; he was arrested but eventually received a suspended sentence. The police were so thorough that they even placed a Tokkō shadow on the Ōhara Institute's director, ex-professor Takano.[12] If these events were not disturbing enough to Ozaki, all he had to do was read the news from Germany during 1933 to believe that his worst predictions about the international situation were coming true. "I thought to myself," he wrote, "that after the Manchurian Incident Japan seemed to be charging frenetically in an unknown direction."[13]

Nevertheless, until the spring of 1934 Ozaki took no personal action to check the drift toward fascism and war. He did make a secret trip to Peking to meet and assist Smedley, but this was more a revival of old Shanghai associations than a new departure for him. It will be recalled that in the spring of 1932 Sorge sent Kawai Teikichi back to north China to report on the continuing struggle in Manchuria. But Kawai did not go to Peking. Having become frightened of arrest, he secretly returned to Tokyo in July, and from there he journeyed to Osaka and contacted Ozaki at his home. In the autumn Ozaki went to Tokyo to help Kawai maintain himself in hiding. At about this time Smedley wrote to Ozaki explaining the need for someone to continue the intelligence collecting in Peking and asking Ozaki to take the job. Instead, Ozaki recommended Kawai and said that he would help establish him in Peking.

By prearrangement, Ozaki left Kobe for Tientsin on December 25, 1932, Kawai having left earlier by a different ship from Yokohama. Ozaki took advantage of his year-end vacation, telling his wife and his newspaper superiors that he was going to visit a friend in Dairen. He met Kawai and Smedley on December 29 in his hotel room in Peking, and the three of them worked out the details of Kawai's operations and arranged for the transmission of reports to Sorge or his successor. This accomplished, Ozaki departed from Tientsin for home on January 3, 1933.[14] He had not seen Sorge, and he would not see Kawai again until March of 1935.

One day in April or May of 1934, while working in his office at the Osaka *Asahi* building, Ozaki received a visitor, a young man whose card read "Minami Ryūichi, artist." "Mr. Minami" told Ozaki that they had a mutual friend, a foreigner who had known Ozaki in Shanghai and wished to see him again. At dinner that evening Ozaki closely questioned "Mr. Minami" (who was Miyagi Yotoku, lately of the United States Communist Party), and the following Sunday he made an excursion to nearby Nara. There he met his old friend Richard Sorge, relaxing on the banks of Sarusawa pond in Nara's deer park.[15] Sorge had been very busy in the intervening years, but he was now ready to attempt the decisive operation in his latest assignment: the recruitment of Ozaki Hotsumi into the Soviet Union's first espionage group in Japan.

Sorge had been to Japan only once during his Shanghai period, and then only for a three-day visit in Tokyo, but he had found the country interesting enough to begin considering it as the locale of his next assignment. In December 1932, after turning over his operations in Shanghai to "Paul," he had returned to Moscow. Sorge described his reception as follows: "When I arrived back from China, I called on the Director of Department Four, Berzin, and his new deputy [Uritskii]. The two of them gave me a heartfelt welcome. They said that my work in China had been eminently satisfactory, and we agreed to meet later to discuss my future activities. . . . After completing my report for Berzin on my China work, he told me that my request for an extended stay in Moscow had been rejected. I was to go abroad again. Half jokingly, I said that I might be able to do some work in Japan, but Berzin said nothing then. Several weeks later, however, he took up my suggestion with enthusiasm."[16]

It was an opportune time to express interest in Japan. The Soviet Union had been extraordinarily concerned about that country since the Manchurian Incident, and Sorge believed that Berzin's instructions for him came from Stalin himself, via Voroshilov.[17] In fact, as we shall see in a moment, Moscow was already sending operatives to Japan when Sorge arrived back from China; it seems likely that Sorge, because of his success in China and his proven abilities, was chosen to lead a mission that had already been planned.

In April of 1933 Berzin set forth for Sorge the questions he was to answer during the first phase of his mission: (1) whether he and his collaborators could secure legal entry into Japan; (2) whether they could maintain contact with Moscow by radio; (3) whether they could establish liaisons with Japanese nationals and other foreigners; and (4) whether they could collect information on future Japanese policies toward the Soviet Union. To accomplish this initial part of the mission he was to have two years, after which he was to report back to Moscow in person. Sorge requested and received the following subordinate collaborators: a foreign national, a Japanese national fluent in English (for translating Japanese materials into a language that could be coded for radio transmission), and a radio technician. The three men made available to Sorge by Moscow, men whom the Comintern was already infiltrating into Japan, were Branko de Voukelitch (1904–1945), Far Eastern correspondent for the Havas Agency of Paris; Miyagi Yotoku (1903–1943), a member of the United States Communist Party and a professional artist; and "Bernhardt," who was Sorge's radio operator between 1933 and 1935, until Max Clausen arrived in Japan.

Branko de Voukelitch, a Croatian, was born the son of an army lieutenant colonel in Osijek, Austria-Hungary. He studied art and architecture at the University of Zagreb, where he also joined the student Marxist club, and he was active in the Croatian independence movement until 1926, when he left Yugoslavia for Paris. He studied law at the University of Paris, but he withdrew without completing the course. In about 1929, he met and married the Danish woman, called Edith, who was with him in Tokyo. He may have joined the French Communist Party sometime during this period; in any case, he associated with French Communists, and in March 1932 he was asked by a Comintern agent—a woman with a Finnish or a Baltic accent identified only as "Olga"—to proceed to Tokyo under the cover of a journalist. He secured appointments as Far Eastern correspondent for the French magazine *La Vue* and the Belgrade daily *Politika*, and he received instructions from "Olga" on how to make his contacts in Tokyo. His first tasks in Japan were to become established and to develop his legitimate cover as a journalist.[18]

Voukelitch sailed from Marseille with his wife on December 30, 1932, and reached Yokohama on February 11, 1933. He was a trained photographer and photo technician, which made him especially valuable to Sorge in later years. He was also a competent newsman, and in April 1935 he was asked to become one of the Havas Agency reporters in the Far East. His formal Communist affiliations are not well known, and after his arrest he gave the Japanese police less cooperation than any member of the ring. Sorge said of him: "Voukelitch had absolutely no connection with the Moscow authorities—that is, with the CPSU, the Comintern, the Red Army's Department Four, etc. All of his contacts with Moscow were indirect. However, it was Moscow that ordered him to leave France and work for me. This meant that he had been recognized by Moscow, although I do not know by what organization. I believe that he was a member of the French Communist Party."[19]

Miyagi Yotoku, who was also selected by the international Communist network to work with Sorge, had a background that is extremely interesting for what it suggests about the political motivations of the Japanese members of the ring. He was born on February 10, 1903, the son of a poor peasant in Agarie village, Nago-chō, in the Kunigami district of Okinawa. In 1905 his father, Yosei, migrated to Davao, Mindanao, in the Philippines; his farming venture there failed, and after about a year he moved, by way of Hawaii, to California, where he eventually established a farm outside the town of Baldwin Park, near Los Angeles.

All this time Yotoku was left behind in Okinawa with his maternal grandparents, and he credits his grandfather, Higa Gichihō, with giving him his first political perspective: "It goes without saying that in my youth I was simply one hundred per cent nationalist [pro-Japanese]. However, my grandfather taught me that one should not 'oppress the weak,' and this provoked in me an antagonism toward the arrogant officials and physicians who came to Okinawa from Kago-shima [Kyushu] at this time. (Doctors, bank officials, and retired bureaucrats from Kagoshima became shrewd usurers, and they exploited the local peasants.) I believe that I acquired my first political consciousness at the age of 14 or 15 as I listened to my grandfather tell of Okinawa's brilliant history. He spoke of our people's flourishing trade with the South Seas and the golden age of our culture some three hundred years earlier, and he compared it with our present spiritually dependent society—a society in which those who work do not eat, a naturally and politically cursed 'palm-tree hell' [*sotetsu jigoku*] of wanton exploitation by Kagoshima capital."[20] Miyagi thus shared with Ozaki an early disgust for Japanese attempts to rule other peoples. Okinawa, although a prefecture and not a colony, was not radically different from Taiwan.

Miyagi was sixteen years old and enrolled in the Okinawa Prefectural Normal School when he discovered that he had tuberculosis. He withdrew from school and decided to visit his father in California, hoping there to pursue his interest in painting and art. He arrived at Seattle in June 1919, and after staying with his father in Baldwin Park until December, he moved to Brawley, in the Imperial Valley of California, where he studied English at the local high school and treated his tuberculosis with the desert air. In September 1921 he moved to San Francisco in order to enroll as a student in the California School of Fine Arts. He studied there for a year but found the moist climate damaging to his lungs, and so in April 1923 he went to San Diego. Between September 1923 and September 1925 he studied at the San Diego Public Art School, from which he graduated. He passed another year on a farm near Brawley nursing his lungs, and then, in September 1926, he moved to the "Little Tokyo" section of Los Angeles. Between 1926 and 1933 he supported himself by painting and by operating, with three Japanese friends, the Owl Restaurant near the city's Union Station. It was in Los Angeles that Miyagi first began to express his long-smouldering resentment against the treatment of Orientals on the West Coast.

Miyagi told the police on April 12, 1942: "My position after coming

to the United States derived from my reading of the classics of anarchism and Marxism and from my companions. However, there were
several practical problems that I believed could not be solved except
by a Communist revolution. These included: the contradictions of
American capitalism; the tyranny of the capitalists and the ruling
classes, and above all their inhuman oppression of Oriental peoples
(particularly Japanese); the spineless diplomacy of the Japanese government; and the contemptuous attitude of the Japanese government's overseas representatives toward immigrants (they referred to
us as the 'discarded people'), their adulation of American capitalists,
and their collusion with leaders of the immigrant community to
oppress Japanese in America."[21]

In Los Angeles, Miyagi read extensively in the works of Gorky, Tolstoy, Bakunin, and Kropotkin, and he and his partners at the Owl
formed a "social science study group." He considered himself an ideological Communist rather than an anarchist as early as 1929, but he
did not join the Communist Party until two years later. He was very
skeptical of the sincerity of the Japanese party members, and he felt
that the working-class movement was overrated in both the United
States and Japan. He states that even after he entered the Party he
intended to participate in the Communist movement mainly "as a
nationalist."[22] It was in the autumn of 1931 that Miyagi became a
member of the Japanese Section, Oriental Department, California
District, CPUSA.

Miyagi was never very active as a party member; his motivations
were primarily personal rather than ideological, and he spent most
of his time painting. He had married a Japanese girl in 1927, and in
1932 he and his wife rented a flat in West Los Angeles from one Kitabayashi Yoshisaburō. Here Miyagi first became acquainted with another party member, Kitabayashi Tomo, his landlord's wife. Like
Miyagi, Kitabayashi Tomo had entered the CPUSA in 1931, but she
returned to Japan in 1936 and later played a central role in the police
exposure of the Sorge ring.

There were many active Japanese members of the United States
Communist Party in 1932–33, despite the arrests of 1930, and there is
no ready explanation for why the Comintern chose Miyagi to meet
its needs. Whatever the reasons, an occidental Comintern agent and
a Japanese party official called on him in late 1932 and asked him to
return to Japan, for only one month, on a special mission for the Com-

intern. They asked him to contact in Los Angeles a foreigner named Roy, who would arrange for his passage and give him instructions.* Miyagi agreed but vacillated for almost a year before departing. (He aided the Los Angeles *Nichi-Bei shimbun* workers' strike during the summer of 1933.) Finally, on October 24, 1933, he left San Pedro on the *Buenos Aires Maru,* bound for Yokohama. Expecting to return soon to the United States, he left his wife and all of his personal belongings behind.[23]

The third member of the Sorge ring recruited by Moscow was a man known as "Bernhardt." Mr. and Mrs. "Bernhardt" (the name was probably an alias) were already established in Tokyo in 1933 when the other members of the ring began to arrive. Sorge wrote that "Bernhardt" had been a member of the German Communist Party in the twenties and had been ordered to Moscow for training at the Moscow Radio School, which was operated by and for the Red Army. He was assigned to Sorge on direct orders from Department Four. "Bernhardt" was not Sorge's own choice as radio specialist; he would have preferred Max Gottfried Friedrich Clausen, whom he did request as a replacement for "Bernhardt" in 1935.[24] There is no evidence that Sorge personally selected Voukelitch or Miyagi, either; he apparently let the Comintern-Soviet apparatus find men to fill his needs. The only man he specifically requested for the ring was Clausen, whom he had known in Shanghai, and the only man he personally recruited was Ozaki.

While these arrangements were being completed in the spring of 1933, Sorge was in Moscow meeting old friends, discussing the difficulties of his forthcoming assignment with top officials, and receiving coding instructions at Department Four. With Berzin's permission, he contacted his former comrades from the Comintern, Piatnitskii, Manuilskii, and Kuusinen, who feared for his safety in Japan but congratulated him on his past successes. Karl Radek of the Central Committee talked with Sorge at length about the general trend of Far Eastern politics, and Foreign Ministry officials who had served in Tokyo briefed him on conditions there. Department Four's code section established his key-lists for him: all messages were to be put into

* Willoughby was mistaken in his suggestion that "Roy" may have been the famous Comintern agent in China, Manabendra Nath Roy. (*Shanghai Conspiracy,* p. 54.) M. N. Roy was out of favor with the Comintern after 1929 and in prison in India after 1931.

English and then encrypted, using numbers taken from the 1933 and 1935 editions of the German *Statistical Yearbook*; messages were to be transmitted in five-digit word groups. Finally, in May of 1933, Sorge departed for Berlin in order to establish his own cover.

Sorge remained in Germany from May until July of 1933 and accomplished four specific tasks: he became an accredited newspaperman; he obtained an impressive series of letters of introduction to persons connected with the German Embassy in Tokyo; he became a member of the Nazi Party; and he acquired a completely legal passport. Sorge had remarkable luck with the newspaper editors he visited. The *Frankfurter Zeitung*, Germany's most respected newspaper and one of the last to be subjected to full Nazi pressure, made him its accredited representative, which meant that he would automatically become the senior German correspondent in Tokyo. He was also accepted as a correspondent by the influential *Amsterdam Handelsblad*, Berlin's *Tägliche Rundschau*, and a financial journal, the *Berliner Börsen Zeitung*.[25] Moreover, it was during these months in Germany that Sorge established his close ties with Karl Haushofer and Kurt Vowinckel, the editor and publisher, respectively, of *Zeitschrift für Geopolitik*; and they provided him with letters of introduction to several persons at the German Embassy in Tokyo. He also received letters from each of his editors addressed to the Embassy for purposes of identification and other letters to individual Germans in Japan.

Sorge's application for Nazi Party membership was a risk that proved worth taking. Normally, an extensive background investigation was required for a new applicant (to check on Jewish or Communist antecedents), but Sorge applied at an opportune time. The Nazis had just come to power, and a flood of new requests for Party membership was being processed. Sorge said that since he was recommended by two reliable Party members (a colleague and a personal friend, not otherwise identified), "a close investigation was not necessary."[26] Even so, he did not wait in Berlin to hear whether he had been accepted; he received word of his membership after he arrived in Tokyo. Before leaving the German capital he had also obtained a genuine German passport that listed his occupation as a journalist. Thus prepared, he traveled first to Paris and then to the United States. He took a ship from Vancouver, B.C., and eventually arrived in Yokohama on September 6, 1933.

In Tokyo, Sorge called on the German Embassy and the Information Bureau of the Japanese Foreign Ministry (Gaimushō). He contacted Voukelitch and "Bernhardt" and set about to establish himself and his associates and to explore the possibilities of espionage. Miyagi arrived in November, and later that month, by means of a prearranged signal advertisement placed in an English-language Tokyo newspaper, he met Richard Sorge at the Ueno Art Museum. Miyagi was not happy to learn why he had been asked to come to Japan: "It required a good deal of thought for me," he said, "to decide to participate in Sorge's espionage organization. If the work had been in the United States, it might have been different. However, I wondered what my role would be as a Japanese citizen in Japan and whether or not my participation contradicted the emphasis I had placed on racial emancipation. The consideration that led me to agree to assist Sorge was the historical importance of our work—that is, the prevention of a Russo-Japanese war. At first I hoped to discover a replacement, because I had no training in espionage activities; but as time passed it became apparent that no one else would take the responsibility. Of course, I knew that our work conflicted with national statutes and that, in wartime, we risked the death penalty."[27] In the end, the Japanese government never passed sentence on Miyagi. The combination of prison conditions, his attempted suicide (in 1941, in order to protect the other members of the ring), and chronic ill health were enough: he died in prison on August 2, 1943.

Despite his introspection and self-doubt, Miyagi did what Voukelitch did and what Clausen would later do: he responded to a Communist Party order to serve the Communist International. Miyagi agreed to assist Sorge in January 1934, and in April or May of that year the two of them went to Osaka by different routes in order to attempt to enlist Ozaki. Miyagi made the initial contact with Ozaki, and Sorge then met him in Nara park. Precisely what Sorge said to Ozaki is not known; presumably, he asked Ozaki to help him gather information in Japan for the Communist International—information that would be used to fight fascism and aggressive war. Sorge himself undoubtedly believed that this was the ultimate purpose of his mission in Japan, and he probably saw no reason, then or later, to complicate his request by mentioning Department Four of the Red Army, General Berzin, or any of the other details of his Moscow affiliations. Ozaki listened to Sorge, argued with him briefly, and then accepted.

The reasoning behind Ozaki's acceptance still intrigues and disturbs Japanese scholars. In his twenty-first interrogation by the prosecution's investigator, on March 7, 1942, Ozaki responded to a question concerning his reestablishment of contacts with Sorge: "I readily accepted his proposal" (*dōnin no mōshi-ire o kaidaku shite*).[28] The word *kaidaku* ("ready acceptance") is simply unacceptable to Japan's most thorough investigators of the Sorge case. Ozaki Hotsuki argues that here the word means "without hesitation," adding that "if it is said that Ozaki's heart did not falter, it is a lie."[29] Kazama Michitarō implies that the statement was made under police pressure and that, in any case, it was not true.[30] Aochi Shin contends: "First of all, we have strong feelings about the word 'spy.' If the object of espionage were another nation, one might feel differently; but the betrayal of one's fatherland is the most despicable of acts. In Ozaki's case he did not engage in espionage for money but for his ideology and beliefs. Nevertheless, it must have been a heavy mental burden for him. . . . At the time, Ozaki was making his debut as a young China critic, and he had a bright future ahead of him. Under such circumstances it is a blasphemy against humanity to believe that he headed blindly toward his death without hesitation."[31]

There is only slight evidence to support these views. In the third and fourth questionings of October 1941, Ozaki said that he reminded Sorge that they were in Japan, not China, and that the Japanese police were considerably more capable than their Shanghai counterparts.[32] Nevertheless, he did agree, then and there, to assist him. His reasons, certainly, were not those of Voukelitch, Clausen, "Bernhardt," or Miyagi. He had no organizational responsibility to the Party, he was not under anyone's orders, and he had not cut his ties with his native land; unlike Miyagi, he was a rising member of the Japanese elite and had a good career ahead of him. Obviously, he did not decide to commit treason impetuously; what appears to be overlooked by those who boggle at the word *kaidaku* is Ozaki's previous intellectual development. He could say *kaidaku* because he was the sort of man, rare in any culture, who held his own counsel. His agreement to assist Sorge was the act of an educated person whose whole experience had convinced him of the need for political action.

Ozaki was an experienced political analyst with genuine confidence in his own judgments. In his first *tenkōsho*, he wrote: "The crux of my anger over contemporary Japanese politics is that the political leaders of Japan have no coherent understanding of the direction in which the world is moving. . . . Since the Manchurian Incident, the military has continued relentlessly to seize political leadership; but the politicians have shown themselves lacking in the discernment and ability necessary to control the situation. The militarists' goal in foreign policy is close cooperation with Germany—even if this provokes a war with the U.S.S.R. as well as with Britain and America. It is absurd that Japan has galloped furiously into this catastrophic war. . . . Ten years have passed since I began concrete leftist activities . . . but my basic beliefs have never changed during that time. As the global situation developed, I saw my beliefs increasingly proved true, and this strengthened my confidence. My confidence, in turn, helped me overcome my fears and become braver. Thus I continued to engage in espionage work, which was the direct expression of my left-wing involvement."[33]

The meeting at Nara ended Ozaki's peaceful family life in Kansai. Sorge knew that before he could begin collecting meaningful information he needed to know much more about Japanese politics, and so he asked Ozaki to move to Tokyo and work as a private tutor. Ozaki made it clear that he would not leave the *Asahi*, but said he would try to arrange for a transfer. Then fortune smiled on the conspirators: Ozaki was unexpectedly invited to join one of the most important research and policy-making bodies in Japan.

In September 1934 the *Asahi shimbun* established in Tokyo the East Asia Problems Investigation Association (Tōa Mondai Chōsa Kai), a semi-independent research bureau affiliated with the *Asahi*.[34] Its purpose was to investigate continental problems in anticipation of Japan's deepening involvement in Manchuria and China and to serve as a common forum for representatives of government and industry concerned with Asian policy. The *Asahi* staff members included Ogata Taketora (1888–1956), the *Asahi*'s editor and president of the association; Ōnishi Itsuki, a China specialist and a member of the *Asahi* editorial board; Takeuchi Ayayoshi, a specialist on Chinese and Mongolian economics; Kaji Ryūichi, an Asian and Soviet expert; and Masuda Toyohiko, an *Asahi* political analyst. In addition to these men, the Foreign Ministry's chief information officer, officials from the Colonial Office (Takushokushō) and the Finance Ministry, the Army and Navy press officers, representatives of the General Staff and the Navy, Mitsui and Mitsubishi executives, and professor Takagi Yasaka of Teidai participated in the deliberations. When the association was founded in the autumn of 1934, Ozaki was asked to come to Tokyo to become one of its staff members, which put him in an excellent position to gather information for Sorge.[35]

Before leaving Osaka, Ozaki hurriedly completed his translation of Smedley's *Daughter of Earth*. He had been working on it sporadically for more than two years, but the writing had not gone well, and so he enlisted the help of two colleagues at the Osaka *Asahi* office (Kikunami Katsumi and Fukazawa Chōtarō) and finished it during the summer of 1934. *Onna hitori daichi o yuku,* translated by Shirakawa Jirō, appeared in the Tokyo bookstores in mid-September, just as he, Eiko, and Yōko were establishing their new household there.[36] Ozaki had not heard from Agnes Smedley since the spring of 1933, when she left China for the Caucasus to enter a rest sanitarium. Before 1933 Smedley had been the *Frankfurter Zeitung*'s China correspondent, but with the rise to power of the Nazis, the newspaper came under the financial control of the I. G. Farben interests, who bought up Smedley's contract. She had trouble finding a new employer, and in the autumn of 1934, on her way back to China, she unexpectedly called on Ozaki at the *Asahi* offices during her ship's stopover in Yokohama. She inquired about the possibility of finding magazine commissions in Japan and told him that she was going to China to enter the guerrilla areas in Kiangsi, which had recently been evacuated by the Communists. Ozaki probably obtained from Smedley at this time some manuscripts that he promised to translate and publish in Japan. Sorge, however, instructed him not to associate with her in the future because she was known to the police. Ozaki never met Agnes Smedley again, and she had no further involvement with the Sorge case until General Willoughby brought his accusations against her in 1949.

In Tokyo in 1935, Ozaki quickly became one of the central figures of the *Asahi*'s Tōa Mondai Chōsa Kai, and during the summer and autumn of that year he made his third trip to China since returning from Shanghai. (The other two were his meeting with Smedley and Kawai in Peking in December 1932, and his trip to Dairen, Mukden, and Harbin in 1933 to report on Japan's recognition of Manchukuo; he was accompanied by Moriyama Takashi of the *Asahi* on the latter trip.)[37] The 1935 visit was a joint inspection mission by members of the Tōa Mondai Chōsa Kai under the leadership of Ōnishi Itsuki. The Japanese specialists toured north China, and in June 1936 they published their observations in the first of a series of perceptive volumes on contemporary Chinese politics, *Genchi ni Shina o miru* (*China Seen Firsthand*).[38] Ozaki contributed the chapter on Shantung and the record of his interview with Yin Ju-keng, the Japanese puppet in east Hopei. (He also interviewed Sung Che-yüan and Han Fu-ch'ü on this trip.) The following year, in February 1937, the Tōa Mondai Chōsa Kai published an even more valuable book, and one that had a good deal of influence among Japanese liberals. This was *Utsuri-yuku Shina* (*Changing China*), to which Ozaki contributed the chapters on Chinese economic problems, on the Chinese Communist Party, and on the role of the Great Powers in China.[39] Ozaki's knowledge and influence had increased rapidly since 1935, when his first independent articles had appeared in *Chūō kōron*,[40] and he was beginning to be respected in policy-making circles. He was becoming the perfect complement to Sorge, who was himself already well-established within the German Embassy and beginning to get leads on the Anti-Comintern pact, then under secret negotiation.

Sorge chose the period of Ozaki's 1935 trip to China for his own trip to Moscow to report on the establishment of the ring. He left Tokyo in July and traveled to Russia via New York.[41] In the Soviet Union, he reported to General Berzin's successor as head of Department Four, General M. S. Uritskii—a Stalinist who as a young Red officer cadet had participated in the suppression of the Kronstadt Mutiny in 1921. Sorge told Uritskii of his success in organizing the ring in Tokyo, and he mentioned the name of Ozaki Hotsumi to his superiors for the first time.[42] Uritskii approved Sorge's selection and use of Ozaki, and he assigned Ozaki the code name "Otto." Sorge went on to insist that he be given an absolutely free hand in cultivating his contacts at the German Embassy, to which Uritskii also assented.

Finally, Sorge asked to have "Bernhardt" replaced. In his second confession, he explained: "Speaking technically, his [Bernhardt's] work was quite unsatisfactory. I could send only very short messages, and those only infrequently. Not only that, he became completely panic-stricken at the thought that our two stations could not be insured against detection. When Clausen arrived in Japan, everything changed. He had unlimited ability and enthusiasm for his work. Also, while Bernhardt was here, I had to do all of the encoding of messages, a very time-consuming job; however, after Clausen arrived, I obtained Moscow's permission to teach him the codes."[43]

Even before arriving in Moscow Sorge had probably sent a message asking Uritskii to assign Max Clausen to him in Tokyo; at any rate, Uritskii promptly informed him that Clausen was available. Uritskii talked at length with Sorge about the importance of his work and warned him not to proceed too rapidly. After consulting with Party leaders and obtaining instructions for Sorge—namely, to warn the U.S.S.R. against a Japanese attack on Siberia and to keep Moscow informed of trends in Japanese foreign and domestic policy—Uritskii arranged for Sorge's immediate return to Tokyo. Sorge made his way to Berlin, and then flew to Tokyo, arriving on September 26, 1935.*

Max Clausen followed Sorge, reaching Yokohama via Europe and America on November 28, 1935.† Clausen was one of the more unusual figures in the Sorge case because he apparently lacked strong Communist beliefs. Only his extraordinary abilities as a radio technician led Sorge to request him and Department Four to approve him for service in Tokyo. Clausen was in serious trouble with Department Four in 1933, when Sorge first asked for him, because of his unapproved liaison with Anna Wallenius (later his wife); and in Tokyo his bourgeois habits often conflicted with his responsibilities to Sorge. Max and Anna Clausen both felt at home with and greatly enjoyed the life their Tokyo cover provided them: he was ostensibly the prosperous, Mercedes-driving German businessman, the president of "M. Clausen Shōkai," sales representatives for German blueprint machines in Japan. After his arrest he talked far more than any other member of the ring in order to save himself. When the Allies declared their amnesty for all political prisoners in 1945, Max Clausen was the only one of the top five within the ring to walk out of prison free. In early 1946 he and Anna disappeared from Japan, and it has been said, but never confirmed, that they now live in East Germany.[44]

* Willoughby contends that Sorge went to Moscow in 1935 in order to attend the Seventh Congress of the Comintern (July 25 to August 20, 1935). (*Shanghai Conspiracy*, pp. 73–74.) However, Sorge testified that Manuilskii told him over the telephone that he was strictly forbidden to attend and that the only person he saw from the Comintern while in Moscow was Kuusinen. Piatnitskii was ill and unavailable for consultation during Sorge's 1935 visit. (*Gendai-shi shiryō*, I, 210.)

† Willoughby follows his Japanese translator in consistently misspelling Clausen's surname as "Klausen." The correct form is clearly shown on Clausen's Shanghai driver's license (photo, *Shanghai Conspiracy*, p. 75), typewritten letters by Clausen, and in Clausen's signature (frontispiece photos, *Gendai-shi shiryō*, III). In the U.S. Army volume, *A Partial Documentation of the Sorge Espionage Case*, Clausen's name is spelled with a "K" in the text and with a "C" in the photo captions.

Max Clausen was born on February 27, 1899, the son of a poor merchant on Nordstrand Island in the North Sea, a part of the province of Schleswig-Holstein. Having completed his basic schooling, he was drafted into the German Army in April 1917. He joined a radio unit and fought on the Western front. After the war he served an apprenticeship as a blacksmith, and in 1921 he became a merchant seaman working out of Hamburg. He was strongly influenced by both left- and right-wing propaganda during the period of Germany's economic inflation and political upheaval, but he did not join the German Communist Party until July or August of 1927. In February 1929, two Comintern representatives asked him, on the basis of his wartime training and his knowledge of radio, to become a radio operator for the Communist International. Clausen agreed, but after reaching Moscow he learned that he was to be trained by and attached to Department Four of the Red Army. He received only a few weeks of radio instruction, and in April 1929 he was dispatched to Shanghai as a radio operator for one of the groups in Asia other than Sorge's.[45]

Clausen worked in China and Manchuria for Department Four until August 1933. He built radio sets and sent messages for agents in Shanghai, Canton, Harbin, and Mukden during this period; he also met Sorge in Shanghai, although he never worked directly for him. While operating out of Shanghai, Clausen fell in love with a young widow, Anna Wallenius, whom he eventually married in August 1936, after joining Sorge.

Anna Clausen was born April 2, 1899, of Finnish parents, in Novonikolayevsk (the pre-1925 name of Novosibirsk), Siberia. At the age of 16, she married Edward Wallenius (the brother of Kurt Wallenius, who later became a General in the Finnish Army), and they moved to Finland. Soon thereafter Edward Wallenius became a salesman for Finnish electric generators and they returned to Russia, to live near Semipalatinsk in Kazakhstan. At the time of the Bolshevik revolution, Edward gave up his job and the couple fled to China. After passing a year in Urumchi, they moved, in 1921, to Tientsin. In 1924 Anna's husband bought a small lumberyard in Shanghai, and they transferred their household to that city. In 1926, just as their fortunes were improving, Edward Wallenius succumbed to a heart attack.

Anna was thus left alone, a White Russian refugee living in Shanghai. For the next four years she made her living as a nurse and took in boarders. One of these boarders was Max Clausen, who rented a room from her in July 1930. They fell in love, but Anna—who hated the Bolsheviks—was distressed when she eventually discovered that Clausen was not an automobile mechanic, as he had told her. She continued to disapprove of his politics and his work, but she remained loyal to him nevertheless. She left with him for Russia in August 1933 (although at the time she thought they were going to Germany), and in November, after vacationing for a few weeks by the sea at Odessa, Max entered one of Department Four's radio schools near Moscow.

In January of 1934, quite without warning, Clausen was told by Department Four that "the results of his work in China were unsatisfactory" and that he was to be punished with a period of "reform through labor."[46] He and his common-law wife were sent to the Volga-German Autonomous Soviet Socialist Republic, where Max went to work in the machine tractor station.* Anna later told the Japanese police that life there "was on an extremely low standard,"[47] and Max complained of having to attend ideological lectures along with the German peasants. Max and Anna Clausen remained in the Volga-German Republic from January 1934 until April 1935. It was for this reason that Department Four reported Clausen as unavailable when Sorge requested him during the formative period of the Tokyo ring. Clausen never knew, or never told the Japanese police, precisely what had been unsatisfactory about his work in China; presumably, it was because he was on intimate terms with Anna Wallenius, a known anti-Bolshevik, and had told her the nature of his mission.

The Clausens were fortunate that Max was known to Sorge and had a reputation as an excellent radioman. Had Sorge not requested him, they might have remained in the Volga-German Republic and have been shot or deported to Siberia in 1941. Sorge apparently requested Clausen as a replacement for "Bernhardt" even before he

---

* The Volga-German A.S.S.R. was a colony of Germans who had begun settling in the area around Pokrovsk (after 1932, known as Engels) as early as 1762; it had been Catherine II's idea to encourage German immigrants to settle on the lower Volga in order to block Asiatic penetration. The Bolsheviks created the Volga-German A.S.S.R. in January 1924, during the early period of Soviet nationalities policy, and the small enclave was enthusiastically pro-Soviet until the Second World War. Nevertheless, on September 2, 1941, the Volga-German Republic was abolished by decree, and all of its inhabitants were forcibly deported to Siberia. See Robert Conquest, *The Last Empire* (London, 1962), pp. 50–52, 61–63.

arrived in Moscow; the Clausens later said that the message ordering Max's recall to Moscow arrived in the Volga Republic in April or May of 1935. (Clausen even said that the order was signed by Voroshilov himself.)[48] After reaching Moscow, the worried pair were relieved to hear that they were going overseas; Max thought that it would probably be to the United States, but Sorge told him personally that the mission was to Japan. Clausen received more radio instruction in Moscow between May and September of 1935 and then left for Japan via Europe and America. He carried forged Austrian and Canadian passports, in addition to his own valid German passport, in order to disguise his passage. Anna was kept in Moscow as a hostage and a virtual prisoner until March of 1936, when she was finally allowed to travel by train to Vladivostok and by ship to Shanghai. Max Clausen and Anna Wallenius were reunited in Shanghai in August 1936 and were married by the German consul there. Max took Anna back to Tokyo with him, and she later assisted him in his work by carrying microfilm reels under her clothing to Shanghai and by helping him in his periodic moves of the transmitter around Tokyo.[49]

With Clausen's arrival in Tokyo, the main structure of the Sorge ring had crystallized. At the center was Richard Sorge, the man who collected information from the other four members and compiled it into one basic report for transmission to Moscow by radio or courier. His own prime sources of information were the German Embassy and his private researches. Second in importance to Sorge, and the man with whom Sorge tested and verified all of the rumors he heard at the German Embassy, was the senior Japanese journalist and political publicist, Ozaki Hotsumi. Ozaki's sources, as we shall see in the next chapter, were the Konoye cabinet and the South Manchurian Railroad Company. To this Sorge added: "Ozaki was a superbly educated man. His extensive knowledge and sound judgment made him one of those rare persons who are sources of information in themselves."[50] Miyagi Yotoku cultivated a wide variety of minor informants connected with the Japanese Army, and he translated Japanese documents into English for Sorge. Voukelitch drew upon his associations with French and British journalists and the Dōmei News Agency, and he made a valuable trip to the front at the time of the Nomon-Han Incident (see Chapter Seven); he also did photocopying tasks for the group. Max Clausen performed miracles of surreptitious high-frequency radio transmission and also managed to bring in blueprints of military equipment manufactured by Mitsubishi, Mitsui, Nakajima, and Hitachi, who were clients of his business firm.[51]

This espionage group—probably the most important example of its kind prior to the cold war—had been patiently and carefully constructed. Sorge's attention to details of cover and security was painstaking, and the espionage work itself did not begin until everything was in perfect readiness. As Sorge explained: "In the period from the autumn of 1933 until the spring of 1935, any execution of our duties was completely out of the question. This time was spent in preparing to grapple with the especially difficult Japanese situation. We had to organize the group and lay a foundation before beginning positive operations. Moreover, we foreigners in the group first had to learn the subject matter that was the object of our mission; it was impossible for us to know all of the related problems from the beginning. Miyagi himself needed a good deal of time to acquaint himself with Japan, and those of us who were foreigners needed a proportionately longer period. Espionage work did not begin in earnest until after I returned from Moscow in 1935, and the group's real strength and abilities did not become manifest until the autumn of 1936."[52]

Sorge took elaborate precautions against the ever-present Japanese police—not only the Tokkō, but also the common policemen, who, in prewar Japan, took notes on meetings between Japanese and foreigners, and enlisted maids and neighbors as informants. Sorge's associates were to have absolutely no contact with Japanese Communists or fellow travelers (a weakness that eventually destroyed the ring), and never under any circumstances were the members of the ring to associate with Russians. Code names were used in all communications, written and wireless, including codes for the addressees: "Wiesbaden" for their Siberian receiving station (Vladivostok or Khabarovsk) and "Munich" for Moscow. In the early years of the ring, elaborate efforts were made to avoid all meetings between the top five members that could appear as anything other than coincidental. However, as the possibility of a Japanese-Russian war became more acute, they had to meet often. Sorge and Clausen met at the German Club, Clausen and Voukelitch developed a Franco-German friendship, Miyagi was commissioned by Ozaki to paint his wife's portrait, and Ozaki and Sorge met as senior journalists of allied nations.

Each of the primary members of the ring cultivated his own sources of information and occasionally enlisted an outsider as a member of the ring directly subordinate to himself. These lesser members of the group were not known to the other primary members; Sorge says that he had to trust to the discretion and ability of his associates in this respect and that he purposely avoided inquiring about the names of their satellite informants.[53] Miyagi had the greatest number of followers; but Kitabayashi Tomo, who eventually betrayed him, was only briefly one of these. One man who apparently knew all the members of the Sorge group was the British newspaperman Günther Stein, and his connection with the ring requires some explanation.

Günther Stein (b. 1900), a German who had become a naturalized British subject, was a prominent left-wing correspondent who wrote extensively on Far Eastern politics.[54] He was a correspondent in Europe and Moscow for the *Berliner Tageblatt* until 1933, when, as an anti-fascist and a Jew, he left Germany for London. Between 1934 and 1944, he served as the Far Eastern correspondent for the London *Financial News*, the London *News Chronicle*, the London *Daily Telegraph*, and the Boston *Christian Science Monitor*. He gained considerable recognition during the war as the special Chungking reporter for the International Secretariat of the Institute of Pacific Relations, whose headquarters were in New York. He was naturalized by the British government in Hong Kong on August 6, 1941, and obtained a valid British passport there on September 2. He was highly regarded as an economic and financial reporter, although it was known that as a German refugee he held strong anti-Nazi and anti-fascist views.

Stein was in Tokyo from early 1936 until mid-1938. During that time he met Sorge and helped him gather information on Japan. Possibly more significant, Max Clausen built and operated his first transmitter in Stein's house in Tokyo (where it was located until August 1938).[55] Stein's sources of information—noted and praised by Sorge—were the British Ambassador; the Commercial Counsellor of the British Embassy (1925–40), and the West's best-known historian of Japan, Sir George Sansom; various British and American journalists; and the Dōmei News Agency. On various occasions during his stay in Tokyo, he met all five of the main members of the ring. According to Sorge, "Because he [Stein] had also studied seriously the Japanese economic situation and had written excellent books on that subject, he was himself an important source of information. His researches clarified several aspects of the economic situation that were previously quite misunderstood. His specialty was Japan's foreign trade and financial problems."[56]

On August 4, 1942, the Japanese police asked Sorge directly, "What was the position of Günther Stein?" Sorge replied, "He cooperated with us only as a sympathizer."[57] The importance of Sorge's answer lies in the fact that General Willoughby named Stein as a "Soviet agent" in his *Shanghai Conspiracy* and characterized him as a member of the Sorge spy ring before the McCarran Committee when it was investigating the Institute of Pacific Relations.[58] Shortly after the release of the SCAP report, Stein, who was living in the United States at the time, left for Paris; there, on October 18, 1949, he produced a registered press card identifying himself as the representative of the *Hindustani Times* of New Delhi. He remained in Paris until November 14, 1950, when he was arrested and charged by the French police with being a Soviet espionage agent. He was then deported to Great Britain. Willoughby may have been involved in urging the French police to take such action; he admitted to the McCarran Committee that he had corresponded with the French Ambassador in Tokyo about the Stein case.[59] In London, Stein denied that he had been involved in any Russian spy ring either before or during World War II, and added that the accusations made by Willoughby and the French "secret police" were false.[60]

The documents suggest that both Willoughby and Stein are partly correct and partly wrong. Stein certainly must have thought that he was assisting the Comintern by aiding Sorge, but he probably did not know—any more than Ozaki and the others knew—that Sorge was an agent of the Red Army. Willoughby, however, consistently interpreted the available information to indicate that Stein was a Moscow agent, and this cannot be sustained by the evidence. Sorge and Clausen both identified Stein as a "sympathizer."[61] Furthermore, Sorge once asked Moscow to accept Stein as a member of the ring, but Moscow turned him down.[62] Willoughby's own questioning of Tokkō Police Inspector Ōhashi Hideo, one of the leaders of the police group that broke the case, is inconclusive as to Stein's role.[63] Stein's motivations were probably those of the Soviet collaborators known and described by Hede Massing: "The common basis was the hatred for fascism. The belief was that only the international Communist party

understood the real danger and was able to fight successfully. Dead as
the German fascist issue is today, if we do not recall the menace it
represented and the general appeal to fight it in 1933, we fail to understand the very root of the development that, in its final stage, led men
like those [her collaborators] to commit espionage for the Soviet
Union."[64]

Sorge's group attracted not only men like Stein, who were motivated by political principles, but also a few adventurers and opportunists. The foremost among these was Kawai Teikichi. Kawai had been
busy in China since his meeting with Ozaki and Smedley in December of 1932: he had established liaisons with Chinese informants in
Peking, Tientsin, and Dairen, and he himself had opened a bookstore
opposite the office of the Kwantung Army's Tokumu Kikan (Special
Affairs Unit) in the Japanese concession of Tientsin.*

Kawai became friendly with some of the civilians associated with
the Tientsin Tokumu Kikan, notably with Fujita Isamu, a right-wing
adventurer (uyoku rōnin) who had played a part in the murder of
Chang Tso-lin in 1928. In fact, Kawai became so engrossed in Fujita's
activities that he gradually lost contact with his Communist superiors.
When he returned to Japan in March 1935, he lived with and at the
expense of Fujita, and the two of them associated intimately with
members of the "imperial way" faction of the Army, who revolted in
Tokyo on February 26, 1936.

It was presumably because he thought Kawai could give him inside
information on the plans of these military conspirators that Ozaki
enlisted him as a subordinate member of the spy ring. There is no evidence that Kawai himself supported the right wing ideologically, but
he never brought Ozaki any valuable information on the right wing's
intentions. It appears today that during this period Kawai was willing
to support anyone in the political demimonde who would in turn
support him financially and eliminate the necessity for steady employment. Sorge himself remarked, "Kawai should be thought of as one
of Ozaki's subordinates, but it would be closer to the truth to say that

---

* The Tokumu Kikan were the political organs of the Japanese Army in China—the
units that organized the provocations which in turn provided the pretexts for further Japanese penetration below the Great Wall between 1933 and 1937. The most
famous of the Japanese political-military plotters of the period and the officers who
actually gave the orders to the Tokumu Kikan were the Colonels, later Generals,
Itagaki Seishirō and Doihara Kenji, both of whom were executed by the International Military Tribunal for the Far East.

Ozaki was Kawai's means of support."[65] In 1940 Ozaki and Sorge turned Kawai over to Miyagi for training and supervision, but Miyagi became so exasperated at Kawai's "insincerity" and his limitless absorption of allotments that he returned him to Ozaki.[66]

It is possible that Ozaki befriended and helped Kawai in gratitude for an early act of loyalty to the ring. In January 1936, after Kawai had been back in Japan for less than a year, he was suddenly arrested and sent to the Japanese police in Ch'angch'un (Hsinking), Manchuria. The police had apprehended Fukujima Ryūki, a member of the Manchurian intelligence network that Kawai had organized, and Fukujima had implicated Kawai to the Tokkō. Kawai received a merciless third-degree interrogation in Ch'angch'un, but he said nothing about the Sorge ring. The Tokkō, unable to decide whether he was a rightist or a leftist, released him after ten months in jail with a three-year suspended sentence for violating the Peace Preservation Law. Kawai remained in Tientsin working with Funakoshi Hisao until September 1940, when he again returned to Tokyo. Ozaki and Miyagi tried to use him for almost a year, but finally, in July 1941, Ozaki obtained a job for him with Mizuno Shigeo's pulp firm in Hokkaidō. During this entire period, Ozaki helped Kawai financially; and after the war Kawai became one of Ozaki's strongest champions in the general left-wing dispute over the Sorge case.[67]

Among the many other subordinate members of the ring were Shinozuka Torao and Mizuno Shigeru. Ozaki recruited Shinozuka in 1935, and both Ozaki and Sorge believed that he would become their military expert. As it turned out, however, he was interested only in selling information to Sorge, and he was dropped before he had learned too much.[68] Mizuno, it will be recalled, was one of Ozaki's Tōa Dōbun friends in Shanghai. He was of much greater importance to the ring and to Ozaki personally than either Kawai or Shinozuka. Ozaki had obtained a position for him at the Ōhara Institute in late 1933, but Mizuno resigned from it in 1936 and came to Tokyo. He was not an ideal person to be recruited by Ozaki: he had participated in the secret Japanese Communist Party rebuilding movement in Osaka in 1935, and he was arrested and released in December 1936 on suspicion of violating the Peace Preservation Law.[69] Nevertheless, Ozaki liked Mizuno personally and included him among his subordinates in the ring.

Most of Mizuno's work for the ring was private research rather than direct espionage. Although Mizuno was again arrested and given a suspended sentence in February 1938 for violating the Peace Preservation Law, Ozaki secured an important staff post for him in the China Research Office (Shina Kenkyū Shitsu) in 1939. Ozaki's behavior with regard to both Kawai and Mizuno was neither deliberately foolhardy nor careless. It reflected his extraordinary loyalty to personal friends and, apparently, a belief that it was not very dangerous for him to associate with persons who had political police records.

There was another reason, besides the necessity for careful advance preparation, why the ring's real successes began, as Sorge said, in 1936. That year brought a major turning point in Ozaki's life, an event that made him the most valuable of Sorge's partners and also established him in his own right as an important man in Japan: he attended the Yosemite Conference of the Institute of Pacific Relations as a member of the Japanese delegation.

The IPR was an influential international organization committed to research and exchange of information on a broad range of political, social, economic, and technical problems confronting the nations bordering on the Pacific Ocean. It was organized on the basis of national councils, and these national units sent carefully selected delegations to several IPR conferences. During the period when Sino-Japanese and Japanese-American relations were deteriorating, IPR conferences naturally became forums for expressing differences of national policy. The 1936 conference, held in Yosemite National Park in California, was the last one in which the Japanese genuinely tried to influence world public opinion through the IPR.

The Japanese delegation to the 1936 meeting included the former Foreign Minister Yoshizawa Kenkichi as chairman; Yamakawa Tadao of the Foreign Ministry as vice-chairman; Takayanagi Kenzō, a legal specialist from the Imperial University in Tokyo; Kanai Shōji of the South Manchurian Railroad, who was later an adviser to the Japanese-controlled Mongolian autonomous government; and Lieutenant General (retired) Banzai Rihachirō, an expert on Chinese military affairs. The youngest regular delegate was Ozaki Hotsumi, a specialist on the China problem.[70] The Japanese Council of the IPR had chosen their spokesmen well; Ozaki's paper, written in English and entitled "Recent Developments in Sino-Japanese Relations," was as forceful and cogent a presentation of the Japanese case for its continental policies as could have been made at the time. There is no indication that

Ozaki was insincere when he wrote: "Japan has become a world power; yet, a still more important fact is that she is in a special position as an important Asiatic power. Japan's economic relations with the continent of China are incomparably closer than those of Great Britain or the United States. It is true that the Chinese markets have important significance both for Great Britain and the United States, but the importance of the China market for these countries is not so urgent as it is in the case of Japan. Hence it is natural that Japan's activities should be more expressive than those of the other two countries."[71]

In dealing with the Manchurian and Shanghai Incidents, Ozaki drew attention to the world economic crisis, the disorders in Manchuria after the death of Chang Tso-lin, the attempt by Chang Hsüeh-liang (with the aid of Chiang Kai-shek) to build railroads that would compete with the South Manchurian Railroad, the Nanking government's demands for the abolition of foreign concessions, the new Chinese tariff of January 1931, and China's protectionist policies toward its own industries.[72] Ozaki knew quite well that it was the pressure of Chinese nationalism that lay behind these policies, and that both the Chinese and the foreigners would have to compromise if the outstanding issues were to be settled. Nevertheless, it seems strange to read Ozaki Hotsumi, the "Comintern spy," repeating so forcefully the very rationalizations then being used by Japanese militarists in support of further aggression in China. Certainly, some parts of Ozaki's paper assume standard and "official" positions; but, as we shall see, the main thrust of his argument in this paper reflected the curious blend of Marxism and Asian nationalism that he was beginning to espouse.

In his Yosemite paper Ozaki approached Sino-Japanese relations with unusual candor; indeed, some postwar academicians have credited him with helping to free the whole study of Asian politics in Japan from the cultural and literary *gestalt* which had restricted it up to that time. The paper began: "It is idle to look toward such phrases as 'the same race and the same culture' or 'the goodwill of neighbors,' as has often been done in the past between the peoples of the two countries. . . . The two nations are standing face to face on the edge of a precipice. . . . In studying Sino-Japanese relations, let us also bar an idealistic method and adopt an economic and social approach."[73] This was perhaps more than candid. If Ozaki had been committed first and foremost to espionage, he would have seen no reason to champion an objective political and sociological study of the Chinese revolution; and surely he was endangering his "cover" when, at Yosemite, he praised the Lytton Commission's report on Manchuria, the very document that had precipitated Japan's withdrawal from the League of Nations.[74]

Attendance at the IPR conference signified Ozaki's acceptance into the ranks of the civilian political elite of Japan, and his selection as a member of the delegation marked him as a recognized spokesman for Japan's China policy. Moreover, on board the ship en route to California Ozaki made the acquaintance of two very highly connected young men who later gave him access to official circles. They were Saionji Kinkazu, grandson of the *genrō*, Prince Saionji; and Ushiba Tomohiko, soon to be one of the two private secretaries to Prince Konoye in the Prince's first cabinet. Saionji had graduated from Oxford University in 1930, and Ozaki had known Ushiba at Ichikō before Ushiba had also gone to Oxford to study. These two men were the secretaries of the Japan Council of the IPR, and since Ozaki was of their age, and all three shared a mutual respect for each other, they formed a natural group on board ship.

Ozaki's lifelong personal friendship with Saionji began at the IPR conference, and it was an attachment that certainly did not hinder his rapid advancement as a government adviser.[75] But it would be wrong to suggest that he cultivated Saionji only to advance his espionage work. Both of them were invited into the Breakfast Society because they were men of proven ability, and Saionji maintained his friendship with Ozaki after he was arrested in 1941. Saionji never knew that Ozaki was a spy, and when the Sorge case was exposed Saionji himself was arrested for having revealed to Ozaki secrets from the Foreign Ministry, where he was a consultant. Nevertheless, Saionji has steadfastly maintained since the war that Ozaki's motives were patriotic; and he provided the calligraphy that was engraved on Ozaki's tombstone in Tama cemetery.

The year 1936 marked the beginning of Ozaki's double life. The IPR conference and his meeting with Saionji were the beginning of his public career, a career of such great activity and commitment that it is impossible to believe that it was merely a "cover." On the other hand, 1936 was also the year in which valuable information first began to flow from Tokyo to Moscow. Attempts to reconcile these contradictory commitments within the context of Japan's steady descent into war with China would occupy Ozaki until the day of his arrest.

Chapter Six
Spy and Scholar

✵ ✵

The Shōwa Research Association (Shōwa Kenkyū Kai) was founded in November 1936 through the efforts of Gotō Ryūnosuke, who had been a close personal friend of Prince Konoye Fumimaro since both were students together at Ichikō. The Association was intended to bring the best civilian thinkers in Japan into a high-level, policy-planning brain trust; thus organized, it was hoped that these men could hammer out concrete measures for checking the drift toward war and fascism and define Japan's national interests in a way that would provide alternatives to the abject acceptance of *faits accomplis* engineered by military officers. The beneficiary of this concentrated intellectual activity was to be Prince Konoye (1891–1945), probably the most enigmatic of Japan's wartime statesmen, who in 1936 was contemplating accepting the premiership. At the time of the army mutiny in February 1936, which had dramatically illustrated the need to bring responsible men back into the government, Konoye had declined to serve. Nevertheless, he was widely regarded among civilians as "the last trump" (*saigo no kiri-fuda*) with which to forestall a total seizure of power by the militarists; and at the same time he was not wholly unacceptable to the military, for he came of impeccable lineage and was clearly an Asian nationalist. The Shōwa Research Association was to be the personal mentor and research bureau of this prospective standard-bearer of Japanese "liberalism" and constitutional government.

Gotō's efforts succeeded in at least one respect: he did bring together the leading political thinkers of the period, and he did place them at the service of Prince Konoye. Among the members of the Association, besides Ozaki, were: Kazami Akira (1886–1961), Konoye's first Chief Cabinet Secretary; Rōyama Masamichi (b. 1895), a Teidai political scientist; Miwa Jusō (1895–1956), Japan's most prominent labor lawyer and the translator of Kautsky's *Erfurt Program*; Sassa Hiroo (b. 1896), the assistant chief editor of the *Asahi*; Yabe Teiji (b. 1902), a Teidai professor of political science; Ryū Shintarō (b. 1900), an Ōhara Institute staff member and *Asahi* editorial writer; Ōkōchi Kazuo (b. 1905), a Teidai sociologist; Tachibana Shiraki (1880–1945), one of the South Manchurian Railroad's best-known Sinologists; Taira Teizō (b. 1894), a writer on politics and economics; Matsumoto Shigeharu (b. 1899), the chief editor of the Dōmei News Agency and Japan's translator of Charles Beard; Inaba Hidezō (b. 1907), an economist for the Cabinet Planning Board (Kikakuin); Wada Hiroo (b. 1903), an agricultural specialist; Gotō Fumio (b. 1884), a former Agriculture and Home Minister; Hosokawa Karoku (b. 1888), an Ōhara Institute analyst; Miki Kiyoshi (1897–1945), one of the most influential philosophers of the day; Tōhata Seiichi (b. 1899), an agricultural economist who had studied under Joseph Schumpeter; Nakajima Kenzō (b. 1903), a literary critic; Miyahara Seiichi (b. 1909), a professor of education; and the "reform bureaucrats" Kaya Okinori (b. 1889) and Taki Masao (b. 1884).[1] They were an imposing group, both on paper and in terms of their respective individual talents; but a more heterogeneous, mutually incompatible, and hopelessly indecisive group of liberal intellectuals intending to influence politics can hardly be imagined.

Ultimate responsibility for the failure of this group is commonly, and not inaccurately, placed on its leader, Konoye Fumimaro. But although Prince Konoye was certainly an ineffective leader, both personally and politically, the failure of his group cannot be blamed wholly on his own inadequacies. Of greater significance were the contradictory motives that brought the members together, the peculiar style in which they communicated with each other, and the particular policies they espoused. The Shōwa Research Association, which occupied as much of Ozaki's time and energy as did his work for Sorge, represented the main stream of the Japanese intellectual response to militarism and war; and before we can attempt to judge Ozaki and his role in the Sorge incident, we must understand the nature of that response and Ozaki's own part in it.

It must be understood, first of all, that the members of the Shōwa Research Association were desperate men. The Association was not a seminar called upon to explore problems affecting its members only distantly; it was more akin to a conspiracy, but one in which the conspirators dared not reveal their true motives to each other. Its members included liberals, ultra-nationalists, Communists, Marxists, opportunists, and several men committed only to bureaucratic roles. These men had no basis of mass support, no place to seek political asylum, and no freedom even in silence. They were under direct attack from the numerous extremists, so pervasive as to seem almost invisible, who were demanding a totalitarian state and a racist war in East Asia. They chose a policy of limited resistance that had little chance of long-term success, and each of them chose it for a different reason. They decided to support Prince Konoye as a means of gaining political leverage against the irresponsible authorities who had sought to neutralize and ultimately seize control of the Japanese government since 1930. They failed in the end, and even made a certain contribution to Japanese totalitarianism, but theirs was the only serious effort to challenge the militarists before the creation of a police state in 1941.

Japanese opinion on the Association is mixed. Aochi Shin has argued that "the activities of the Shōwa Research Association during the war [1937–40], which strongly influenced Konoye, epitomize in their complexity how the Japanese intellectual tried to cope with war and fascism. [The Association's] intellectuals, with their backs to the wall, stood on a narrow border area between cooperating with the war and criticizing it."[2] Shigemitsu Mamoru holds Konoye personally responsible for the Pacific War and suggests that the only importance of the Shōwa Research Association was that it allowed traitors like Ozaki to discover military secrets.[3] Yabe Teiji, who was a member of the Association, contends that it was definitely intended to work against "militaristic fascism."[4] Furuta Hikaru, who has written the best intellectual history of this period, shows an acute awareness of the dilemma of the intelligentsia but nevertheless holds the intellectuals responsible: "The failure of Konoye's appeasement policy, which was intended to exercise a negative control by means of cooperation with militaristic fascism, is a historical fact; at the same time, it was also a failure for the intellectuals who cooperated in his brain trust."[5]

Two main policies were advanced by members of the Shōwa Research Association: the New Structure Movement and what they chose to call the "East Asian Cooperative Body." Since the Japanese government used both of these policies to rationalize aggression in East Asia and to mobilize the home front for total war, a perplexing question arises: how could the intelligentsia, bent on avoiding total war, support such ultra-nationalistic programs? To find the answer, we must consider again the pressures on Japanese intellectuals in the mid-thirties. Japanese nationalism has its roots in the Meiji period, but it began to take a fascist turn only in the early thirties, after the Manchurian Incident, with the rise of several ultra-rightist organizations. A good example of the type—one that concentrated on purging democratic, liberal, Marxist, and neo-Kantian thought from the universities—is the Genri Nihon Sha (Fundamental Japan Society), which existed from February 1925 to January 1946. In the thirties it was headed by three dissident professors (Minoda Kyōki of Keiō University, Mitsui Kōno of Kyushu University, and Takata Shinji of Tokyo Teidai), and it received strong backing from the Education and Home Ministries and from the Procurator's Bureau.[6]

After 1931 the Genri Nihon Sha demanded that all academicians support the two basic rationalizations of the fascists' policy for Japan: "universal brotherhood" (*hakko ichiu*), which meant the expansion of the Japanese empire to include all of East Asia, and "clarification of the national polity" (*kokutai meichō*). The latter idea meant the redefinition of the respective roles of the Emperor and his subjects; concretely, it legalized the absolute sovereignty of the Emperor (and of his military commanders) and rejected the organic, or functional, theory of the Emperor (*tennō kikansetsu*). The Genri Nihon Sha began to purge the universities in approximately 1932. It was the prime mover in the Takikawa Incident of 1933, and its assault on scholars was completed in 1935 with the indictment of professor Minobe, the prime exponent of the organic theory, on a charge of lese majesty. After that time virtually all liberals, Communists, freethinkers, and non-conformists lived in forced retirement or became "converts" (*tenkōsha*). All the members of the Shōwa Research Association had chosen to remain active in public life by going through the motions of supporting *hakko ichiu* and *kokutai meichō*. They could work only as apparent converts to ultra-nationalism, as Japanese who seemed to differ with the militarists and fascist societies only over the best means to achieve common ends.

There was one insuperable difficulty in using this disguise: it was virtually impossible for one true *gisō tenkōsha* (disguised convert) to reveal himself fully to a fellow thinker without risking a miscalculation of the other's position. The result was that liberals had only a very limited communication among themselves, and that all of them, including Ozaki, put their published writings into an esoteric language that could be read in different ways by different men.[7] The belief by many members of the Shōwa Research Association that Konoye himself had made a *gisō tenkō* was ultimately their undoing: Konoye simply did not have the courage of his own convictions, whether ultra-nationalist or liberal. Nevertheless, it was in this context that many different persons, for very contradictory reasons, came together to support the East Asian Cooperative Body and the totalitarian state. They all hoped to achieve different results—from Ozaki's Asian Communist utopia to a holy war against the Americans and the English—through the implementation of these policies. What they actually helped promote was the total isolation of Japan from the other peoples of Asia, and, finally, the destruction of Japan itself in the bombings of 1945.

Furuta Hikaru and Miyakawa Tōru, the biographer of Miki Kiyoshi, have stated that the three most important theorists of the East Asian Cooperative Body were Miki, Rōyama Masamichi, and Ozaki Hotsumi.[8] Although many other Japanese specialists would dispute this list, all three men were outstanding for their liberalism, their ingenious rationalizations of rightist policy, and their ultimate failure to influence the course of events in any significant way. Miki's views were the most representative, and his influence may be detected in the works of all the other members of the Shōwa Research Association.

Miki Kiyoshi was trained in humanistic and idealistic philosophy. While a student at Ichikō in 1916, he read Nishida Kitarō's *Zen no kenkyū* (*A Study of the Good*), and the following year he entered the philosophy department of Kyoto University to study under him. Between 1922 and 1925 he attended universities in Germany and Paris as a student of Heinrich Rickert and Martin Heidegger; he specialized in the thought of Leibnitz, Aristotle, and Pascal. Unable to find suitable employment after returning to Japan, Miki became a journalist in Tokyo. He studied Marxism during this period but did not become a Party member; nevertheless, he was arrested in 1931 for donating money to the Japanese Communist Party. During the nineteen-thirties he wrote many books, as well as a daily column for the *Yomiuri shimbun,* and participated in the Shōwa Research Association. After the outbreak of the Second World War, he was conscripted as an army journalist and sent to Manila. On March 28, 1945, Miki was again arrested in Tokyo for allegedly helping a man wanted by the police (the Marxist, Takakura Teru); he died at the hands of the police in prison on September 26, 1945, after the war had already ended.[9]

The essence of Miki's views on the East Asian Cooperative Body (*tōa kyōdō tai*)—the phrase used by the intellectuals in preference to the New Order in East Asia (*tōa shinchitsujo*) or the Greater East Asia Co-Prosperity Sphere (*daitōa kyōei ken*)—was to insist that a Japan-centered theory of East Asia conflicted with the nationalism of other Asian peoples. (Ozaki's main contribution was to demonstrate this point with regard to the Chinese.) Miki advocated that a "new order" be established on the basis of an anti-capitalist, anti-imperialist liberation of the colonized peoples in Asia and the creation of a pan-Asian culture "analogous to Hellenism." Japan, he said, was to serve only as midwife in bringing this about: "Japan itself must conform to the principles of 'cooperativism,' which will naturally limit Japanese nationalism."[10] Here was the heart of the matter: a real cooperative body demanded that the Army place itself under civilian control and refrain from spreading "cooperativism" at the point of a bayonet. In the hope that the Army might heed their warning that the war was only accelerating the latent nationalism of the area rather than laying the foundations of Asian unity, the members of the Shōwa Research Association supported the puppet state of Manchukuo, denounced the Kuomintang as anti-Japanese and soft on Communism, and merely shook their fingers at the rape of Nanking and similar incidents. They ended up by approving of the Greater East Asia Co-Prosperity Sphere, which in practice meant only aggression.

Miki's views typified the orthodox Association position and were reflected in all of its publications.[11] This "liberal" position is usually contrasted to the right-wing philosophy of the "imperial way" (*kōdō tetsugaku*), which held that the East Asian Cooperative Body simply meant the extension of the Emperor-centered national myth of Japan to all of East Asia. For example, Kanokogi Kazunobu, a leading right-wing philosopher, asserted: "The basic principle of the East Asian Cooperative Body is actually nothing more than the 'nation-building spirit of Imperial Japan.' "[12] Nevertheless, as we shall see when we turn to Ozaki's position, there was at least one other view, namely, that the cooperative body should be the vehicle for driving European imperialists from Asia and promoting Communist revolutions in this area. Although Ozaki was mistaken in his belief that Japan itself would someday participate in a new Communist community of Asian nations, his ideas came close to predicting the ultimate historical reality: Japan's New Order did provoke such a furious war in China that it led to a Communist revolution.

The complement to the intelligentsia's backing for the East Asian Cooperative Body was their support for the New Structure Movement (Shin Taisei Undō). This was another, less idealistic attempt to create a strong political instrument on the Japanese domestic scene that could force the military to heel. As a consultant in the first Konoye cabinet (June 4, 1937, to January 5, 1939), Ozaki actually drafted the first organizational plan for the New Structure, and he supported its launching in 1940—a gesture that greatly perplexed Sorge.[13] The New Structure Movement, as envisioned by the Shōwa Research Association, was to fight fire with fire: since Nazism and European fascist ideas were permissible models for Japanese society during this period, the liberals proposed to create a totalitarian party of the masses that could impose its will on the Army and on the Army-dominated bureaucracy.

Clothing their ideas in *kokutai meichō* terminology, the Association's theorists advocated dissolving the existing political parties, creating a series of functional component organizations (mass bodies of workers, farmers, young people, etc.), and establishing a supreme directorate controlled by Prince Konoye. The liberals, of course, were not agreed on what to do with this "new party." Konoye was primarily interested in avoiding a domestic revolution that might topple the Emperor; Ozaki believed that the New Structure contained the germs of a Leninist party, which could replace the decimated and tactically bankrupt Japanese Communist Party; and many conservatives (who provided the financial backing of the Shōwa Research Association) supported it as a desirable duplication in Japan of the one-nation, one-party principle of the Nazis. They all agreed, however, on one point: the venal and faction-ridden traditional political parties had to be abolished.

During the period of the first Konoye cabinet, when Ozaki was involved in the initial planning of the movement, the Shōwa Research Association raised the New Structure idea and dropped it as too extreme. However, during his second premiership (July 22, 1940, to July 18, 1941) Konoye proclaimed the single political party to be a necessary condition for the "strong political leadership" he had promised for so long. The Army easily adjusted to this; it ignored the proposal insofar as it touched upon internal Army affairs, and it supported and subverted the civilian New Structure as a convenient organizational device for placing the economy on a wartime basis. As Shigemitsu has noted: "The political world [in mid-1940] was in a state of confusion in which the two opposing reactions of decomposition and recombination were taking place. On the one hand, right- and left-wing agitators were poised ready to seize their opportunity. On the other, the power of the politicians was crumbling, and the tendency to fall in line with the militarists and to cling onto their coattails was gaining the day."[14]

The result of the proposals of Konoye and his brain trust was the formation of the Imperial Rule Assistance Association (Taisei Yokusan Kai) on October 12, 1940. Count Arima Yoriyasu, one of the financial backers of the Shōwa Research Association, was its first secretary-general, and for a short time he managed to implement some of the Research Association's ideas; but he was ousted in late March of 1942, and the Assistance Association rapidly degenerated into a very inefficient mass mobilization instrument of the Army. While it owed some of its inspiration to the Nazi party, the Imperial Rule Assistance Association never became a genuinely totalitarian organization; it can be compared accurately only to the Concordia Society in Manchukuo (the Hsieh Ho Hui, founded in July 1932) and to the Hsin Min Hui, the puppet political party in Japanese-occupied north China, on which it was partly patterned. No proposal by the "liberals" backfired more resoundingly than the New Structure Movement; in October 1940, after the Imperial Rule Assistance Association came into being, the Shōwa Research Association itself was dissolved and denounced for trying to smuggle "Red" principles into the Japanese body politic. Konoye did his best to forget about the Imperial Rule Assistance Association, and it lived out the war as an institutional pigeonhole for men who could make no other contribution to the state than talk.[15]

Ozaki Hotsumi became a member of the Shōwa Research Association in April 1937 on the recommendation of Sassa Hiroo of the *Asahi shimbun*'s editorial committee.[16] Sassa invited Ozaki to join the group primarily because of his renown as a China expert. Besides having been a delegate to the IPR conference in California, Ozaki had been very well known since December 1936 for his astonishingly prescient articles on the Sian Incident. As a member of the brain trust, Ozaki entered the "China Problem Department," headed by Kazami

Akira.* (The Shōwa Research Association was subdivided into twelve research departments, among which were departments for politics, economics, diplomacy, labor, agriculture, education, science, and China.) There were eight or nine associates in the China Problem Department, and Ozaki became the department head in June 1937, when Kazami entered the Konoye cabinet. Ozaki retained this position until the dissolution of the Shōwa Research Association in the autumn of 1940.

Four months after joining the Shōwa Research Association, Ozaki had another opportunity to demonstrate his remarkable insight into the dynamics of Far Eastern politics. On the night of July 7, 1937, Chinese and Japanese troops clashed at Lukouch'iao, near Peking, and the Japanese Army decided to use this incident as a pretext for destroying the Chinese nationalist movement once and for all. That it was this decision that led to the full-scale Japanese invasion of China, and eventually to World War II, did not cross the minds of Japanese leaders in Tokyo for some time, and the true consequences of the Sino-Japanese war began to be understood by Western politicians only during the nineteen-fifties.[17] But Ozaki's grasp of the social, political, and economic forces at work in China allowed him to predict the denouement of the Lukouch'iao incident almost immediately. On July 12, 1937, he wrote: "In all probability, most people in China and Japan believe that no very grave consequences will follow from this incident, but I myself am convinced that it can hardly fail to develop on such a scale as to prove of the utmost significance in world history."[18] This was a prediction that Ozaki elaborated upon and continued to repeat until the day of his execution: that the po-

* Kazami (1886–1961) was one of the most influential politicians with whom Ozaki worked during the China Incident period. As a youth, Kazami had been influenced by the Meiji nationalist teacher Sugiura Shigetaka, and he had later associated with Huang Hsing, the Chinese revolutionary in exile in Tokyo. Kazami was an old-fashioned Asian nationalist with a strong interest in the Chinese revolution. He was the Chief Cabinet Secretary during the first Konoye cabinet and Minister of Justice (July 22 to December 21, 1940) in the second. Before the war Kazami maintained an essentially nationalist position (he had supported Mori Kaku, and it was Shiga Hijikata who introduced him to Konoye); but after abandoning his self-imposed retirement in 1952 he became a strong champion of Communist China, and in 1955 he joined the Socialist Party. He served many terms in the lower house of the Diet as a representative from Ibaraki prefecture. Kazami maintained from 1941 until his death that Ozaki was a patriot. See Suda Teiichi, "Kazami Akira no hito to shisō" ("The Personality and Thought of Kazami Akira"), Sekai, No. 207 (March 1963), pp. 264–72.

litically significant aspect of World War II in the Far East was the conflict between China and Japan, and not that between Japan and the Western powers.

Ozaki was not merely a lucky forecaster; his analyses were based upon an acute insight into the clash between regional and unifying forces in China and, above all, upon an awareness of the growing strength of Chinese nationalism. In September 1937 he wrote: "The greatest of the disasters now taking place in China is not that the Nanking government is on the verge of collapse; it is rather that the Chinese nationalist movement is rapidly turning to the left."[19] In dealing with the question of whether Japan could do anything militarily without accelerating this trend, Ozaki was constrained to avoid attacking the Army frontally once the invasion was under way; nevertheless, he often pointed out, with no excess of subtlety, that it had taken the Mongols about 45 years to defeat the Sung dynasty and that the Manchus had needed almost that much time to subdue the Ming dynasty.[20] Ozaki's initial reaction to the war was total opposition; his book *Arashi ni tatsu Shina* (*China Facing the Storm*), published in September 1937, was devoted to proving that the Japanese people knew next to nothing about contemporary Chinese political trends and that indulging in open aggression was like pouring gasoline on the fires of Chinese nationalism. Needless to say, the militarists did not heed his warning.

Two important men, however, were very interested in Ozaki's views. Richard Sorge accepted unconditionally Ozaki's prediction that the China Incident would lead to a protracted war, and he transmitted Ozaki's views to Moscow. He also repeated them as his own to German Ambassador von Dirksen and Military Attaché Ott. At the time, both Germans trusted their Japanese informants, who had told them that the Kuomintang was unpopular and feeble and that the war would end quickly with a Japanese victory; when Sorge was proved correct, his prestige and importance as an adviser to the German Ambassador rose considerably.[21] Another man who placed a high value on Ozaki's analytical capacities was Premier Konoye's Chief Cabinet Secretary, Kazami Akira, who was sufficiently impressed to secure a position for Ozaki in the government.

In June of 1938 the Foreign Ministry asked Ozaki to accept a post as economic consultant to the Japanese Embassy in Peking. Ozaki was seriously contemplating this offer, and he discussed it with Ushiba

Tomohiko, one of Konoye's personal secretaries and a friend from the IPR conference and the Shōwa Research Association. Ushiba told Kazami that Ozaki would probably go to Peking, and Kazami quickly proposed to Ozaki that he remain in Tokyo as a cabinet consultant (*naikaku shokutaku*). Kazami subsequently recommended Ozaki to the Premier and he later took full responsibility for having him appointed to this post.[22] Ozaki resigned his position at the *Asahi* to accept Kazami's offer. From July 1938 until January 1939 he occupied an office in the Premier's official residence, and he enjoyed relatively free access to the Cabinet Secretariat.

On the face of it, it might seem that when Ozaki assumed this position any semblance of security within the Konoye government became impossible. But this was not the case. There is no convincing evidence that Ozaki used his government post to steal war plans, and he was not formulating national policy. As we shall see when we examine the operations of the Sorge ring during this period, Ozaki's espionage reports were primarily analytical statements reflecting his own views, analyses which he checked carefully in his numerous conversations with members of the Shōwa Research Association and the Breakfast Society. Matsumoto Shigeharu believes that Ozaki used his position in the cabinet mainly to research and write his immense quantity of magazine articles (which often duplicated his espionage reports).[23] In any case, the importance of the unofficial adviser (*shokutaku*) within the Japanese government has been exaggerated by some Western writers on the Sorge case.[24] Ozaki did discover and pass on to Sorge some valuable secret information, but he neither used nor needed to use his cabinet position solely for this purpose. He did obtain some information more quickly than if he had had to work entirely outside government circles; but his entry into the cabinet certainly did not make all of Japan's military secrets an open book to Stalin.[25]

Ozaki described his governmental position to the police as follows: "My appointment read 'unofficial consultant on research affairs,' and I served primarily as an assistant to Chief Cabinet Secretary Kazami. I did not make decisions, but instead presented reports giving my own views on ways to control the China Incident. I studied various methods of terminating the war, including the possibility of working with Great Britain and the potentialities of the Wang Ching-wei operation; and I made plans for the national reorganization [the New

Structure Movement]. Although I was dealing with fairly important matters, I made absolutely no attempt to use my position during this period to realize my political proposals. Policies had already been established, and I merely recommended concrete measures for their realization. . . . Of course, any information that I did obtain in the cabinet I passed on to Sorge."[26]

The most important position achieved by Ozaki, one which afforded opportunities for both espionage and personal influence, was not in the cabinet but in the Breakfast Society. When speaking of the Konoye brain trust, we must distinguish two organizations with overlapping memberships. One, the Shōwa Research Association, was a large, well-endowed research organization with its staff and its own suite of offices (located in Marunouchi); it published many books and pamphlets in order to acquaint the public with its policies. The other, the Breakfast Society (Asameshi Kai, also called the Suiyō Kai, or Wednesday Society), was more strictly a group of personal advisers—what is called a "kitchen cabinet" in the United States. Both groups were organized by Konoye's supporters with his permission, but only the Breakfast Society was in direct personal contact with the man who was three times Premier of Japan. The Breakfast Society came into existence in November 1937 as an informal discussion group among the younger men in the Konoye cabinet and their close friends in the Shōwa Research Association.[27] The two central figures of the Society were Ushiba Tomohiko and Kishi Michizō, Konoye's brilliant young private secretaries (both were 37 years old in 1937).*

In the autumn after the Lukouch'iao incident, Ushiba and Kishi arranged a series of meetings at which a group of young intellectuals discussed policy alternatives that might be useful to the Premier. At first the group included only Ushiba, Kishi, Saionji Kinkazu, and Ozaki, and it met at the offices of the Cabinet Secretariat. Very soon

---

* Ushiba and Kishi are today very prosperous Japanese industrialists. Ushiba first met Konoye when he accompanied him and Rōyama Masamichi on a trip to the United States in 1934. Ushiba and Ozaki were classmates at Ichikō, and Ushiba—as an official of the Japanese Council of the IPR—had urged Ozaki's selection as a delegate to the IPR conference in 1936. Kishi Michizō was another of Ushiba's classmates at Ichikō; and when Ushiba became Konoye's personal secretary at the time the cabinet was formed in 1937, he obtained Kishi's recall from China in order to join him. Kishi was trained as a mining engineer at Tokyo Teidai, and he worked in China before the war as a South Manchurian Railroad consultant and in a Japanese investment enterprise in Canton. He is today the president or vice-president of numerous Japanese mining concerns.

it expanded to include Sassa Hiroo and Ryū Shintarō of the *Asahi*, Rōyama Masamichi of Teidai, Taira Teizō of the South Manchurian Railroad, and Watanabe Sahei of Hōsei University's economics department. In late 1939 three more members were invited: Matsumoto Shigeharu and Matsukata Gisaburō (the son of the Meiji politician, Matsukata Masayoshi), both of the Dōmei News Agency, and Inukai Ken of the Diet and the Foreign Ministry. In mid-1938 the group began meeting twice a month for breakfast, and beginning in 1939 it held regular breakfast discussions on Wednesday mornings. Kazami Akira occasionally attended these gatherings, but Konoye himself did not participate. A summary of the discussions was conveyed to Konoye by his secretaries. During 1939, 1940, and 1941 the Breakfast Society met at the Mampei Hotel, the Premier's residence, Saionji's Surugadai residence in Tokyo, or various restaurants. On the very day that Ozaki was arrested (October 15, 1941) Ushiba, Kazami, Sassa, Taira, and Saionji had already begun eating without waiting for the others, when Kishi burst in with the electrifying news that the police had arrested Ozaki as a spy.[28]

They could not believe their ears at the time, but these men later had good reason to recall soberly what had been said at Breakfast Society meetings in Ozaki's presence. It was here that Ozaki learned some of Japan's most important wartime secrets, and here that his influence on Japanese policy was most directly felt. The one time when a Japanese leader was known to have been suspicious of Ozaki (and then only by hindsight) was at one of the breakfast meetings. Ozaki asked Ushiba whether it was true that the United States had made an offer in the U.S.-Japanese negotiations of mid-1941. Ozaki explained that he had the information from journalistic sources, but Ushiba feigned ignorance. Ushiba remembers that at the time only the Premier, the Foreign Minister, and the War and Navy Ministers even knew that negotiations were under way, and that he was greatly surprised at Ozaki's knowledge of such top secrets.[29]

The reason the Breakfast Society afforded more opportunities for espionage than any of Ozaki's other affiliations is clear from the nature of Ozaki's reports to Sorge. Ozaki was not the sort of spy who would photograph documents stolen from locked files or plant microphones under conference room tables; he was a high-level political analyst who wrote objective reports on political trends, and his greatest "espionage" need was to verify his personal opinions by testing them on actual decision-makers. On April 1, 1942, the prosecutor Tamazawa Mitsusaburō asked Ozaki: "What were your espionage techniques?" Ozaki, apparently rather surprised by the question, replied at length: "If you are referring to my attitude toward collecting information, or the distinctive features of it, I must say that I have never given any thought to the so-called technical aspects of espionage. You might say that my non-technical attitude was a technique in itself. I am a sociable person and I like to mix with people from all walks of life; I find great sources of information just by being gregarious. My espionage work did not consist of collecting and compiling fragments of information; instead, I made my own judgment on a particular matter and then checked it against items of information that fitted into a general picture of the situation and its probable development. Consequently, persons who met me never suspected that I was collecting information from them. On many occasions people asked me to listen to certain bits of information in order to obtain my opinion."[30]

Ozaki went on to argue that isolated bits of information were useless in a period of great flux and confusion. He stated that he had always ignored temporary situations in order to try to appraise the attitudes of Army and government leaders, and that he had also tried to relate daily developments to his own objective analysis of underlying trends. He was different in this respect from the Japanese statesmen themselves, who have been characterized by many Japanese and Western writers as primarily followers rather than makers of policy.[31] The only single piece of pure information for which Ozaki was always on the lookout was "the timing of a Japanese attack on the Soviet Union."[32]

Forced to give his own opinion on the qualities that make a good spy, Ozaki listed the following two points, which accurately characterize himself: "The greatest secret of success is to win the trust of others as a human being and to create situations in which one obtains information naturally. Closely connected with that is preparing oneself, through exhaustive study and experience, to become a source of information and of sound judgments."[33] It was precisely as a well-informed man of sound judgment that Ozaki held his positions in the Shōwa Research Association, the cabinet, and the Breakfast Society. Professional espionage agents are continuously concerned with matters of "cover," but Ozaki, strictly speaking, never maintained a cover. He was a genuine political analyst and a participant in the disaster of prewar Japanese politics. He tried to warn his government —as did many other Japanese intellectuals—of the folly of a policy of aggression; but he also took independent action, through Sorge, to affect international politics in a way he thought would cushion the probable failure of the liberals' efforts. No other interpretation can logically account for the inconsistency between the concept of a spy's "cover" and Ozaki's public involvement, particularly as it was expressed in his published writings.

Ozaki's books and articles written during the war in China are devoted to three topics: the East Asian Cooperative Body, the New Structure Movement, and the development of Chinese nationalism. His published works on the first two subjects do not reveal his actual motivation in advancing these policies, but they are not mere camouflage. As a *gisō tenkōsha*, he could not reveal his true intentions (as he later did in prison); but he believed in these two measures for private reasons, just as did Konoye, Rōyama, Miki, and various others. The ironic aspect of his writings on these two topics is that he probably did more to convince military activists that they were morally right than to advance his own private vision. Just before his execution as a war criminal in 1949, General Itagaki composed this poem:

> Keep in mind, my friends,
> My friends of the land of Kara
> That even now there is but one,
> One East Asia.*

Ozaki might have agreed with Itagaki's sentiment, but no two men could have been further apart on what was meant by "one East Asia"; Ozaki consistently argued that the major obstacle to its realization was men like Itagaki.

Ozaki published his most famous piece on the East Asian Cooperative Body in the January 1939 issue of *Chūō kōron* (which was reprinted in that journal's seventy-fifth anniversary issue of November 1960).[34] This article is squarely in the tradition of Miki Kiyoshi and the Shōwa Research Association except that it is more concerned with China than with the rest of Asia. The war in China was then entering

---

* "Kara" is an archaism for China or Cathay. This poem is quoted by Hanayama Shinshō, the Buddhist chaplain at Sugamo prison, in *The Way of Deliverance, Three Years with the Condemned Japanese War Criminals* (New York, 1950), p. 241.

its nineteenth month, and Ozaki stressed that the policy of military force was bankrupt. It could never hope, he said, to overwhelm the Chinese people's unlimited capacity for resistance. He insisted that the only possible way to terminate the China Incident was for Japan to identify itself with the true interests of Chinese nationalism; if such cooperation could be realized, it would automatically provide the foundation for an Asian bloc of states united against European imperialism.

In this article Ozaki also voiced grave reservations about Premier Konoye's proclamation of the New Order in East Asia (December 22, 1938), which he had helped to draft as a cabinet consultant.[35] Like other *gisō tenkō* intellectuals, Ozaki felt that the Konoye declaration had put the cart before the horse. Konoye's statement itself asserted that "the Japanese government desires to make public its basic policy for adjusting the relations between Japan and China in order that its intentions may be thoroughly understood both at home and abroad. Japan, China, and Manchukuo will be united by the common aim of establishing the New Order in East Asia and of realizing a re-lationship of neighborly unity, common defense against Communism, and economic cooperation. For that purpose it is necessary first of all that China should cast aside all narrow and prejudiced views belong-ing to the past and do away with the folly of anti-Japanism and re-sentment regarding Manchukuo."[36] In response to this statement, Wang Ching-wei and some forty-four of his followers fled Chungking for Hanoi and Hong Kong, where they proclaimed their desire to make peace with Japan. The result was the establishment, in March of 1940, of the Japanese puppet government at Nanking, under Wang Ching-wei.

Ozaki was not a defender of Chiang Kai-shek or the Kuomintang, but he accurately pointed out that Wang Ching-wei, despite his life-long reputation as a true Chinese nationalist, was merely so much baggage unless he could get rid of the label of Chinese traitor. And, Ozaki stated, Wang could not do that (as historically he proved unable to) so long as the Japanese Army interfered with his attempts to create a stable regime. Ozaki did not believe that the Army could be re-strained, and so he regarded the Konoye statement as premature; he suggested that the realization of the domestic Japanese New Structure Movement was a prerequisite for the success of any "New Order."

It is difficult to know whether Ozaki really believed that the New

Structure Movement could become a counterfoil to the Army. In a very carefully hedged article written in English at the time of the establishment of the Imperial Rule Assistance Association, Ozaki alluded to his own role in planning the New Structure (in the first Konoye cabinet) and to the failure of its ulterior purpose of checking the Army: "After the fall of Hankow and Canton in November [October] 1938, the Konoye cabinet began to consider seriously the reorganization of the political structure, though at that time it was called a 'reorganization of the people.' Various plans were discussed, and a number of proposals were advanced by Kazami Akira, then Chief Cabinet Secretary, Count Arima Yoriyasu, and Admiral Suetsugu [Nobumasa], then Home Minister, but before any action could be taken the first Konoye cabinet resigned *en bloc* at the beginning of 1939. . . . In what relation the new national structure as a whole stands with the high military command is another serious question left unanswered. In this connection, the Army has clarified its position by not participating in the Central Headquarters [of the Imperial Rule Assistance Association]."[37] What the Army's "clarification" meant—as Ozaki, Konoye, Kazami, and the others knew only too well —was that the Imperial Rule Assistance Association (and the East Asian Cooperative Body) was a failure.

According to Saionji's memoirs, Kazami Akira was the guiding power behind the New Structure in the first Konoye cabinet, and Ozaki, working directly for him as a consultant, drew up a concrete plan for its realization. The purpose was to check the military cliques, and, if that goal were attained, to provide a possible way to end the China Incident on a basis favorable to Japan (via the East Asian Cooperative Body).[38] The police apparently found these plans highly treasonable, for they published Ozaki's organization chart on the New Structure along with their summary of the evidence against him.[39]

It seems certain that Ozaki's own views on the New Structure and the East Asian Cooperative Body changed between 1938 and 1941. Ozaki himself reflected on his liberal involvements from his prison cell: "I have believed for a long time, together with many other intellectuals, that the positive policy of force (imperialism) was driving Japan to its destruction. Moreover, I believed that I had to do anything I could in order to interrupt this trend. I cooperated with the Shōwa Research Association and other organizations because I placed trust in the honesty and serious intentions of the other intellectuals who had joined them."[40] However, Ozaki also said in prison that he had hoped that these two policies, when combined with his collaboration with Sorge, would bring about a Communist revolution from above in Japan and lead to the unification of all of Asia under Communist auspices. It seems likely that this occurred to him only after both policies had been subverted by the militarists, at which time he concluded that a long and disastrous world war was inevitable and that it would leave Communist regimes in its wake in China, Japan, and the ex-colonies of Asia—still a utopian goal, but one to be gained at a terrible cost and one that was distinct from his pre-1940 position.

After the fall of the Konoye cabinet in January 1939, Ozaki found himself temporarily unemployed. He spent the first half of the year writing the book for which he is best known today, *Gendai Shina ron* (*On Modern China*); it appeared as the tenth volume in the influential red-cover New Library series of Iwanami publishers and was an expansion of a series of public lectures he delivered at Tokyo Imperial University in the spring of 1939.[41] Ozaki himself, although proud of *On Modern China,* believed that *Shina shakai keizai ron* (*On Chinese Society and Economy*), published in June 1940, was his best book. These books were neither "cover" nor propaganda, and they contain some of the best analysis of the Chinese revolution ever written in Japan. Ozaki himself wrote to Eiko in 1943: "As the authorities acknowledge, my writings are not considered to contain dangerous thoughts. Therefore, I can leave them to Yōko."[42]

On Modern China is a treatise on the transitional nature of twentieth-century Chinese society, particularly on the descent into warlordism that followed the collapse of the Empire and on the efforts of Chinese nationalists to reestablish unity through either elitist or mass movements. To put it simply, Ozaki was interested in the meaning of the "semi-feudal, semi-colonial" description commonly applied to China, and in discovering the conditions under which China's political disintegration could be overcome. His study ranges from a critique of the "Asiatic mode of production" theory to a consideration of the interim nature of the Nanking government (1927–37). He analyzes the activities of gentry, secret societies, peasants, nationalist intellectuals, and warlords in a historical and sociological perspective, and he insists that their twentieth-century roles belong neither to classical Chinese political theory nor to the modern nation-state.

With regard to the government of Chiang Kai-shek, Ozaki considered it an unstable coalition of transitional political powers, powers which were generated by and flourished as a result of the decomposition of traditional Chinese society. He wrote: "Certain characteristics of the former Kuomintang government at Nanking should be noted: first, it is in the nature of a guild based upon the blood and regional relationships of its members; second, important positions are held by powerful provincial elements of a feudalistic tendency, namely, the military cliques [Yen Hsi-shan of Shansi, Li Tsung-jen and Pai Chung-hsi of Kwangsi, Han Fu-ch'ü of Shantung, Liu Hsiang of Szechwan, etc.]; third, the controlling influence is wielded by a group of Chekiang financiers; fourth, the regime is under the influence of various foreign powers."[43] Ozaki did not believe that it was impossible for Chiang Kai-shek to repair the internal fissures of the Nanking government, given sufficient time; but he was certain that the rising pressure of Chinese nationalism would either transform the Nanking government from within or overthrow it from without.

On Modern China concludes by stating that the awakening of the Chinese masses from their "semi-feudal, semi-colonial" existence was inevitable, and that if Japan possessed farsighted leaders they would adopt policies in harmony with China's awakening; the results of such policies, Ozaki said, would be a true Asian renaissance and the demise of European influence. These ideas, as outlined here, are as old as Sun Yat-sen; Ozaki's contribution was to develop them analytically and to add an important statistical dimension (particularly in On Chinese Society and Economy). Most important, he courageously declared that the China Incident had given an uncontrollable turn to the development of Chinese nationalism, and he predicted that the Chinese Communist Party would be the final beneficiary.[44] This was not in itself a development unwished for by Ozaki, but he deplored the fact that Japan had made itself the enemy of Chinese nationalism. His analysis, however, was cogent, carefully reasoned, and unimpassioned, and it was because of this that neither Saionji nor Ushiba ever suspected that he was a Communist.[45] Needless to say, Ozaki's views differed fundamentally in spirit and detail from those of the Comintern and the Chinese Communist Party during this period.[46]

During the spring of 1939, when Ozaki was writing On Modern China, he continued to meet with the Breakfast Society and work in the Shōwa Research Association. He was asked to join several other departments of the Association in addition to its China section, which he headed, and he also participated in its adult school. The Shōwa

Academy (Shōwa Juku) was a heavily endowed public school—some-times called the "officers' school for new bureaucrats"—for dissemi-nating the Association's ideas. Gotō Ryūnosuke, Kazami Akira, and Taira Teizō supervised its operations, and Ozaki served as a regular lecturer there.[47]

Another of Ozaki's projects during 1939 was a new China research organization. In December 1938, just before the dissolution of the first Konoye cabinet, Ozaki, Inukai, and Saionji proposed to Kazami that they establish an independent China research bureau, which would investigate Sino-Japanese relations and make concrete pro-posals aimed at restoring friendly relations between China and Japan. The members were particularly concerned with finding ways to bolster the position of Wang Ching-wei as a means of ending the China Incident; their first project was a study of Sun Yat-sen's *San-min chu-i (Three Principles of the People)*, from which they hoped to establish an ideological foundation for Wang's pro-Japanese policy, based on Sun's heritage. Kazami Akira furnished the funds for the group, and offices were established at Tamaike-chō, in the Akasaka district of Tokyo. Inukai was named the formal head of the new in-stitute, which was called the China Research Office (Shina Kenkyū Shitsu), and Kazami later indicated that he provided money for this group primarily because Inukai had lent his name to it.[48] Within a short time Inukai became Japan's chief civilian negotiator with Wang Ching-wei; he was holding the post of adviser to the puppet Nanking government when he was arrested in connection with the Sorge case on April 4, 1942.*

* Inukai Ken (1896–1960) was one of Japan's most prominent politicians of the Shōwa period. After withdrawing from Tokyo University's literature department, he became a promising novelist of the White Birch Faction of modern Japanese art and literature, which was strongly influenced by Tolstoy and Romain Rolland in literature and by Cézanne and Rodin in painting and sculpture. In 1930 Inukai abandoned his literary interests for politics. He was elected to the Diet four times during the nineteen-thirties, and in 1939 the Abe cabinet appointed him pleni-potentiary to the Wang government; he also held many other advisory positions in the Foreign and Communications Ministries during the war. After the war he took part in politics as a conservative and was Minister of Justice in the Yoshida cabinets of 1952 and 1953. He was implicated in the Sorge case for unknowingly (but illegally) divulging the results of his negotiations with Wang Ching-wei to Saionji and Ozaki. *Gendai-shi shiryō,* I, 82; Asahi Shimbun, ed., *Nihon o ugokasu sambyaku nin (The Three Hundred Men Who Move Japan)* (Tokyo, 1948), p. 7; and Inukai, *Yōsukō wa ima mo nagarete iru (The Yangtze Still Flows)* (Tokyo, 1960), pp. 32–33. (The title article of this book was published in *Bungei shunjū,* June 1959, pp. 260–75. Inukai's book is concerned with his part in the Wang operation.)

It is doubtful whether Ozaki placed much faith in the Wang operation, but he did secure positions for many of his friends in the China Research Office. It was through his influence that Hosokawa Karoku became the group's manager and that Mizuno Shigeru was employed to work on a Japanese translation of Sun Yat-sen. Other members brought in by Ozaki included Horie Yūichi and Matsumoto Shin'ichi, who joined the group after being released from prison in late 1939. The dominant figures in the organization were Ozaki, Saionji, and Inukai, and they became very close personal friends as well as valuable sources of information for each other. The group functioned until Ozaki's arrest, when, according to Hosokawa, the police confiscated all of its records and closed its office.[49]

The troubles of Matsumoto Shin'ichi (1901–1947), Ozaki's friend from the time they were students together at Ichikō, also occupied Ozaki throughout much of 1939. After leaving college Matsumoto had become an ardent Communist sympathizer; he was first arrested in 1931 for having contributed to the Noulens Defense Committee fund. In 1933 he was working closely with the Japanese Communist Party's Information Section, and he associated with the well-known Party leaders Noro Eitarō (killed by the police in 1934), Kazahaya Yasoji, and Miyamoto Kenji (both of whom later became members of the JCP's Central Committee). Matsumoto was arrested a second time for violating the Peace Preservation Law on February 16, 1934, and his arrest led to the unusual prosecution of William Maxwell Bickerton, the first foreigner arrested under the Peace Preservation Law.[50] Matsumoto was in jail for nearly two years, until November 26, 1935, and throughout that time Ozaki supported his family financially.

Between 1935 and 1938, Matsumoto worked as a member of the editorial staff of the English-language journal *Contemporary Japan* and the Japanese magazine *Kokusai hyōron* (*International Review*). Both periodicals were published by the Foreign Affairs Association (Gaiji Kyōkai), a conservative, semi-official public body affiliated with the Foreign Ministry. Ozaki published many articles in both journals, although it is not clear whether this was at Matsumoto's request. After the outbreak of the war with China, Matsumoto joined the antimilitarist "peace movement"—a Communist front—and he was arrested again on November 29, 1938, as a leader of what was called the Tokyo-Yokohama Communist Group. He was held in Sugamo prison without trial for almost a year before receiving a suspended sentence; during this time Ozaki again supported Matsumoto's family financially and brought as much pressure on the police as he dared in order to obtain his release.

When Matsumoto regained his freedom in late 1939, Ozaki secured him a job with Hosokawa and Mizuno at the China Research Office. Matsumoto was not one of Ozaki's subordinates in the spy ring, and he was never arrested in connection with the Sorge case. However, as Ozaki's oldest friend, he directed Ozaki's defense during the treason trials, and his wife aided Eiko in every way that she could. After the war Matsumoto helped edit *Love Is Like a Falling Star,* and he published many articles describing Ozaki as a "great Communist" and blaming himself for not being able to delay his execution longer. Matsumoto had a long record as a Communist sympathizer (he became a Party member after the war), and Ozaki, in coming to his aid, had ignored Sorge's warning not to associate with known leftists.[51]

Ozaki also exposed himself to the police in another case, one that did not concern a personal friend. This was his defense in court of the very prominent novelist Ishikawa Tatsuzō (b. 1905) and his novel *Ikite iru heitai (Living Soldiers).* After the outbreak of the China Incident, several publishing houses sent novelists to the front in order to write on-the-scene reports. Ishikawa, who was sent by Amemiya Yōzō, the chief editor of *Chūō kōron,* arrived in central China in early December of 1937 and witnessed the assault on Nanking. After he returned to Japan he wrote a war novel for *Chūō kōron* in which he "portrayed battlefield atrocities as atrocities."[52] The result was that the Home Ministry prohibited distribution of the March 1938 *Chūō kōron,* which contained Ishikawa's novel, and on August 4, 1938, the Tokyo prosecutor's office entered a case against Ishikawa, Amemiya, and Makino Takeo, the publisher of *Chūō kōron;* they were charged with printing falsehoods and disturbing the peace. Ishikawa and Amemiya received sentences of four months in prison (with suspended sentences of three years) and Makino was fined 100 yen ($28.50). The prosecutor, however, was displeased with these relatively light sentences, and he appealed the case, asking four-year prison terms for Ishikawa and Amemiya.

It was at the appeal, in February 1939, that Ozaki testified in Ishikawa's defense. He had read Ishikawa's novel, and when the *Chūō kōron* editorial board asked him to be a witness he quickly agreed.

In substance, his testimony was limited to saying that he did not believe the novel conveyed anti-war sentiments, but this in itself was a very dangerous thing for him to do. Ishikawa's case was not an isolated incident that might go unnoticed; it was part of a general police campaign against left-wing and pacifist literature at this time. Ozaki's decision to testify reflects his genuine concern with Chinese matters and his feeling that, as a *tenkō* liberal with connections in the Konoye circle, he could afford to be more outspoken than most men of his persuasion.

On June 1, 1939, Ozaki returned to work for the government as a consultant to the Investigation Department of the South Manchurian Railroad (Mantetsu Chōsa-bu), the capacity in which he was serving on the day of his arrest. Ozaki's employment at the South Manchurian Railroad apparently disturbed the police more than any of his other affiliations, and the Tokkō later made a thorough investigation of everyone Ozaki had known at the Tokyo and Dairen offices of that organization. It was indeed a sensitive position that Ozaki held with the South Manchurian Railroad, and he exploited it fully in his espionage activities. It was not a post that of itself would have met his and Sorge's needs; but combined with his membership in the Breakfast Society, it provided Ozaki with an opportunity to verify some of the most important secret decisions made by Japan during this period.

The South Manchurian Railroad was the most prominent of Japan's "national policy companies" (*kokusaku gaisha*), firms that were partly owned and staffed by the government and used as instruments for Japanese expansion. (These companies proliferated after the Manchurian Incident; before that time they included—in addition to the South Manchurian Railroad—the Bank of Japan, the Yokohama Specie Bank, the Bank of Taiwan, the Hokkaidō Development Bank, Taiwan Electric, and the Bank of Chōsen.) The South Manchurian Railroad was created after the Russo-Japanese war in order to develop Japan's newly won properties, and the Japanese government put up fifty per cent of the original capital investment. Over the next thirty years, the South Manchurian Railroad created the only industrial complex on the mainland of the Far East—the iron, steel, mining, and manufacturing enterprises of southern Manchuria and the Liaotung Peninsula. In 1936 there were more than eighty satellite companies of the South Manchurian Railroad, which was, for all practical purposes, an arm of the Japanese government.

Moreover, the Railroad cooperated closely with the Kwantung Army (originally created to defend the Japanese rail network in Manchuria); its investigation bureaus received the Kwantung Army's operational plans and even helped draw up many of them. If there was to be a war between Japan and Russia, the Kwantung Army would have to move over the rail lines of the South Manchurian Railroad; Ozaki was thus in a good position to discover any unusual troop concentrations along the Manchukuo-Soviet border.

The South Manchurian Railroad's head office was in Dairen, with branches in Shanghai, Tokyo, and many other locations. Ozaki went to work in 1939 for the Tokyo branch of the Investigation Department, whose offices were on the fourth floor of the Mantetsu Building at Toranomon (which now houses the U.S. Embassy Annex). His main assignments were to serve as a consultant to the staff committee that was measuring the war potential of China and to write and compile research materials on the contemporary international situation. In addition, he was expected to attend the major conferences of the entire South Manchurian Railroad research staff, usually held in Dairen or Shanghai. Ozaki also maintained close liaison with other research groups, including those of the military, the Cabinet Planning Board, and the Mitsui combine.

Ozaki's daily work consisted chiefly of writing reports for the political sections of the Investigation Department's highly classified periodical, the *Current Materials Monthly Report* (*Jiji shiryō geppō*), which was intended only for internal circulation among executives and various selected agencies of the government and the Army. Ozaki told the police that he was "truthful and objective" in all of his writing for this journal, but the investigators were aghast to hear that he had passed along all of the 1940 and most of the 1941 issues to Sorge.[53] (Ozaki actually gave the materials to Miyagi, who then made English translations for Sorge.) The police were painstaking in their examination of Ozaki's young assistant at the Tokyo office, Kaieda Hisataka, who actually compiled each issue of the *Monthly Report*; it is from his testimony that we know the exact articles that Ozaki wrote for the South Manchurian Railroad.[54] Needless to say, Kaieda never suspected that Ozaki was anything other than a distinguished expert on China and international politics.

One of Ozaki's chief functions with the South Manchurian Railroad was to travel to the mainland in order to keep abreast of the latest developments. His last trip to China before joining the Railroad had been to Shanghai and Hong Kong in December of 1937, when he had been sent by the *Asahi* to survey the possibilities of a Sino-Japanese peace after the fall of Nanking. In his new post he was sent to the continent five times: once in 1939, three times in 1940, and once again in 1941. These visits, all made in his official capacity, provided him with some crucially important information for Sorge. In the summer of 1939, just after becoming an Investigation Department consultant, he went to Hong Kong, Shanghai, and Hankow in order to explore the potential strength of the Chinese resistance. He was accompanied on this trip by Saionji Kinkazu, who was on a special mission for the General Staff to investigate potential Chinese support for Wang Ching-wei when Wang's government was formally inaugurated.[55] In Shanghai, Ozaki introduced Saionji to Nakanishi Ko, who was then employed at the South Manchurian Railroad office, and in Hankow they visited Funakoshi Hisao, the adviser to the military government of the city. Saionji had no idea that Nakanishi was one of Ozaki's old comrades from the Japan-China Struggle League and that Funakoshi was Ozaki's successor as the Comintern spy in Shanghai.[56]

In March of 1940 Ozaki went to Shanghai as the official delegate of the Tokyo Investigation Department to attend the Department's second Conference on Measuring China's Ability to Resist. The topics discussed included the strength of the military forces affiliated with the Communist Eighth Route Army in Jehol province, and Ozaki had an opportunity to talk with military officers, railroad officials, and Japanese representatives from all over China and Manchuria.[57] In September of the same year, Ozaki was back in Manchuria to observe the Sixth Congress of the Concordia Society (Hsieh Ho Hui). It was at this time that the Imperial Rule Assistance Association was being launched in Japan, and the South Manchurian Railroad asked Ozaki to write an article on the Concordia Society, which was widely regarded as a model for the Assistance Association. In December, shortly after returning from this assignment, Ozaki left again for Shanghai, where he participated in the third session of the conference on China's resistance potentiality. He learned a great deal about the Wang Ching-wei government on this trip, and he also made, for his own use, a major survey of political and military conditions in China. He returned to Tokyo by ship and train, passing through Tsingtao, Peking, Mukden, and Dairen.

Probably the most important of Ozaki's trips was the one he made to Dairen only a month before he was arrested. On September 5–6, 1941, Ozaki and another official from the Tokyo Investigation Department attended a major conference at the Dairen office; this conference, entitled The Influence of the New Situation on the Politics and Economics of Japan, Manchukuo, and China, dealt with such matters as the American-Japanese confrontation and the Russo-German war, and it enabled Ozaki to obtain the latest information on Japan's mobilization and on her relations with the Soviet Union. By this time, Sorge and Ozaki had already transmitted to Moscow the news that Japan intended to advance southward and honor the Russo-Japanese non-aggression pact of April 13, 1941. To make certain that this was not solely a Tokyo decision and that the Kwantung Army did not have plans for independent action against the U.S.S.R., Ozaki did some traveling in Manchuria on his way home. He took the railroad north to Mukden and Hsinking (Ch'angch'un), calling on as many friends and colleagues as he could find in the South Manchurian Railroad offices in these cities. He determined from actual observation, railroad movement orders, general economic indicators, and information on military logistics that no Japanese movement to the north was in the offing.[58]

This piece of information was the last major contribution that Ozaki and Sorge made to the defense of the Soviet Union. On the eve of Japan's strike south, with Russia free to fight undisturbed on one front, their work was essentially finished. For Richard Sorge, the ring's final messages to "Wiesbaden" must have provided the satisfaction of seeing a difficult job well done, but for Ozaki Hotsumi there was no end in sight. As a Japanese nationalist as well as a Communist idealist, he could not bring himself to go into exile in the autumn of 1941, as Sorge proposed. It was a dilemma that would soon be solved for him by the Japanese police.

Chapter Seven

The Fruits of Espionage

⚜ ⚜

While Ozaki was advancing to high positions in the Breakfast Society, the Shōwa Research Association, and the South Manchurian Railroad, Richard Sorge was developing equally valuable sources of information on his own. As in China, Sorge cultivated informants primarily among the overseas German community. Between 1933 and 1939, his contacts included German businessmen, consulting engineers on assignment in Japan, members of the Nazi Party, and correspondents of the DNB (Deutsches Nachrichten Büro) and the Transocean News Agency. But the most important of his sources—so important that he paid no attention to any others after 1939—was the German Embassy.[1] From the time of the Japanese Army revolt in 1936, and particularly after General Eugen Ott replaced Herbert von Dirksen as German Ambassador (on April 28, 1938), Sorge held a position within the Embassy second only to the Ambassador himself. He not only learned the Ambassador's secrets; he attempted to influence the course of world politics from within the Embassy's walls, and he used the Embassy building as a convenient place to store espionage materials that he dared not leave in his own house.

Sorge prepared himself in precisely the ways recommended by Ozaki: he won the trust of informants on a personal basis, and he made himself an authoritative source of political information. Between 1933 and 1936, Sorge devoted most of his time to winning friends. After presenting his valuable letters of introduction to the German Ambassador, he quickly discovered that he and the Military Attaché, Eugen Ott, had both fought in Belgium during the First World War. Ott was an old soldier with a good deal of political experience: he had served for ten years as chief of the political department in General Schleicher's Reichswehr Ministry. Having been somewhat tainted by this involvement in the late Weimar Republic, Ott had sought a change of scene. At his request he was appointed an official German observer to the Japanese Army from June to December of 1933. In March of 1934 Hitler made him Senior Military Attaché to the German Embassy in Tokyo.* Ott and Sorge liked each other personally from their first meeting, but Ott's receptiveness to Sorge's proffered friendship also derived from Sorge's position as a representative of Germany's most famous newspaper and a member of the Nazi Party.

Sorge's first opportunity to make himself useful to the Embassy's staff came with the February 26 Incident. The revolt of the young Japanese officers in Tokyo perplexed the German Embassy as much as it did the Japanese government and civilian leaders; the Germans did not understand the roots of the Army protest, and they were mystified by the vacillation of the government and the senior officers in suppressing it. Sorge put Ozaki and Miyagi to work at once compiling all available materials on the young officers' movement and making translations for him of relevant pamphlets and newspaper articles. The gist of Ozaki's own explanation of the episode was as follows: the revolting troops were influenced by the poverty of the agricultural classes, from which most of them came; the rebel ideology (as expressed by Kita Ikki and others) was neither left-wing nor Communist, but anti-capitalist and revolutionary; the movement signified another rapid increase in right-wing influence in Japan, as had the assassination of Inukai; and among the likely foreign-policy consequences would be a more pronounced anti-Soviet position.[2]

Sorge wrote up these views as his own and gave copies of his final

---

* Ott was the chief Military Attaché from March 1934 until March 1938. In April of 1938 he became the German Ambassador to Tokyo following von Dirksen's transfer to London. He held the post of Ambassador until January of 1943, when he was relieved by Heinrich Stahmer. Ott claimed after the war that he tried to return to Germany in 1943, but it has been widely presumed that he did not try too hard for fear of Hitler's wrath over the Sorge case. Ott and his wife lived as private citizens in Peking between 1943 and 1947. He was never accused as a war criminal, but he did give a deposition to the defense in the trial of Shiratori, one of the authors of the Tripartite Pact, who was given a life sentence as a Class A war criminal. See International Military Tribunal for the Far East, Exhibit No. 3579; Herbert von Dirksen, *Moskau, Tokio, London* (Stuttgart, 1949), p. 157; and Erich Kordt, *Nicht aus den Akten* (Stuttgart, 1950), pp. 425–35.

report to Dirksen, Ott, and the Naval Attaché, Captain Paul W. Wenneker.* The Embassy staff was impressed by Sorge's knowledge of Japanese politics and sociology; they were even more impressed when his study was published in the May 1936 issue of professor Haushofer's *Zeitschrift für Geopolitik*. Haushofer's journal was the most influential strategic and analytical periodical in Nazi Germany, and he himself was an authority on Japan. The Embassy henceforth treated Sorge with a high degree of respect and trust, and members of the staff—particularly the military attachés, who were directly concerned with Japanese Army developments—sought his opinions on Far Eastern politics. Needless to say, Sorge also sent his report on the February 26 Incident to Moscow, where Karl Radek eventually had part of it translated and published in *Pravda*.[3] The February 26 Incident, besides being a turning point for political life in Japan, started Sorge on his way to becoming an influential spy within the German Embassy.

In the period before Ott became Ambassador, Sorge attempted to obtain information from a variety of German and other foreign sources. He collected data on the patents Germany was selling to Japan from representatives of German machinery and chemical concerns, and he associated with engineers of the Heinkel Aircraft Company, who were helping the Japanese to manufacture Heinkel engines on license. He met these persons and many others like them at the German Club, at Embassy receptions, or at the German Chamber of Commerce in Tokyo. However, he later wrote: "After 1938 or 1939, these sources no longer figured in my intelligence work, and I took no more notice of them. The strengthening of Japanese laws to protect state secrets after the China Incident made people afraid of committing violations, and they refused to cooperate. Moreover, the information that businessmen possessed suddenly became much more restricted."[4]

Sorge's other contacts in the pre-1938 period included many close friends among the German and foreign press agencies. He knew Relman Morin of the Associated Press and James Cox of Reuters (who was killed by the Japanese police in 1940).[5] He was naturally very close to the German reporters, and he ran the DNB Agency while its chief, a friend of his, was away on a leave of absence. However, Sorge

---

* Wenneker was German Naval Attaché in Tokyo, 1934–37 and 1940–45; between 1937 and 1940, he commanded the pocket battleship *Deutschland*. He, too, was a valuable source of information for Sorge.

said that he never learned anything of value from other newsmen and that they had no suspicion of his espionage activities or real political convictions. Moreover, he never passed on to other journalists any of the information he obtained from his collaborators or from the German Embassy (although he did include some of Ozaki's analyses in his own well-researched articles for the *Frankfurter Zeitung*). After about 1939, he left the task of maintaining contacts with foreign journalists and the official Japanese Dōmei News Agency primarily to Voukelitch.

Sorge had also established close ties with the Dutch community upon his arrival in Tokyo, but these were severed by the Dutch as the European political situation grew serious. He knew all of the local Nazis and listened to their opinions on Russia in order to evaluate the future of German-Russian relations. When the Japanese government released its press announcement on the Sorge case on June 16, 1942, the chairman of the Nazi Party in the Tokyo-Yokohama area, the manager of the Agfa photographic firm, was asked by the Home Ministry for a statement. His answer was: "I was surprised at the news because I have known Sorge personally for a long time. Men are apt to expose themselves inadvertently, but Sorge—despite the fact that he was a heavy drinker—never gave anyone the slightest suspicion about his activities. . . . He joined the Party before 1935, when I assumed my present position. . . . However, he had never exerted himself for the development of the Party."[6] The local Nazi chief went on to comment that he considered Clausen a buffoon who could not possibly hold ideological convictions of any sort.

When Eugen Ott became Ambassador, Sorge became an unofficial Embassy adviser, and he let all of his other contacts languish. He was given a private office in the Embassy building, and he made daily reports to the Ambassador on the news from abroad and on the latest developments in Tokyo. He usually spent from 6 until 10 o'clock every morning going over press dispatches and other reports received by the Embassy in preparation for his briefing with the Ambassador. Sorge was also given access to various files in the Embassy, including those of the Economic Section and the Air Attaché.[7]

It would be wrong to suppose that Sorge achieved his powerful position within the German Embassy primarily on the basis of personal friendship (and that Ott was therefore an extraordinarily bad judge of character). Sorge was not only a Communist, a journalist, and a spy; he held the highest academic degree granted in Germany. While in Japan, he devoted himself to a rigorous program of private study of Japanese history, language, economics, and art, and he built up a library of about a thousand volumes on Asian subjects. He also became an expert on Japanese agriculture. He traveled extensively in Honshu, Kyushu, and Shikoku when it was still possible to do so (until about mid-1938), and he spent every Sunday hiking in the countryside around Tokyo looking at the crops. He had a great interest in Asian art, which dated from his China days, and he and Miyagi, who frequently met in museums, often spent more time talking about Oriental art than about political questions. The editors of the *Frankfurter Zeitung* and professor Haushofer had both been pressing him for years to write a book, and he had written about 300 pages in manuscript at the time of his arrest.[8]

There was a personal drive behind these labors (he berated himself, for example, for failing to master Japanese), but he never forgot their practical purpose. "My research on Japan," he said, "had great intrinsic value for my espionage work, but at the same time it was indispensable as a part of my cover. If I had not studied Japan thoroughly, I could never have acquired the strong position I held in the German Embassy or in German journalistic circles. My acceptance at the Embassy was not acquired solely through personal friendship with its officials. Certain members of the Embassy staff were opposed to my having considerable influence in the Embassy. I acquired my position in the Embassy chiefly through my general fund of information, my knowledge of China, and my concrete research on Japan."[9] Sorge probably underestimated the opposition to him within the German Embassy; Meissner hated him and says that many other junior officials regarded him with a mixture of awe and resentment.[10]

Regardless of the feelings of the junior staff members, the leaders of the Embassy considered Sorge's services indispensable for their mission. Ambassador Ott repeatedly asked Sorge to accept an official position, probably one at the ministerial level, and in mid-1939 the Wilhelmstrasse offered Sorge the post of Embassy press officer. Sorge explained: "Although I politely refused these offers, Ambassador Ott took a long time in getting over his indignation. However, I did agree to continue my services as informal political consultant to the Ambassador; and in October [1939], after the outbreak of the second European conflagration, I promised to collaborate with the Embassy's press and propaganda section on analyzing the reports received by the Embassy. I did not at any time become a formal member of the Embassy staff."[11] The reasons for his refusal, Sorge said, were that an official post would have kept him too busy to meet his responsibilities to the Soviet Union and that a Foreign Ministry request for a background check on him might have exposed his early membership in the German Communist Party. In any case, his refusal appears only to have made him an even more desirable confidant in the eyes of Ambassador Ott.

There is one aspect of Sorge's influence within the German Embassy that he does not elaborate on in his memoir: the extent to which he owed his reputation to Ozaki and Miyagi. Sorge's position within the Embassy suggests he gave a good deal of technical information acquired by the ring to the German military attachés. In his written statement for the police, Sorge said: "I prepared reports for the Military Attaché and myself using materials gathered by the Embassy"; and at another point he refers to "reports that I prepared for Military Attaché Matzki." (Colonel Matzki was Ott's replacement as Military Attaché from April 1938 until December 1940; he was succeeded by Colonel, later Major General, Kretschmer, with whom Sorge also worked.)[12] He may have based these reports solely on information available in the Embassy, but there is good reason to believe that he supplemented them with valuable data of his own. Lieutenant Colonel Fritz von Petersdorf, Assistant Military Attaché in Tokyo from December 1938 until January 1943, testified before the International Military Tribunal for the Far East that the German correspondent, Richard Sorge, was one of the German Embassy's major sources of information on the strength of the Kwantung Army, and that he told the Embassy things not revealed by the Japanese General Staff.[13] There is only one way Sorge could have acquired this sort of information: from the South Manchurian Railroad via Ozaki.

The von Petersdorf testimony has become famous in the Sorge case because the Russian prosecutor, General Vasiliev, objected violently every time the defense counsel, Mr. Cunningham, mentioned the name of Richard Sorge.[14] The court, considering testimony about Sorge irrelevant to its cases, ruled against Cunningham, and Sorge was never discussed again before the tribunal. More interesting than Vasiliev's objections, however, is what von Petersdorf said in his affidavit: that Sorge was regarded by the German military staff as a prime source of intelligence. While there is no evidence to suggest that Sorge was a "double spy" impartially serving both Germany and the Soviet Union, it does seem that he supplied the German Embassy with concrete military information he collected from Ozaki and Miyagi. Moreover, Sorge undoubtedly contributed to the German Ambassador's understanding of the Japanese political situation by telling him things reported by Ozaki from Breakfast Society gatherings. In return for such information, Sorge did not hestitate to ask Ambassador Ott about the negotiations for the Triple Alliance or about probable German actions during the period of the Molotov-Ribbentrop pact. In a sense, Sorge traded information on Japan for clues to major Axis policy decisions that affected the Soviet Union. As we shall see, he made a good bargain.

Sorge's position within the German Embassy was based on his credentials, his abilities, and the fact that he possessed high-level Japanese informants not available to any other foreign journalist in Tokyo. He used his own position and that of Ozaki to send an incredible amount of information to the Soviet Union. Much of it was routine political background information, although of a much higher quality than is normally collected by most nations' embassies; but on questions related directly to the security of the Soviet Union, Sorge's reports were of inestimable value. Nowhere is this better illustrated than in the ring's efforts to report the Japanese side of the Russo-Japanese border clashes at Chang-ku-feng and Nomon-Han.

Chang-ku-feng (literally, "Broad Drum Peak") is a spot of high ground along the Tumen River near the intersection of the borders of Manchukuo, the Soviet Union's maritime provinces, and Korea. On the map it is about 70 miles southwest of Vladivostok. Until the summer of 1938, the top of the ridge line of Chang-ku-feng was regarded as the Russo-Japanese border. During that summer the Kwantung Army, in order to make the border more defensible, claimed that the entire ridge was within Manchurian territory; the Russians, to demonstrate their disagreement, dug in and reinforced their side of the ridge. The result was an attempt by the Japanese Army to dislodge the Soviet forces, since known to the Japanese as the Chang-ku-feng Incident and to the Soviet Union as the Lake Khasan Operation (July 12 to August 11, 1938). It was the first of two great Soviet-Japanese clashes during 1938–39, and it produced some of the most furious fighting in the Far East prior to the Pacific War.

The Chang-ku-feng Incident was the first occurrence to demand the undivided attention of the ring. Was Chang-ku-feng a pretext for a Kwantung Army invasion of Siberia? What was the strength of reinforcements sent to the Kwantung Army? What was the attitude of the Tokyo government? These were precisely the sort of questions that Sorge had been sent to Japan to answer, and the ring performed well. Ozaki attended cabinet discussions (he was a cabinet consultant at this time), read reports from the Governor General of Korea, and then told Sorge that Japan had no intention of allowing the incident to develop into a war. Ozaki further provided an expert analysis of why Japan did not want the incident to expand: the Army was then concentrating its large force in central China for the assault on Hankow, and the Kwantung Army had already transferred several divisions to the Yangtze area; in addition, Japan planned a landing near Canton simultaneously with the Hankow operation. But Ozaki urged further investigation: "I pointed out to Sorge that immediately after the Chang-ku-feng Incident had broken out the flow of information between the military and the cabinet was completely cut off, and that this was characteristic of politics in Japan."[15]

Therefore Sorge also checked with Miyagi, who in turn consulted his wide range of military observers. Yamana Masazane, Miyagi's subordinate in Hokkaidō, indicated that no large troop movements were under way.[16] This corroborated Ozaki's prediction that the Kwantung Army would come to terms. Sorge meanwhile figured out the divisional strength and location of the Japanese Army from German Embassy sources, and Clausen transmitted all of this information to "Wiesbaden."[17]

It is impossible to know how the Soviet Union used Sorge's intelligence, for an official Russian history of these operations has never been written.[18] Nevertheless, it should be noted that Maxim Litvinov stood firm and made no compromise proposal to the Japanese; he told Ambassador Shigemitsu that the only way to avoid war was to restore the status quo as of July 29, 1938. The Kwantung Army agreed, and that ended the incident. Although the Russians sustained many casualties at Chang-ku-feng and the Kwantung Army penetrated as far as four kilometers into Soviet territory, the Chang-ku-feng Incident is usually considered a Soviet victory. The Soviets had conducted some 700 aircraft sorties into Korea and Manchuria, behind the Japanese lines; and, more important, they had succeeded in gaining their diplomatic point.

Besides reporting on Japanese intentions, the Sorge ring had another task to perform in connection with the Chang-ku-feng Incident, a task that would result in a personal triumph for Sorge. On June 13, 1938, just before fighting broke out on the border, G. S. Lyushkov, a general (third grade) in the State Political Department (GPU), defected from the Soviet Far East Army and crossed into Manchukuo. He was arrested by the Kwantung Army and taken to Tokyo, where the Japanese government announced his desertion on July 1, 1938.[19] Lyushkov stated that he was disillusioned with the Soviet Union, but Sorge believed that he probably feared being killed in the purges of the Red Army and the GPU, which were then in full swing. Lyushkov possessed a great deal of political and military information on the Soviet Far East, and the Japanese intelligence officers were delighted to have him under their wing. They lodged him in Miyakezaka—the Tokyo headquarters of the Imperial General Staff—and began to interrogate him.

Moscow was definitely upset; in one of its rare radio transmissions from "Wiesbaden" to Clausen, it sent this message: "The ring must make maximum efforts to acquire the report on Lyushkov."[20] The report to which Moscow referred was not one prepared by the Japanese Army. Imperial General Headquarters intelligence had decided that it did not have an officer competent enough to get everything from Lyushkov that he might know, and so the Japanese requested that Germany send a military expert on the Soviet Union to Tokyo for this purpose. Ambassador Ott complied with the request, and in October or November of 1938, Admiral Wilhelm Canaris's Abwehr, the German intelligence service, sent a colonel to Tokyo to interrogate Lyushkov. Sorge became informed of the whole affair during the summer through the German Assistant Military Attaché, Lieutenant Colonel Schol (von Petersdorf's predecessor). It was the report of the colonel from Berlin (whom Sorge never identified by name) that Moscow wanted to see.

Sorge had already learned from Schol everything that the Japanese had learned from Lyushkov, and he sent this information to Moscow by radio. Sorge's report included Lyushkov's personal statement of his anti-Communist attitude, his opinion on the extent and strength of anti-Moscow factions within the Soviet Far East Army, his criticism of Stalin and of the Central Committee, and details of the disposition of troops in Siberia and of the codes used for military communications. Sorge's preliminary compilation, which he transmitted in the late summer of 1938, may very well have contributed to the execution of the Russian commander at Chang-ku-feng, Marshal Vassili K. Blyukher (Blücher), the famous Comintern figure of the Chinese revolution known as "Galen." Blyukher may have been implicated by Lyushkov in an anti-Party plot. John Erickson observes: "As for Blyukher himself, there is no way of establishing with any certainty the date on which he was removed from the Far East and dispatched to Moscow. On November 9, 1938, however, Blyukher was dead. Most probably this proletarian Marshal of the Soviet Union, soldier, diplomat, and the lord of Eastern Siberia, was the victim of a persistent and deadly intrigue, from which neither Voroshilov nor Mekhlis emerges with any honor. At the death of Blyukher there were no trumped-up charges, no orders of the day, no talk of tribunals— only a complete and utter silence which remained unbroken for some twenty years. It was the epitome of personal vengeance."[21] Erickson's explanation may be accurate—Blyukher may have been purged without cause—but the fact that his death did not receive the usual purge publicity raises the possibility that Sorge's report had implicated him in one plot that was not fabricated by Stalin.

After having radioed his initial findings, Sorge intercepted the Abwehr report on Lyushkov at the German Embassy. He photographed it in its entirety during one of his early morning sessions in his office. (Sorge used a Leica for his extensive copying of documents at the German Embassy.) The film was then dispatched to Moscow during January 1939, in one of the ring's regular courier packages.[22] Yoshikawa Mitsusada, the chief prosecutor in the Sorge trials, believes that Sorge's performance in the Lyushkov case played a large part in the genuine defeat dealt the Kwantung Army by Marshal Zhukov later in 1939 at Nomon-Han.[23] Thanks to Sorge, the Soviet Union knew the Japanese Army's exact estimate of Soviet military strength in Siberia before the Japanese launched their drive into Mongolia.

If Chang-ku-feng was a big "incident," the fighting around the village of Nomon-Han on the Mongolian-Manchurian border was a small war. Known to the Russians as the battle of Khalkhin-Gol, the Nomon-Han Incident (May 11 to September 15, 1939) was a major battle of the Second World War in the Far East. It produced the Far East's first evenly matched aircraft and tank engagements, and it established the reputation of one of Russia's most famous commanders, Marshal G. K. Zhukov. The undefined border between Manchukuo and the Mongolian People's Republic was the immediate cause of the dispute, but in a larger context Nomon-Han was a major probing operation by the Kwantung Army's military adventurers. During the first half of 1939, they had made repeated raids into Outer Mongolia to test the possibilities of annexing more territory to Manchukuo and to discover whether the Soviet Far East Army would come to the aid of its Mongolian ally.

The Japanese got their answer to the second question at dawn on the morning of August 20, 1939. Marshal Zhukov, in a painstakingly well-prepared counterattack involving tanks, aircraft, artillery, and infantry, surprised the invaders and drove them from Soviet-Mongolian territory by the end of the month. Japan's only logical recourse after this defeat would have been to declare war, but just as she was losing the battle, she was betrayed by her German ally: on August 23, 1939, the Molotov-Ribbentrop Pact was signed, and on September 1, the Germans and Russians together invaded Poland. The Kwantung Army's politically naïve officers withdrew into Manchukuo and tried to make sense of these startling diplomatic developments. (As is well known, Japan remained as perplexed by Germany's reasons for signing the agreement as foreign Communists were by Stalin's purposes.) The Russians and the Japanese negotiated an armistice on September 16, 1939; the Mongolia-Manchukuo border was established on the battle lines as of 1 P.M. Moscow time, September 15. Nomon-Han was without question a Soviet victory, and it greatly accelerated the reorientation of Japanese ambitions toward the south.

The Sorge ring contributed to the Soviet victory in several ways. Ozaki questioned Japanese journalists returning from the front and reported to Sorge the results of the Breakfast Society's discussion of the incident. His conclusion was that Prince Konoye wanted to avoid war with Russia at all costs, and that the Army was being restrained by the ferocity of the Russian counterattack. Ozaki also obtained accurate information from the South Manchurian Railroad on the size of the Kwantung Army and of the reinforcements being sent to it. Furthermore, Mizuno Shigeru, whose family was living in Kyoto, discovered that the Kyoto army division that was suddenly transferred during July and August of 1939 was going to Anhwei, in central China, rather than to Nomon-Han. This, too, was reported to Sorge through Ozaki.[24] Voukelitch visited the Nomon-Han battlefield between July 3 and July 15 as the Havas representative and a guest of the Japanese Army. He discovered that the Japanese military commanders regarded the action as having limited objectives, and he informed Sorge of the numbers and types of aircraft and tanks at the disposal of the Japanese forces.[25]

It was Miyagi, however, who supplied the most valuable information on Nomon-Han. He had more subordinate informants than any member of the ring, and the most important among them was Kodai Yoshinobu (b. 1911). Kodai was an ex-soldier. He had been conscripted in March of 1936 and sent to Manchuria; after the outbreak of the China Incident he had fought in Peking, Inner Mongolia, Suiyüan, and in the T'aiyüan campaign; and after a period of garrison duty in Korea he was released to the reserves on March 9, 1939. Kodai thus knew a great deal about the Army in Manchuria and Korea, and he had many friends still on active duty. He was one of the few subordinate informants whom Sorge had met and in whom he had placed great trust.[26]

During the early summer of 1939 Kodai and Miyagi worked together to establish precisely the strength and location of Japanese units that might be used to reinforce the Nomon-Han front. They discovered the presence of about one division at Hailaerh (Jehol) and another at Tsitsihar, details of troop movements in and around Harbin and Hsinking, the numbers of aircraft and tanks concentrated at Kungchuling (near Mukden), and the unit strength of all other forces in western Manchukuo. Miyagi gave this intelligence to Sorge for transmission in July 1939, and after the Soviet counterattack in August Miyagi and Kodai reported all new mobilizations that might indicate an expansion of the battle into a full-scale invasion.*

Sorge contributed his own analysis. He had learned from the German military attachés, who had had conversations at Imperial General Headquarters, that Nomon-Han was not the first stage of a scheduled invasion, and he reported this intelligence in detail to Moscow. The Soviet forces undoubtedly used Sorge's technical information, but the Nomon-Han Incident was one of the few occasions when Mos-

---

* Kodai, a graduate of the law department of Meiji University (March 1935), achieved the rank of corporal before his release to inactive duty in March 1939. He worked with Miyagi on military problems until July 26, 1941, when he was called back into the Army. In the summer of 1941 he was sent to Manchukuo and then, in October, to the area around Canton. He was arrested on April 11, 1942, and sentenced to fifteen years imprisonment for his part in the Sorge case. He was released in the amnesty of October 8, 1945. See *Gendai-shi shiryō*, I, 17; III, 657–60, 704. Willoughby misromanizes Kodai's name as "Koshiro"; *Shanghai Conspiracy*, pp. 85–87. Cf. Ozaki Hotsuki, *Zoruge jiken*, p. 211.

cow expressed skepticism about Sorge's general appraisal of the situation. Sorge later wrote: "The Soviet Union, observing the Japanese Army's obvious role in and attitude toward foreign policy after the Manchurian Incident, held the deepest suspicion that Japan was planning an attack on the Soviet Union. This suspicion was so strongly held that the Moscow authorities sometimes found my analyses to the contrary unacceptable. Two specific instances of this were during the Nomon-Han battle and the great mobilization of the summer of 1941."[27] Nevertheless, Sorge's analyses proved to be correct in both instances. As we shall see later, there is a conspicuous lack of correspondence between the intelligence he is known to have sent to Moscow and Soviet actions during that time. One of the greatest unresolved questions still surrounding the Sorge case is the part that the ring's reports played in Kremlin decision-making.

Sorge and Ozaki sent literally hundreds of reports to Moscow in the years between 1934 and 1941. Sorge spoke at one point of a packet of thirty rolls of film comprising more than 1,000 pages being dispatched in one courier bundle, and the composite lists of each member's espionage activities prepared by the police fill long sections of the Sorge case materials.[28] An exhaustive analysis of this intelligence would amount to a political history of the Far East during the decade prior to the war in the Pacific. The Tokkō credit Ozaki alone with studies of the assassination of General Nagata by Colonel Aizawa, the failure of General Ugaki to form a cabinet, the composition of the first Konoye cabinet, the establishment of Imperial General Headquarters, the appointment of General Itagaki as Minister of War in 1938, the New Structure Movement, the formation of the Hiranuma cabinet, Anglo-Japanese negotiations on the Tientsin concession, the policies of the Abe and Yonai cabinets, the impact of the China Incident on Japan's rural economy, the revised table of organization of a Japanese Army division (1941), Japan's gold holdings, and many, many other events.

Sorge testified to the police: "The most important intelligence reports furnished me by Ozaki concerned: (a) the peace negotiations and the peace treaty between Japan and China [Wang Ching-wei]; (b) Foreign Minister Matsuoka's mission to Europe [spring 1941]; (c) Japan's position after the outbreak of the Russo-German war; (d) the huge mobilization of Japanese forces [summer 1941]; and (e) the negotiations between the United States and Japan." The first item relates to Ozaki's China specialization, while all the others constitute the subject matter of the ring's primary mission: predicting the timing and direction of Japanese aggression in Asia.

Ozaki's intelligence on Japan's use of the Wang Ching-wei government ultimately led to the involvement of his friends Saionji and Inukai as defendants in the Sorge case. Ozaki made many reports to Sorge on the defection of Wang Ching-wei and Japan's intention of using him as a puppet. Saionji and Inukai were implicated because Ozaki possessed a copy of the treaty between Wang and Japan a good three months before the Wang government was established at Nanking (March 30, 1940) and almost a year before it was formally signed at Nanking (November 30, 1940). Inukai Ken, the chief civilian negotiator with Wang throughout 1939, actually completed the draft treaty governing future relations between China and Japan in December of 1939, after which he flew home to Tokyo. Early in 1940 his friend Saionji Kinkazu visited him at his Yotsuya home, and Inukai allowed Saionji to make a handwritten copy of the treaty. Saionji then showed his copy to Ozaki. Saionji testified: "When Ozaki was a consultant to the Konoye cabinet, he had presented his recommendations on China policy to the government through Cabinet Secretary Kazami Akira. He had also participated in drafting the Konoye statement of December 22, 1938. Although Ozaki was not directly involved in the work to influence Wang Ching-wei, he was a well-known authority on China, and I had often consulted him on Chinese problems and the Wang operation since the middle of 1938. . . . Thus, when he visited me at Surugadai [a section of Tokyo] in January 1940, I mentioned the treaty and showed my copy of it to him at his request."[29]

Ozaki, of course, sent the gist of the treaty and his analysis of it to Sorge, who sent it to Moscow. This treaty and the Wang operation were of vital interest to the U.S.S.R. Had Japan really compromised with China and established an independent government under Wang, Chiang Kai-shek might have capitulated, leaving the entire Japanese Army free for an attack on Russia. But the Inukai treaty offered no threat in that direction. It was based on the original Konoye statement, and it securely established Wang as a puppet of Japan. Japan had to give Wang genuine but independent support if it hoped to end the China Incident. This treaty did not give Nanking such independence, and the Soviet Union was aware of it long before Wang's reliance on Japan became obvious to the Chinese resistance forces themselves.

The Sorge ring accomplished its greatest feats of espionage on the eve of the Pacific War. It is an oversimplification, however, to say only that Ozaki and Sorge warned the Soviet Union of the German attack on Russia, which occurred on June 22, 1941, and that Ozaki discovered the results of the meeting held in the Imperial Palace on July 2, 1941, when Japan decided to advance south rather than join Germany in its assault on the U.S.S.R. Ozaki and Sorge did do these things, of course, and the fact is recited in virtually every book or article on the Sorge case.[30] But Sorge and Ozaki were not the only Soviet spies to report the German attack, and they contributed more to Japan's "Southern Advance" than simply telling Moscow about it. The involvement of the Sorge ring in the great issues of peace and war was highly complex, and it cannot be reduced to two items of intelligence.

The great objective of Sorge and his associates had always been to warn the Soviet Union of an attack. Despite their diverse motives, the members of the ring kept everything subordinate to this goal. As Miyagi said under interrogation: "Sorge told us that if Japan's attack on Russia could be forecast two months ahead, it could be avoided by diplomatic maneuvers; if one month in advance, the Soviet Union could have large forces on the border and its defenses ready; if two weeks ahead, a first line of defense could be constructed; and if only a week ahead, losses could be reduced."[31] However, in order to warn the Soviet Union of an attack, the ring had to know as much as possible about all of Japan's foreign relations—including those with Germany, China, and the United States.

The threat of a coordinated German-Japanese attack on the Soviet Union had existed since the Anti-Comintern Pact of 1936. Stalin had deferred it with the Molotov-Ribbentrop agreement of 1939, and he further strengthened his hand during Foreign Minister Matsuoka Yōsuke's mission to Europe in March and April of 1941 (a mission that included among its members Saionji Kinkazu). It is impossible, even today, to rationalize Axis diplomacy during 1941. Whatever the Triple Alliance was intended to accomplish, it presumably did not include triple suicide. Nevertheless, Hitler simply didn't tell Foreign Minister Matsuoka, when he visited Berlin in March of 1941, that plans for the German invasion of Russia had already been laid; Matsuoka thereupon proceeded to Moscow, where on April 13, 1941, he negotiated a treaty of neutrality with their presumed mutual ally. There are many possible explanations for this: that Japanese policy was based on the need to advance toward the resources in southeast Asia regardless of German actions; that Hitler made his greatest miscalculation of the war; that the mild German response to Matsuoka's treaty was only a façade to disguise the coming invasion of Russia; or that, as professor Maruyama suggests, this treaty and subsequent German-Japanese actions derived from a near-lunatic ignorance of strategic possibilities on the part of the Axis leaders.[32] The Russo-Japanese neutrality treaty was the beginning of a series of events that led Japan to declare war on the United States precisely at a time when the Russian defense of Moscow was beginning to be stiffened with troops from Asia. Whatever else can be said about Japanese policy and policy-makers in 1941, Matsuoka's treaty unwittingly saved Soviet Russia from almost certain destruction.

Ozaki later recalled: "Sorge was jubilant over the signing of this pact. He had been very worried what Japan's reaction would be should Germany attack the Soviet Union, but this treaty to a certain extent separated Japan from Germany. He took it as a diplomatic victory for the Soviet Union. Our main concern after the conclusion of the Russo-Japanese neutrality pact was whether or not Japan would abide by it in the event of a German invasion of Russia. Very shortly after the promulgation of the treaty, I discovered that there were two main schools of thought in Japan concerning the relationship between the neutrality pact and the Triple Alliance [September 27, 1940]. On the one hand, the so-called pro-Axis faction maintained that since Japan's national policy vis-à-vis the Triple Alliance had been determined by Imperial Rescript, the neutrality pact could not take precedence over it. On the other hand, the legalistic faction—concentrated mainly in the Foreign Ministry—contended that since the Triple Alliance excluded the Soviet Union and the neutrality pact defined a new area of obligation, the pact should be given priority over the Alliance."[33] Sorge and Ozaki met almost daily throughout the spring and summer of 1941 and tried to follow up these trends. Ozaki discovered at a Breakfast Society meeting that most of the Konoye circle already belonged to the legalistic faction, but he continued to support and advocate their position in an attempt to ensure its acceptance.

Sorge, meanwhile, was busy at the German Embassy. He managed to learn the details of the German attack on Russia from three different military sources.[34] The first was Colonel Kretschmer, Matzki's successor from December 1940 as Senior Military Attaché. In late April of 1941 Kretschmer told Sorge that Germany's preparations for war with Russia had been completed. Then, in May, two special military emissaries came to Tokyo for the purpose of briefing the Ambassador on the forthcoming war. The first of these was "special envoy Niedermayer," whom Sorge identifies elsewhere as "a colonel in the [former] Reichswehr and one of Germany's authorities on the Soviet Union."[35] This could only have been Colonel Oskar Ritter von Niedermayer, who was in Russia throughout the nineteen-twenties as one of the chief Reichswehr figures in the Soviet-German military collaboration of that period; Niedermayer's old friend Herbert von Dirksen, the German Ambassador to Moscow before being assigned to Tokyo, gave Niedermayer a letter of introduction to Richard Sorge before he departed from Berlin.[36] Niedermayer saw Sorge in Tokyo and told him that a Russian-German war was inevitable and gave three reasons for the planned attack: Germany required the breadbasket of the Ukraine for its war effort; it wanted to capture from one to two million Russians to supplement the German labor shortage in agriculture and industry; and it wanted to eradicate the threat Russia posed to its eastern frontiers.[37]

The second special envoy was Lieutenant Colonel Schol, von Petersdorf's predecessor as Assistant Military Attaché in Tokyo (prior to December 1938), who was then on his way to a new post as German Military Attaché at Bangkok. He traveled via the trans-Siberian railroad (Germany and Russia were, of course, still allies in May 1941), and he brought Ambassador Ott the date of the German attack and details on Germany's strategy. Schol told Ott and Sorge that the invasion would occur on June 20 (it actually took place June 22, 1941), that the German force would consist of between 170 and 190 largely mechanized divisions, and that the main thrust would begin toward Moscow and Leningrad and then turn toward the Ukraine. Sorge states that all of this information was radioed to Moscow by Clausen; but, as we shall see, Clausen betrayed Sorge during this period and only part of it got through. Nevertheless, Sorge did some of the transmitting himself, and the Soviet Union may have been forewarned successfully. Sorge claims to have received a message of thanks and congratulations from Moscow after the Russo-German war had broken out, but this message is not included in Clausen's later reconstruction of "Wiesbaden"-to-Tokyo radio traffic.[38]

With the Russo-German war in progress, the ring devoted itself to the next decisive question: would Japan decide to "shake hands with Hitler in the Urals" or would it pursue its already well-laid plans for the conquest of Singapore and the Dutch East Indies? As Ozaki explained, the Japanese government was divided on this issue. The invasion of Russia marked the second time that Japan's German ally had acted without prior consultation (the first being the conclusion of the Molotov-Ribbentrop pact during the Nomon-Han battle). Nevertheless, Matsuoka reversed his policy of the previous April and urged that Japan enter the war. Added to his voice were those of the Nazis—at least of Ribbentrop and Ott, if not of Hitler himself—who now demanded a Japanese attack on Siberia despite the fact that they had calmly allowed Matsuoka to conclude the neutrality pact only two months earlier. The Konoye circle's position, strongly supported by Ozaki, won out: Japan would advance southward regardless of what Germany did, and it would not renounce the neutrality pact with Russia (it never did); the Germans had miscalculated if they believed that they could embarrass Japan as they had on June 22 and still call for support. It was this combination of German arrogance and Japanese pride that led to the eventual destruction of both states.

The decision to advance south was made on July 2, 1941, in a conference in the presence of the Emperor. Ozaki had already reasoned that this was the course his nation was most likely to pursue, but he was unable to obtain the details of the July 2 decision at once. He learned through South Manchurian Railroad sources that the Army itself was divided. Most Army officers wanted to attack Russia, but the Kwantung Army was not confident about the Japanese internal economic situation, and the hesitancy of its Manchurian armies made the General Staff cautious. Ozaki discovered that the Kwantung Army would consider an attack only on two conditions: if it had a three-to-one superiority in troops over the Soviet Far East Army, and if the German invasion produced disunity and broken morale among the Siberian forces. The memory of Nomon-Han had obviously made the Kwantung Army more wary.

Ozaki did not learn the details of the Army's decision not to attack Russia until late August. At that time he had lunch with Saionji Kinkazu at the Asia Restaurant on the sixth floor of the Tokyo South Manchurian Railroad building. The Breakfast Society had not been told of the July 2 decision, and so neither Saionji nor Ozaki knew about it officially. However, a few days earlier a certain Lieutenant Colonel Fujii of the War Ministry had unofficially confirmed Saion-ji's belief that the Army had decided not to enter the Russo-German war. During their luncheon, Ozaki expressed *his* belief that the Army would not attack Russia, and Saionji told him that his hunch was correct.[39]

Ozaki conveyed this information to Sorge, who had come to the same conclusion on the basis of clues within the German Embassy. Ambassador Ott had tried frantically to convince Foreign Minister Matsuoka of the need for Japan to enter the war; but on July 16, 1941, the second Konoye cabinet resigned *en bloc* and reconstructed itself two days later without Matsuoka—which could only mean a Japanese decision against Ott. Sorge had been transmitting these developments to Moscow throughout the summer of 1941, and Ozaki's information now allowed him to confirm the view that Japan had decided against war with Russia. In early October of 1941, Sorge sent his definitive message: "There will be no attack until the spring of next year at the earliest."[40]

As Sorge indicated in his confession, the Soviet Union was unwilling to accept his appraisal until autumn because of the large Japanese troop mobilization during the summer of 1941: Japan had called up some 1,300,000 men for military service during July and August. Sorge was certain that these forces were being readied for the Southern Advance, but he had to investigate the United States–Japanese negotiations of 1941 in order to reassure Moscow. His only source of information on this subject was Ozaki. At the Dairen conference of the South Manchurian Railroad's research staff in September, Ozaki acquired the figures on Japan's oil stocks: two million tons in civilian hands, two million tons held by the Army, and eight million tons in naval reserves. The non-military supplies could sustain Japan's economy for only six months, and so it was clear that a decision for or against war with the Anglo-American powers had to come soon.[41] Ozaki also knew from Saionji the details of the Roosevelt-Konoye exchanges throughout 1941, but his own appraisal of the economic situation made him pessimistic about their outcome.[42] He reported to Sorge that Konoye was trying to avoid war with the United States, but that the economic situation appeared hopeless. The Soviet Union received a virtual confirmation of Ozaki's analysis on October 18,

1941, when General Tōjō replaced Konoye as Premier. Ironically, this was also the day on which Richard Sorge was arrested.

It is impossible to say with precision exactly how the Soviet Union used the Sorge ring's 1941 espionage. The U.S.S.R. has never so much as acknowledged the existence of Richard Sorge; and we do not know how many of Sorge's reports got through to "Wiesbaden" or what relative weight was given to them in comparison with reports from other Soviet spies. From the timing and course of the German invasion of Russia, it would appear that the efforts of the *Rote Kapelle* ring operating within Göring's Air Ministry in Berlin were as important as Sorge's.[43] In this writer's opinion, the Sorge ring's reporting of the Southern Advance was its single most important act of espionage, and a contextual analysis of the use Russia made of this information is possible.

It has been argued that Sorge's reports predicting the Southern Advance were not crucial to Russia because Stalin did not send large reinforcements from the Far Eastern Army to the western front until mid-autumn.[44] However, the record of Sorge's and Ozaki's activities indicates that such a view misinterprets their contribution. Although he sent reports throughout the summer, Sorge did not send a definite "no attack" message until late September or early October of 1941; it was precisely at that time that almost half of the ground strength of the Far Eastern armies was moved from east to west, to join in the defense of Moscow by the early part of December.[45] The relevance of this transfer to the course of the Soviet-German war is unchallengeable. In the words of John Erickson: "Out of the east loomed the threat of possible Japanese intervention at a time when the Soviet western frontiers were beginning to cave in. The Soviet-Japanese Neutrality Pact was merely a scrap of paper and Stalin knew this only too well. . . . The *Stavka* [General Headquarters] stood in desperate need of those Red Army troops in the eastern hinterlands and on the eastern borders." Sorge was unable to say in July or August that these forces could be moved. But by autumn he informed Moscow that eastern Siberia was safe for the time being because Japan was going to declare war on the United States and England. Then "those reserves which the German high command thought it [the Red Army] could not possibly possess" entered the war in the west.[46]

It may well be, however, that Sorge's and Ozaki's major contribution to frustrating German-Japanese collaboration against Russia did not involve espionage at all. During 1941 both of them made active efforts to prevent a joint German-Japanese attack on Russia by exerting their influence on Axis leaders. This was an extremely dangerous venture, requiring the greatest prudence and sensitivity, and Moscow never gave explicit approval of it. Nevertheless, both Sorge and Ozaki felt that their high positions required that they not only collect intelligence on political decisions but also attempt to ensure the desirability of the decisions themselves. Ikoma Yoshitoshi, the prosecution's German translator, writes that during conversations in prison and in his appeal of the death sentence, Sorge argued that exercising political influence was more important to his work than espionage.[47] As for Ozaki, it was undoubtedly because of his attempts to sway decisions in favor of the U.S.S.R. that he later believed that he had established something of a claim to recognition by Stalin; in the event of a successful Communist revolution in wartime Japan, he hoped to lead his country into alliances with China and Russia.

When the police asked Ozaki about his political maneuvering, he explained: "Sometime in 1939 I met Sorge at a restaurant in Tokyo and spoke to him essentially as follows: 'As a critic of the China problem, I have a certain power of persuasion; and within my circle of acquaintances there are several groups that are very powerful politically. Should I attempt to influence them in ways that would serve the defense of the Soviet Union?' Sorge replied that this was not included in our duties, and he was very apprehensive lest I become labeled pro-Soviet and compromise my usefulness for our espionage work. Nevertheless, after the outbreak of the Soviet-German war on June 22, 1941, I discovered that even within the Breakfast Society, persons like Ushiba, Kishi, and Matsumoto expected Leningrad and Moscow to fall within three to six weeks. Their analyses were based on a belief that Soviet society would collapse internally. I therefore took it upon myself to point out that this view was oversimplified."[48]

There were four essential points in Ozaki's line of argument. First, even if the Soviet Union were defeated militarily, the Bolshevik revolution had created a degree of cohesion within Soviet society that could not be destroyed; the Germans had underestimated the capacity for resistance among the Russian masses (just as Ozaki may well have overestimated their loyalty to the Bolsheviks). Second, Siberia could never be made independent of European Russia, and this dependence would persist even if Japan occupied eastern Russia. Third, Siberia offered little in the way of natural resources, whereas southeast Asia was rich in rubber and oil; Japan should therefore advance southward. Fourth, even if Germany should defeat Russia, Japan could always obtain Siberia by diplomatic means; in short, it was simply unnecessary for Japan to enter this war.[49] Ozaki used these arguments in discussions with members of the Breakfast Society and officials of the South Manchurian Railroad throughout the summer of 1941.

Sorge explained in his confession that the orders he received in Moscow in 1935 explicitly forbade him and members of his group to engage in propaganda or organizational activities. However, prompted by Ozaki's belief that they could exert some meaningful influence, Sorge asked Moscow by message in 1941 that both of them be allowed to advocate a policy of peace between Japan and the Soviet Union. The reply did not prohibit such activities outright, but it did state that they were unnecessary. Sorge clearly understood that Moscow's response was negative; but on his own initiative he construed the answer as not ruling out all attempts at political persuasion. He told Ozaki to proceed with activities intended to influence the second and third Konoye cabinets, and he himself spoke out on the Russian war within the German Embassy and to his Japanese friends.[50]

Sorge and Ozaki tailored their arguments to suit the opinions and predilections of their listeners. With Ambassador Ott, German residents in Tokyo, and members of the Nazi party, Sorge invoked Bismarck in support of the theory that Britain and France were Germany's real enemies and argued that a Russo-German war would only serve the interests of the Western Powers. When speaking with Japanese, he argued that the Red Army existed solely for defensive purposes; or, conversely, he drew attention to Japan's failures to subdue the Red Army, from the Siberian Expedition of 1918–21 to Nomon-Han. Ozaki frightened his fellow Breakfast Society members by suggesting that Britain and the United States would welcome a Russo-Japanese war as a way of getting rid of two dangerous states at once. He argued that the Anglo-American powers would wait until Japan had exhausted its oil and iron reserves and then strike at Japan in order to end the war in China. Ozaki also vehemently denied the possibility of an early Soviet collapse; Ushiba remembers a Breakfast Society gathering at which Ozaki did so, and Ozaki was convinced that his arguments on this point were quoted to Premier Konoye.[51]

It is impossible to determine the extent, if any, to which the political efforts of Sorge and Ozaki influenced the course of history. Sorge argued—perhaps in his own defense, but plausibly enough by any standards—that Japan's decision to advance to the south was based not on his and Ozaki's efforts, but on objective realities: the war with China; the isolation of Japan from the United States, Britain, and the Netherlands; the oil and scrap iron embargoes; and so forth.[52] On the other hand, during the crucial period between the German invasion (June 22) and the council in the Imperial Presence (July 2), Premier Konoye undoubtedly welcomed opinions from all sides. It is not inconceivable that arguments put forth by Ozaki—a man whose analysis of the China Incident had been proved absolutely correct—served to increase the caution of the already cautious prince. If this is what happened, Ozaki performed a service of inestimable value to the Soviet Union. It is by no means certain, of course, that an Axis victory would have been ensured by a Japanese invasion of Russia, but it is quite certain that the policy actually pursued by Japan—the one Ozaki advocated in order to save Russia and drive his own nation to revolution—was disastrous. Ozaki cannot be held solely responsible for the Konoye government's decision, for his influence was never decisive; but he did commit treason in order to prevent Japan from joining the invasion of Russia.

Between 1933 and 1941 Sorge employed two methods of contacting Moscow: personal couriers and radio transmissions. He used both throughout the period, but couriers were more important between 1933 and 1939 and radio became the primary means of communication between 1939 and 1941. Before 1939 all meetings between Sorge's agents and special couriers from Moscow took place in Shanghai or in Hong Kong, but after that it became too dangerous to travel to China bearing microfilm. Arrangements were then made with Moscow for couriers to be contacted in Tokyo, and during the last months of the ring's operations surreptitious meetings took place between Clausen and officers of the Soviet Embassy in Tokyo. The details of time, place, and recognition signals for courier meetings were worked out with Moscow in advance by radio. Sorge described in his confession some of the many ways couriers identified their contacts: A man standing in a restaurant holding an unlighted cigar would be approached by a courier holding an unlighted pipe; after glancing at each other, both would light up, and one would follow the other from the restaurant to a park, where they would exchange code words. Another device was for one courier to carry a red package and the other a yellow one; they would identify each other at a restaurant and meet later at a safe location.

Shanghai was an ideal place for courier meetings because there were persons of many nationalities living there and the city was relatively easy to enter. Still, Sorge sent as couriers to Shanghai only persons who had logical business in the city or who might be considered tourists. Thus, the courier missions were undertaken by Clausen, his wife Anna (a former resident of Shanghai), Günther Stein, a woman friend of Stein's, and Sorge himself. The courier from Tokyo carried tightly wound spools of 35 millimeter film strung on a cord suspended inside his clothing. This film included reports written by Sorge and documentary materials gathered by members of the ring; the photographs were taken with a Leica or a similar camera (Sorge used a Leica) and processed by Voukelitch in his laboratory. Both Sorge and Voukelitch were accomplished amateur photographers.

The courier from Moscow was usually a functionary unknown to the members of the Sorge ring; occasionally he would give his contact the details of the next meeting in order to avoid excessive use of the radio. The Moscow courier usually turned over to Sorge's agent a large sum of money—often $5,000 in U.S. currency—for the ring's operating expenses. Sorge's needs for funds included fairly large salaries for Clausen and Voukelitch; a bribe for Voukelitch's divorced wife, Edith, before she left Japan in 1939; nominal sums for Ozaki and Miyagi, with most of Ozaki's money going to maintain Kawai; and cash for the purchase of film, radio parts, and photographic chemicals. The money was first deposited in American banks in Shanghai in the name of Clausen's firm and later transferred to Japan through the Mitsui, Mitsubishi, Yokohama Specie, or Hong Kong and Shanghai banks. Clausen's company, which had many foreign trade transactions, served as a front for all Soviet funds entrusted to Sorge. Sorge sent financial statements of his disbursements to Moscow by courier at intervals of six months to a year.

Some of the most extraordinary courier missions were made by Sorge himself. Ambassador Ott occasionally asked Sorge to deliver various reports to the German Embassy in China when Sorge was making a trip there, and Sorge was only too happy to oblige: he could take advantage of his freedom of movement within Ott's Embassy to seal a pouch of his own and carry his films past Japanese customs inspectors in packages bearing the seals of the German Foreign Ministry. Sorge himself admitted using this device late in 1938, on a trip to Manila and Hong Kong, and again in April of 1941, when Ott specifically asked him to go to Shanghai; he might well have used it on every one of his many trips to the continent after Ott became Ambassador, for it was a foolproof method of smuggling.[53]

Radio communications were entirely Clausen's responsibility, and he proved to have a genius for the task. He had been told in Moscow to build an entirely new radio set in Japan in order to replace the old "Bernhardt" radio, which had performed poorly. He brought no radio materials with him, however, and it would have been dangerous to buy the various components at a radio store, so he bought most of the parts he needed at the Mazda Lamp Shop on the Ginza in Kyō-bashi (except for the transmitter key, which was probably purchased in Shanghai); he made his own tuning coils from copper gasoline tubing for automobiles, which he bought in a hardware store. All of his parts were of Japanese manufacture except for the RCA transmission tubes. For a source of power he used ordinary household AC current, which he stepped up to 800 volts with a homemade transformer. His radio had to be entirely portable and capable of sending and receiving within a radius of 2,000 kilometers from Tokyo. After arriving in Japan in November 1935, Clausen set to work immediately and completed his first radio in February 1936. After only a week of experimental broadcasting from Günther Stein's house, he established firm contact with "Wiesbaden."

Engineers of the Japanese Communications Ministry (Teishinshō) estimated that Clausen's transmitter produced about 20 watts of power and was capable of transmitting 1,500 km. during the day and 4,000 km. at night. Clausen always broadcast in the evening in order to obtain the most favorable atmospheric conditions (and also to get daytime servants out of the house). Because his transmitter used AC current, government engineers assumed that the transmissions could not have been very clear; but Clausen testified that contact was always established within ten minutes and he never mentioned portions of messages being missed. Sorge and Clausen both believed that monitoring of their broadcasts was unavoidable, but they correctly calculated that the source could never be pinpointed closer than within a radius of a few kilometers. Against the possibility of a house-to-house search, the transmitter was always moved in a large briefcase immediately after each transmission.

Clausen's receiver was an ordinary three-tube radio modified for short-wave reception and equipped with headphones. The only part of the entire apparatus that was not portable was the transformer; Clausen therefore built several concealed, stationary transformers—one at each of his different broadcasting locations—and moved the transmitter and receiver from station to station to make his broadcasts. He actually built his radio and first transformer in Günther Stein's house, but he later established transmitting posts at his own house, at Voukelitch's house, and at the house of Voukelitch's ex-wife, Edith; he also had a last-resort station at Sorge's house. In each case he transmitted from the second story of a frame building in order to avoid terrestrial magnetism. He did not install outdoor antennae that could be seen from the street; instead, he suspended two tin-plated copper wires, each seven meters long, within the room. For reception, he used only a single one-meter wire. The police estimated that he could set up his station in ten minutes and dismantle it in five.

The police did indeed monitor Clausen's transmissions. The Communications Ministry, the Tokyo Metropolitan Communications Bureau, the Osaka Communications Bureau, and the Communications Bureau of the Governor General of Korea had all been aware since at least the summer of 1938 that illegal radio transmissions were emanating from the Tokyo area. They believed that the broadcasts made before 1940 were beamed toward Shanghai and only after that time toward the Soviet areas of the Far East. The exact location of Moscow's receiving station, however, was never ascertained, and it was not known by any member of the ring. It is reasonable to assume, as Clausen did, that "Wiesbaden" was somewhere near Vladivostok. The police monitors, of course, could not understand Clausen's coded messages, and the government's cryptographers never cracked Sorge's codes. On January 19, 1942, Clausen gave a demonstration before Nishizaki Tarō, an engineer of the Communications Ministry, and Hirai Shigeru, a clerk of the Tokyo Metropolitan Communications Bureau who had previously worked as one of the monitors of Clausen's broadcasts. Both men testified that Clausen put the set together in a very short time and that it was capable of sending and receiving. Hirai also confirmed that the rhythm and tune of Clausen's transmissions were similar to those he had monitored.

One of the most amazing aspects of Clausen's radio talent was his ability to dispense with special equipment. His only instructions when he arrived in Tokyo were that he should transmit on a wave length of 37 to 39 meters and receive messages on the 45- to 48-meter band. Since he had no instruments for measuring wave length, he had to rely entirely upon his own experience in building the set. Nevertheless, he established contact after only a week of intermittent experimentation. Once he was ordered to change his transmission wave length to 38 meters, but after that the radio required no further modification.[54]

Clausen may have been one of the Soviet Union's most gifted radio technicians, but he was not its most reliable follower politically. He had been a Communist since the early twenties and had gained considerable experience in clandestine activities in China and Manchuria between 1929 and 1933; but he testified to the police that he had never made a deep study of Marxist theory, and his life in the Volga Republic seems to have left him somewhat jaundiced about the workings of a "dictatorship of the proletariat." By 1941 Clausen was in the process of becoming the most unreliable member of the ring.

There were at least two powerful reasons for Clausen's gradual change of heart. One of them was that he greatly enjoyed his "cover" role as a German businessman, and he worked hard to make his business succeed. As he told the police: "I started this business [the blueprint firm] entirely for the purpose of camouflage, but I did not like being a spy. My Communist beliefs began to falter."[55] Undoubtedly, his loss of conviction was abetted by his wife. Anna had always despised the Bolsheviks, and she feared the loss of their Mercedes and other comforts once they should have to leave Japan; on one occasion Sorge became furious with her for attempting to influence Edith de Voukelitch with anti-Communist propaganda. Clausen never came to the point of breaking with Sorge, and in fact the actual strength of his belief in Communism, as revealed during his interrogations by the police, has been underestimated by certain writers, notably Meissner.[56] Nevertheless, he was disposed to take fewer and fewer chances as the years wore on.

The second reason is even more understandable: shaky as his beliefs were, Clausen had to take greater risks and possess tougher nerves than any other member of the ring. By 1941 his nerves were ragged. He had had many close calls when moving the transmitter or making courier trips to Shanghai. He spoke in his confession of policemen grilling him while he was taking a train to Nagasaki; of a fantastic trip he and Voukelitch took to Lake Yamanaka in order to drop "Bernhardt's" bulky old transmitter into the lake; of losing his wallet, which contained a message ready for coding and transmission, in a Tokyo taxi; and of a policeman once stopping his car in Roppongi. On the latter occasion, Clausen had his radio in the car with him and he was instantly convinced that the policeman had seen it; the policeman merely told him to turn on his lights. Max Clausen had a strong sense of his own guilt, and he found it almost impossible to behave normally when confronted by the police. After six years as a spy, he was a badly frightened man.

After Sorge's motorcycle accident of May 13, 1938, Clausen had been entrusted with most of the coding, as well as the transmitting, of messages, and he therefore became aware of their contents. In 1941 he began to edit them occasionally. Sometimes, if he disagreed with them, or was afraid to leave his house in order to go to one of his stations, or was passing through one of his anti-Communist phases, he simply didn't transmit them at all. Sorge, of course, assumed that Clausen followed his orders to the letter. But speaking of a part of Sorge's intelligence on the German invasion of Russia, Clausen told the police: "Sorge ordered me to transmit this message at once. Although I realized that it was of genuine importance, I was somewhat influenced by the policies of Hitler's Germany at the time, and I did not send it."[57] According to Clausen's diary, which the Japanese police checked thoroughly, he made 50 transmissions during 1939, a total of 23,139 word groups; 60 transmissions during 1940, of 29,179 word groups; and only 21 transmissions during 1941, of 13,103 word groups.[58]

It is impossible to know whether the small figure for 1941 reflects greater caution on Sorge's part or the effects of Clausen's censorship. Under detailed interrogation by the police, Clausen admitted that he actually did send most of the very important messages. Often, if the message were of great importance, Sorge would supervise the transmission in person, and a portion of the 1941 intelligence was passed on microfilm to a Soviet courier from the Russian Embassy. Moreover, it is quite possible that Clausen gave false answers to the police in order to diminish his own guilt. Nevertheless, it must be presumed that some portion of the Sorge ring's espionage during 1941 never reached its destination.

Relations within the ring were strained during the final months of its operation. The two intellectuals of the group, Sorge and Ozaki, remained firmly committed to their ideals and were engrossed by the great events preceding the outbreak of the Pacific War; Clausen and Voukelitch, however, were losing faith and growing apprehensive. Voukelitch had divorced his European wife in 1939 in order to marry his Japanese mistress, and his new wife, combined with his success as a Havas correspondent, dampened his taste for espionage. Clausen explicitly stated that Voukelitch was dissatisfied with working for Sorge prior to his arrest.[59] He also said that Branko and Edith de Voukelitch had never enjoyed a satisfactory marriage, and that Branko became much happier after his remarriage. Edith was paid a large sum of money by Moscow, which Sorge and Clausen augmented with money of their own, in order to leave the country, and she went to Australia in 1939 or 1940.[60] Miyagi, the artist, should be included with Ozaki and Sorge as possessing an unshakable conviction in the justice of his activities. Although he entered the ring with the greatest misgivings, he performed his tasks without faltering throughout the years, and he tried to commit suicide after his arrest in order to save his associates.

By mid-October of 1941 Sorge had decided that his mission in Japan was finished, and he began to discuss with members of the ring the possibility of their going into exile. According to Ozaki Hotsuki, Sorge had even drafted a message requesting Moscow's permission for them to leave the country.[61] The message was never sent. On October 15 Sorge told Clausen that Miyagi had not kept his appointment two days earlier, and that Ozaki, who had arranged to meet him for lunch that very day at the Asia Restaurant, had also failed to appear. They were apprehensive, but they dared not try to contact Ozaki and Miyagi directly. In the early morning of October 18 three special squads of the foreign section of the Tokkō, acting simultaneously, arrested Voukelitch, Clausen, and Sorge.

Chapter Eight
Arrest, Trial, and Execution

※⽕ ⽕※

The Sorge ring operated for eight years without interference from the Japanese police. Not until a major member of the ring was under arrest did the police begin to suspect high-level espionage, and not until after the eight-month pre-trial investigation were they fully convinced that Sorge was a Soviet spy. Of course, the Japanese police do not bear sole responsibility for failing to detect the ring's existence. The chaotic political conditions of prewar Japan were ideal for espionage, and conducive also to treason on the part of Japanese nationals. Sorge and Ozaki throve on the disintegration of responsible government in Japan.

The Home Ministry's Special Higher Police (the Tokkō) actually had clues to the ring's existence as early as mid-1938, in the form of reports from the Communications Ministry and the Government of Korea telling of unauthorized, nighttime radio transmissions from Tokyo. A year later, Navy authorities complained that a secret study entrusted by the Navy to the South Manchurian Railroad's Investigation Department had been compromised, and asked the Tokkō to scrutinize the South Manchurian Railroad for a possible break in security.[1] Other agencies complained of secrets being leaked to the press, and the Tokkō made routine investigations. By 1940 they were beginning to think about the possibility of espionage, but they did not seriously believe that a spy ring was operating in their midst. Despite their notorious penchant for calling every tourist with a camera a spy, they proved unable to conceive of genuine espionage by a man such as Ozaki.

Rather than looking for spies, high police officials worked to tighten up laws against the disclosure of state secrets. Two new statutes were introduced suddenly and passed without debate in the 76th Diet session during the spring of 1941. These were the National Defense Security Law (Kokubō Hōan Hō), effective May 10, 1941; and the modified Peace Preservation Law (Chian Iji Hō), effective March 10, 1941. Everyone arrested in connection with the Sorge case was tried under both of these acts, and Sorge and Ozaki received the death penalty in accordance with their provisions.

The National Defense Security Law was designed to protect state secrets of a diplomatic, economic, or political nature (military secrets were covered by earlier legislation). Japanese were forbidden to disclose to any foreigner the proceedings or decisions of conferences before the Throne, conferences of the Privy Council, cabinet meetings, or secret sessions of the Diet. Article Three read: "Persons who have divulged to foreign countries (including persons who act on behalf of foreign countries and foreigners, both of whom shall hereinafter be regarded alike) or who make public state secrets which they have acquired or which have come into their possession in the course of their own business, shall be condemned to death, or punished with penal servitude for life or not less than three years."[2]

The modified Peace Preservation Law was a drastic expansion of the original one promulgated in 1925, with the death penalty added in 1928. An anti-subversive measure, the Peace Preservation Law made it an offense to attempt to change the "national polity" (kokutai) or to oppose the "private ownership system." In the 1941 version, the penalties for violating the law were made more severe, the public prosecutors and the Tokkō were given virtually unlimited powers of investigation, and the court was authorized, on demand by the public prosecutors, "to detain 'thought criminals' who have been released from prison but who have failed to give sufficient evidence of reform [tenkō], in order to prevent further offenses by them."[3] Agents of the Communist International—an organization that demonstrably intended to alter the kokutai—were the chief object of the Peace Preservation Law from the time it was first enacted.

Despite the severity of these laws, they were intended more to strengthen totalitarian rule than to support counterespionage. The police no doubt bore in mind the possibility of espionage, but they made no concerted search for a spy ring; they were looking chiefly for crypto-Communists or for the few Communists who might have escaped earlier police actions against the Party. The search for left-wing sympathizers had brought the names of Ozaki and Sorge to police attention by 1941, but neither man was initially suspected of espionage. The Sorge case itself was broken entirely by accident.

One of the most promising leads that came to the attention of the Japanese police originated in Berlin with Walter Schellenberg, chief of the foreign intelligence section of the SS Reichsicherheitshauptamt (RSHA) under Heinrich Himmler. Sorge, from about the time that he was offered the post of press attaché in the Tokyo Embassy, had been sending intelligence reports on Far Eastern politics to the German government—reports that came to Berlin in the form of personal letters to Wilhelm von Ritgen of the Nazi Party's Reich Press Department and chief editor of the "NS Partei-Korrespondenz."[4] Von Ritgen considered Sorge's reports indispensable to Germany's evaluation of British and American policies in the Far East and of Japan's intentions. However, according to Schellenberg (who received Sorge's reports from von Ritgen), the Nazi Party was "creating difficulties" for Sorge during 1940 because there were doubts about his political past. More in order to protect Sorge than to incriminate him, von Ritgen asked Schellenberg to investigate the Gestapo files. What Schellenberg found there raised genuine suspicions about Sorge's Nazi *bona fides,* though it did not show conclusively that Sorge was a former member of the KPD or a Soviet agent.

Concerning his actions after making this inquiry, Schellenberg writes: "Von Ritgen finally concluded that even if we assumed that Sorge had connections with the Russian Secret Service, we must, after safeguarding our own interests, find ways of profiting by his profound knowledge. In the end, we agreed that I should protect Sorge from attacks by the Party, but only on condition that he included in his reports intelligence material on the Soviet Union, China, and Japan. Officially he would work in this direction only with von Ritgen. I reported this plan to Heydrich, who agreed with it on condition that Sorge should be placed under the closest surveillance and that his information should not go through normal channels, but should be subjected to special scrutiny, for we had to assume that at the decisive moment he would try to introduce misleading material."[5]

The problem was to maintain surveillance over Sorge without attracting his suspicion. Schellenberg did not trust his own inexperienced agents in Tokyo to handle so delicate an assignment, and chose instead Joseph Meisinger, a colonel in the Gestapo, who had just been assigned to the German Embassy in Tokyo as security officer. Meisinger, better known as the "Butcher of Warsaw" (he was flown from Tokyo to Poland in 1945 and executed as a war criminal), was generally despised; according to Schellenberg, he was sent to Tokyo primarily in order to get him out of Berlin. Schellenberg nevertheless briefed him on the Sorge problem prior to his departure, and ordered him to make a discreet investigation of Sorge's activities.

Meisinger arrived in Tokyo in late 1940. Shortly thereafter, he reported back to Berlin that Sorge enjoyed the highest reputation in the German Embassy and was trusted completely by the Ambassador. However, Meisinger for some reason intimated to officers of the military police (the Kempei) that Sorge was under surveillance. Meisinger's main duty in Japan was to identify and control any Jewish or anti-Nazi elements in the German community, and it probably never occurred to him that Sorge might be a spy; but from whatever he said, the Kempei inferred that the German Embassy might be a possible source of their security leaks.

Schellenberg was furious to discover that Meisinger had allowed suspicion to be drawn to Sorge; he writes: "In the spring of 1941 I received my first shock. A Japanese police commission was visiting Berlin, and in the course of our conversation, their chief asked me whether Meisinger was placing certain German nationals under surveillance. . . . Meisinger, of course, denied later that he had ever spoken a word about Sorge to the Japanese security organization. But it was clear that he had worked very clumsily, and had drawn the attention of the Japanese police toward Sorge. . . . Meanwhile, Sorge's intelligence material grew more and more important to us, for in 1941, we were very keen to know more about Japan's plans concerning the United States. Already Sorge predicted that the Three Power [Axis] Pact would prove of little real—meaning military—value to Germany. And after the beginning of our campaign in Russia he warned us that in no circumstances would Japan denounce her nonaggression pact with the Soviet Union."[6]

The Kempei placed Sorge on their list of possibly untrustworthy foreign nationals, and they began to keep records on all persons—particularly Japanese—with whom he associated. In the spring of 1941, a Justice Ministry prosecutor named Funatsu Hiroshi discovered that the Kempei had Sorge under surveillance. Out of loyalty to his civilian colleagues, Funatsu passed this information on to the Tokkō, who forthwith began their own investigation of Sorge.[7] Both Japanese police agencies appear to have had only one piece of concrete information on Sorge, namely, that his Nazi loyalty had been questioned. The chief prosecutor in the Sorge case, Yoshikawa Mitsusada, told the U.S. House Committee on Un-American Activities that the police had considered Sorge a possible Nazi agent as well as a possible Soviet agent.[8] The former opinion had by far the greater currency in Tokyo political circles immediately after Sorge's arrest.

The Tokkō's independent investigation of Sorge went considerably beyond the Kempei's. Agents from the Toriizaka police station placed Sorge's nearby house under constant watch, and in this way the Tokkō learned the identity of his mistress. One evening in August 1941, a police officer asked Ishii Hanako (whose *nom de plume* is Miyake Hanako) to accompany him to the Toriizaka police station. There she underwent a long harangue—a Tokkō officer accused her of being a disgrace to Japan for associating with a foreigner—and the police tried to obtain information on Sorge's activities. When she told Sorge what had happened, he became quite upset; he proposed that she either go to Shanghai or that he marry her. Ishii Hanako, however, knew nothing of Sorge's espionage work, and she was unable to incriminate him in any way. With his customary aplomb, Sorge disarmed the chief of the Toriizaka police station by inviting him to dinner and criticizing him for having frightened a "friend" of a representative of Japan's ally. After his arrest, Sorge asked prosecutor Yoshikawa to try to avoid implicating Ishii Hanako, and following a short police investigation she was exonerated of any involvement in the ring's operations.[9]

During 1940 and 1941, the Tokkō and the Kempei also began to investigate Ozaki. As we have seen, Ozaki had taken an outspokenly liberal position within the Konoye circle and the Shōwa Research Association, and after he joined the South Manchurian Railroad's Investigation Department as a consultant, the police began to wonder whether he might not be a security risk. Ozaki's liberal articles in *Chūō kōron* and *Kaizō* caused the Kempei, in particular, to want to remove him from politics by an application of the Peace Preservation Law; Ozaki's writings, of course, were submitted to official censorship before being printed, but his published views on China were decidedly contrary to those of the Army. For this reason, according to Ōtani Kenjirō, the Kempei detachment commander at Akasaka (in Tokyo), Ozaki's books and articles were placed under close scrutiny beginning in 1940. The Kempei believed (and hoped) that Ozaki might prove to be one of the *gisō tenkō* Communists who were rumored to have infiltrated the Shōwa Research Association and its school, the Shōwa Academy.[10]

The Tokkō also began to have doubts about Ozaki. Complaints from the Navy and other agencies suggested the presence of a spy in the South Manchurian Railroad's Investigation Department. Ozaki himself was never suspected, but it was thought that a spy might be using him as a source. Beginning in about June of 1941, the Tokkō began to record the names, addresses, and business affiliations of everyone who called on Ozaki at his office in the South Manchurian Railroad building.[11] They also attempted to place a police spy—Itō Ritsu—in Ozaki's office.

Itō Ritsu was born in 1913 in Gifu prefecture, the region of Ozaki's ancestral home. Although destined by birth and antecedents to become a peasant, he was discovered in school to be intelligent beyond his station. In 1930, at the age of 17, he was admitted to Ichikō in Tokyo as a candidate for the Imperial University. He drifted into left-wing activities and in December 1932, in his third year at Ichikō, he was arrested as a member of the Japanese Communist Youth League. He was in prison from early 1933 until April 16, 1935; according to one source, he was released only after recanting his Communist beliefs.[12] Between 1936 and 1939 he was active as a Communist peasant organizer, and between August 1937 and November 1939, he worked as a key member of the Preparatory Committee for Rebuilding the Japanese Communist Party. Another member of this Committee was Kamiyama Shigeo, who played a minor role in the "postwar Sorge incident."

On the recommendation of various friends, Itō was employed on August 1, 1939, as a research assistant in the Investigation Department of the South Manchurian Railroad. (Ozaki had joined the Department as a consultant on June 1.) It is not clear whether Itō already knew Ozaki at this time. According to the detective-story writer Matsumoto Seichō, who has made a thorough study of the Itō Ritsu case, Itō met Ozaki in 1932, shortly before his first arrest. Itō allegedly introduced himself to Ozaki on that occasion as a fellow native of Gifu and a student at Ozaki's *alma mater,* Ichikō; and Ozaki is supposed to have received him warmly.[13] At all events, while both were employed at the South Manchurian Railroad, Ozaki and Itō worked very closely together. Ozaki was Itō's superior, and he asked the younger man to prepare various reports for him on Japanese agriculture and on the economies of the southeast Asian colonies.[14] Ozaki doubtless knew of Itō's left-wing political views, but, in any case, he trusted him completely; he invited him to his home several times, and Ozaki's daughter Yōko remembers the visitor as "Uncle Itō."[15]

In November of 1939 Itō was again arrested by the Tokkō. It has been said that he was chief of organization for the new Proletarian Youth League in the Kanda area, and that he was picked up at Shōka Daigaku (Commercial University), located at Hitotsubashi in the Kanda district of Tokyo.[16] Itō himself later claimed that he was arrested as a member of the Communist Party Rebuilding Committee,[17] but this may or may not be true. The Tokkō claim that they began their arrests of the Rebuilding Committee members in June 1940, seven months after Itō's arrest, and Kamiyama Shigeo, the leading figure of the renascent JCP organization, was not arrested until May 1941.[18] Odder still is the fact that Itō, upon his release in August 1940, immediately returned to work at the South Manchurian Railroad. Itō later explained that he was sentenced under the Peace Preservation Law in early 1940 but was released because he had contracted tuberculosis—an extremely unlikely reason for the prewar Japanese police to show clemency.[19] Even if his explanation is true, it seems inconceivable that the South Manchurian Railroad should reemploy him at the very time it was being investigated as a source of security leaks. Itō continued to work in Ozaki's office until September 29, 1941, when the Tokkō again took him into custody; on November 17, 1942, he gave evidence concerning Ozaki's work at the South Manchurian Railroad, evidence that was used in the trial of Ozaki and Sorge.[20] Kazama sees Itō's release of August 1940 as an example of the incompetence of the prewar Japanese government, but others see in it something considerably more sinister. It seems likely today that Itō was released because he had agreed to report to the police on Ozaki's activities at the South Manchurian Railroad.

There are two sources of information that implicate Itō with the police, both of them uncovered several years after Ozaki and Sorge had been executed. The first is a document that reportedly came into the hands of Nashiki Sajirō and Sekiguchi Kihachirō, director and secretary respectively of the leftist Union of Free Jurists (Jiyū Hōsō Dan). In January or February of 1946, these two men visited the Tokyo Metropolitan Police Agency in order to obtain certain documents, books, and magazines that constituted the library of their organization, which had been confiscated by the police during the war. When the police subsequently returned two truckloads of printed matter to them, a curious document came to light. It was an application to the Home Minister for a meritorious service citation for Assistant Inspector Itō Taketora of the Tokkō (no relation to Itō Ritsu); he was being recommended for the citation because he had uncovered the first clue leading to the exposure of the Sorge-Ozaki case. Attached to the statement of outstanding service were a record of Inspector Itō's interrogation of Itō Ritsu and an affidavit signed by Itō Ritsu. The two lawyers were so startled by their discovery, in view of the high position then held by Itō Ritsu in the Communist Party, that they delivered their find personally to Political Bureau member Shiga Yoshio at the JCP's Yoyogi headquarters. Unfortunately, nothing has been heard about the whereabouts of the papers since that time.[21]

The second source of information is a press conference given by Shida Shigeo, a member of the JCP Secretariat, about six weeks after the Party's Sixth National Consultative Conference (VI Zenkyō) of July 28, 1955. At that conference Itō's expulsion from the Party, which had occurred in 1953, was reconfirmed; but the statement released to the public had dealt only in generalities, and Shida therefore gave the press some details on Itō's offenses.[22] Among the mass of charges against Itō was the statement that he was released by the Tokkō in 1940 on the condition that he report monthly on the activities of "progressive elements" to Tokkō Inspectors Itō Taketora, Miyashita Hiroshi, and Iwasaki Gorō. Itō allegedly spied on liberals employed by the South Manchurian Railroad, including Ozaki, and then reported to Inspectors Miyashita and Iwasaki at their homes. According to Matsumoto Seichō, who attended Shida's press conference, Inspector Miyashita probably saw Itō at the Meguro police station in approximately May of 1940; Itō, then suffering from tuberculosis, offered to become a police spy in return for his release, and Inspector Miyashita agreed.[23]

Neither of these two pieces of information has ever been confirmed through independent sources. It is perfectly possible that the charges against Itō were manufactured by the Party as a cover for his purge (see the Appendix); Itō was removed in a power struggle within the JCP Central Committee (and possibly because of his alleged betrayal of Communists to SCAP in postwar Japan), not because he was involved in the Sorge-Ozaki case. At the same time, even if Itō was a police spy, which seems likely, his surveillance of Ozaki and the "progressive elements" in the South Manchurian Railroad was not what led to the exposure of the Sorge ring. Itō was a good friend of Ozaki's, but he testified that he knew nothing of Ozaki's "Comintern" activities or his association with Sorge and the other members of the ring.[24] His name is not mentioned once in the hundreds of pages of testimony given by Sorge, Ozaki, Miyagi, and Clausen. Itō's real contribution to the breaking of the Sorge case came about by chance.

During 1940, as relations with the United States were steadily deteriorating, many Japanese were returning to their homeland from America, and the Japanese police began to fear the presence of Communists and Socialists among these long-absent expatriates. One of Inspector Itō Taketora's questions of Itō Ritsu was whether he knew any members of the Japanese Section of the United States Communist Party who had returned to Japan.[25] In the short, cryptic introduction to the official Tokkō report on the Sorge incident, the decisive clue in the case is explained: "Itō Ritsu (aged 29, an employee of the Investigation Department, Tokyo Office, South Manchurian Railroad) was a quick-witted, extremely devoted Communist; for several months after his arrest he refused to confess his crimes. However, despite great difficulties, the severe but at the same time kind-hearted investigation of the police authorities led him to renounce Communism and make a full confession. In the course of his confession, Itō Ritsu stated that he suspected that a woman member of the Japanese Section of the United States Communist Party had returned to Japan and was working as a spy. This woman was Kitabayashi Tomo, aged 56."[26]

The First and Foreign Sections of the Tokkō immediately launched an extensive secret investigation to locate Kitabayashi Tomo. Their search probably began in June 1940, about the time Itō first mentioned her name to the police, for by July 1940 she had been found. She was living in the town of Kokawa, in her native province of Wakayama, awaiting the imminent return to Japan of her husband Yoshisaburō. After he arrived, the Tokkō kept both Mr. and Mrs. Kitabayashi under surveillance for more than a year. According to Kobayashi Gorō's study of the Tokkō, this surveillance revealed nothing significant, and so on September 28, 1941 (the day before

Itō was rearrested), the police decided to take the couple into custody for questioning. They were arrested and transferred to the Roppongi police station in Tokyo, where they were intensively interrogated about the activities in Japan of Japanese members of the U.S. Communist Party.

It will be recalled that Kitabayashi Yoshisaburō became Miyagi Yotoku's landlord in Los Angeles in 1932 and that his wife, Kitabayashi Tomo, had joined the Communist Party of the United States in 1931, at the same time Miyagi had become a member. When asked to list U.S. Communists who had returned to Japan, Kitabayashi Tomo named Miyagi, whom she had briefly assisted as one of his many subordinates during 1938. She did not have to mention his name twice to the Tokkō. Miyagi had often appeared on the lists of persons associating with Ozaki Hotsumi or Richard Sorge. His house was immediately placed under continuous surveillance, and after several of his current subordinate informants had been identified, Miyagi himself was arrested on October 10, 1941. At first he refused to talk, but two things soon led him to confess. The police discovered in his house a secret document belonging to the Investigation Department of the South Manchurian Railroad—probably an issue of *Current Materials Monthly Report* that Ozaki had given him to translate for Sorge—and they took him to Tsukiji police station in Tokyo, where they undoubtedly tortured him. During his ordeal Miyagi leaped from the second-story window of the police building, but instead of killing himself, as he had intended, he merely broke his leg. Only then did he begin to tell the police about a "very important spy group," and about Ozaki Hotsumi.[27]

On the morning of October 15, 1941, the Tokkō came to Ozaki's home in Meguro to arrest him; he was reading in his library when they arrived. After a few hours of intensive questioning he gave them the name of Mizuno Shigeru, and Mizuno was arrested on October 17. From Ozaki and Miyagi the police also acquired the names of the three other main spies, and they, too, were arrested, on the morning of October 18; at Clausen's house the Tokkō discovered the radio and coding materials. The police still knew very little about the men they had arrested, or what these men had done; but they had smashed the Sorge spy ring.[28]

The exposure of the ring proved the soundness of the rule laid down by Sorge in the very beginning: no member, under any circumstances, should associate with known or suspected Communists. The rule was not actually violated, except possibly by Ozaki, when he helped his left-wing friends; but the Communist past of one of the ring's own members was fatal. Miyagi was not the only vulnerable member, of course; Sorge was already under strong suspicion during 1940 and 1941, and Schellenberg could have sacrificed him at any time he considered him no longer valuable. The only member of the ring with a truly impeccable past was Ozaki; he was the only one who had never belonged to a Communist Party.

Between October 18, 1941, when Sorge was arrested, and June 16, 1942, when the government released a statement on the case to the press, the Japanese authorities did not publicly acknowledge any of the arrests. Naturally, rumors were rife. The third Konoye cabinet resigned and was replaced by the Tōjō cabinet on the same day Sorge was arrested, and this coincidence alone was enough to give rise to speculation. The fact that Ozaki was involved in the case seemed to confirm the opinion that the arrests were connected with a cabinet crisis. For several months after the initial arrests, Prince Konoye himself believed that the incident was an indirect attack on him by the militarists. Iwabuchi Tatsuo, former chief editor of the *Yomiuri shimbun* and a close personal friend of Konoye's, writes that he saw the prince genuinely depressed only twice: on the day of Ozaki's arrest, and on the day of Japan's surrender.[29]

There was a certain logic behind the rumor that the Army was trying to discredit Konoye by arresting Ozaki. Konoye was working hard to avoid a war between Japan and the United States, and the militarists probably wondered whether he would actively oppose the Southern Advance. Even six months after Ozaki's arrest, Konoye and Kazami thought that the Sorge incident might have been contrived by the Army simply to banish the ostensibly pacifist Konoye from political life. Kazami remembers that Judge Takada Tadashi, who had returned from Germany early in 1942 (and later served as the presiding judge at Ozaki's trial), told him that this was a persistent rumor in Berlin.[30] It was repeated seriously in Japan as late as February of 1963.[31]

The rumor was not true, but when Konoye and Kazami learned that Ozaki was really a spy, they became genuinely afraid that the

Sorge incident might banish Prince Konoye from political life. Saionji Kinkazu and Inukai Ken were the only members of the Konoye circle, except Ozaki, who were actually arrested, but Konoye and Kazami expected that they, too, would be taken into custody.[32] Kobayashi recalls that several high-ranking Army and Navy officers demanded Konoye's arrest when the details of the case were first revealed.[33] Konoye, however, was protected from arrest by his connections, which led all the way up to the Throne, and he used his influence to secure suspended sentences for Saionji and Inukai. His only actual involvement in the case was his testimony as a witness, in which he stated that he did not know Ozaki as a personal friend (which was true) and that he had met Ozaki only three or four times, always in the company of Saionji or Ushiba (which was not true).[34] Ozaki himself gave the police detailed accounts of meeting Konoye on at least five occasions, all of them after leaving the cabinet.[35] In view of Kazami's close association with Ozaki, his avoidance of arrest can be explained only by Konoye's protection and the fact that the militarists would have gained no political advantage by implicating him, since he was already in virtual retirement.

The arrest of Richard Sorge caused similar soul-searching elsewhere. In Berlin, Schellenberg had "a long and uncomfortable session with Himmler," and in Tokyo, Ambassador Ott gave strict orders to his staff not to mention the name of Sorge.[36] Ott tried to see Sorge within a fortnight after his arrest, but Sorge, having already made his initial confession, refused to meet anyone from the German Embassy. The Japanese police did not keep their German allies informed of the progress of their investigation; except for the scraps of information that Meisinger could collect, the German Embassy and government learned nothing about the seriousness of the evidence against Sorge until after the preliminary court completed its case on December 15, 1942. After Sorge's conviction, Himmler told Schellenberg that Hitler would have to be informed; Schellenberg writes: "In a confidential discussion between Hitler and Himmler, Hitler agreed that no blame could be placed on the German Secret Service in this affair. However, Himmler was never able to allay Hitler's deep suspicion of Ott. Hitler held to the opinion that a man in Ott's position should never allow trust and friendship to carry him so far as to reveal confidential political information. It was lucky for Ott that Hitler took such an objective view of the matter."[37] Ott did not press his luck. When he was relieved as Ambassador in January of 1943, he and his wife chose to pass the remainder of the war in retirement in Peking.

The actual investigation of the five main suspects was extremely thorough because of the keen competition among various branches of the Japanese police and the Justice Ministry. Immediately following his arrest on October 18, Sorge was interrogated by Inspector Ōhashi Hideo of the Tokkō. Sorge refused to talk, but the prosecutors demanded that a confession be obtained from him before October 25, when he was scheduled to be visited in prison by Ambassador Ott. According to prosecutor Yoshikawa Mitsusada, Ōhashi broke down Sorge on October 24: Sorge allegedly wept and stated that this was his first defeat since joining the Communist movement.* The prosecutors then sought to take Sorge's confession themselves, but Sorge refused to confess to anyone but Inspector Ōhashi.[38] His confession began, "I have been a Comintern agent from 1925 to the present."[39] After making this first revelation, Sorge canceled his meeting with Ott; and he never contacted anyone from the Germany Embassy after his arrest.

Sorge's initial confession was obtained so quickly that it raises the question of Japanese police methods used in the case. In 1950 General Willoughby insisted that there was no suggestion in any of the Sorge case materials that torture was used to gain confessions; with characteristic simplicity, he attempted to prove this by getting former police officers and prosecutors to sign affidavits denying that they had tortured suspects, and by soliciting statements in support of his contention from Western lawyers stationed in Japan.[40] However, in 1952 he wrote: "[Voukelitch's] early death in prison raises the question of torture. He was only forty-one when he died, and the record does not show that he was physically below par before his arrest. It is very

* The verbatim transcript of Ōhashi's interrogation of Sorge is not included in the Gendai-shi shiryō; instead, there is a summation of it, known today as Sorge's first shuki (memoir). (Gendai-shi shiryō, I, 113–35.) However, Mr. Obi Toshito, the editor of Misuzu Shobō, has informed me by letter (October 31, 1963) that copies of Sorge's interrogation by Ōhashi and his record of radio messages have been discovered in Japan, and that Misuzu will publish these during 1964 as a supplement to volumes one to three of Gendai-shi shiryō.

possible that he was firm in his refusal to talk, and was treated accordingly."[41]

Voukelitch was not the only member of the ring to die in prison: Kawamura Yoshio died on December 15, 1942; Miyagi died August 2, 1943; Funakoshi Hisao died February 27, 1945; and Mizuno Shigeru died on March 22, 1945. Chief prosecutor Yoshikawa, testifying before a committee of the U.S. House of Representatives, referred to Sorge's "poor health" during the week following his arrest.[42] Furthermore, we know that the Japanese police were using torture on prisoners in precisely this period; the description of the treatment of *New York Times* correspondent Otto Tolischus during January and February of 1942 is a particularly impressive example.[43] It seems probable, in short, that the Japanese police did compel some of the Sorge ring members to confess. This does not invalidate the confessions, however, and in any case Ozaki and Clausen probably were not tortured. Clausen began to act almost like a prosecution witness after his arrest, and Ozaki's responses display a self-confidence and a willingness to defend his position not found in the statements of Sorge and Miyagi.[44]

Inspector Ōhashi, who obtained Sorge's first confession, himself became the subject of a minor dispute within police circles because of the trust that Sorge placed in him. On March 7, 1942, Sorge wrote a now-famous letter in English to Ōhashi thanking him for his kindness in conducting the questioning; the letter was later used by SCAP as prime evidence that Ōhashi had not tortured Sorge.[45] Whatever the circumstances that led Sorge to write this letter, his personal regard for Ōhashi caused other officials to suspect that Ōhashi was not being properly impartial or thorough in his work. As a result, the main responsibility for examining Sorge passed within one week from the Tokkō (under the Home Ministry) to the Prosecutor's Office of the Tokyo District Criminal Court (under the Justice Ministry). (Inspector Ōhashi continued questioning Sorge in the mornings, but prosecutor Yoshikawa interrogated him each afternoon from the day after he confessed. Ozaki, on the other hand, remained under exclusive Tokkō questioning until March 11, 1942, when the prosecution took over.) There was another reason why the Justice Ministry quickly established jurisdiction in the Sorge case. The Kempei (under the War Ministry) were beginning to hear rumors that the ring was affiliated with Department Four of the Red Army, and they believed

The Ozaki family in Taiwan at the time of Eiko's visit (1917)
(*Left to right*, Hotsumi, Honami, Hotsuka, Kita, Eiko, and Hotsuma)

Ozaki and Yōko
Shanghai, c. 1932

Ozaki Hotsuki

(Below) Richard Sorge boating
at Hakone, Japan, c. 1938

Ozaki Hotsuki

Sorge, 1937 passport photo

Wide World

Wide World

Agnes Smedley, February 1949

Prince Konoye, October 1938

Wide World

Kazami Akira, postwar

Kyodo

Inukai Ken, postwar

Saionji Kinkazu, postwar

Ozaki Hotsuki

Wide World

(*Upper left*) Miyagi Yotoku
prison photo, c. 1942

(*Upper right*) Branko de Voukelitch
prewar passport photo

Max Clausen
prewar passport photo

General Eugen Ott, April 1938

Fox, London

(*Below*) Sugamo prison,
Tokyo, postwar

(*Above*) Itō Ritsu, postwar

(*Left*) General Charles A. Willoughby testifying before the House Committee on Un-American Activities, August 22, 1951

Yoshikawa Mitsusada (*left*), chief investigator in the Sorge case, testifying before the House Committee on Un-American Activities, August 9, 1951, and his interpreter, Andrew Y. Kuroda (*right*)

that if the prisoners were military criminals, they should be given jurisdiction.

The Tokyo District Criminal Court set up a special team of prosecutors to uncover the facts in the case. The supervisor of this group was Nakamura Tōneo, chief of the Thought Department in the Prosecutor's Office, but the actual investigation was carried out under the guidance of prosecutor Yoshikawa Mitsusada, who became well-known in America in 1951 as a witness before the House Committee on Un-American Activities and the Senate committee investigating the Institute of Pacific Relations. Yoshikawa personally interrogated Sorge from immediately after his initial confession (October 24, 1941) until March 27, 1942. During this period Yoshikawa employed the services of Ikoma Yoshitoshi, a professor of German at Tokyo Foreign Languages University, as his interpreter. According to Ikoma, after Sorge had confessed most of the details of the case, Yoshikawa gave Sorge a typewriter in his prison cell at Sugamo and suggested to him that he write out his life history and the details of his espionage activities. Sorge took the suggestion, and there still exists today a Japanese translation of the German original of Sorge's memoirs. (The German version was destroyed in the bombing of the Justice Ministry, on March 7, 1945; only fragments that were in the personal possession of Yoshikawa have survived.)

One of Yoshikawa's most perplexing problems was discovering Sorge's real organizational affiliation with Moscow; it seemed to him that because the statements of the various prisoners did not jibe, someone must be lying. Clausen insisted that he was employed by Department Four of the Red Army, but Ozaki, Miyagi, and Voukelitch all stated their genuine belief that they were workers for the Comintern. In the early part of his interrogation, Sorge would say only that he reported to "the Moscow authorities" or "the Moscow center." Yoshikawa, to make sure that the case would not be taken away from the Justice Ministry, interpreted "Moscow authorities" to mean the Comintern. However, Sorge reversed himself in the typewritten memoir he prepared for Yoshikawa; there he went into great detail on the theory of "capitalist encirclement," and he insisted that working for the Red Army was no different from working for the Comintern. After his memoir was translated, the discrepancy was discovered; and on June 24, 1942, during the preliminary trial, Examining Judge Nakamura Mitsuzō asked Sorge directly to whom he had sent his reports. In the course of his answer Sorge stated explicitly that he had been separated from the Comintern in 1929 and had worked ever since for Department Four of the Red Army.[46]

Sorge's reasons for not stating at the outset his affiliation with Department Four are perfectly clear: had he done so, he would have been turned over to the Kempei, who might have executed him without trial. In his testimony, he made specific reference to cases of other foreigners in Japan who had fallen into the hands of the Kempei.[47] (He may have been thinking of James Cox of Reuters, who allegedly "committed suicide" in 1940 by jumping from the second story of a Tokyo police building.) During the first week of his interrogation by Tokkō Inspector Ōhashi, Sorge had requested that the Soviet Embassy be contacted, in the hope that he might be exchanged through diplomatic negotiation. When the police refused to notify the Soviet Embassy and told him about the provisions of the National Defense Security Law, Sorge was frightened; he became convinced that only by being tried as a violator of the Peace Preservation Law did he have a chance to save his life. According to Ozaki Hotsuki, Sorge made his full written confession only after he was informed that he would be charged with Communist activities in violation of the Peace Preservation Law.[48] In the end, Sorge's maneuvers did not matter: the Justice Ministry chose to characterize the Sorge ring as a Comintern espionage group for its own reasons, but it charged Sorge personally with violations of both the Peace Preservation Law and the National Defense Security Law. Both laws carried the death penalty.

On June 16, 1942, the Justice Ministry released to the press its first official statement on the case. It was one of the most carefully scrutinized of all wartime Japanese press releases; and it remained, technically speaking, the only official document concerning the Sorge case available to the Japanese public until Misuzu Shobō published the entire court records in 1962. Discussions within the government concerning the public announcement had begun on May 17, when the Justice Ministry laid down its ground rules: the announcement was to come solely from the Justice Ministry, and newspapers would be allowed to report on the case in the future only within the framework of the Ministry's official statements. The Supreme Court and the Foreign Ministry added other restrictions to the disclosure: the word "important," used to describe the intelligence gathered by the ring, had to be deleted; Saionji's basic beliefs could not be described as "patriotic," nor could the title "consultant to the Foreign Ministry" be used with his name; and no photographs were to be published. Before the final version was released, the government cut out all references to the South Manchurian Railroad (except in listing Ozaki's employment) and to "high political figures" as sources of information. A dispute within the government then developed, with certain agencies insisting that the Justice Ministry was playing down the importance of the ring. The final version of the statement emphasized the guilt and treason of the principal spies, but it did not mention the responsibility of Japanese and German officials in supplying them with information.[49]

The most important single item in the announcement was the government's characterization of the Sorge group as "a Red spy ring under the orders of Comintern headquarters."[50] The Justice Ministry knew full well when the statement was released that the ring was technically under the control of Department Four of the Red Army and that Sorge had never correctly identified his immediate superiors to Ozaki, Miyagi, and Voukelitch. The Ministry deliberately chose to describe the Sorge group as a Comintern espionage unit for three reasons: First, Japan and the Soviet Union were at peace in 1942, and a treaty of non-aggression was in effect between the two countries; by maintaining the fiction of the international status of the Comintern, the government could avoid antagonizing the Soviet Union. Second, the Justice Ministry preferred to make its case under the old and familiar Peace Preservation Law, for it feared that cases resting solely on the new National Defense Security Law might be overturned. In order to charge the main spies and their subordinates with having violated the Peace Preservation Law, the prosecution had to show that they were members of a Communist Party, or the Comintern, or some subversive organization that intended to change the *kokutai,* or "national polity." Every Japanese member of the group, particularly Ozaki, was questioned closely about his attitude toward the *kokutai.* Third, cases brought under the Peace Preservation Law were clearly within the domain of the Justice Ministry; if that law were not used, the War Ministry might argue that it should have jurisdiction.[51]

Since the war many Japanese have contended that Sorge did not receive a fair trial. They argue that he was not guilty of violating the

Peace Preservation Law and that a valid case could not have been made against him under the National Defense Security Law alone; that he personally gathered his intelligence at the German Embassy, which was not in violation of either law so long as no state of war existed between Japan and the Soviet Union; and that if he had been charged only with conspiring to violate the National Defense Security Law, the validity of the death penalty would have been doubtful.

Regardless of the laws involved, the adjudication of all criminal cases in prewar Japan was heavily weighted against the defendant. The judicial system created during the Meiji period was constructed chiefly on the French model, particularly in its criminal code. In a criminal case tried in a district court, the "procurators" (state's attorneys, here called "prosecutors") first carried out an investigation in conjunction with the police in order to establish the facts of the case. After this investigation was completed, a hearing, or *yoshin*, was held by one "examining judge" from the district bench. According to Harold Quigley: "This [the *yoshin*] takes the place of investigation by a grand jury, and it may consume months or even years if the accused is obdurate in maintaining his innocence of the offense charged, since it is the object of the state, represented by the procurator, to obtain a confession before the case is tried. In the absence of *habeas corpus* procedure, the accused is helpless and frequently is kept in jail for a lengthy period, being subjected to questioning from time to time. Prior to indictment, the persons under examination may not employ counsel. Preliminary examinations are conducted *in camera*."[52]

After establishing during the *yoshin* whether or not a crime had been committed, the examining judge either transferred the case to a local court, declared lack of jurisdiction, released the accused, or reported the case for trial in the district court (which constituted an indictment). The essential difference between Anglo-Saxon and continental courtroom methods is that the latter are not adversary proceedings; the primary fact-finding responsibility rests with the trial judge. Quigley's description of a prewar trial in a district criminal court is as follows: "The public trial [it did not have to be public] is marked by the prominent part taken by the presiding judge. He has the evidence previously obtained before him, and it is he who conducts the examination of the defendant and the witnesses. The hearing begins with a statement by the procurator, who, from his position [seated above the defendant and his counsel] and costume, is scarcely distinguishable from the judges. . . . The defendant is examined first, very minutely. . . . The presiding judge in criminal trials appears to become in effect a prosecutor, since upon him falls the responsibility of eliciting every item of evidence unfavorable to the defendant. The defendant's counsel may cross examine only through the judge, and in practice the amount of questioning by counsel is almost negligible. . . . Defendant and witnesses are required to stand while giving testimony. The atmosphere of the courtroom is unfavorable to the defendant, his own counsel appearing to be awed by the forces arrayed against him and to accept in a rather apologetic way any opportunities extended to him for cross examination."[53] The greatest single drawback for the defendant in such a trial was the fact that the record of the *yoshin* judge was admitted without challenge.

Prewar Japanese courts did not employ official court reporters, and no official reports were published. Thus, the records available today in the Sorge case are the pre-trial interrogations of the prosecutors and the *yoshin* judge—not the transcripts of the trials themselves. The jury system was infrequently used in prewar Japan, except in special types of cases (arson, for example), and judgments were normally reached by a panel of judges. Juries were not called in the Sorge trials, and the courtrooms were closed except to a few specially invited persons. The decisions in the cases of both Sorge and Ozaki were automatically appealed to the Supreme Court (Taishin-in), as required by the National Defense Security Law; but the appeal brief written by Sorge's counsel, Asanuma Sumitsugu, was invalidated because it was submitted one day too late—Asanuma had not been given the correct deadline for its submission.[54] In Sorge's trial and appeal the question of *tenkō* (recantation) was never raised or considered (as it was in Ozaki's) because he was a foreigner.

The forty-seventh and last recorded interrogation of Sorge by prosecutor Yoshikawa took place on March 27, 1942. On June 24, after the public statement had been released, the preliminary investigation (*yoshin*) began under Examining Judge Nakamura Mitsuzō. Nakamura, who also conducted Ozaki's *yoshin*, went over the same ground covered by Yoshikawa in order to establish a clear, orderly case against Sorge. He completed his interrogations (forty-five of them) on December 5, and on December 15, 1942, he made his decision in favor of a trial in the Tokyo District Criminal Court. Sorge remained in prison under indictment until May 1943, when his trial began. The trial itself continued throughout the summer before a panel of three judges headed by Judge Takada Tadashi. The courtroom proceedings were conducted entirely in Japanese, and Sorge received only intermittent translations from Ikoma. The evidence against him—Yoshikawa's and Nakamura's interrogations and Sorge's own written statement—was already in the hands of Judge Takada. In accordance with the provisions of the National Defense Security Law, Sorge's attorney was permitted to look at the evidence against his client only after obtaining the permission of the presiding judge; on no account was he allowed to copy any of it. The Tokyo court rendered its verdict on September 29, 1943: *"Hikokunin o shikei ni shosu"*—"the defendant is condemned to death."[55] An appeal to the Supreme Court was made automatically and denied, just as automatically, in a one-line decision on January 20, 1944. The case had really been decided in the examining rooms of Sugamo prison, where Yoshikawa and Nakamura—alone, without witnesses, and with no cross examination—had interrogated Sorge for more than a year.

Ozaki's case followed a pattern basically similar to Sorge's but with several significant differences. Ozaki was a citizen of Japan; he had many friends, no language problem, and expert legal advice. Most important, in addition to committing espionage he had become a traitor to the Japanese state, and his relationship to the *kokutai* therefore came into question. Ozaki produced two written statements while in prison; but these were not memoirs (*shuki*), as Sorge's had been. Ozaki did not begin his first statement until after his trial had already opened, and the prosecution had not asked him to write it for the purpose of eliciting evidence. Ozaki's prison statements were *tenkōsho* (documents of conversion), and they were explicitly considered and rejected in the decision of the Supreme Court.

The recanting of crimes is certainly not unknown in Western political systems (as in the practice of applying for official pardons), but it is not an integral part of Western legal philosophy. Communist China offers a much closer parallel, and a contribution to the understanding of Chinese Communist *ssu-hsiang kai-tsao* (thought reform) might be made by comparing the treatment of ideological offenders in postwar China and prewar Japan. Although no one ever suggested calling it "brainwashing" (a possible indication of the caution with which serious students ought to approach that term), the prewar Japanese institution of *tenkō* bears striking similarities to contemporary

Chinese practice. Persons arrested for violations against the *kokutai*—a summary word composed of the characters for "nation" and "body" and symbolizing the unity between Emperor and people, which was dear to the hearts of Japanese nationalists—were never simply convicted and allowed to serve their sentences. In prison they were pressured to think about their crimes and to write *tenkōsho*. This practice was particularly enforced against Communists, who were said to have "left the Japanese race"; it produced the sensational recantations, in 1933, of two famous Communists, Sano Manabu and Nabeyama Sadachika. A belief in Communism, defined as a crime against the *kokutai* in the Peace Preservation Law, was not merely a felony; it was a blasphemy, an intolerable offense in a group-relating, anti-individualist society strongly infused with nationalism. Ozaki might have saved his life had his own *tenkōsho* been sufficiently abject; as it was, he won the admiration of the judges who sentenced him to death because he occasionally went back on his own recantations.[56]

On the day Ozaki was arrested, Eiko immediately called on Kishi Michizō, a member of the Breakfast Society, and asked what the suspicions against her husband were; Kishi telephoned a former classmate in the Home Ministry and discovered that Ozaki was implicated in a Communist case. On October 17, Takane Yoshisaburō, a judge of the Tokyo District Civil Court and a classmate of Ozaki's at Ichikō, visited Eiko and offered to help her arrange for defense counsel. The next day Eiko and Takane met with Miwa Jusō, one of Japan's most famous attorneys and an associate of Ozaki's in the Shōwa Research Association, and he agreed to help them employ suitable counsel when Ozaki's case came to trial. Another friend of Ozaki's who came forward at once was Matsumoto Shin'ichi. Matsumoto had had a great deal of personal experience in "Communist" cases, and he undertook to advise Eiko on the best strategy for helping Ozaki. Matsumoto's wife also assisted Ozaki's family during this period.

Eiko did not see Ozaki from the day he was arrested (October 15, 1941) until early 1943, after his *yoshin* had been completed. However, between November 1941 and November 1944, Ozaki wrote more than 200 letters to her, and these letters, published in 1946 under the title *Love is Like a Falling Star (Aijō wa furu hoshi no gotoku)*, have become the most famous correspondence in postwar Japanese literature. It is through them that we know what Ozaki read in prison, his thoughts on the trial, his ideological development, his turn toward

Zen in 1944, and his attitude toward making a *tenkō*. More than any other documents in the Sorge case, these letters reveal that Ozaki was a uniquely gifted and independent man.

Following his arrest Ozaki was taken to the Meguro police station, where he was held until November 1. His preliminary investigation was conducted by Tokkō Inspector Takahashi Yosuke, under the supervision of prosecutor Tamazawa Mitsusaburō. Matsumoto Shin'-ichi believes that the police tortured Ozaki while he was at the Meguro police station,[57] but this seems implausible. The general director of the prosecutors in the Sorge case, Nakamura Tōneo, was a classmate of Ozaki and Judge Takane at Ichikō; he specifically refrained from interrogating Ozaki personally because of this tie, and it seems unlikely that he would have allowed the police to use duress on his friend.[58] Furthermore, Ozaki's answers in the interrogation do not sound like those of a man under extreme pressure.

On November 1, the police transferred Ozaki from Meguro to Sugamo prison, and the police-prosecution phase of the investigation began in earnest. Inspector Takahashi questioned Ozaki until March 11, and then prosecutor Tamazawa took over personally. He continued the interrogations until May 8, 1942. Kempei officers also examined Ozaki during this period in order to learn precisely what military secrets might have been compromised. During June 1942, after the Justice Ministry disclosed the Sorge case, Ozaki's family encountered certain personal difficulties. Most of Ozaki's former associates—with the notable exception of Matsumoto—tended to shun the family of a traitor, and Ozaki's daughter, Yōko, experienced a degree of embarrassment at school. Ozaki was distressed about his family's public position, but he was more apprehensive about what his wife and daughter would feel when they discovered that he had been charged with espionage. To their mutual credit, they always remained loyal to him; Eiko's respect never wavered, and Ozaki Yōko, at the age of 19, was one of the speakers who eulogized her father at the "Ozaki-Matsumoto Memorial Meeting" of November 1948.

Prosecutor Nakamura Tōneo delivered his report on the police investigation and asked for a *yoshin* on May 16, 1942, and on June 16 Judge Nakamura Mitsuzō began his interrogation of Ozaki. The *yoshin* lasted until November 27, and it probed deeply into Ozaki's political beliefs and attitude toward the Emperor system (*tennō-sei*). Nakamura was especially troubled by Ozaki's theory of a Communist

New Order in East Asia and by his frank contention that the Emperor system had become a mere cover for militarist rule in Japan. During the preliminary interrogation, Ozaki had presented his personal vision of the future of East Asia and it so startled his listeners that nothing he said later was able to mitigate its influence on them. On February 24, 1942, he had stated:

"In my opinion, just as World War I gave birth to the Soviet Union, World War II will bring forth many socialist nations, beginning on the side that is defeated or exhausted in the war. The result will be world revolution. I have believed since at least July of 1941, and I have explained to Sorge, that it will probably take the following course: (1) The Soviet Union, by means of a peace policy, ought to and will remain outside of the wars between the imperialist states. (2) The war between the Axis and the Anglo-American states (a war of modified imperialist nations versus genuine imperialist nations) will be protracted and will result in their mutual ruin. The victory of one side will cause social revolutions in the other. (3) Because of the comparative increase in the strength of the Soviet Union, even the victorious side may well be forced by circumstances to transform itself into a socialist state. As for Japan, its position in the Far East and in the China Incident will mean that no matter what it does— attack Russia, cooperate with England and America, or carry out the Southern Advance and even gain a temporary military victory over England and the United States—it will probably undergo an internal socialist revolution as a result of complete national exhaustion. The first stage of Japan's transformation will begin, at the earliest, during 1942. Because the internal, revolutionary strength of Japan will be weak during the transitional period and because it will be difficult not only to realize but also to stabilize the revolution in Japan—particularly while fighting Anglo-American imperialism—I believe that it will be necessary for Japan, having freed itself from the capitalist structure, to cooperate with the Soviet Union and those parts of China under the hegemony of the Chinese Communist Party. This is what I have meant by the New Order in East Asia."[59]

In essence, Ozaki believed (and hoped), after the outbreak of war in 1941, that the Japanese militarists would drive the country to revolution. Once that had happened, Japan could ally itself with Russia and Communist China in order to stop the fighting in the Far East and begin constructing a socialist order. Ozaki's prison statements on the Emperor system were equally novel and iconoclastic; they derived from his acceptance of Marxist sociological concepts and from his chagrin at the failure of the New Structure Movement. He said:

"It is doubtful that the 'Emperor system' is an accurate term for describing the essentials of the present political system of Japan. The basic characteristic of Japanese capitalism today is not so much its late development as its internal imbalance. What was formerly a strong feudal element in Japanese politics has been transformed into a strong capitalist force. The nucleus of political power is the combination of the capitalists and landlords with the militarists and bureaucrats. In the long run it is the capitalists who benefit most from Japan's policy of imperialism. Actually, the capitalist class and its spokesmen (the political parties) are not active advocates of imperialism, nor do they exercise direct leadership over this policy. The militarists and the bureaucrats believe that they are serving their own immediate interests—not those of the capitalists. But despite what the militarists believe, it is actually the capitalist class that benefits most. . . . Thus viewed, the [role of the] Emperor system in the contemporary Japanese political system is a fiction."[60]

These statements, combined with his own interrogations of Ozaki, led Judge Nakamura to conclude that Ozaki was an ideological Communist and had been one since late 1925.[61] On December 15, 1942, Nakamura found that Ozaki had violated the Peace Preservation Law, the National Defense Security Law, and several other military security statutes, and he sent the case to the Tokyo District Criminal Court.

Between December and the opening of Ozaki's trial on May 31, 1943, Matsumoto Shin'ichi and attorney Miwa Jusō met often to plan their courtroom strategy. Miwa argued that Ozaki's best defense was to adopt an attitude of recantation and that his friends and counsel should refrain from attempting to challenge the indictment or the prosecutors. To his everlasting regret, Matsumoto accepted this advice, and he allowed the court to appoint Ozaki's defense counsel.[62] Ozaki's first lawyer was Kobayashi Shunzō, a distinguished defender who later became a judge on the Supreme Court. He was not at all sympathetic to Ozaki's espionage activities, and he agreed to defend him only if he could base his case on Ozaki's political beliefs. He also insisted that Ozaki write a statement of these beliefs—in effect, a *tenkōsho*—that would be submitted to the presiding judge, Takada.

Ozaki began his first letter to the court on June 1, 1943. Before starting to write, on Kobayashi's advice, he reread Satō Tsuji's famous book, *Philosophy of the Imperial Way* (*Kōdō tetsugaku*). (Satō was an eminent scholar of German philosophy and an official of the Ministry of Education's Education Training Institute.) Kobayashi also lent Ozaki a copy of *State and Economy* (*Kokka to keizai*), by the economist Naniwada Haruo. Ozaki wrote to Eiko: "My lawyer, Mr. Kobayashi, has recommended that I read several books before I start to write my personal account. He seems to fear that, as a journalist, I will approach this problem too light-heartedly; however, no one can imagine just how serious my present state of mind really is."[63]

Ozaki's first *tenkōsho*, dated June 8, 1943, was a 30,000-word document addressed to Judge Takada Tadashi. In it he made a valiant effort to square his life and activities with the *kokutai* while at the same time retaining his self-respect.[64] The first few pages, in which he deals with his early personal development, contain a prophetic observation: "As I look back on my life, I see that it was really fatal for me to have met Miss Agnes Smedley and Richard Sorge."[65] After giving his early personal history, Ozaki divided the *tenkōsho* into four separate essays: "My Arrest and the Outbreak of the Second World War," "Progress of the Pacific War and Reflections on the Kokutai," "The New Significance of Nationalism and the Breakdown of Internationalism," and "My Present Frame of Mind."[66]

Ozaki's discussion of nationalism in his *tenkōsho* reveals the extent to which he was willing to engage in a critique of Marxism. He spoke not as a recanter or a Marxist but as a political analyst when he wrote: "World War II has made increasingly clear the fundamental importance of nationalism, or statism. The war is demonstrating that nationalism is the basic structure of the contemporary world system. In the final analysis, the organization of the supreme struggles—those in which men risk their lives and fortunes—rests solely upon the particular configurations of nationalism. Even the various united fronts amount to nothing more than alliances of convenience by particular states. Today I believe that the Marxist theory of nationalism was mistaken in its estimate of the actual strength of nationalism and statism, or that by abstracting on the basis of temporary developments it too hastily reached an idealistic conclusion. In any case, it is completely erroneous on this point."[67]

Although Ozaki sought to understand the roots of Japanese imperialism in China in terms of a Marxist analysis of Japanese *capital-ism*, he was aware that this imperialism was producing a radical nationalist reaction in China and that Japan was incapable of adjusting to Chinese nationalism because of its own national upsurge. Ozaki thought that the Chinese Communists might become the carriers and beneficiaries of Chinese nationalism, but he did not confuse such a development with a genuine acceptance of Marxism by the Chinese people.

Ozaki placed great hopes on his letter to Judge Takada, and he apparently believed that he would receive nothing worse than a long prison term. On September 11 he wrote to Eiko that he was shaken, though without losing his composure in the courtroom, when he heard the prosecutor ask for the death sentence; he simply had not expected it. He went on to say that he believed the judges would not adopt the prosecution's whole view of the case.[68] But on September 27 he wrote again to Eiko: "My verdict will be handed down the day after tomorrow. Although I urged you earlier to have faith in the common sense of the presiding judge, I realize that this is an era not to be comprehended by common sense. I am trying to anticipate the worst."[69] The worst came to pass on September 29, 1943, when Judge Takada sentenced Ozaki to death.

Matsumoto was appalled. In 1946 he wrote that he bitterly regretted not having fought the government's case against Ozaki simply in order to prolong the proceedings. He did not realize until 1944, when it was too late, that the only way he could save Ozaki was by keeping the case before the courts until after Japan's probable defeat in the war.[70] After the verdict was returned, Matsumoto fired counsel Kobayashi and turned from the liberal Miwa to his leftist friends for advice. He talked with Shinoda Hideo, Kazama Michitarō, Kozai Yoshishige, and Saionji Kinkazu. To write the appeal to the Supreme Court, Matsumoto and his friends selected Takeuchi Kintarō, an experienced lawyer who had defended Matsumoto and Kozai in one of their earlier arrests under the Peace Preservation Law, and Horikawa Yūhō, a lawyer sympathetic to Ozaki's case.[71] Ozaki was quite pleased with these two men. He wrote that at their first meeting Takeuchi was moved to tears, and protested that the government should have been allowing Ozaki to serve Japan in its hour of peril instead of throwing him in prison to face execution.[72]

In preparing for the appeal the most difficult problem facing

Ozaki's lawyers, and Eiko, was to convince Ozaki of the need to write a second *tenkōsho*. By early 1944 Matsumoto realized that Ozaki's execution might be delayed until after Japan's defeat, or that the Supreme Court, if impressed by Ozaki's sincerity, might commute his sentence to life imprisonment. Ozaki, on the other hand, was becoming increasingly resigned to his fate, and life in prison was sapping his energy and his acumen. Matsumoto therefore asked Eiko to make a personal plea to her husband to write another *tenkōsho*. Eiko writes that Ozaki was indignant when she first made the suggestion and expressed disgust with the idea of composing a false statement in order to save his life. But before leaving the case, Ozaki's first lawyer, Kobayashi, had also advised him to write another confession and encouraged him to expand on his discussion of the *kokutai*; and so at last, although reluctantly, Ozaki agreed.[73]

Instead of stalling for time, as his friends expected him to do, Ozaki wrote his second *tenkōsho* rapidly, as if to get it over with as quickly as possible. Before writing this document, which was more than twice as long as the first one, Ozaki sought inspiration by rereading certain classics of ancient history, Shintō, and nationalism, such as the *Kojiki*, the *Nihon shoki*, and the works of Motoori Norinaga and Hirata Atsutane.[74] But inspiration failed him. He began to compose on February 1, 1944, and in his letter to Eiko of February 8, he admitted that he could not write the confession of a true convert.[75] The second *tenkōsho*, in which he mentioned that he had begun the study of Zen, was nevertheless much more self-critical than the first. Ozaki argued that he had been simultaneously a nationalist and a Communist, but that in his present frame of mind he was much more a nationalist than a Communist; he believed, he said, that he had made considerable progress in understanding his particular relationship to Japan and its *kokutai* since writing his first statement. He divided his second *tenkōsho* into six chapters: "On Writing a Personal Account Again," "My Family and My Country," "My Reverence for the Nation and for the Sublimity of the Kokutai," "Confronting Death," "The Eternal Obligation of Loyalty," and "Thoughts on the Prospects of the War."

An important section of Ozaki's second recantation dealt with his attitude toward the Communist International and his reaction to its dissolution (on May 15, 1943). He wrote: " 'The world' is an idealized and abstract entity; realistically and concretely, it exists only as a pattern of 'international' relations between a congregation of states. Therefore, universalism or a one-world philosophy (*sekai-shugi*), as a historical reality, must assume the form of 'internationalism.' The course of world history illustrates this fact most bluntly. My own universalism consisted in dreaming that a harmonious world society could be realized through the machinery of international cooperation [provided by] the Third International. However, the Soviet Union, which was the main prop and the driving force of the Third International, emphasizes the supremacy of the state on grounds of actual political conditions. Now it has dissolved the Comintern itself. Although the demise of the Comintern was dictated by concrete realities, its passing is a crushing blow to the ideal of a universalist utopia."[76]

Ozaki completed his statement on February 29, 1944, and it reached the Supreme Court on March 13. The Court specifically took notice of this second *tenkōsho* in its extremely long decision, handed down on April 5, 1944.[77] After refuting the points of law raised in the brief submitted by Ozaki's attorneys, the Court found that Ozaki was still fundamentally a Marxist. His second *tenkōsho*, they said, showed encouraging signs of change, but these did not outweigh the strong objections to the Japanese forms of government and social organization that he had expressed during the preliminary interrogations. The Court therefore rejected his appeal. In a letter of April 7, Ozaki wrote that he was not surprised by the verdict; he said he realized that his death sentence was a consequence of his activities but that he still believed that those activities were justified by the times in which he and Eiko lived, and he concluded by thanking the many friends who had worked to save him.[78] After the war, Matsumoto stated that this *tenkōsho* had not swayed the Court because Ozaki had been unable to dissimulate in the manner expected of him, and Eiko expressed regret at having urged him to write it.

Even after all legal remedies had been exhausted, Ozaki's friends did not give up hope. The Sorge case was more political than legal, and Japan's impending defeat in the war encouraged Matsumoto and others to believe that the condemned men might still be saved. Several proposals for using Sorge and Ozaki in the war effort, none of them confirmed, were raised within the Japanese government during 1944. One rumor, which circulated after the meeting in Moscow between Molotov and Japanese Ambassador Satō Naotake (September 16, 1944), was that Sorge would be sent to the U.S.S.R. as an emissary of peace.[79] Another story was that Kwantung Army staff officers had advised against executing Sorge on the grounds that it would anger the Soviet Union. According to a third rumor, Japan and Russia had agreed to exchange agents: General Doihara Kenji was to turn Sorge over to Russian officials in Macao in November 1944 and in return take custody of certain Kwantung Army spies being held by the Soviet Union.

One of the wildest rumors concerned Ozaki. Sometime during September 1944, the Koiso cabinet allegedly discussed the need for making peace with the Communists in China. A leak suggested that Kodama Hideo and others in the cabinet were planning to send one of two *tenkō* Communists, Sano Manabu or Nabeyama Sadachika, on a secret mission to Yenan as a special plenipotentiary of the Japanese government. Taira Teizō, Saionji, and Matsumoto heard this story and entered into negotiations with the government to have Ozaki sent instead. They argued that he was eminently better qualified for such a mission than either of the old JCP members. But the Justice Ministry would not guarantee a stay of execution until after arrangements with Yenan had been completed, and Ozaki was hanged just as the government was beginning to pay serious attention to the proposals of Saionji, Taira, and Matsumoto.[80]

During his three years in prison Ozaki himself kept busy by reading an enormous number of books. Eiko brought the books to him, and they found that the ones in foreign languages passed the censor more easily. He finished most of Goethe's works in German, Nehru's autobiography, a biography of Benjamin Franklin, Machiavelli's *Prince*, and innumerable Japanese books on China, international trade, and politics. Ozaki's letters to Eiko included long passages on his reading, particularly on his thoughts about the so-called "Asiatic mode of production," or "Oriental despotism," theory of traditional Chinese society. He commented at length on A. N. Poliak's studies of middle eastern feudalism and compared them with the theory that irrigation and flood control had supported the bureaucracy of classical China. He concluded one letter to Eiko with the observation that she might not be very interested in this subject, but he returned to it in the next letter. Ozaki came to feel dissatisfied with the characterization of Chinese society he had given in his book *On Chinese Society and Economy*, but he was unable to accept either the "feudal" or the "hydraulic" theory *in toto*. He sought, in his letters, to reach a synthesis between the two.[81]

Ozaki was a life-long collector of postage stamps, and even after the rejection of his appeal he wrote to his wife asking her to send Yōko to a certain shop to buy him some philatelic books. (One of Yōko's most vivid memories was of Ozaki showing his collection to visitors at their home and lecturing them on various stamps.)[82] His interests, however, became more serious as 1944 wore on. As early as March of 1943 he had asked his wife for some books on Zen; and in his second *tenkōsho* he mentioned that he was studying Zen in order to acquire the composure needed to meet his death.[83] Tsurumi Shunsuke has called attention to the similarity between certain Zen riddles and some of Ozaki's remarks in his second *tenkōsho*.[84] Ozaki had been interested in Zen Buddhism since his youth, but he denied that he was a religious man; he preferred intellectual studies, such as Suzuki's *First Principles of Zen*, to the more enigmatic writings of the Zen masters themselves.[85]

Like many prisoners before him, Ozaki became interested in the weather outside. He once mentioned reading Okada Takematsu's *Fragments From Meteorology* with fascination while listening to the rain, and he usually closed his letters to Eiko with a comment about the weather. In the final months of his life, he wrote extensively on a vast range of subjects—including philosophy, religion, and art criticism—for a collection he called *Reflections on a White Cloud (Hakuun roku)*. He entrusted these essays to Ichijima Seiichi, the warden at Sugamo; but they were lost in the bombings of 1945. We know of their existence only because Ozaki referred to them in his letters and mentioned them to his lawyer, Takeuchi.[86]

Ozaki was a Marxist, a spy, and a traitor, but these labels lose their meaning when he is studied as an individual man of politics. He was simply not typical, for his country and his age, as a Communist, an intellectual, or a politician. Probably the most distinguished student of Japanese politics, Maruyama Masao, has written of the militarist period that "from the apex of the hierarchy to the very bottom it was virtually impossible for a truly free, unregulated individual to exist."[87] Ozaki was the exception to this rule. He lived, thought, and acted from within the hierarchy, but his ideals were his own, and he drew the principles of his behavior from an independent, personal evaluation of the crucial events of his time. As he wrote to Eiko: "I am not first and foremost a Communist."[88] The most significant tribute to his independence was paid him by his judge, Takada Tadashi. After the trial, Takada privately said that Ozaki was a man of virtue, devoted to his ideals, and the very model of a patriot.[89]

The sentences given to the other members of the Sorge ring were not particularly severe. Max Clausen and Branko de Voukelitch received life imprisonment, but Anna Clausen was sentenced to only three years. The Court gave Kawai Teikichi ten years in prison, but Saionji received only two years (and this was suspended). All the members of the ring who were still alive in October 1945 were released by the Allied occupation forces. Only Sorge and Ozaki had been executed. It is not clear why the Supreme Court waited more than six months after rejecting the appeals by Sorge and Ozaki before ordering their sentences to be carried out; political considerations may have been involved, and perhaps there was some official reluctance, even then, to believe that the two had actually been spies. Sorge and Ozaki were not told when they would be executed until the day had arrived; Ozaki's wife was visiting her daughter, then living in the countryside to escape the bombing of Tokyo, on the day of her husband's death. It was on the morning of November 7, 1944, the anniversary of the Bolshevik revolution, that Richard Sorge, aged 49, and Ozaki Hotsumi, aged 43, were hanged at Sugamo prison.

Chapter Nine
A Hero of Our Time

Within a year after Ozaki's death Japan lay in ruins. Battered Imperial troops were returning home from Burma, China, and U.S. prisoner-of-war camps, and the United States Army's occupation forces were at work throughout the country. At first it was difficult for the Japanese people to comprehend that the Americans intended to subvert the old order and replace it with a "democratic" one; but they were genuinely stimulated by the iconoclastic instructions that began issuing from General MacArthur's SCAP headquarters. The climate of social renovation also led them to ask who had been to blame for the war and how to prevent another disaster like it. SCAP blamed the militarists and proposed democracy as the best defense against the revival of military rule. The Japanese people were not averse to experimenting with this imported political philosophy, but they also insisted upon examining other alternatives to the discredited theory of *kokutai*.

One major alternative was Communism. On October 4, 1945, General MacArthur's headquarters abolished the Peace Preservation Law, disbanded the Tokkō, released all political prisoners, and proclaimed citizens free to criticize the Emperor system. Out of prisons all over Japan walked about 3,000 political offenders, among them Max Clausen, Anna Clausen, Kawai Teikichi, and the long-incarcerated leadership of the Japanese Communist Party. On October 19 in Osaka the new Party leader, Tokuda Kyūichi, after eighteen years in prison, made his first speech on the policy of the Communist Party; on the next day, the first issue of *Red Flag* (*Akahata*) appeared on the street corners of Tokyo. During the next few months, the Party made its policies for the occupation period known to every adult citizen of

Japan: to overthrow the Emperor system, to unite with the masses in order to transform Japan, to carry out a "peaceful revolution" at the polls and through labor organizations. For a time, these policies were attractive to many Japanese; they seemed to be in harmony with the democracy that SCAP was encouraging from the Dai Ichi building, and the Communist Party's ties with the Soviet Union, which might have created suspicions, were carefully concealed until the end of the occupation period.

It was natural that the Sorge case should have been injected into this general ferment, for Ozaki's part in it bore directly on the questions of who was to blame for the war and whether Communism was desirable for Japan. Unfortunately, no one in Japan knew the full story of the Sorge spy ring. SCAP officers apparently read about it for the first time in the *Yomiuri shimbun* and the English-language *Nippon Times* during the autumn of 1945,[1] and the Japanese people possessed only the fragmentary report that the Justice Ministry had published in June of 1942. But there were numerous survivors of the incident, such as Kawai, and men who had known Ozaki at the *Asahi*, in politics, and as personal friends; and they all began to tell their stories.

The case was of intense interest to the public: Ozaki had been executed as a traitor to the very system they were in the process of dismantling. Had he really been a great patriot? As much as they wanted to know who should be blamed for the war, the Japanese people were just as vitally interested in the obverse question: who were the men who had fought, and died, to prevent it? The national press took up the Sorge case with enthusiasm, and popular interest appears to be as strong in 1964 (although for different reasons) as it was in 1945. The Sorge case became an integral part of Japanese popular culture, and it was transformed many times in the process.

The first hard information on Ozaki and the Sorge case came from Ozaki's left-wing friends who had rallied to his defense during the war. Matsumoto Shin'ichi (his former counselor) and Kazama Michitarō (who had known Ozaki before the war) did not possess the official records of the Sorge case, but they did have access to Ozaki's letters to Eiko. Immediately after the surrender, these two men began to read Ozaki's correspondence; and they soon selected some 238 letters for publication.[2] During February of 1946 some of these letters appeared in the left-wing journal *Jinmin hyōron (People's Review)*, which

Matsumoto controlled as chairman of its editorial board.* The read-ing public responded with enthusiasm; here was a man who had taken personal action against the militarists and who had perished at their hands. It was also clear, however, that the *Jinmin hyōron* was using Ozaki's letters to popularize the Communist Party, which was then actively trying to portray itself as a patriotic party of the masses. The apotheosis of Ozaki as a great Communist had begun, although it soon set in motion a reaction by persons who had known him better than the Communists.

In September 1946 the Sekai Hyōron (World Review) Company published the first book-length edition of *Aijō wa furu hoshi no goto-ku,* or *Love Is Like a Falling Star.* Printed on the coarse brown paper then used in Japan, it contained 73 of Ozaki's letters, a foreword by Eiko entitled "I Believe That the Dawn Is Approaching," and two postscripts, one by Matsumoto and one by the well-known woman novelist and Communist Party member, Miyamoto Yuriko.[3] This first edition sold out immediately (it is today a collector's item), and *Aijō* remained the leading best seller in Japan from 1946 through 1948. Japanese literary scholars have since awarded it a place in the history of Shōwa literature as one of the sources of inspiration for the "human-istic school" of postwar writing.[4] As of 1963, *Aijō wa furu hoshi no gotoku* had been published in at least seven different formats or editions.[5]

Contrary to the expectations of *Aijō*'s Communist editors, the pop-ular fascination with Ozaki was not based entirely, or even primarily, on the fact that he had been a Marxist; it was his individualism, his introspection, and his courage that stimulated popular interest in him. Those Communists who had been closest to him, particularly Matsumoto and Nakanishi Kō (not to mention the JCP hierarchy itself), were disconcerted that he had apparently emerged from *Aijō* more as a "humanist" than as a "Communist." Matsumoto at first hoped to resolve the problem by labeling Ozaki a "fighting human-ist."[6] Then, in December of 1946, he wrote an article for the influ-ential journal *Sekai (The World)* in which he tried to hand down an

---

* The *Jinmin hyōron* represented a union of Communist and left-socialist views during the united front period of postwar Japanese politics; besides Matsumoto, who was a member of the Japanese Communist Party, its editorial board included two socialists, two labor leaders, and another Communist—Ozaki's old friend from Tōa Dōbun, Nakanishi Kō. See *Jinmin hyōron,* November 1947, p. 3.

official opinion on Ozaki and to explain the obvious discrepancies between the man who wrote *Aijō* and the stereotyped Communist of the
Stalinist period. He admitted that Ozaki was no ordinary Communist, and added that he had tried to encompass too much and was
too compromising and too flexible; but he concluded that Ozaki "was
a true Communist from the time he joined the *Asahi shimbun* in
1926."[7] At the time he wrote this article, Matsumoto also received
strong support in the pages of *Red Flag* for his attempt to portray
Ozaki as an ideal Communist martyr.

There were other Communists ready to give their versions of Ozaki.
Except for members of the police, probably the last man to see Ozaki
alive was Kamiyama Shigeo. Kamiyama (b. 1905), who is today one
of the pillars of the JCP establishment, was arrested three times before the war under the Peace Preservation Law. The third time was
on May 1, 1941, when he was taken into custody as the leader of the
Communist Party Rebuilding Committee in the Tokyo area. He was
held throughout the war in Sugamo prison, where he steadfastly refused to make a *tenkō*. After the war he became a member of the
Party's Central Committee, headed its labor union department, and
became known as a doctrinaire leftist theorist of Leninism and Stalinism. He was purged by the Party in 1954 but reinstated in 1958 during the Party's reunification movement.[8]

During the year preceding Ozaki's death, Kamiyama often met and
talked with Ozaki in the exercise yard or while working on cleaning
details at Sugamo prison. The two men shared a bond of companionship because they had both lived in Taiwan at one time and because
certain prison guards mistreated them. According to Kamiyama, certain guards considered them the two biggest criminals in Sugamo:
the one a Communist spy and the other the last leader of the JCP.
In the November 9, 1946, issue of *Red Flag*, Kamiyama wrote the first
version of an often reprinted article dealing with Ozaki's life in
prison.[9] This article reappeared, in an expanded form and under its
best-known title "Saigo no akushu," or "The Last Handshake" (with
Ozaki), in the November 1947 issue of *Jinmin hyōron*.

Kamiyama argued that there were only two unrecanting political
prisoners in Sugamo: himself and Miyamoto Kenji (who today re-
presents the doctrinaire left of the Party). But he added that Ozaki,
too, was essentially unrepentant, despite his two *tenkōsho*. After
Ozaki's death sentence had been confirmed, Kamiyama urged him to

declare his true beliefs and to announce his reconversion to the Communist cause. Ozaki did not listen to this advice, but Kamiyama claimed that even some persons in the "enemy camp" knew that Ozaki had not written a real *tenkōsho*. Ozaki continued to act like a convert (*tenkōsha*), and in Kamiyama's opinion this had a deleterious effect on him: he grew very thin, his voice became hoarse, and he suffered from various ailments. Kamiyama tried to instill in him the will to live; but although they both believed that Japan's defeat was imminent, Ozaki had given up hope. Nevertheless, according to Kamiyama, Ozaki was at heart an unrepentant Communist, one who should have been in the ranks of the Party leaders who emerged from prison in 1945 after decades of incarceration.[10]

Unofficially, the Communist Party was thus trying to establish that Ozaki was one of them and to use the public's fascination with his life to dignify the Communist movement. As individuals, the liberals who had known Ozaki before the war and who joined the Communist Party after the war probably did not intend to falsify the record of his life; they honestly believed that Ozaki had responded correctly to militarism in Japan and that they were merely carrying on in a way he would have approved. In the years of intense political iconoclasm right after the war, the belief that Ozaki was both a great patriot and a great Communist brought together many diverse personalities. On November 7, 1946, the second anniversary of Ozaki's execution, some thirty former friends and admirers gathered beside his grave in Tama cemetery.* This group included Shiga Yoshio, one of three top leaders of the postwar Communist Party (along with Tokuda Kyūichi and Nosaka Sanzō); Inukai Ken, of the (conservative) Progressive Party; Tsuge Hideomi, a scientist; Horie Yūichi, of the JCP; Yamasaki Ken, Ozaki's old philosophical acquaintance at Tokyo University; Kazama Michitarō, another prewar acquaintance; and Matsumoto Shin'ichi.

---

* Ozaki's wake in the autumn of 1944 had drawn only six people: Eiko, Yōko, Takeuchi Kintarō (Ozaki's second lawyer), Matsumoto Shin'ichi, Saionji Kinkazu, and a fellow worker of Saionji's. Saionji himself drew the characters of Ozaki's name that are the only words engraved on his tombstone. (Saionji, *Kizoku no taijō*, p. 55; Kazama, *Aru hangyaku*, p. 142.) Saionji Kinkazu's loyalty to Ozaki rests on his belief that Ozaki correctly analyzed the Chinese revolution. After the war Saionji revived the Japanese Council of the Institute of Pacific Relations, and he was elected to the House of Councilors in 1947. Following the Korean War, he moved permanently to Peking, where he resides today. (See the articles by Saionji in *Sekai*, June 1959, April 1960, and September 1961.)

At Matsumoto's suggestion, the group organized itself as the Ozaki Hotsumi Biography Compilation Committee.[11] Shiga's presence clearly indicates that the Communist Party initially approved of this enterprise, and the work went ahead on the understanding that Matsumoto would actually write the final biography. The committee soon discovered that it was going to be very difficult to obtain the records of the Sorge case; every inquiry they made to the government was turned away with the reply that the records had all been destroyed in the B-29 raids. Matsumoto busied himself during 1947 tracking down leads, but little real progress was made. Then, on November 26, 1947, Matsumoto, who was also active as a Communist labor leader in the postwar period, died unexpectedly of pneumonia.

One of Matsumoto's last published articles was an attempt to strengthen the image of Ozaki as an "iron Communist." In the September 1947 issue of *Asahi hyōron*, Kaji Ryūichi, one of Ozaki's old newspaper associates, had written that "since the war there have been some persons who have consciously attempted to make a revolutionary out of Ozaki." Matsumoto felt that he had to answer this charge, which he did in a sensitive and well-balanced article for *Jinmin hyōron*. He admitted that Ozaki had not been a Party member and had had no experience in mass struggles; Ozaki's "duties" had forced a "bourgeois life" on him, and Ozaki did not "hate such a life." Nevertheless, Matsumoto argued that Kaji did not appreciate Ozaki's most important trait: his incredibly strong will. Ozaki could have been wealthy and comfortable, but instead he chose a path that led to prison and to the gallows. Here was the test of a genuine revolutionary.[12] Despite its Communist intent, the article was a fitting tribute by one of Ozaki's most devoted admirers. Matsumoto lies buried today next to Ozaki in Tama cemetery.

The high point of the extreme left's apotheosis of Ozaki came on November 27, 1948, with the Ozaki-Matsumoto Anti-Fascist Memorial Meeting, held in the lecture hall of Meiji University. The speakers included Ozaki Eiko, Ozaki Yōko, Matsumoto Toshiko (Matsumoto's widow), Kamiyama Shigeo, Yamasaki Ken, Kozai Yoshishige, Hosokawa Karoku, Nakanishi Ko, Horie Yūichi, and various other Party members who spoke on anti-fascist and anti-imperialist topics. The proceedings, recorded stenographically, were published in 1949 under the title *The Great Love* (*Idai naru aijō*). The introduction by the editors, Horie Yūichi and Kozai Yoshishige, both middle-ranking officials of the JCP, proclaims: "We send this book into the world: For the memory of Ozaki and Matsumoto! For freedom, peace, and independence! For the overthrow of the new fascism!"[13]

The Great Love's greatest value to the history of the Sorge case lies in Ozaki Eiko's notes on the organization of her husband's defense after his arrest. However, the book also makes clear the uses influential Communists were prepared to make of Ozaki's reputation and fame. Kamiyama's "Last Handshake" was reprinted in the volume, and several speakers recalled Ozaki's predictions about the course of the Chinese revolution and related these to the spectacular advances that the People's Liberation Army was then making on the mainland. Nakanishi Ko, very much aware of the traditional Japanese antipathy for Russia, perpetuated the old description of the Sorge ring as a Comintern espionage unit. He wrote: "The fact that Ozaki was affiliated with the Comintern does not necessarily mean that he was connected with the Soviet government."[14] The Communist Party, for reasons of its own, was being as cynical with the truth as the Justice Ministry had been in 1942.* By calling the Sorge group a "Comintern spy ring" it neatly obscured both Ozaki's treason and its own organizational subservience to the U.S.S.R. Nakanishi also said that "although Ozaki did not belong to the JCP, he never for a moment forgot about the working masses of Japan" (Ozaki's writings do not suggest that he ever gave the working masses, as such, an instant of his thought); and he warned readers of *Love Is Like a Falling Star* not to judge Ozaki's revolutionary qualities on the basis of that particular book.[15] Possibly the only person at the meeting who remembered the real Ozaki was his daughter, Yōko, who told the audience of her father's fondness for Chinese tea and Chinese music, and paid tribute to the complexities of his personality as reflected in his letters.[16]

Although its work was interrupted by the death of Matsumoto, the Biography Compilation Committee did not disband; instead, in a move that certain JCP members would later regret, it entrusted the investigation of the Sorge incident to one of its actual participants and an old friend of Ozaki's, Kawai Teikichi. Kawai, still undisposed to find regular employment, had time on his hands, and he undertook the project in collaboration with Ozaki's younger half-brother, Ozaki

---

* Nakanishi was an influential figure in the JCP until January 10, 1950, when he was purged for criticizing the leadership from an extreme leftist point of view.

Hotsuki. The two researchers rented an office in Yūrakuchō and deco-
rated their door with a sign reading "The Association to Investigate
the True Facts of the Ozaki-Sorge Incident." Somewhat surprisingly,
they began to uncover a few official reports on the incident—reports
that led them to ask some embarrassing questions.

It was in 1942, when he was 13 years old, that Ozaki Hotsuki had
first read of the charges against his elder brother in a Taiwanese newspaper. The Ozakis had been ostracized by their associates in T'aipei
because of the case, and this made Hotsuki intensely curious about
the brother he had never met. In 1946 Hotsuki came to Tokyo, where
he met his sister-in-law Eiko and the family friend Itō Ritsu, who was
then one of the most powerful figures in the Japanese Communist
Party. Before leaving Taiwan, Hotsuki had inquired about materials
on the Sorge case from a certain judge Asakawa. The judge mentioned
that a pamphlet issued by the Justice Ministry gave details on the
incident, and suggested that Hotsuki try to find a copy in Tokyo. It
seems that the judge also gave Hotsuki some ideas about how the case
had been broken.[17] But when Ozaki Hotsuki quoted these views to
"Uncle Itō," his sister-in-law, and Matsumoto, they all told him that
such reports were biased and that he shouldn't rely on them. (At the
time, neither Matsumoto nor Eiko had the slightest knowledge of how
the Sorge case had been exposed.)

In November 1946 Itō Ritsu secured a job for Hotsuki as a journalist on the *Chūbu mimpō,* a JCP organ in Nagoya. He also urged
Hotsuki to join the Party, but Hotsuki did not do so until early 1948.
After a short period in Nagoya, Hotsuki returned to Tokyo to cover
the capital as a reporter for the *Chūbu mimpō.* In early 1948, after
the death of Matsumoto, he met Kawai Teikichi, his brother's old associate and the newly appointed biographer of Ozaki Hotsumi. Hotsuki and Kawai had many long discussions about the case, and Kawai
passed on to him some gossip about Itō Ritsu's "scandalous" behavior
in prison.[18] Later Kawai confided to Hotsuki that he believed the ring
had been betrayed, because of a chance remark made by a police officer when he himself was placed under arrest in October 1941.[19]

Hotsuki liked Kawai and was intrigued by his suspicions, and so
he agreed to cooperate with him in investigating the case for the
Party-affiliated Biography Committee. During the spring of 1948 Hotsuki contacted some of the judges and prosecutors in the case, and
he learned that SCAP was also investigating the Sorge incident. He

befriended a reporter named Nagahama Retsu, then covering the Metropolitan Police, and Nagahama loaned him a copy of the original Justice Ministry–Tokkō study of the case. Although the first two parts of this report, which dealt with the breaking of the case, were missing, Ozaki Hotsuki was getting close to the truth. He was also beginning to notice certain unusual occurrences.

The Sekai Hyōron Company, which had asked Nagahama to contribute a series of articles on Ozaki, suddenly canceled its request in late 1948. Similarly, Kawai had written several articles on his recollections of Sorge, Smedley, and Ozaki for the October and November 1948 issues of *Companion of the Masses (Minshū no tomo)*, the organ of the Japanese Federation for a Democratic Culture, but these, too, were rejected without explanation.[20] Hotsuki concluded that someone within the Communist establishment was trying to suppress any further discussion of Ozaki. This opinion has since been confirmed by Kazama Michitarō. Kazama writes that he does not know whether the charges made against Itō in Hotsuki's book, *The Living Judas,* are true, but that he, too, ran afoul of Itō in 1948. After the death of Matsumoto, Kazama conceived the idea of writing an independent biography of Ozaki, and he therefore began to gather materials, record anecdotes, and talk to Ozaki's old acquaintances. While thus engaged, he encountered Itō, who warned him that his investigation of the Ozaki case might get him into trouble with the American authorities. Kazama recalls that he wondered at the time why a member of the Political Bureau of the Japanese Communist Party—a man not noted for his fear of the Americans—should have said such a thing. Later, a friend told Kazama that Itō had a "guilty conscience" about Ozaki.[21]

In early 1949, however, Kawai and Hotsuki were still collecting data at their Yūrakuchō office and had not turned up the name of Itō Ritsu. Then, on February 10, 1949, Major General Charles Willoughby released to the press his famous report, "The Sorge Spy Ring, A Case Study in International Espionage in the Far East." On February 11, every newspaper in Japan carried a digest of the SCAP report; and there, for all to read, was the phrase "Itō Ritsu, unwitting Judas." The U.S. Army's purpose in releasing its study probably had no direct bearing on Itō or his position within the Communist Party; its intention was rather to influence the political handling of certain cold war issues within the United States.

SCAP based its report on original copies of the Japanese police and *yoshin* interrogations, but it never made these records available in their original form to the general public. Instead, it used the documents as sources for various condensed studies which, as we have seen, contained numerous inaccuracies. Shortly after the occupation was established SCAP had asked the Japanese government for the Sorge case materials, and it had been told that the records held in Tokyo had all been destroyed in the bombings. Occupation authorities later discovered, however, that copies had been stored in Kōfu city, Yamanashi prefecture, and these were impounded by SCAP and turned over to Lieutenant Colonel T. P. Davis of the Civil Intelligence Section, G-2, U.S. Army Far East Command, for examination and analysis. Colonel Davis then wrote the first version of the SCAP report, which he completed on August 5, 1947. According to General Willoughby, Davis's study was edited by a civilian, Dr. H. T. Noble of the Civil Intelligence Section, G-2, before it was published.[22] SCAP printed the Davis-Noble report in final form as part of its *Civil Intelligence Section Periodical Summary,* No. 23, December 15, 1947. The Army's purpose in writing the Sorge report was to present it as a case study that could be used in the training of U.S. Army intelligence officers.*

During 1948 General Willoughby sent copies of this report to the Military Intelligence Division of the War Department in Washington; and late that year Pentagon officials disclosed parts of it to certain American journalists. Rumors spread about various persons implicated by the report, and the press criticized SCAP for having freed all Japanese political prisoners in 1945 without prior scrutiny. In order to silence some of the rumors and accusations, the Department of the Army persuaded General MacArthur's headquarters to

---

* More than ten years after the end of the occupation, the Davis-Noble report was still in use as one of the standard texts at the U.S. Army Intelligence School, Fort Holabird, Maryland. See U.S. Army Intelligence School, Department of Field Operations Intelligence, *The Sorge Spy Ring, A Case Study in International Espionage in the Far East* (Fort Holabird, Maryland: "Supplemental Reading," no classification, n.d.). All of the non-existent characters mentioned earlier—e.g., General "Olitsky" and Max "Klausen"—are perpetuated, and the misspellings and inconsistent usages of words in Japanese, Chinese, and German are endless. According to the note on sources (p. 85f.), the report has been brought up to date to include new research; however, there is no indication that it differs in any fundamental way from the 1947 version. For the text of the 1947 version, see U.S. 81st Congress, First Session, *Congressional Record,* Vol. 95, Part 12, Appendix, pp. A705–A723.

release the sections of *Civil Intelligence Section Periodical Summary* No. 23 that dealt with the Sorge case. This was done on February 10, 1949.

In Tokyo as well as in the United States, the reactions to the SCAP report were instantaneous. On February 11, *Red Flag* published an interview with Shiga Yoshio in which he denounced the occupation's study of the Sorge case as cold war propaganda, denied that the JCP had any connection with the Sorge ring, and explicitly stated that Itō Ritsu and Nakanishi Ko were not involved in any way. On February 13, *Red Flag* published an interview with Itō entitled "I Have No Connection." But the Party could no longer regard these disclaimers as sufficient, for it was beginning to realize that the Ozaki-Sorge case was a two-edged sword: it might be used by the Party to enhance its own popularity, but SCAP might also use it against the Communists. In addition to characterizing Itō Ritsu—the most important subordinate of Party Secretary-General Tokuda Kyūichi—as an "unwitting Judas," the SCAP report insinuated: "Can it be that the Japan Communist Party and the Soviets do not know who really betrayed the ring and so killed Richard Sorge and Hosumi [Hotsumi] Ozaki?"[23] This question, which was printed in the *Pacific Stars and Stripes* of February 11, 1949, was interpreted by the JCP Political Bureau as an open attempt by SCAP to split the Party's leadership.

In his February 11 interview, Shiga, speaking as one of the Party triumvirs, stated that the Party had investigated Itō's connection with the Sorge case in March of 1946 and had found him blameless. He even said that the Party now believed that the entire Sorge incident itself was something the Tokkō and Kempei had "cooked up" in order to advance militarist rule.[24] Obviously, the Communist Party wanted nothing more to do with the ghosts of Ozaki Hotsumi and Richard Sorge. Within a few weeks after February 10, the Party's Political Bureau called a special meeting of the Biography Compilation Committee at Ozaki's old family residence in Tokyo, and Hotsuki was specifically asked to attend. (Whether Kawai was also present is not clear.) Horie Yūichi announced to the assembled friends of Ozaki that the Political Bureau had decided that the "Association to Investigate the True Facts of the Ozaki-Sorge Incident" must suspend its work at once.[25] Despite considerable disagreement, the group agreed that it was in the interests of the Communist cause to do so, and Ozaki's biographers ceased their formal association forthwith.

The Party's directive was not the only interruption in the work of Kawai and Hotsuki. Another blow to the research was being generated across the ocean. In the United States, Agnes Smedley had vehemently denied the truth of the SCAP report. Her reaction, and the fact that the Occupation's sources had not been transmitted to Washington, led the Department of the Army to repudiate the report publicly less than ten days after it had been released to the press. According to UP and INS dispatches, "The Army's Public Information Division said flatly . . . that it was wrong and in error in charging that Agnes Smedley, an American writer, was a Russian spy. [Colonel] Eyster [the Public Information Division's spokesman] said, 'The Division has no information to back up the spy charges. The report was based on information from the Japanese police and the report should have said so.' . . . Eyster said that the report was prepared by intelligence officers in Tokyo and that the 'young fellows that did it proceeded to philosophize and add their opinion of its effect.' "[26]

It was this particularly humiliating rebuff by his Washington superiors that drove General Willoughby into the arms of the House Committee on Un-American Activities.[27] The Committee wanted to investigate Agnes Smedley, and it asked Willoughby to find documentary evidence implicating her—the evidence that Colonel Eyster said did not exist. Willoughby agreed to this request, and he spent the rest of 1949 tracking down substantive data that would prove that Smedley had been a member of the Sorge ring. In the course of his investigation, Willoughby took one action that directly influenced the course of postwar research in Japan on the Sorge case: he arrested Kawai Teikichi and held him as a possible witness against Agnes Smedley.

According to Willoughby, he first interrogated Kawai on February 18, 1949, and "two American lawyers" then interrogated him again on March 31 and April 1, 1949.[28] Willoughby suggests that Kawai agreed voluntarily to become a witness against Agnes Smedley; as he put it: "A sort of Whittaker Chambers of Japan, Mr. Kawai has since turned against Communism and is now willing to 'tell all.' . . . Mr. Kawai was under no pressure so far as this Headquarters was concerned; in fact, he appeared grateful to his American liberators. His collaboration was entirely voluntary."[29] Kawai's friends Ozaki Hotsuki and Kazama Michitarō deny this. They say that Kawai was not a willing informant against Smedley, and assert that SCAP held Kawai under house arrest for two months at the Iwasaki villa in Bun-kyōku (then being used as a U.S. Army officers' billet.)[30]

The truth of the matter is complex. Kawai, who was never much of an organization man, had indeed turned against the Party, but he never completely renounced his belief in the Communist cause. Kawai, Kazama, and Ozaki Hotsuki all bitterly resented the Party's breaking up the Biography Committee, and they believed that the person responsible for it was Itō Ritsu. Kawai, in particular, was infuriated by Shiga's statement that the Sorge case had simply been "cooked up" by the Tokkō; after all, he had been arrested as a member of the ring and had served a long prison term because of his work for Ozaki and Sorge. Therefore, on February 18, he voluntarily contacted SCAP headquarters and reaffirmed under oath the accuracy of the information the police had obtained from him in October of 1941.[31] Six weeks later, after the Smedley controversy had developed in the United States, SCAP again came to see him and took him into custody as a witness against her. By this time, he had been expelled from the Party as a "right-wing spy" for contradicting the Party line on the genuineness of Ozaki's and Sorge's activities.[32] He may well have welcomed SCAP's protection in mid-1949 because he feared that the Party might put further pressure on him; but he never gave any testimony against Agnes Smedley (who died on May 8, 1950).

Kawai's behavior on this occasion was not out of character. His first loyalty, from the day they had met, was to Ozaki Hotsumi, and he never forgot that Ozaki had supported him in 1940 and 1941. He believed that the Party was mistaken (or worse) in denying that the Sorge ring had ever existed, and so he took personal action to see that Shiga's pronouncement did not go unchallenged. Moreover, after he was released by the Americans, he decided to write a book giving his story of the Sorge case. His *Memoirs of a Revolutionary* (*Aru kaku-meika no kaisō*), which appeared in December 1953, remains today the sole account by an actual participant written after the event. It is a straightforward, factual statement of his activities in Shanghai, his friendship with Ozaki and Smedley, and his work in Manchuria. His book was specifically intended to refute the JCP's assertion that the ring was something deliberately fabricated by the Tokkō, but it did not take up the problem of Itō Ritsu. Kawai ended his account with his own arrest in October of 1941.

Kawai Teikichi is still basically a Marxist, but one severely disillusioned with the Communist movement. In 1962 he published a short statement giving the fundamental reasons for his antagonism to organized Communist parties, and they are reasons that speak for a generation of leftists. He had thought that he was working for the Comintern when he was assisting Sorge and Ozaki. After his arrest, when he discovered that Sorge was an agent for Department Four of the Red Army, he believed that he and Ozaki had been betrayed. He had nourished a strong emotional commitment to the idea of the Comintern, but after the war he came to realize that the Comintern had been an instrument of Soviet foreign policy since at least 1928. He concluded that this was "an instance of Soviet national egotism."[33] To this extent, Willoughby is right when he states that Kawai "turned against Communism."

Although Kawai did not take up the problem of Itō in his book, his partner on the defunct Biographical Committee, Ozaki Hotsuki, did. The SCAP report served to confirm his earlier suspicions that Itō had betrayed his brother. As we have seen, Hotsuki was already close to believing that Itō had played a dishonorable role in the case when the occupation released its study. His own knowledge of the Party's attack on the Biographical Committee and other incidents made him unwilling to accept SCAP's contention that Itō was an *"unwitting Judas"*; the mere fact that Itō was mentioned in the SCAP report, which was based on official documents not then available to any left-wing Japanese, was sufficient proof to him that Itō had been a traitor to Communism. Although interrupted by a prolonged illness, Hotsuki continued to gather all available information on Itō for several years, and he published his findings in 1959 under the title *The Living Judas (Ikite iru yuda)*. The weight of his argument is that Itō had suppressed all discussion of the Ozaki case in postwar left-wing circles and that he had done so because of his fear of exposure as Ozaki's betrayer.

Unfortunately for Hotsuki, Itō himself disappeared in June 1950, when the entire Central Committee of the JCP went underground. In 1959 Itō could not be held to account for the charges Hotsuki made against him, and he could not defend himself. In fact, there is a distinct possibility that Itō Ritsu, if a Judas, was no longer a living Judas by 1959. He was purged from his official posts within the Party in 1953 and expelled from the Party in 1955; he remains today the only member of the JCP Central Committee who went underground at the time of the Korean War and who did not reappear (or become otherwise accounted for) when the old leadership again took up the reins in 1955. The accusations made against him by Ozaki Hotsuki have never been confirmed, and it does not seem possible that they ever will be. Itō's role in the ring's exposure and the reasons for his disappearance after 1950 will probably remain the greatest mystery in the case.[34]

Since the end of the war, the Sorge case has provided the basis for at least two motion pictures, one play, innumerable novels, several fictionalized accounts, and about half a dozen journalistic studies.[35] In addition to the books by Kawai and Ozaki Hotsuki, Kazama Michitarō, another member of the Biographical Committee and one of the editors of *Love Is Like a Falling Star*, wrote a valuable biography of Ozaki designed to show that he was a great patriot.[36] This outpouring reflects the intrinsic interest of the incident, but it was also encouraged by the fact that no official records were made available to the general public until 1962. In the absence of facts, myths and romantic interpretations flourished. It was said that Sorge was exposed by one of his mistresses, who was then assassinated by Soviet agents in Shanghai after the war. It was claimed that Ozaki was not really a "spy" but a martyred patriot. It was argued that the whole case had nothing to do with espionage or treason and was instead an early manifestation of the "peace movement"—the pacifist activities that have absorbed so many postwar Japanese intellectuals.[37] There has even been a difference of opinion about Sorge's last words.*

Since 1962, when the Sorge case records began to be published in the Misuzu Shobō Company's *Materials on Modern History*, many of the myths have been dispelled. But Ozaki's ghost is still abroad in Japan, and his old friends are still perplexed by it. Ryū Shintarō remembers how Ozaki enjoyed laughing and drinking with his companions. Could such a man, at that very time, have been risking his life for his politics? Kazami Akira has said that Ozaki was "as warm

---

* Yoshikawa Mitsusada states that Sorge shouted "Three cheers for the Red Army and the Communist Party of the Soviet Union!" According to General Willoughby, he said "I thank you [the prison officials] for all your kindnesses." (Cf. *Gendai-shi shiryō geppō*, No. 1, p. 5; and *Shanghai Conspiracy*, p. 127.) The most interesting, but surely the most apocryphal, version is given by Meissner, who has Sorge say "To hell with mankind!" (*The Man With Three Faces*, p. 235.)

as jade and as charming as dew," but this is not the man one finds
in the record of the Tokkō interrogations. Tsurumi Shunsuke cannot
forget that Ozaki was a genuine friend and confidant to several of
Japan's highest ranking leaders during the Sino-Japanese war, and
he is forced to conclude that Ozaki was the most extreme example of
"disguised conversion" in the militarist era.

For thousands of Japanese who never knew him, and for all who
want to grasp the meaning of his life and times, Ozaki will remain a
difficult man to judge dispassionately. Some of his hopes now seem
utopian, some of his actions futile. But he saw, as few of his contem-
poraries did, that the Sino-Japanese war would transform the Orient:
he predicted that a genuine Chinese nation-state would arise from
the ruins of classical Chinese society, and he saw the folly of his own
government's militaristic opposition to the tide of the Chinese revolution. What is most important in human terms, he was not content
to remain an observer. He staked his life on his convictions.

ACCORDING TO HIS VIRTUE

LET US USE HIM

Appendix

Was Itō a Judas?

Itō's role in the Sorge case is extremely complex and not well understood even today. In order to evaluate his suspected activities as a police spy, one must bear in mind certain other details of his career. First, Itō Ritsu did *unwittingly* provide the clue that broke the Sorge case; but his information bore no relation to Ozaki at the time, and the clue he provided was in the hands of the Tokkō in early 1940. Second, his involvement with the Sorge case is related to one of the greatest postwar scandals of the Japanese Communist Party—the purge of Itō in 1953–55. After the war, Itō became an influential member of the Political Bureau and Secretariat of the JCP, and he was chief of the Party's agrarian section. The accusation by the Party's Central Committee that he had been a police informer for more than ten years still reverberates within Japanese left-wing circles. Third, the Japanese police have remained very taciturn about the details of their pre-arrest investigation of the Sorge case, and the recently published official records on the incident do not resolve all of the outstanding issues. Therefore, the only way of checking the JCP's accusations against Itō—and these accusations are themselves extraordinarily cryptic—is to compile every rumor, conjecture, and occasional remark that has come from police, prosecutors, and Party members interested in the Sorge case.

Kitabayashi Tomo was arrested on September 28, 1941, and she received a sentence of five years in prison, for having occasionally supplied information to Miyagi; she was released on February 9, 1945, because of illness, and she died shortly thereafter. Itō Ritsu was taken into custody on September 29, 1941, but the police held him without returning an indictment. He was released on June 28, 1942 (four days after Sorge's *yoshin* had begun), and on November 17, 1942, he supplied the prosecutors with information on Ozaki and his work at the South Manchurian Railroad. Itō's employment after the summer of 1942 and during most of 1943 is not known, but he may have been called up for military training and released because he had tuberculosis.[1] Matsumoto Seichō believes that he continued to communicate with Tokkō Inspectors Miyashita Hiroshi and Itō Taketora during this period.[2] He was rearrested in late 1943 on an unspecified charge—presumably under the clause of the Peace Preservation Law that allowed the police to take previous violators into custody as a preventive measure—and he was given a three-year jail sentence on November 11, 1943. He spent some time in Sugamo prison and was then transferred to Toyotama prison, where he stayed until the war was over. Kamiyama Shigeo recalls that Itō asked him, before leaving Sugamo, to look after Ozaki.[3]

After his release in 1945, Itō worked with Nakanishi Ko to establish the Jinmin Sha publishing house, and both of them began to participate in the movement to rebuild the Communist Party. Itō was recommended for admission to the Party by Komatsu Yūichirō, an old friend from the Communist Youth League, and Kamiyama Shigeo, the Party's labor-union bureau chief. According to Political Bureau member Shiga Yoshio, Itō voluntarily confessed his connection with the Sorge case before the Party leadership in March 1946, and the Party accepted his explanation.[4] Itō then advanced very rapidly within the postwar JCP structure, apparently for two reasons. First, Party leaders needed the assistance of young Party members who had participated in the immediate prewar Communist movement. Tokuda and Shiga had been in prison since 1928, and they were completely out of touch with the people and the mood of the nation; and Nosaka Sanzō had spent the war years working with Mao Tse-tung in Yenan, and had not returned to Tokyo until January 12, 1946. Second, Itō was both young (32 years old in 1945) and talented. He strongly supported the "lovable Party" line during the occupation period, and he seemed adept at predicting the next moves by SCAP. Itō represented the "leadership generation of men in their thirties," and he made a genuine contribution to building a mass base for the postwar Party.[5]

The Party—and especially its Secretary General, Tokuda Kyūichi—repaid Itō for his services with rapid promotions. At the Fifth Party

Congress (February 24–26, 1946) Itō was elected a member of the Central Committee; and on February 27, when the Central Committee created its own Political Bureau and Secretariat, Itō was also elected to the Secretariat. (Political Bureau: Tokuda, Nosaka, Shiga, Hakamada, Miyamoto, Kim Ch'ŏn-hae; Secretariat: Tokuda, Nosaka, Shiga, Kuroki, and Itō Ritsu.)[6] Critics of Party leadership during the 1945–50 period date the development of Tokuda's iron grip over the "Party center" (the Political Bureau and Secretariat) from the time of these appointments. Tokuda emerged supreme over his two chief rivals, Nosaka and Shiga, because—in the best Stalinist tradition—he controlled the Secretariat: Kuroki and Itō were his devoted followers.

Tokuda's machinations should not be understood as springing solely from a desire for personal advancement. It was logical that the Party should bring young and capable organizers into the leadership at this particular time. However, Itō's rapid advancement under Tokuda took place at the expense of many older men, men who were veterans of the underground-prison period, and this put him in an exposed position. At the second plenary session of the Fifth Central Committee (May 6–9, 1946), Itō moved up to the Political Bureau (along with Hasegawa Hiroshi and Kasuga Shōjirō) while retaining his post in the Secretariat. Moreover, in the spring of 1946, Tokuda and Itō began to strengthen their so-called "bureaucratic control" over the Party by allowing unrestricted admissions and by working to eliminate non-Party direction of the various mass organizations.

The climax of Itō's rapid advance and the ascendancy of the Tokuda-Itō faction occurred at the Sixth Party Congress (December 21, 1947). Itō was one of eight members of the Congress's platform committee, and he was elected to its 25-member Central Committee. At the Central Committee's organization session (December 25), Itō was named to the Political Bureau and the Secretariat, as well as being made director of the Party's agrarian section and assistant chief editor of *Red Flag*. Although twenty years younger than Nosaka and ten years younger than Shiga, Itō was virtually the deputy Secretary General of the Party under its "patriarchal leader," Tokuda Kyūichi.

During 1948 and 1949 the membership of the Japanese Communist Party, which then totaled 100,000, became more the servant of the Political Bureau than vice versa, and it was Itō who had brought about this centralization under Tokuda and his faction. He isolated old-time Communists like Kamiyama, Miyamoto, and Shiga, and he filled the Party center with his own supporters. Itō has been described, no doubt accurately, as suave, clever, eloquent, businesslike, quick to judge a situation; certainly he had a knack for human relations.[7] These qualities were especially valuable to the Party shortly after the war, when the Communists were trying to ally themselves with the socialists in a united front dedicated to "peaceful revolution." In the elections of January 1949, the Communists placed 35 representatives in the lower house of the Diet. This was a triumph for the Tokuda-Itō faction; but, strangely enough, it was the beginning of the end for the younger man.

By 1949 Itō Ritsu already had many enemies. Part of the criticism of him was based on envy and factional politics, but part of it was based on principle. There had been too many rumors over the years about Itō's dissipated living and his violations of the moral code of Communists (particularly as interpreted by the old, long-imprisoned leaders) for these to be ignored.[8] Miyamoto Kenji, head of the Party's Control Commission, often suggested that his group should investigate Itō's alleged flouting of Party rules and his "insincere life." The Tokuda faction was always able to force the majority of the Control Commission to side with it, and all charges against Itō (including those whispered by Kawai and Ozaki Hotsuki) were successfully suppressed. However, the bureaucratization of the Party center and the toleration of Itō's excesses were slowly producing a split in the Party that has never been successfully healed, even to this day. In January 1950, when criticism of the Party came from a source that could not be suppressed — namely, from Stalin himself — these festering grievances split the Party wide open.

The JCP's postwar policy of "peaceful revolution" had been more successful than any it had pursued in its history, but it had one crucial flaw: it required that the JCP not come into open conflict with the occupation authorities. As the cold war developed, Stalin decided that the JCP's peaceful policies were not producing tangible results, and he therefore chose to use the Party against the Americans for purposes of his own global strategy. On January 6, 1950, the Cominform journal in Bucharest published an attack on the JCP's "gradualist" strategy of revolution. Stalin's criticism split the Japanese Communist Party into two factions: the "main current" faction, which tried to refute the Cominform's charges; and the "internationalist" faction, which argued that Stalin was correct and that the Party should become more militant. The main current group was led by Tokuda and Nosaka, and the more leftist international faction by Shiga and Miyamoto. Throughout early 1950 the two groups hurled charges and countercharges at each other, and then the main current faction, ably defended by Itō, excommunicated Miyamoto and other prominent figures on the left.

Having silenced the Party members who sought to capitalize on Stalin's attack, Tokuda and Nosaka proceeded to adopt Stalin's line. Party organs denounced "American imperialism," and action groups of young Party members battled Japanese and U.S. Army policemen with Molotov cocktails and homemade bombs. The Japanese Communist Party had obviously dropped its "lovable" façade. The shift in tactics produced two results. The Japanese people realized that the Party was following policies dictated by Moscow, and this discredited it as a force in Japanese politics from then on; and General MacArthur banned the Party's leadership from political life for the duration of the occupation. On June 6, 1950, MacArthur ordered Premier Yoshida to purge the twenty-four members of the Central Committee. According to SCAP regulations, this meant that these men were prohibited from holding public office and were to report regularly to local police authorities. When the Korean War broke out on June 25, 1950, *Red Flag* published pro–North Korean propaganda and was promptly banned by the occupation. Rather than conform to the purge order, the Central Committee, which was the "main current" faction, went underground.

For the next five years no one in Japan knew the exact whereabouts of the Central Committee or its composition. On the evening of August 11, 1955, with the greatest possible dramatic flair, Nosaka Sanzō and two associates walked into a rally of 3,500 Party members at Meiji Outer Garden, Tokyo. Before the rally was over, some 500 police and members of the press corps had surrounded the hall, and when Nosaka came out the police arrested him. By this time the occupation was a thing of the past, and the Party was in the process of shifting its line back to the earlier, more popular "peaceful revolution" tactic. On August 16, Nosaka was released by the Tokyo District Court for lack of evidence against him; three days earlier he had told the press: "We were forced to go underground by General MacArthur, who started the Korean War. The last five years, however, have proved that our stand was correct."[9] After the rally, on August 14, the editor of the *Mainichi* had written: "Nosaka's dramatic reappearance recalls his almost triumphant return to Japan from Red China after the end of the war. He is a man who knows how to make newspaper headlines. . . . Among the Japanese Communist leaders who went underground, Itō Ritsu alone remains unaccounted for."[10] And so it has been ever since.

The summer of 1955 produced another piece of spectacular news about the Communist Party. As late as July 15, 1955, Party members in Japan still believed that Secretary-General Tokuda, not heard of since 1950, was alive and their leader. On that date—the thirty-third anniversary of the founding of the JCP—an estimated 27,000 Party members gathered at the Kuramae Kokugikan sports arena in Tokyo, and "a portrait of the Party's top boss, Tokuda Kyūichi, was unveiled amid deafening applause. . . . The showing of the portrait of the fierce revolutionary leader was interpreted as giving the lie to all the reports that somebody else had replaced Tokuda in his Secretary-Generalship, or that Tokuda has been critically ill."[11] But only two weeks later, newspaper headlines proclaimed: "Japan Red Boss To-kuda Dies in Peking in 1953."[12]

This startling development was apparently unknown even to the Party leadership. When asked to say when Tokuda's death first be-came known to the Party leaders in Japan, Shiga Yoshio (formerly of the anti-Tokuda "internationalist" faction) said that it was "only re-cently and came as a bolt from the blue."[13] Even Tokuda's wife had not known where he was.[14] The announcement of Tokuda's death ex-plained the convocation of the Sixth National Consultative Confer-ence (VI Zenkyō) on July 27–29, 1955. The Party was coming out of hiding, and it needed a new formal policy and a new leadership. The Sixth Consultative Conference witnessed the reunification of the "in-ternationalist" and "main current" factions and issued a denuncia-tion of "inner-Party bureaucratism." On August 17, six days after his reappearance, Nosaka was elected the new First Secretary of the JCP, and he became the Party's undisputed leader. Stalin was dead, Japan was beginning peace talks with the U.S.S.R., and Nosaka reactivated the Party's policy of "peaceful revolution."

One problem, however, remained unsolved: where was Itō Ritsu? On September 14, 1955, the JCP announced that he was "living abroad"; the police believed that this announcement was made chiefly to prove that the Party had not murdered him.[15] Whether Itō was actually living in China in 1955 or whether the Party had executed him much earlier may never be known. But certain Party pronouncements and the conscientious scholarship that has gone on in Japan since 1955 make it possible to offer at least an educated guess about Itō's fate.[16]

Sometime after July or August of 1950, the purged Central Committee fled from Japan, via underground Communist channels, to Peking. Rumors suggest that one of the Party's chief financiers, a Tokyo dentist, sold his land near the capital for half a million yen, and that this money was used to support the Central Committee in exile.[17] In China, the "main current" faction split into three subfactions as the exiled leaders began to argue among themselves about who was responsible for the Party's disastrous mistakes. The first subfaction was made up of Tokuda Kyūichi, Itō Ritsu, Hasegawa Hiroshi, Takakura Teru, Itō Ken'ichi, and Matsumoto Saneki. The second group included Shida Shigeo, Shiino Etsurō, Nishizawa Ryūji, Konno Yojirō, Iwamoto Iwao, and Takenaka Tsunesaburō. The third faction was composed of Nosaka Sanzō, Kasuga Shōichi, Okada Bunkichi, and others.[18] Technically speaking, all three of these groups were united under Tokuda; but individual members of the first two began to be picked off in the factional warfare that proceeded underground for three years. Even the Chinese Communist Party took a hand in trying to bring order into the ranks of their divided comrades.[19] The two main warring factions proved to be the Tokuda-Itō group and the Shida group.

On February 23, 1951, the Party's Fourth National Consultative Conference (IV Zenkyō) was opened underground. At that time Tokuda formally abandoned the "peaceful revolution" line and adopted the militaristic tactics that had proved so disastrous to the Communists' mass base in Japan. The chief proponent of violent measures had been Shida Shigeo; and as a result of his success, Itō, who had long been identified with the "peaceful revolution" line, was forced to write a self-criticism.[20] Itō was thus already on the run when Shida began to attack him in earnest that autumn. According to Ozaki Hotsuki's most recent research on this period (1963), Shida organized the votes at the Fifth National Consultative Conference (October 16–17, 1951) in order to have Itō thrown out of the Political Bureau.

Because of Itō's weakness in the factional battle, it appears today that Tokuda decided to throw him to the wolves. Shida's group was clearly displacing Itō's, and Tokuda himself had shifted to support of the militarist tactics. Sometime in late 1951, a committee headed by Nishizawa Ryūji (of the Shida faction) was appointed to investigate Itō and his past. Nishizawa collected a large amount of derogatory information on Itō, and he publicized this within the Party center in early 1953. Nosaka and his group, who had remained neutral during the battle between Itō and Shida, sided with Shida in 1953. Authorities conclude that the Shida faction had ousted all of Itō's followers from positions of strength by April 1953—well before Tokuda's death.[21]

The stage had thus been secretly set for the biggest shock that ordinary Japanese Communists were to receive during the underground period. On September 21, 1953, *Red Flag* (once again being legally published in Tokyo) ran as its lead story a "Statement Concerning the Disposition of Itō Ritsu."[22] A note stated that the editorial board of *Red Flag* had received the statement *by mail* on September 19; the statement itself was signed by the Central Committee of the Japanese Communist Party. Individual Party members in Japan, who had no knowledge of the struggles within the "main current" faction or of Nishizawa's investigation, could hardly believe the charges against Itō. According to the statement, he had betrayed individual Party members to the enemy, he had degraded the Party's policies into bourgeois policies, he had formed a faction within the Party, he had infiltrated American spies into the Party center, and he had ruined the JCP's agrarian program. The most sensational claim was that he had confessed to having been a police spy during the prewar period and to having sold out his comrades to the police on two different occasions. The Sorge case, however, was not mentioned by name.

Itō's behavior in Toyotama prison was also cited. He had been assigned educational work in jail during 1944 and 1945 (unheard of for a political prisoner); he had written a war poem that served the cause of fascism; and he had written an essay on Japan's agricultural productivity for the government. As a consequence of the Control Commission's investigation (led by Nishizawa) and Itō's own confession, the Central Committee had decided unanimously to remove him from all positions in the Party. At the same time, according to the rules of the Party, the Central Committee resolved to await the next national Consultative Conference in order to propose Itō's formal expulsion from the Party.

The statement of September 21 was all that regular Party members heard about Itō between July 1950 and July 1955. Not until the Sixth Consultative Conference, when Tokuda's death was announced, was Itō formally and unanimously expelled from the Party. Itō's case was not widely discussed because of the excitement generated by Nosaka's return and the news of Tokuda's death. Clearly, however, it was the two men who strode into Meiji Outer Garden along with Nosaka on the night of August 11 who had brought down Itō and inherited his influence: Shida Shigeo and Konno Yojirō. The formation of a new "unity" Secretariat was announced on August 17, 1955: it consisted of Nosaka, Konno, Shida, and Miyamoto. Not long after Shida had been elected to the Secretariat, he decided to tell the press something about his defeated foe. Thus, on September 14, 1955, Shida expanded upon Nishizawa's investigation and gave several new reasons for Itō's purge in 1953. He asserted that Itō had worked as a police spy in 1940 against Ozaki Hotsumi; that he had provided evidence for the prosecution in the Sorge case; and that he had betrayed about 150 Communists to the police in the prewar, wartime, and postwar periods. When asked about Itō's present whereabouts, Shida remarked that he believed Itō "was abroad."[23]

The real meaning of these sensational developments is still being argued in Japan. One view is that they were only a manifestation of power politics within the Communist Party. Professor Maruyama, for example, considers the charges against Itō so hyperbolic as to be an insult to the intelligence. He suggests that the purge of Itō resembles the Beria affair and that it was carried out in the worst Stalinist tradition. (Itō was compared to Beria by the Communists themselves in their statement of September 21, 1953.)[24] Evidence supporting this view is found in the fact that Itō's attacker was Shida Shigeo. Shida differed little from Itō in the way he served the revolutionary cause, and he was expelled from the Party on July 4, 1958, for corruption and Trotskyism.[25] He, too, has "disappeared." It could be, then, that Itō fell victim to his own dangerous game of playing high politics within a Stalinist party; he rose fast and was toppled by his own methods as soon as the aura of success began to leave him.[26]

On the other hand, it is perfectly possible that the most important charges against Itō are correct. Ozaki Hotsuki, in his latest study of the Sorge case, asserts that Nosaka Sanzō once told another Communist that Itō was really guilty of only two things: he betrayed the Sorge ring, and he betrayed certain Communists to SCAP in 1947. (On

February 19, 1947, Itō made a violently anti-U.S. speech following the occupation's interdiction of the general strike the JCP had planned for February 1, 1947. SCAP police arrested Itō, and in order to obtain his release Itō allegedly gave them the names of certain Party members.)[27] The novelist Kishi Yamaji was allowed to publish a short column in *Red Flag* on September 27, 1955, commenting on the recently ended Sixth Consultation Conference. Kishi wrote that he was greatly relieved to see that the Party had finally thrown out Itō, for he had been unable to trust the leadership during the immediate postwar period because of Itō's powerful position. He asserted that those who knew the real Itō knew that he was corrupt and that he had blackened the name of the Party. However, Kishi went on to criticize Nosaka for having allowed only vague declarations about Itō's purge to be made public. "The Party," he wrote, "has failed to credit the common sense of the masses: everybody knows that Itō Ritsu was the one who exposed the Sorge ring."[28]

What Kishi says may be true, but it does not prove that Itō deliberately betrayed the ring; no one, in fact, has ever proved that Itō so much as suspected the ring's existence. He did sell out Kitabayashi Tomo, but he could hardly have guessed what this would lead to.*

It is my own opinion that Itō sought a way out of his difficulties by serving as a police spy in 1940 and 1941, but that he became a devoted Stalinist-type Party leader after 1945. He was purged in the period when a scapegoat had to be found, and the old rumors against him were used to obscure the real reasons for his expulsion; had he remained on top, or had he died early enough to be considered a martyr to the Communist cause (like Tokuda), the charges against him, whether true or false, would never have been printed by the Party. This explanation, however, can no more be confirmed today than any other. There are many stories about Itō's present whereabouts (he would have been fifty years old in 1963). It has been said that he is in Japan under Party arrest, that he died in Japan, that he is in China under arrest, and even that he is in the United States. It has also been said that he was executed in China on Party orders, and this is the rumor most frequently heard in Japan today.

---

* Willoughby suggests that Itō betrayed Kitabayashi "out of malice and jealousy," because he considered her a "party traitor." But there is no evidence that Kitabayashi was a "party traitor" or that Itō thought so, and no one in Japan who knows the case believes that Willoughby's interpretation is accurate. See *Shanghai Conspiracy*, p. 117.

Notes

〰〰

CHAPTER ONE

1. *Gendai-shi shiryō, Zoruge jiken* (Materials on Modern History, The Sorge Incident) (Tokyo: Misuzu Shobō, 1962), 3 volumes (1,835 pages total).

2. "The Sorge Spy Ring—A Case Study in International Espionage in the Far East," released to the press and published in the *Congressional Record*, February 9, 1949, U.S. 81st Congress, 1st Session, Vol. 95, Part 12, Appendix, pp. A705–A723. Cf. Douglas B. Cornell, "Mighty Russian Spy Ring Revealed," *Pacific Stars and Stripes*, Tokyo, February 11, 1949. Also see U.S. Army, Far East Command, Military Intelligence Section, *A Partial Documentation of the Sorge Espionage Case* (Tokyo: "Confidential. Private Printing. Not for Circulation. Prepared for the House of Representative [*sic*]. Committee on Un-American Activities"; Toppan Printing Co. Ltd., May 1, 1950). (Copy in Documents Department, General Library, University of California, Berkeley.)

3. Major General Charles A. Willoughby, *Shanghai Conspiracy, The Sorge Spy Ring* (New York, 1952), p. 39. Because of Willoughby's erratic romanization of Japanese, it is advisable to use his book in conjunction with its Japanese translation: *Sekishoku supai dan no zenbō, Zoruge jiken,* Fukuda Tarō, trans. (Tokyo, 1953).

4. Both books were combined in one volume and published as *Chūgoku shakai no kihon mondai, Ozaki Hotsumi senshū* (Basic Problems of Chinese Society, Selected Works of Ozaki Hotsumi) (Tokyo, 1949), which includes essays on Ozaki by Hosokawa Karoku and Horie Yūichi. *Shina,* the derogatory prewar Japanese word for China, was changed throughout to *Chūgoku,* the term used by the Chinese.

5. See Marius B. Jansen, *The Japanese and Sun Yat-sen* (Cambridge, Mass., 1954).

6. See my *Peasant Nationalism and Communist Power, The Emergence of Revolutionary China, 1937–1945* (Stanford, 1962).

7. Kazama Michitarō, *Aru hangyaku* (A Case of Treason) (Tokyo, 1959), p. 67.

8. Nineteenth interrogation of Ozaki by the Tokkō. *Gendai-shi shiryō,* II, 128.

9. Kawai Teikichi, *Aru kakumeika no kaisō* (Memoirs of a Revolutionary) (Tokyo, 1953), pp. 308–9.

10. See the work of Sassa Hiroo, himself a leading member of the Konoye circle, *Shōwa seiji hishi* (The Tragic History of Shōwa Politics) (Tokyo, 1946), pp. 34–35.

11. See the article by Ozaki Hotsuki, Ozaki Hotsumi's younger half-brother, "Kakumei—densetsu, henkaku, to yutopia" (Revolution—Legend, Reform, and Utopia), *Shisō no kagaku* (The Science of Thought), No. 13 (April 1963), p. 12.

12. Representative of Ozaki's many articles on the New Structure and the East Asian Cooperative Body (see the Bibliography for the complete list) are: (1) " 'Tōa kyōdō tai' no rinen to sono seiritsu no kakkanteki kiso" (The Idea of an "East Asian Cooperative Body" and the Objective Basis for its Realization), *Chūō kōron,* No. 616 (January 1939), pp. 4–18; reprinted in the 75th anniversary issue of *Chūō kōron,* November 1960, pp. 400–411; (2) East Asia Political Research Subcommittee, Shōwa Research Association, *Tōa shinchitsujo no riron to hōsaku* (The Theory and Policy of Establishing the New Order in East Asia) (Tokyo, June 1940); and (3), in English, "The New National Structure," *Contemporary Japan,* IX:10 (October 1940), 1284–92.

13. Aochi, *Gendai-shi no magarikado,* p. 190. Also see Tsurumi Shunsuke, "Yokusan undō no sekkeisha" (Planners of the Assistance Movement), in Science of Thought Research Association, ed., *Tenkō* (Conversion) (Tokyo, 1960), II, 113, n. 28.

14. Kazami Akira, *Konoye naikaku* (The Konoye Cabinet) (Tokyo, 1951), p. 259. Cf. Kiya Ikusaburō, publisher of *Seikai ōrai* (Comings and Goings in the Political World) and a friend of Konoye's, *Konoye kō hibun* (Private Conversations with Prince Konoye) (Takano, Wakayama Prefecture, 1950), pp. 161–64.

15. For a short, perceptive study of Japan's left-wing intelligentsia, see Robert A. Scalapino, "The Left Wing in Japan," *Survey,* No. 43 (August 1962), pp. 102–11.

16. "Prison Memorandum I"; June 8, 1943. *Gendai-shi shiryō,* II, 7.

17. *Ibid.*

18. Lu Hsün, *A-Q seiden (A Q cheng chuan;* The True Story of Ah Q) (Tokyo: International Proletarian Library, Shiroku Shoin, October 1931), translated by Shen Tuan-hsien (pseud. for Hsia Yen), Lin Shou-jen (pseud. for Yamakami Masayoshi), Mizuki Ryōsaku, and Shirakawa Jirō (pseud. for Ozaki Hotsumi).

19. Kazama, *Aru hangyaku,* p. 104. On the "first Shanghai Incident," see China Research Institute, *Gendai Chūgoku jiten* (Tokyo, 1959), p. 259; and W. C. Johnstone, Jr., *The Shanghai Problem* (Stanford, 1937).

20. First published in 1929. I have used the revised edition with the foreword by Malcolm Cowley (New York, 1935).

21. Ozaki Hotsuki, *Zoruge jiken* (The Sorge Incident) (Tokyo, 1963), pp. 113–14.

22. See the important but not wholly accurate memoir by Hans-Otto Meissner, Third Secretary and Chief of Protocol in the German Embassy in Tokyo from July 1936 until the spring of 1939, *The Man With Three Faces* (New York, 1955).

23. *The Schellenberg Memoirs* (London, 1956), Chap. XV, "The Case of Richard Sorge," pp. 175–81. Alan Bullock believes that these memoirs are genuine, and he discusses their history in his introduction to this volume.

24. *Gendai-shi shiryō*, I, 47.

25. R. S. [Richard Sorge], "Die Armeerevolte in Tokio," *Zeitschrift für Geopolitik* (Heidelberg and Berlin), XIII:5 (May 1936), 307–17; "Japanische Agrarfragen," *ibid.*, Part I, XIV:1 (January 1937), 18–24; Part II, XIV:2 (February 1937), 132–38; Part III, XIV:3 (March 1937), 211–21.

26. Cf. Meissner, *The Man With Three Faces*; and the article by Ikoma Yoshitoshi, Professor of German at Tokyo Foreign Languages University and the prosecution's translator in their interrogations of Sorge after his arrest, "Zoruge kaisō" (Recollections of Sorge), *Misuzu*, IV:3 (March 1962), 12–22.

27. Cf. Matsumoto Shin'ichi's epilogue to *Aijō wa furu hoshi no gotoku* (Love Is Like a Falling Star) [Ozaki's letters to his wife from prison] (Tokyo: Sekai Hyōron Sha ed., 1946); and Kazama, *Aru hangyaku*.

28. See Kainō Michitaka, "Dokuso kaisen no nazo" (The Puzzle of the Outbreak of the Russo-German War), *Asahi Journal*, V:8 (February 24, 1963), 56–57; and Otto D. Tolischus, *Tokyo Record* (New York, 1943), p. 251 (diary entry for September 14, 1941).

29. For the Russians' statements, see *Gendai-shi shiryō*, I, 102.

30. See "Zoruge, omae wa nanimono da!" (Who Was Sorge?), *Shūkan sankei*, May 15, 1961, pp. 66–69. Miyake Hanako is the pseudonym for Ishii Hanako; she was employed in 1935 at the Rheingold Cabaret, owned by the German restaurateur Ketel, and Sorge met her there. See *Ningen Zoruge, Aijin Miyake Hanako no shuki* (The Man Sorge, Memoirs of His Mistress Miyake Hanako) (Tokyo, 1949).

31. Shigemitsu Mamoru, *Shōwa no dōran* (The Upheavals of the Shōwa Era) (Tokyo, 1952), II, 92–98. Full details of the Ozaki case are omitted from the English translation of Shigemitsu's memoirs, but Ozaki's treason is mentioned in the English version. See *Japan and Her Destiny*, O. White, trans. (London, 1958), pp. 157, 245. For an analysis committed to the view that Ozaki and the Shōwa Research Association contributed materially to Japan's losing the war, see Mitamura Takeo (formerly of the Home Ministry Police

Bureau), *Sensō to kyōsan-shugi, Shōwa seiji hiroku* (War and Communism, the Secret Record of Shōwa Politics) (Tokyo, 1950).

32. Horie Yūichi, "Chūgoku hyōronka to shite no Ozaki Hotsumi" (Ozaki Hotsumi as China Critic), in *Chūgoku shakai no kihon mondai*, p. 303.

33. Cf. Saionji Kinkazu, *Kizoku no taijō* (Exit of the Nobility) (Tokyo, 1951), pp. 45–56; Inukai Ken, "Yōsukō wa ima mo nagarete iru" (The Yangtze Still Flows), *Bungei shunjū*, June 1959, pp. 260–75; Kazami Akira, "Ozaki-kun no omoide" (Recollections of Ozaki), epilogue in the Mikasa Bunko edition of *Aijō wa furu hoshi no gotoku* (Tokyo, 1951), Volume I; *Idai naru aijō* (The Great Love) (Tokyo, 1949), the record of the Ozaki-Matsumoto [Shin'ichi] Memorial Meeting, held in the lecture hall of Meiji University, November 27, 1948; and Kazama, *Aru hangyaku*, p. 157.

34. See Suda Teiichi, "Nitchū mondai ni shōgai o kakete, Kazami Akira no hito to shisō" (A Life Staked on the Sino-Japanese Problem; Kazami Akira, the Man and His Thought), *Sekai*, No. 207 (March 1963), pp. 264–72.

35. "Chō Gaku-ryō kūdeta no igi, Shina shakai no naibu-teki mujun no bakuhatsu" (The Significance of Chang Hsüeh-liang's Coup d'Etat, the Explosion of the Internal Contradictions in Chinese Society), *Chūō kōron*, No. 590 (January 1937), pp. 406–14.

36. Meissner, *The Man With Three Faces*, pp. 186–91.

37. *Shanghai Conspiracy*, p. 93.

38. Aochi Shin, "Janarizumu to kyōfu" (Journalism and Terror), *Shisō*, No. 360 (June 1954), pp. 67–71; and [A Foreign Correspondent], "Covering the War From Tokyo," *Contemporary Japan*, VII:2 (September 1938), 269–79. Otto Tolischus's extraordinarily brutal treatment at the hands of the police before his repatriation in 1942 probably owed something to the Sorge case, for by that time the Tokkō were convinced that all reporters were espionage agents for one or another of Japan's enemies.

39. Answer to question 30, interrogation number 12; *Gendai-shi shiryō*, I, 476.

40. Matsumoto Shin'ichi, "Kaji-shi no 'Ozaki Hotsumi ron' " (Mr. Kaji's "Essay on Ozaki Hotsumi"), *Jinmin hyōron* (The People's Review), III:6 (November 1947), 45.

41. The best study is Furuta Hikaru, "Dai-ni-ji taisenka no shisō-teki jōkyō" (Ideological Conditions During World War II) in *Kindai Nihon shisō shi* (Tokyo, 1956), III, 679–733, particularly pp. 704–5.

42. The most thorough analysis of "conversion" for political reasons in Japan was made by the Science of Thought Research Association between 1954 and 1959. In a later chapter we will make use of Tsurumi Shunsuke's study of Ozaki's career as an instance of *gisō tenkō*. See Shisō no Kagaku Kenkyū Kai, ed., *Tenkō* (Tokyo, 1959), in three volumes.

43. Testimony by Willoughby. U.S. 82d Congress, First Session, House

Committee on Un-American Activities, *Hearings on American Aspects of the Richard Sorge Spy Case* (Washington, 1951), pp. 1162–63.

44. *Aijō wa furu hoshi no gotoku*, p. 121.

CHAPTER TWO

1. Kyoto University, National History Research Institute, ed., *Nihon kindai-shi jiten* (A Dictionary of the Modern History of Japan) (Tokyo, 1958), pp. 200, 204, 358–59; Ozaki Hotsuki, *Zoruge jiken*, pp. 10–22.

2. See, for example, Leonard Woolf, *Growing* (London, 1961), the second volume of his autobiography, in which he recounts his experiences as a colonial administrator in Ceylon.

3. *Gendai-shi shiryō*, II, 5.

4. Matsumoto Shin'ichi, "Ozaki Hotsumi ni tsuite" (Concerning Ozaki Hotsumi), quoted in Kazama, *Aru hangyaku*, p. 9.

5. *Zoruge jiken*, p. 21. For conditions in Taiwan, also see Ozaki Hotsuki, *Ikite iru yuda* (The Living Judas) (Tokyo, 1959), pp. 26–32; and *Nihon kindai-shi jiten*, p. 626.

6. Ozaki Hotsumi, "Tenkōsho I," in *Gendai-shi shiryō*, II, 5; Kazama, *Aru hangyaku*, pp. 3–4. For Hirata Atsutane, see D. M. Brown, *Nationalism in Japan* (Berkeley, Calif., 1955), pp. 65–66.

7. Letter of July 20, 1943. *Aijō wa furu hoshi no gotoku*, p. 85.

8. "Share-otoko Ozaki Hotsumi" (Ozaki Hotsumi, a Bel Esprit), in *Bungei shunjū*, June 1955, pp. 122–26.

9. Ozaki Hotsuki, *Zoruge jiken*, p. 19.

10. Ichinose Masayuki, *Nihon kyōsantō* (The Japanese Communist Party) (Tokyo, 1954), pp. 46ff.

11. One of the best political and sociological interpretations of this period is Robert A. Scalapino, *Democracy and the Party Movement in Prewar Japan* (Berkeley, Calif., 1953), Chapter 8, "The Rise and Decline of the Left."

12. *Gendai-shi shiryō*, II, 6.

13. Noel F. Busch, *Two Minutes to Noon* (New York, 1962), p. 54.

14. *Ibid.*, p. 111.

15. Eduard Bernstein, *Ferdinand Lassalle, eine Würdigung des Lehrers und Kampfers* (Berlin, 1919).

16. Kazama, *Aru hangyaku*, p. 43.

17. Quoted in *ibid.*, p. 27. Also see Matsumoto Shin'ichi, "Nihon teikoku-shugi to Ozaki Hotsumi" (Japanese Imperialism and Ozaki Hotsumi), *Sekai*, December 1946, p. 86.

18. Kazama, *Aru hangyaku*, p. 43; Ozaki Hotsuki, *Zoruge jiken*, p. 26.

19. See Asahi Shimbun, Political-Economic Department Associates, ed., *Nihon o ugokasu sambyakunin* (The Three Hundred Men Who Move Ja-

pan) (Tokyo, 1948), pp. 131–33, under "Morito Tatsuo." Also see *Nihon kindai-shi jiten,* p. 597; and Hugh Borton, *Japan's Modern Century* (New York, 1955), p. 318.

20. *Gendai-shi shiryō,* II, 6–7.

21. Kazama, *Aru hangyaku,* p. 45; Ozaki Hotsuki, *Ikite iru yuda,* p. 33.

22. The primary purpose of the seminar was to explore Bukharin's further development of Lenin's theory of imperialism. For a thorough analysis of Bukharin's importance in this period, see Sidney Heitman, "Between Lenin and Stalin: Nikolai Bukharin," in *Revisionism, Essays on the History of Marxist Ideas,* L. Labedz, ed. (New York, 1962), pp. 77–90.

23. *Gendai-shi shiryō,* II, 7.

24. Ozaki Hotsumi, "Rintenki o kiku" (Listening to the Rotary Press), *Ichikō dōsōkai kaihō* (Bulletin of the Ichikō Alumni Association), No. 5, June 15, 1927, pp. 24–27.

25. Epilogue in Mitamura Takeo, *Sensō to kyōsanshugi, Shōwa seiji hiroku* (War and Communism, Confidential History of Shōwa Politics) (Tokyo, 1950), pp. 339–40.

26. "Tenkōsho I," *Gendai-shi shiryō,* II, 7; and interrogation, II, 100. For Rōdō Hyōgikai, see Scalapino, *Democracy and the Party Movement,* pp. 327, 331, 335.

27. Kazama, *Aru hangyaku,* p. 60.

28. *Ibid.,* pp. 53–58; Ozaki Hotsuki, *Zoruge jiken,* pp. 30–32.

29. Letter of October 15, 1943. *Aijō wa furu hoshi no gotoku,* pp. 116–17.

30. Kazama, *Aru hangyaku,* p. 57; Ozaki Hotsuki, *Zoruge jiken,* p. 32.

31. Matsumoto, *Jinmin hyōron,* III:6 (November 1947), 45; Kawai Teikichi, *Aru kakumeika no kaisō,* p. 165.

32. When the Ōhara Institute lost its unlimited capital source in 1937, it terminated the serviecs of its paid researchers and moved to Tokyo. Most parts of its library and offices were destroyed in the bombings of 1945, but the Institute began reconstruction after the war. In 1949 it was absorbed by Hōsei University and reorganized as an autonomous research organization within the university.

33. Kazama, *Aru hangyaku,* pp. 48–49, 60–61.

34. Letter of March 23, 1944. *Aijō wa furu hoshi no gotoku,* p. 163.

CHAPTER THREE

1. Figures supplied by Liu Shao-ch'i to Nym Wales (pseud. for Helen Foster Snow) in the nineteen-thirties. *The Chinese Labor Movement* (New York, 1945), pp. 60–61. John Lewis records slightly different, but comparable, figures—i.e., 950 for 1925 and 57,967 for 1927. *Leadership in Communist China* (Ithaca, N.Y., 1963), p. 110.

2. See, for example, Liang Hsiao-ming, *Wu-sa yün-tung* (May 30 Movement) (Peking, 1956), p. 14.

3. G. E. Sokolsky, *The China Year Book 1926–27* (Tientsin, 1927), p. 958.

4. F. L. Hawks Pott, *A Short History of Shanghai* (Shanghai, 1928), pp. 290–91.

5. Quoted in Harold R. Isaacs, *The Tragedy of the Chinese Revolution,* 2d rev. ed. (Stanford, 1961), p. 272.

6. For a valuable study of the May 30 Movement and of the anti-Japanese boycotts from a Japanese point of view, see Japanese Chamber of Commerce, Shanghai, *Hōjin bōseki higyō jiken to gosanjū jiken oyobi kakuchi no dōyō* (Japanese Spinning Industry Strikes and the May 30 Incident; Disturbances Elsewhere) (Shanghai, September 30, 1925), Volume I [microfilm, East Asiatic Library, University of California, Berkeley].

7. S. T. King and D. K. Lieu, *China's Cotton Industry* (Shanghai, 1929), p. 3.

8. Spinning mills were not, of course, the only type of industrial investment made in China by Japan or Great Britain. There is an extensive bibliography on this subject; for one important sector, steel, see Marius Jansen, "Yawata, Hanyehping, and the Twenty-One Demands," *Pacific Historical Review,* XXIII (1954), 31–48.

9. Treaty of February 6, 1922, art. I, par. 4. See G. E. Hubbard, *British Far Eastern Policy* (New York, 1943), p. 85.

10. See, for example, Sir Meyrick Hewlett, former British consul at Amoy, *Forty Years in China* (London, 1944), p. 159.

11. See Paul A. Varg, *Missionaries, Chinese, and Diplomats; The American Protestant Missionary Movement in China, 1890–1952* (Princeton, 1958).

12. E. O. Hauser, *Shanghai: City for Sale* (New York, 1940), p. 149.

13. Kazama, *Aru hangyaku,* p. 63; Ozaki Hotsuki, *Zoruge jiken,* p. 71.

14. Letter of May 3, 1944, *Aijō wa furu hoshi no gotoku,* pp. 193–94.

15. Kazama, *Aru hangyaku,* pp. 66–67.

16. Inukai Ken, "Yōsukō wa ima mo nagarete iru" (The Yangtze Still Flows), *Bungei shunjū,* June 1959, p. 270.

17. Kazama, *Aru hangyaku,* p. 70.

18. Interrogation, July 21, 1942; *Gendai-shi shiryō,* II, 315.

19. Ozaki Hotsuki, *Zoruge jiken,* pp. 72–73.

20. *Gendai-shi shiryō,* II, 316.

21. *Ta-chung wen-i* appeared intermittently between September 20, 1928, and June 1, 1930 (Vol. 2, No. 6). Yü Ta-fu was editor only until mid-1929. See C. T. Hsia, *A History of Modern Chinese Fiction 1917–1957* (New Haven, 1961), p. 110; and Ozaki Hotsuki, *Zoruge jiken,* p. 74.

22. *Gendai-shi shiryō,* II, 316.

23. For an analysis of *Senki* and its influence, see Ara Masato, *et al., Shōwa bungaku shi* (History of Shōwa Literature) (Tokyo, 1956), I, pp. 54–58.

24. *Selected Works of Lu Hsün* (Peking, 1959), III, p. 22. For the split in leftist literary ranks, see C. T. Hsia, *op. cit.,* pp. 49–50. For Lu Hsün's views on proletarian literature, see T. A. Hsia, *Enigma of the Five Martyrs, A*

Study of the Leftist Literary Movement in Modern China (Berkeley: Center for Chinese Studies, 1962), pp. 42–43.

25. Quoted by Ozaki Hotsuki, *Zoruge jiken*, p. 80.

26. *Gendai-shi shiryō,* II, 319.

27. Ozaki Hotsuki, *Zoruge jiken,* pp. 74–76. Also see *Gendai Chūgoku jiten,* pp. 50, 300. In 1929, T'ao organized the I-shu Chü-she (Art Dramatic Society) with Hsia Yen, Feng Nai-ch'ao, Cheng Po-chi, and others. This organization was a leader in the leftist theater movement in China.

28. The complexities of this incident, including the possibility that the victims may have been betrayed to the police by the CCP itself, are thoroughly and sensitively analyzed by T. A. Hsia in *Enigma of the Five Martyrs* (Berkeley: Center for Chinese Studies, 1962). (The so-called Li Li-san Line was overturned within the Party at its Fourth Plenum, January 15, 1931. Three organizations were filled with Li Li-san followers: the League Against Imperialism, the International Red Aid [MOPR], and the Young Communist League. All three were purged by the CCP.)

29. *Hōki,* Ou Tso-ch'i, trans. (Tokyo: International Proletarian Library, Shiroku Shoin, October 1931). See also *Gendai-shi shiryō,* III, 706.

30. Lu Hsün, *A-Q seiden* (The True Story of Ah Q), Lin Shou-jen (Rin Shu-jin), trans. (Tokyo: International Proletarian Library, October 1931). Cited in *Gendai-shi shiryō,* III, 705–6. This particular translation is included in the exhaustive bibliography of Lu's work and researches on him by Shen P'eng-nien. See *Lu Hsün yen-chiu tzu-liao pien-mu* (Bibliography of Lu Hsün Research Materials) (Shanghai, 1958), p. 102, with Lin Shou-jen listed as translator. Yamakami later published his translation of *The True Story of Ah Q* separately under his real name, and it also appeared in the Kaizō Company's collected works of Lu Hsün (1936–37).

31. See Gunther Nollau, *International Communism and World Revolution,* (London, 1961), pp. 154–56.

32. Inukai Ken, "Yōsukō wa ima mo nagarete iru," p. 270. Mizuno's translation, based on Chou Fu-hai's text and commentary, was entitled *San-min shugi kaisetsu* (Explanation of the Three Principles of the People) (Tokyo: Iwanami Shinsho, 1939).

33. He was elected to the Central Committee at the JCP's Seventh Congress (July 1958), and reelected to the Central Committee at its Eighth Congress (July 1961). Anzai was born May 20, 1905, and was four years younger than Ozaki. See Kōan Chōsa Chō (Public Safety Police Investigation Office), *Nihon kyōsantō dai hakkai taikai ni tsuite* (Concerning the Japanese Communist Party's Eighth Congress) (Tokyo, September 1961), pp. 103, 247.

34. Nankanishi Ko, *Chūgoku Kyōsantō shi* (Tokyo, 1949).

35. *Tōa dōbun shoin daigaku shi* (History of the East Asia Common Script University) (Tokyo: Koyūkai [literally, "Friends of Shanghai Association"], privately published, July 1955), pp. 244, 321. For Anzai, see p. 320;

for Nakanishi and Kawamura, p. 321; and for Mizuno, p. 322. The primary sources of information on Ozaki's friends at Tōa Dōbun are his replies to police interrogations, in which he mentioned Mizuno, Nakanishi, Anzai, and Katō. *Gendai-shi shiryō,* II, 100. (The character written down by the police for Katō's given name is read "Yonetarō." This error was repeated by Ozaki Hotsuki in *Zoruge jiken,* p. 80, but caught by Kazama in *Aru hangyaku,* p. 70. There was no "Katō Yonetarō" at Tōa Dōbun.) Kawamura is mentioned elsewhere in Ozaki's testimony in connection with the spy ring's activities. A sixth friend of Ozaki's, Shirai Yukikara, supposedly a student at Tōa Dō-bun, is named by Kazama (p. 70) and by Ozaki Hotsuki (p. 81), but I have been unable to identify him. He is not listed as a student at Tōa Dōbun in this period, but he undoubtedly did exist: he is mentioned, along with Ozaki and others, in the dedication of Nakanishi Ko's *Chūgoku kyōsantō shi,* and Kawai Teikichi mentions him in *Aru kakumeika no kaisō* (Reminiscences of a Revolutionary), p. 11.

36. Kasumigaseki Society, *Gendai Chūgoku jinmei jiten* (Biographical Dictionary of Modern China) (Tokyo, 1957), p. 30; *Gendai-shi shiryō,* II, 317.

37. *Gendai-shi shiryō,* II, 100, 317.

38. Foreign Ministry, Asia Bureau, *Shina oyobi Manshū ni okeru kyōsan undō gaikyō* (A Survey of the Communist Movement in China and Manchuria) (Tokyo, December 1932), pp. 74–76 on the Nisshi Tōsō Dōmei. A copy of this document is in the East Asiatic Library, University of California, Berkeley (EAL Film M-37). Nishizato is also named by Kawai as a leader of the Struggle League; *Aru kakumeika no kaisō* (1953), p. 11.

39. Foreign Ministry, *Shina oyobi Manshū,* p. 75; *Tōa dōbun shoin daigaku shi,* p. 318.

40. Kazama, *Aru hangyaku,* pp. 71–73; Foreign Ministry, *Shina oyobi Manshū,* p. 75.

41. Kawai Teikichi, *Aru kakumeika no kaisō,* p. 10.

42. Foreign Ministry, *Shina oyobi Manshū,* p. 76.

CHAPTER FOUR

1. According to the Shanghai Municipal Police, the Shanghai Zeitgeist Bookstore opened in November 1930. See U.S. Army, Far East Command, Military Intelligence Section, *A Partial Documentation of the Sorge Espionage Case* (Tokyo, 1950), p. 47. Ozaki, however, recalled going there to browse as early as the summer of 1929, and this date is probably more accurate because it also matches Kawai's recollection. *Gendai-shi shiryō,* II, 319; Kawai Teikichi, *Aru kakumeika no kaisō,* p. 21; Kazama, *Aru hangyaku,* p. 76.

2. Nollau, *International Communism and World Revolution,* pp. 122, 184–85.

3. Interrogation of July 22, 1942; *Gendai-shi shiryō,* II, 319.

4. *Ibid.*

5. Letter of October 28, 1943; *Aijō wa furu hoshi no gotoku*, p. 127.

6. Agnes Smedley, *Onna hitori daichi o yuku*, Shirakawa Jirō, trans. (Tokyo: Kaizō-sha, August 1934; Tokyo: Kantō-sha, October 1951; Tokyo: Kadogawa Shoten, 2 volumes, December 1957 and January 1958).

7. Kantō-sha ed., p. 1. Ozaki appears to suggest that this was his first meeting with Smedley, but that is contradicted by his own statements elsewhere and also by Kawai; he was probably indulging in an author's embellishments.

8. Nohara Shirō, "Sumedore" (Smedley), *Gendai Chūgoku jiten*, p. 353.

9. G. D. Overstreet and M. Windmiller, *Communism in India* (Berkeley, 1959), pp. 36–37.

10. Agnes Smedley, "Indien als Entscheidener Faktor der Weltpolitik," *Zeitschrift für Geopolitik*, II:6 (June 1925), 385–403.

11. Facsimile of Shanghai Municipal Police file cards, reproduced in *A Partial Documentation of the Sorge Espionage Case*, facing p. 27. These cards contain several inaccuracies, including Smedley's date of birth, period of residence in Shanghai after 1934, etc.

12. In 1937 Ozaki translated and published one other manuscript by Agnes Smedley, a tract on the importation of opium into China, but he probably obtained it from her in 1932 or during their one-day meeting in 1934. Ozaki used his pseudonym. See Agnes Smedley, "Makao—'Tōyō no shinju'" (Macao, "Pearl of the Orient"), Shirakawa Jirō, trans., *Chūō kōron* No. 600 (special number), October 1937, pp. 414–22.

13. Willoughby, *Shanghai Conspiracy*, pp. 243–50.

14. U.S. 82d Congress, First Session, House Committee on Un-American Activities, *Hearings on American Aspects of the Richard Sorge Spy Case* (Washington, 1951), Willoughby testimony, August 22, 23, 1951; pp. 1161 *et seq.*

15. Agnes Smedley, "The Tokyo Martyrs," *Far East Spotlight* V:3 (March 1949), 3. (*Far East Spotlight* was the organ of the Committee for a Democratic Far Eastern Policy.)

16. See "Zoruge jiken to reisen" (The Sorge Incident and the Cold War), *Gendai-shi shiryō*, I, 549–55; International Military Tribunal for the Far East, *Proceedings*, pp. 38, 413–88 (defense interrogation of Lt. Col. Fritz von Petersdorf, former Assistant German Military Attaché, Tokyo, concerning Richard Sorge; and continuous Russian prosecutor's objections); and U.S. Senate, 82d Congress, First Session, Committee on the Judiciary, *Institute of Pacific Relations Hearings* (Washington, 1951), Part II, pp. 499–505 (testimony of former Japanese prosecutor Yoshikawa Mitsusada concerning the Sorge case).

17. *Battle Hymn of China* (New York, 1943), p. 10.

18. *Gendai-shi shiryō*, I, 155.

NOTES TO PAGES 67–84

19. *Ibid.,* 160.

20. *Ibid.,* 207–8.

21. *Ibid.,* 214.

22. *Ibid.,* 215.

23. *Ibid.,* 216.

24. *Ibid.,* 218.

25. *Ibid.,* 220.

26. *Ibid.,* 139.

27. *Ibid.,* 140.

28. *Ibid.,* 8.

29. *Ibid.,* 141–42.

30. *Ibid.,* 153.

31. David Dallin, quoting his mysterious "D Papers" (anonymous informants), *Soviet Espionage* (New Haven, 1955), p. 89; Ozaki Hotsuki, *Zoruge jiken,* pp. 54–55.

32. *Shin Doitsu teikokushugi,* Fuwa Rinzō, trans. (Tokyo, May 1929); see Ozaki Hotsuki, *Zoruge jiken,* p. 57.

33. *Gendai-shi shiryō,* I, 222.

34. *Ibid.,* 221–22.

35. *Ibid.,* 201.

36. The best study of traditional German attitudes toward the Far East as well as the shift to a pro-Japanese policy under the Nazis is Ernst L. Presseisen, *Germany and Japan, A Study in Totalitarian Diplomacy* (The Hague, 1958).

37. *Gendai-shi shiryō,* I, 158. Also see F. F. Liu, *A Military History of Modern China, 1924–1949* (Princeton, 1956), pp. 74–75.

38. *Gendai-shi shiryō,* I, 166.

39. *Ibid.,* II, 321. Kawai, in his memoirs, remembers Yang as "Chiang." *Aru kakumeika no kaisō,* pp. 52ff.

40. *A Partial Documentation of the Sorge Espionage Case,* Appendix, pp. 23–25; Kazama, *Aru hangyaku,* pp. 266–67.

41. *A Partial Documentation,* Appendix, p. 23.

42. *Aru kakumeika no kaisō,* pp. 54–55.

43. *Ibid.,* p. 55.

44. *Gendai-shi shiryō,* I, 160.

45. See W. C. Johnstone, *The Shanghai Problem,* pp. 284ff.

46. *Gendai-shi shiryō,* I, 5, 18; III, 677–82, 704.

47. *Ibid.,* I, 160.

48. *Shanghai Conspiracy,* p. 281.

CHAPTER FIVE

1. See Kinoshita Junji, *Otto to yobareru Nihonjin* (A Japanese Called Otto) (Tokyo, 1963), Act I, scene 4, pp. 74–76. The play was first performed in Sankei Hall, Osaka, June 5, 1962; it was given a total of 52 performances during 1962 in Osaka, Kobe, Kyoto, Nagoya, and Tokyo. It was first published in *Sekai,* No. 199 (July 1962), pp. 209–42; and No. 200 (August 1962),

pp. 393–404. The Chikuma Shobō edition (March 1963), used here, includes a note by the author and two other articles on the play. Kinoshita acknowledges his use of the works of Kazama, Kawai, and Miyake Hanako in writing the play.

2. Kazama, *Aru hangyaku,* p. 95.

3. *Gendai-shi shiryō,* II, 8.

4. Kawai, *Aru kakumeika,* p. 53; Kinoshita, *Otto to yobareru Nihonjin,* pp. 22–23.

5. *Gendai-shi shiryō,* II, 8.

6. *Ibid.,* 9.

7. *Ibid.,* I, 120.

8. *Ibid.,* II, 107.

9. *Ibid.,* 9.

10. Fujiwara Akira, "Kūdetā to guntai" (The Coup d'Etat and the Military), *Asahi Journal,* III:52 (December 24, 1961), 4.

11. Kazama, *Aru hangyaku,* p. 110. Also see Hosokawa Karoku, "Shosai no omoide" (Memories from my Study), *Shisō,* March 1954, p. 111.

12. Hosokawa, "Shosai no omoide," p. 111.

13. *Gendai-shi shiryō,* II, 9.

14. *Ibid.,* I, 14; II, 325; Kawai, *Aru kakumeika,* pp. 167–70; Kazama, *Aru hangyaku,* pp. 110–11.

15. *Gendai-shi shiryō,* I, 28; Twenty-first police interrogation of Ozaki, March 7, 1942, *ibid.,* II, 211; sixth prosecutor's interrogation of Ozaki, August 12, 1942, *ibid,* 326–27; Ozaki Hotsuki, *Zoruge jiken,* p. 98; and Kazama, *Aru hangyaku,* p. 119.

16. *Gendai-shi shiryō,* I, 209.

17. Tenth examining judge's interrogation of Sorge, July 28, 1942, *ibid.,* 348.

18. *Ibid.,* I, 12, 43–44; III, 621–31, 635–53.

19. *Ibid.,* I, 144.

20. *Ibid.,* III, 315.

21. *Ibid.*

22. *Ibid.,* 308.

23. The primary sources on Miyagi are *Gendai-shi shiryō,* I, 10–11, 57–58; III, 249–324, 345–422; and his confession, III, 327–42.

24. *Ibid.,* I, 144, 449.

25. Willoughby lists Sorge's employers, in addition to the *Frankfurter Zeitung,* as "the *Bergen* [Norway?] *Kurier,* the *Technische Rundschau* and the *Amsterdam Handelsblatt.*" *Shanghai Conspiracy,* p. 46. The first two are misreadings of the Japanese court records, and the Dutch word for "commercial newspaper" is misspelled. For Sorge's own statement, see the tenth prosecutor's interrogation (July 28, 1942), question five, in *Gendai-shi shiryō,*

I, 348. Until 1933 the *Börsen Zeitung* was known as the *Börsen Kurier,* and Sorge occasionally called it by that name. Willoughby's translator mistook the Japanese reading of *Börsen Zeitung*—i.e., *"Beruzen Tsaitsungu"*—to mean the city of Bergen, Norway. The *Tägliche Rundschau* was confiscated by the Nazis in December 1933; for Sorge's comments on it, see *Gendai-shi shiryō,* I, 229.

26. *Gendai-shi shiryō,* I, 348.

27. *Ibid.,* III, 317.

28. *Ibid.,* II, 211.

29. Ozaki Hotsuki, *Zoruge jiken,* p. 100.

30. Kazama, *Aru hangyaku,* pp. 119–20.

31. Aochi Shin, *Gendai-shi no magarikado,* p. 188.

32. *Gendai-shi shiryō,* II, 106–8.

33. *Ibid.,* 10–11.

34. Various English translations for the name of this organization have appeared. In an English language article for *Contemporary Japan,* Ozaki is identified as a member of the "Board of Inquiry on Oriental Questions, Tokyo Asahi Shimbun." See Ozaki Hotsumi, "Japan's Friends in China," *Contemporary Japan* IV:2 (September 1935), 252–58. However, at the Yosemite Conference of the Institute of Pacific Relations, Ozaki was listed as a member of the "Asahi Institute for the Far East." See Ozaki Hotsumi, *Recent Developments in Sino-Japanese Relations,* prepared for the Sixth Conference of the Institute of Pacific Relations, Yosemite, California, August 15–29, 1936 (Tokyo: Japanese Council Papers No. 14, 1936). Both of these organizations are, in fact, the Tōa Mondai Chōsa Kai.

35. Kazama, *Aru hangyaku,* p. 137; *Asahi shimbun nanajūnen shōshi* (A Short History of Seventy Years of the Asahi Newspapers) (Tokyo, 1949), p. 235.

36. Kazama, *Aru hangyaku,* pp. 121–22.

37. Moriyama, "Share-otoko Ozaki Hotsumi," *Bungei shunjū,* June 1955, p. 123; *Gendai-shi shiryō,* II, 277.

38. Tokyo: Asahi Shimbun Sha, June 1936.

39. Tokyo Asahi Shimbun, East Asia Problems Investigation Association, ed., *Utsuri-yuku Shina,* Volume One of the series *Asahi jikyoku tokuhon* (Asahi Readers on the Current Situation) (Tokyo: Asahi Shimbun Sha, February 1937), Chapters 7–9, pp. 205–99.

40. Ozaki Hotsumi, "Hoku-Shi jihen no ato ni kuru mono" (Things to Come After the North China Emergency), *Chūō kōron,* No. 573 (August 1935), pp. 97–108; and "Tai-Shi seisaku no suishinryoku to sono genkai" (The Force Behind Our China Policy and Its Limits), *Chūō kōron,* No. 574 (September 1935), pp. 64–70.

41. *Gendai-shi shiryō,* I, 129.

42. *Ibid.,* I, 210; II, 109.

43. *Ibid.,* I, 178.

44. Ozaki Hotsuki, *Zoruge jiken,* pp. 178–79.

45. Information on Clausen is contained in *Gendai-shi shiryō,* III, 3–245, with a useful police synopsis on pp. 132–39. For Sorge's information on other espionage groups in China during the 1930–32 period, see Volume I, pp. 167–70.

46. *Gendai-shi shiryō,* III, 151.

47. *Ibid.,* 456.

48. Max Clausen, *ibid.,* 151, 232–33; Anna Clausen, *ibid.,* 456.

49. For the interrogation of Anna Clausen by the police and other documents, see *ibid.,* 425–77.

50. *Ibid.,* I, 188.

51. *Ibid.,* III, 159–60.

52. *Ibid.,* I, 186.

53. *Ibid.,* 178, 187–90.

54. See Günther (Guenther) Stein, *Made in Japan* (London, 1935); *Far East in Ferment* (London, 1936); *The Challenge of Red China* (New York, 1945); and *The World the Dollar Built* (London, 1952). The last-named work was translated and published in East Germany (*Amerika ist anders,* East Berlin, 1956) and also in Japan (*Doru no uchi-tateta sekai,* Tokyo, 1954).

55. *Gendai-shi shiryō,* I, 86.

56. *Ibid.,* 192.

57. Question 26, *ibid.,* 358.

58. *Shanghai Conspiracy,* p. 77; U.S. Senate, 82d Congress, 2d Session, Committee on the Judiciary, *Institute of Pacific Relations Hearings* (Washington, 1952), Part 2, pp. 353–55, 370–72, 400–401.

59. *Ibid.,* pp. 400–401.

60. *New York Times,* August 11, 1951, p. 5.

61. Sorge: *Gendai-shi shiryō,* I, 146, 191. Clausen: *ibid.,* III, 69–70, 157.

62. *Ibid.,* I, 146.

63. *Institute of Pacific Relations Hearings,* Part 2, pp. 371–72. Ōhashi was questioned on May 2, 1949. Willoughby also misspells Ōhashi's name.

64. *This Deception* (New York, 1951), p. 333. Mrs. Massing is the former wife of Gerhart Eisler. For her comments on Sorge in his Frankfurt days and in Moscow, see her Chapter 5, pp. 68–82.

65. *Gendai-shi shiryō,* I, 189.

66. *Ibid.,* III, 398–99.

67. Kawai's full career could easily fill another book. The sources for the items mentioned here are Kawai, *Aru kakumeika no kaisō* (The Memoirs of a Revolutionary), *passim*; Ozaki Hotsuki, *Ikite iru yuda,* pp. 82–86; Ozaki Hotsuki, *Zoruge jiken,* pp. 103–4; Kazama, *Aru hangyaku,* p. 127; and *Gendai-shi shiryō,* I, 14–15, 145–46, and III, 683–85.

68. *Gendai-shi shiryō*, I, 83, 189. The police mistakenly wrote his name "Shinohara" on p. 189.

69. *Ibid.*, II, 377–78.

70. See W. L. Holland and K. L. Mitchell, eds., *Problems of the Pacific, 1936; Proceedings of the Sixth Conference of the Institute of Pacific Relations, Yosemite National Park, California, 15–29 August 1936* (Chicago, 1936), pp. 436–37.

71. Japanese Council, IPR, Data Paper No. 14, pp. 10–11. Ozaki's English-language paper was based on several of his earlier Japanese articles, particularly "Tai-Shi seisaku no suishinryoku to sono genkai" (The Force Behind Our China Policy and Its Limits), *Chūō kōron*, No. 574 (September 1935), pp. 64–70.

72. Data Paper No. 14, pp. 4–5.

73. *Ibid.*, pp. 3–4.

74. *Ibid.*, p. 4

75 Saionji Kinkazu, *Kizoku no taijō* (Exit of the Nobility) (Tokyo, 1951), pp. 49–50; Interrogation of Saionji, March 16, 1942, *Gendai-shi shiryō*, III, 487.

CHAPTER SIX

1. Twenty-second interrogation of Ozaki, March 8, 1942, *Gendai-shi shiryō*, II, 220–21; Ozaki Hotsuki, *Zoruge jiken*, p. 111; Kazama, *Aru hangyaku*, pp. 143–44; Oda Toshiyo, *Konoye shintaisei no zenbō* (A Full View of the Konoye New Structure) (Tokyo, 1940), pp. 274–75; Sassa Hiroo, *Shōwa seiji hisshi* (The Tragic History of Shōwa Politics) (Tokyo, 1946), pp. 35–36; and Aochi Shin, "Janarizumu to kyōfu," *Shisō*, June 1954, p. 70.

2. Aochi, "Janarizumu to kyōfu," p. 70.

3. *Japan and Her Destiny*, p. 157.

4. Yabe Teiji, ed., *Konoye Fumimaro* (Tokyo, 1952), II, 200.

5. Furuta, "Dai-ni-ji taisenka no shisō-teki jōkyō" (Ideological Conditions During the Second World War), *Kindai Nihon shisō shi* (History of Modern Japanese Thought) (Tokyo, 1956), III, 699.

6. Furuta, "Dai-ni-ji taisenka," p. 683; *Nihon kindai-shi jiten*, p. 160.

7. Tsurumi Shunsuke, "Yokusan undō no sekkei-sha, Konoye Fumimaro" (The Planners of the Imperial Assistance Movement, Konoye Fumimaro) in *Tenkō* (Conversion), Vol. II, Part 2 "Liberals," pp. 82–83.

8. Miyakawa Tōru, *Miki Kiyoshi*, Volume X of the series *Kindai Nihon no shisōka* (Thinkers of Modern Japan) (Tokyo, 1958), pp. 114–15; Furuta, "Dai-ni-ji taisenka," p. 705.

9. I have relied on the works of Miyakawa, Furuta, and Uotsu Ikuo, "Aru jiyūshugi saha no chishikijin, Miki Kiyoshi" (An Intellectual of the Liberal Left, Miki Kiyoshi) in *Tenkō*, I, 366–82. For a useful short study giving a

basic bibliography on Miki, see Yamada Munemutsu, "Miki Kiyoshi," *Asahi Journal* V:14 (April 7, 1963), 88–93.

10. Furuta, "Futatsu no 'tōa shinchitsujo ron'" (The Two "Theories of the New Order in East Asia"), *Kindai Nihon shisō shi*, III, 706–7.

11. See Shōwa Kenkyū Kai, ed., *Shin Nihon no shisō genri* (Basic Principles of Thought in the New Japan) (Tokyo, January 1939); *Kyōdōshugi no tetsugaku-teki kiso* (The Philosophical Basis of Cooperativism) (Tokyo, September 1939); and *Tōa shinchitsujo kensetsu no riron to hōsaku* (The Theory and Method of Constructing a New Order in East Asia) (Tokyo, June 1940).

12. *Sumera Ajia* (The Emperor's Asia); quoted by Furuta, "Dai-ni-ji taisenka," p. 702.

13. *Gendai-shi shiryō*, II, 377–78.

14. *Japan and Her Destiny*, p. 184.

15. See Yabe Teiji, ed., *Konoye Fumimaro*, II, 197–206; Sassa Hiroo, *Shōwa seiji hisshi*, pp. 34–36; *Nihon kindai-shi jiten*, pp. 280, 290–91; Shigemitsu, *Japan and Her Destiny*, pp. 198–200; Aochi Shin, *Shisō*, June 1954, p. 70; Kazama, *Aru hangyaku*, pp. 152–54; and Tsurumi, *Tenkō*, II, 104–5.

16. *Gendai-shi shiryō*, II, 220.

17. Even today, some Western academicians do not seem to have grasped the significance of the Lukouch'iao Incident. See, for example, James B. Crowley, "A Reconsideration of the Marco Polo Bridge Incident," *The Journal of Asian Studies*, XXII:3 (May 1963), pp. 277–91. The authoritative study of the Western reaction to war and revolution in China is Tang Tsou, *America's Failure in China, 1941–50* (Chicago, 1963). For my analysis of the Sino-Japanese war, see *Peasant Nationalism and Communist Power, The Emergence of Revolutionary China, 1937–1945* (Stanford, 1962).

18. Ozaki Hotsumi, "Hokushi mondai no shin dankai" (The New Phase in the North China Problem), *Kaizō*, XIX:8 (August 1937), 94–101 [written July 12, 1937]. Reprinted in Ozaki, *Gendai Shina hihan* (Critical Studies of Modern China) (Tokyo, November 1938), pp. 117–29.

19. *Gendai Shina hihan*, p. 154.

20. "Chōki kōsen no yukikata" (The Methods of Protracted Resistance), *Kaizō*, XX:5 (May 1938), 90–91; "New Far Eastern Diplomacy," *Contemporary Japan*, VII:1 (June 1938), 31–32.

21. *Gendai-shi shiryō*, I, 234–35; for Sorge's statement that he trusted Ozaki's judgment and consulted him on points of general interpretation, see Volume I, p. 202. Also see the Japanese government's analysis of Ozaki's accurate prediction of the outcome of the China Incident, *ibid.*, p. 45.

22. See Kazami Akira, "Ozaki Hotsumi hyōden—junkyōsha e no banka" (A Critical Biography of Ozaki Hotsumi—An Elegy for a Martyr), *Kaizō*, August 1951, p. 78; Kazami, *Konoye naikaku* (The Konoye Cabinets) (1951), p. 260; and Ozaki, *Gendai-shi shiryō*, II, 222.

23. Interview, June 4, 1962.

24. E.g., Meissner, *The Man With Three Faces,* pp. 102, 113–14.

25. See the interrogation of Kazami on this point, November 18, 1942; *Gendai-shi shiryō,* II, 400.

26. Interrogation, March 8, 1942; *ibid., 222.*

27. Police interrogation of Ushiba, May 8, 1942; *ibid.,* III, 539.

28. For a description of this meeting, see Saionji, *Kizoku no taijō* (1951), p. 53. On the Breakfast Society, see *Gendai-shi shiryō,* II, 222–23 (Ozaki); II, 547–48 (police analysis); III, 486–87 (Saionji); and III, 539 (Ushiba).

29. *Gendai-shi shiryō,* III, 540. For Ozaki's analysis of U.S.–Japanese negotiations, see Volume II, 242–44.

30. *Ibid.,* II, 274.

31. See, for example, Maruyama Masao, "Japan's Wartime Leaders," *Orient/West,* VII (May and July 1962), 33–45, 37–53.

32. *Gendai-shi shiryō,* II, 275.

33. *Ibid.*

34. " 'Tōa kyōdō tai' no rinen to sono seiritsu no kakkanteki kiso" (The Idea of an "East Asian Cooperative Body" and the Objective Basis for Its Realization), *Chūō kōron,* No. 616 (January 1939), pp. 4–18 (November 1960, pp. 400–411). See the commentary on Ozaki's article by Aochi Shin, "Tai-Ajia-shugi ni taku-su yume" (The Dream That Went Under the Cover of Great Asiaism), *Chūō kōron,* November 1960, p. 412. Excerpts from Ozaki's article also appear in Mitamura Takeo, *Shōwa seiji hiroku, sensō to kyōsan-shugi* (Secret History of Shōwa Politics, War and Communism) (Tokyo, 1950), pp. 268–71.

35. Statement by Saionji, *Gendai-shi shiryō,* III, 491–92.

36. A slightly different translation is included in John M. Maki, *Conflict and Tension in the Far East, Key Documents, 1894–1960* (Seattle, 1961), pp. 79–80.

37. Ozaki Hotsumi, "The New National Structure," *Contemporary Japan,* IX:10 (October 1940), 1286, 1291. (Form of names slightly altered.)

38. *Kizoku no taijō,* p. 52.

39. *Gendai-shi shiryō,* II, 522–23.

40. From Ozaki's second appeal; *ibid.,* 32. This was written after he was sentenced to death (September 29, 1943) and before his sentence was confirmed by the Supreme Court (March 8, 1944). As we shall see, this document is usually regarded as a *tenkōsho* that his friends forced him to write in a last attempt to save his life. However, this particular excerpt appears to reflect his true feelings at the time of Lukouch'iao and after. Moreover, Ozaki could never bring himself to write a truly abject confession and throw himself on the mercy of the court. For Ozaki's appraisal of the strengths and weaknesses of the Konoye cabinets, see Volume II, pp. 336–37.

41. Tokyo, May 1939. The Iwanami Shinsho series continues to be published today, but with blue covers in order to distinguish it from the prewar

books. For an appreciation of the prewar Iwanami Shinsho series and Ozaki's book (plus a discussion of other important prewar Japanese books on Chinese politics), see Ozaki Hotsuki, "Uketsugubeki isan" (Inheritable Heritages), *Tosho shimbun* (Book News), March 23, 1963. A new edition of Ozaki's *Gendai Shina ron* is to be published in 1964 as No. 13 in the Chūgoku Shinsho (New Library on China) Series of Futsū Sha publishers.

42. Letter of October 28, 1943; *Aijō wa furu hoshi no gotoku*, p. 127.

43. *Gendai Shina ron*, Iwanami ed., pp. 80–81. Cf. Ozaki, "Activities of Wu P'ei-fu and Wang Ching-wei," *Contemporary Japan*, VIII:2 (April 1939), 245–55.

44. *Gendai Shina ron*, Iwanami ed., pp. 202–4.

45. *Gendai-shi shiryō*, III, pp. 488, 586. After the war, Saionji commented, "Ozaki was one of the few men to perceive correctly the trend of events in China," *Kizoku no taijō*, p. 56.

46. For a quotation by Saionji of one of Ozaki's analyses of the China Incident similar to the one given here, see *Gendai-shi shiryō*, III, 505.

47. Kazama, *Aru hangyaku*, p. 147.

48. Statement by Kazami, *Gendai-shi shiryō*, II, 400–401.

49. Hosokawa Karoku, "Shosai no omoide," *Shisō*, No. 357 (March 1954), 112; Kazami Akira, "Ozaki Hotsumi hyōden," *Kaizō*, August 1951, p. 72; Kazama, *Aru hangyaku*, p. 167.

50. Bickerton came from New Zealand to Tokyo in approximately 1923 and secured employment as an English instructor at Ichikō. He became very interested in Japanese proletarian literature, and he probably made the translation of Kobayashi's *Kani kōsen* (The Cannery Boat), published by the English left-wing book firm of Martin Lawrence. Bickerton was a friend of Matsumoto's, and Ozaki once told Matsumoto: "That foreigner was a valuable person; you should have taken better care of him." (*Idai naru aijō*, p. 49.)

After Matsumoto's arrest in February, Bickerton was picked up by the Foreign Section of the Tokkō on March 13, 1934. He has the unique distinction of being the first foreigner arrested under the Peace Preservation Law, and he discovered to his regret what the prewar police were like. He was repeatedly tortured and not allowed to see the British consul until March 23, when his wounds had healed somewhat. The police interrogated him about funds he allegedly gave to Matsumoto and the fact that he had copies of *The Cannery Boat*, the *Daily Worker*, and *Akahata* (Red Flag) in his house. Bickerton was finally released on bail on April 26, and he secretly left Japan for London on July 5, 1934, in order to avoid facing his trial, which was scheduled for July 30.

The repercussions in England included a question in Parliament. Mr. Wilmot (Labor) asked on April 11, "Is the right honorable gentleman aware that this gentleman [Bickerton], who has been a resident in Tokyo for some years and is a highly respected English master at the university, has been informed, unofficially, that his offense is that of harboring dangerous thoughts? (laughter) . . ." *The Times,* April 12, 1934, p. 7. There was no reply from the Government.

Bickerton himself gave a sworn statement to the Foreign Office that he had been beaten across the legs with a baseball bat and otherwise tortured; and he published his own story, "Third Degree in Japan," in the *Manchester Guardian Weekly,* July 27, 1934, p. 78 (reprinted in *The Living Age,* New York, vol. 347, September 1934, pp. 30–34). His later whereabouts are not known. Bickerton's offense appears to have been contributing funds to leftist causes in Japan and translating Communist literature. For Japanese left-wing accounts, see Horie Yūichi and Kozai Yoshishige, eds., *Idai naru aijō* (The Great Love) [A Report of the "Ozaki Hotsumi—Matsumoto Shin'-ichi Anti-Fascist Memorial Meeting," Meiji University Lecture Hall, November 27, 1948] (Tokyo, 1949), pp. 49, 87–88. Also see *The Times,* London, March 28, 1934, p. 13; March 31, p. 9; April 12, p. 12; April 27, p. 13; May 28, p. 13; and June 19, p. 13.

51. Horie Yūichi and Kozai Yoshishige, eds., *Idai naru aijō,* pp. 46–59, 86–90; Kazama, *Aru hangyaku,* p. 168; Matsumoto Shin'ichi, "Nihon teikoku-shugi to Ozaki Hotsumi" (Japanese Imperialism and Ozaki Hotsumi), *Sekai,* December 1946, pp. 81–89.

52. Ara Masato *et al., Shōwa bungaku shi* (History of Shōwa Literature), I, 156, 159–61. Also see Kazama, *Aru hangyaku,* pp. 135, 168–69.

53. *Gendai-shi shiryō,* II, 272–73.

54. The translated titles of Ozaki's articles in *Jiji shiryō geppō* are as follows (for romanized Japanese titles, see the Bibliography):

(1) "Establishment of the Abe Cabinet and Raising the Curtain on the Second Great European War," No. 2, September 10, 1939.

(2) "The Need for Vigilance in the Precarious Internal Situation," No. 9, April 15, 1940.

(3) "The Sudden Change in the European War and the Political Situation," No. 10, May 22, 1940.

(4) "The Problem of the New Party and the Political Situation," No. 11, June 15, 1940.

(5) "The Establishment of the Second Konoye Cabinet and the New Organization of Politics," No. 12, July 30, 1940.

(6) "Concerning the Temporary Stability in the Present Maintenance of Power and the Contemporary Political Situation," No. 18, January 24, 1941.

(7) "The Mist of Uncertainty in the Present Political Situation," No. 19, February 25, 1941.

(8) "The Negotiations with America and the Southern [Asia] Question," No. 26, September 30, 1941.

See the interrogation of Kaieda Hisataka, *Gendai-shi shiryō,* II, 436–39.

For a discussion of the security classifications and distribution of these materials, see *ibid.*, 431–33.

55. *Ibid.*, III, 484.

56. *Ibid.*, 586.

57. *Ibid.*, II, 276–78.

58. Police analysis of Ozaki's trip, *ibid.*, II, 147; Ozaki's account of the Dairen meeting, *ibid.*, 278; interrogation of Gotō Kenshō, a South Manchurian Railroad statistician at the Dairen office, concerning the information that was divulged to Ozaki in September 1941, *ibid.*, 407–9.

CHAPTER SEVEN

1. *Gendai-shi shiryō,* I, 192.

2. *Ibid.*, II, 137.

3. Ozaki Hotsuki, *Zoruge jiken,* p. 105.

4. *Gendai-shi shiryō,* I, 192.

5. *Ibid.*, 196; Otto D. Tolischus, *Tokyo Record* (New York, 1943), p. 67.

6. *Gendai-shi shiryō,* I, 101–2.

7. *Ibid.*, 192–93.

8. Sorge discusses his research at length in *ibid.*, pp. 198–204. The book on which Sorge was working was to have been entitled "Diplomatic History of Japan in Modern Times." When Sorge was arrested, the police confiscated his entire library and two or three boxes containing his typescript; all of this material was destroyed in the air raids when the Ministry of Justice burned. See Obi Toshito, "Zoruge danshō" (Fragments on Sorge), *Gendai-shi shiryō geppō* (Materials on Modern History Monthly Report) (Tokyo: Misuzu Shobō), No. 1, August 1962, pp. 2–3.

9. *Gendai-shi shiryō,* I, 202–3.

10. *The Man With Three Faces,* pp. 77ff.

11. Interrogation of Sorge, February 24, 1942, question 7; *Gendai-shi shiryō,* I, 243.

12. *Ibid.*, 192–93. Willoughby calls Matzki "Makki"; e.g., *Shanghai Conspiracy,* p. 221. The present spelling of the Military Attaché's name is based on General Ott's affidavit for the International Military Tribunal for the Far East (which was available to but apparently unread by Willoughby's investigators).

13. International Military Tribunal for the Far East, *Proceedings,* pp. 38,413ff; 38,469; 38,472; and Exhibit No. 3158 (von Petersdorf affidavit).

14. *Gendai-shi shiryō,* I, 550–52.

15. *Ibid.*, II, 165. Concerning Ozaki's sources on Chang-ku-feng, see also Volume II, p. 85.

16. *Ibid.*, I, 64.

17. *Ibid.*, 40–41, 379.

18. However, John Erickson has carefully analyzed this incident using all available Russian sources. See *The Soviet High Command, A Military-Political History, 1918–1941* (London, 1962), pp. 495–98.

19. *Gendai-shi shiryō*, I, 265ff, 378ff. Erickson refers to Lyushkov as a colonel (*Soviet High Command*, p. 727, n. 84), but Sorge gives his rank as a general (third-grade). Lyushkov himself used the title "general" in the articles that he published during 1939 in Japan. See General G. S. Lyushkoff (Lyushkov), "The Far Eastern Red Army," *Contemporary Japan*, VIII:8 (October 1939), pp. 1022–25 (reprinted from *Kaizō*, September 1939); and Isaac Levine, *The Mind of an Assassin* (New York, 1960), pp. 54–55.

20. *Gendai-shi shiryō*, I, 77. Transmitted during September 1938.

21. *The Soviet High Command*, p. 499; see also p. 836.

22. Sorge interrogation, *Gendai-shi shiryō*, I, 378–79; see also Volume I, p. 36.

23. Testimony before U.S. 82d Congress, House of Representatives, Committee on Un-American Activities, *Hearings on American Aspects of the Richard Sorge Spy Case* (1951), p. 1147. Yoshikawa spells Lyushkov's name "Rushikoff," an adaptation of its Japanese form.

24. For Ozaki's reports on Nomon-Han, see *Gendai-shi shiryō*, I, 50; II, 86, 169–70.

25. *Ibid.*, I, 44, 191, 381–82.

26. See Sorge's memoir, *ibid.*, I, 146, 190.

27. *Ibid.*, 180.

28. Film: *ibid.*, 179. Lists: *ibid.*, 47–57, 58–76; II, 135–56.

29. *Ibid.*, III, 491–92.

30. See, for example, *Shūkan Asahi*, September 7, 1962, p. 18; Aochi Shin, *Gendai-shi no magarikado*, pp. 171–72; Shigemitsu Mamoru, *Shōwa no dōran*, II, 98; and Ozaki Hotsuki, *Zoruge jiken*, pp. 117–19.

31. *Gendai-shi shiryō*, III, 345.

32. *Orient/West* VII:5 (May 1962), 33–34. Cf. Presseisen, *Germany and Japan*, Chap. 10, "Alliance Without Allies," pp. 281–320.

33. Interrogation, March 6, 1942; *Gendai-shi shiryō*, II, 176.

34. Forty-first interrogation of Sorge by Yoshikawa Mitsusada, March 11, 1942; *ibid.*, I, 273–76.

35. *Ibid.*, 249.

36. *Ibid.*, 249, 274.

37. *Ibid.*, 274; Kainō Michitaka, "Dokuso kaisen no nazo" (The Puzzle of the Outbreak of the Russo-German War), *Asahi Journal*, V:8 (February 24, 1963), 56–57.

38. Sorge: *Gendai-shi shiryō*, I, 274. Compare the list of "orders" from Moscow to the ring, *ibid.*, 77–78.

39. Ozaki's statement: *ibid.*, II, 182–83. Saionji's statement: *ibid.*, III, 495–96.

40. *Ibid.*, I, 185.

41. *Ibid.*, II, 246.

42. On Ozaki's knowledge of the Roosevelt-Konoye exchanges, *ibid.*, III, 498–500; on Ozaki's appraisal, *ibid.*, II, 242–44, 361–62.

43. See Erickson, *The Soviet High Command*, pp. 637–38; Dallin, *Soviet Espionage*, Chap. 6, "The Rote Kapelle in Germany," pp. 234–72.

44. Cf. Kainō, "Dokuso kaisen no nazo."

45. Erickson, *The Soviet High Command*, pp. 631–32.

46. *Ibid.*, pp. 599, 632.

47. Ikoma Yoshitoshi, "Zoruge kaisō" (Recollections of Sorge), *Misuzu*, IV:3 (March 1962), 15.

48. *Gendai-shi shiryō*, II, 187.

49. *Ibid.*

50. *Ibid.*, I, 204–7.

51. Ushiba: *ibid.*, III, 540; Ozaki: *ibid.*, II, 188.

52. *Ibid.*, I, 207.

53. On couriers generally: *ibid.*, 28–34, 172–76. On funds and their transmission: *ibid.*, 78–79. On Sorge's trips to the continent: *ibid.*, 175, 278.

54. For information on Clausen's radio, see *ibid.*, I, 86–93 (government study); I, 178–79 (Sorge's comments); III, viii–x (on monitoring); III, 73–82 (tests by Japanese engineers); and Kobayashi Gorō, *Tokkō keisatsu hiroku* (Secret Records of the Special Higher Police) (Tokyo, 1952), p. 233 (on the government's interception of unidentified radio broadcasts).

55. *Gendai-shi shiryō*, III, 159.

56. See *The Man With Three Faces, passim*; note, for example, pp. 164–65.

57. *Gendai-shi shiryō*, III, 191. Cf. Ozaki Hotsuki, *Zoruge jiken*, p. 116.

58. *Gendai-shi shiryō*, I, 88; III, 108–9.

59. From Clausen's confession, *ibid.*, III, 65–67 (on Voukelitch's divorce, see p. 67). The only information on Voukelitch's attitude and personal affairs during this period is contained in Clausen's testimony. Voukelitch's own confession concerned his early, pre-Japan, conversion to Communism. The record of Voukelitch's interrogation has not survived.

60. *Ibid.*, 67, 69.

61. *Zoruge jiken*, pp. 127–28. Also see Sorge's testimony concerning the end of his mission, *Gendai-shi shiryō*, I, 479–80.

CHAPTER EIGHT

1. Kazama, *Aru hangyaku*, p. 189.

2. Dōmei Tsūshin Sha, ed., *Wartime Legislation in Japan* (Tokyo, 1941), English section, p. 4; Japanese section, p. 1. Also see *Gendai-shi shiryō*, I, p. 538; and Kazama, *Aru hangyaku*, pp. 187–88.

3. *Wartime Legislation in Japan*, p. 70 (translation slightly modified).

4. Schellenberg mistakenly remembered von Ritgen as the "head of DNB, the official German News Service." *The Schellenberg Memoirs* (London, 1956), p. 175.

5. *Ibid.*, p. 176.

6. *Ibid.*, pp. 178–79. For Meisinger's contacts with the Kempei, see *Gendai-shi shiryō*, I, 547.

7. *Gendai-shi shiryō*, I, 544; Ozaki Hotsuki, *Zoruge jiken*, p. 124.

8. U.S. House of Representatives, 82d Congress, First Session, Committee on Un-American Activities, *Hearings on American Aspects of the Richard Sorge Spy Case* (Washington, 1951), p. 1144.

9. Miyake Hanako, *Ningen Zoruge* (The Man Sorge) (Tokyo, 1949), pp. 134 *et seq.*, p. 16off.; "Zoruge danshō" (Fragments on Sorge), *Gendai-shi shiryō geppō*, No. 1 (August 1962), p. 4; Ozaki Hotsuki, *Zoruge jiken*, pp. 124–25; and Miyake Hanako, "Watakushi no otto wa supai Zoruge datta ga" (My Husband Was the Spy Sorge), *Shūkan josei* (Women's Weekly), July 1, 1961, pp. 22–25.

10. Ozaki Hotsuki, *Zoruge jiken*, p. 125.

11. Kazama, *Aru hangyaku*, p. 189.

12. *Ibid.* This discussion of Itō's early life is based on the following sources: Matsumoto Seichō, "Kakumei o uru otoko: Itō Ritsu" (Itō Ritsu, The Man Who Sold Out the Revolution), *Bungei shunjū*, June 1960, pp. 194–226; *Gendai-shi shiryō*, II, 395–97; and *Nihon o ugokasu sambyaku nin* (The Three Hundred Men Who Move Japan), pp. 4–5.

13. *Bungei shunjū*, June 1960, p. 207.

14. *Gendai-shi shiryō*, II, 396.

15. Kazama, *Aru hangyaku*, p. 190.

16. *Ibid.*

17. *Gendai-shi shiryō*, II, 395.

18. Concerning the June 1940 date, see *Gendai-shi shiryō*, I, 4; for Kamiyama, see *Nihon o ugokasu sambyaku nin*, p. 43.

19. See Itō's affidavit, *Gendai-shi shiryō*, II, 395.

20. *Ibid.*

21. Kazama, *Aru hangyaku*, pp. 190–91; Ozaki Hotsuki, *Ikite iru yuda* (The Living Judas) (Toyko, 1959), pp. 119–20.

22. The information divulged at this meeting forms the basis of Matsumoto Seichō's study of Itō; *Bungei shunjū*, June 1960, pp. 194–226.

23. *Ibid.*, pp. 194–95, 200.

24. *Gendai-shi shiryō*, II, 397.

25. Kobayashi Gorō, *Tokkō keisatsu hiroku* (Secret Record of the Special Higher Police) (Tokyo, 1952), pp. 235–36.

26. *Gendai-shi shiryō*, I, p. 4. Kobayshi concluded from this that the case was broken by accident; he entitled his discussion "*Gūzen ka ten'yū ka,*"

"Accident or divine assistance?" *Tokkō keisatsu hiroku,* pp. 234ff. Kazami Akira also concluded that the Sorge case was exposed entirely by accident. "Ozaki Hotsumi hyōden," *Kaizō,* August 1951, p. 79.

27. Yoshikawa testimony, *Hearings on American Aspects of the Richard Sorge Spy Case,* pp. 1135–36.

28. For the arrests of the five major members of the ring, see: *Gendai-shi shiryō,* I, 4–5; Kobayashi Gorō, pp. 235–58; Aochi Shin, *Gendai-shi no magarikado,* pp. 194–95; Shigemitsu Mamoru, *Shōwa no dōran,* II, pp. 93–95; Tsurumi Shunsuke, *Tenkō,* II, pp. 84, 113 (note 26); Ozaki Hotsuki, *Ikite iru yuda,* pp. 175, 282; Kazama, *Aru hangyaku,* pp. 191–92; and *Shūkan Asahi,* September 7, 1962, pp. 12–20.

29. Iwabuchi Tatsuo, "Kizoku to seiji to shi to" (Nobility, Politics, and Death), *Bungei shunjū,* June 1954 (Extra issue), p. 122.

30. Kazami, *Konoye naikaku* (The Konoye Cabinets), p. 259.

31. Kainō Michitaka, "Dokuso kaisen no nazo" (The Puzzle of the Beginning of the Russo-German War), *Asahi Journal,* February 24, 1963, pp. 56–57.

32. Kazami, *Konoye naikaku,* p. 260.

33. Kobayashi, *Tokkō keisatsu hiroku,* p. 252.

34. *Gendai-shi shiryō,* II, 402–6.

35. *Ibid.,* 226–27.

36. Schellenberg, *Memoirs,* p. 179; *Gendai-shi shiryō,* I, 100.

37. Schellenberg, *Memoirs,* p. 181.

38. *Gendai-shi shiryō geppō,* No. 1 (August 1962), p. 2.

39. Ozaki Hotsuki, *Zoruge jiken,* p. 134.

40. U.S. Army, Far East Command, Military Intelligence Section, *A Partial Documentation of the Sorge Espionage Case* (Tokyo, 1950), pp. 60–67; Appendix, Exhibit No. 12, pp. 7–12.

41. *Shanghai Conspiracy,* p. 59.

42. *Hearings on American Aspects of the Richard Sorge Spy Case,* p. 1144.

43. Tolischus, *Tokyo Record* (New York, 1943), Chaps. 38 and 39, pp. 335 *et seq.*

44. Ozaki Hotsuki, *Zoruge jiken,* p. 135.

45. A reproduction of the letter appears as the fourth frontispiece to *Gendai-shi shiryō,* III, and in several other works; on SCAP's use of it as evidence, see *Gendai-shi shiryō geppō,* No. 1, p. 2.

46. *Gendai-shi shiryō,* I, 318.

47. *Ibid.,* p. 329 (answer to question four).

48. Ozaki Hotsuki, *Zoruge jiken,* pp. 142–43; *Gendai-shi shiryō geppō,* No. 1, p. 4.

49. *Gendai-shi shiryō geppō,* No. 3 (December 1962), pp. 2–4.

50. The text of the press release is printed in *Gendai-shi shiryō,* I, 539–43.

51. *Gendai-shi shiryō,* I, 543; Ozaki Hotsuki, *Zoruge jiken,* pp. 138–39;

Shūkan Asahi, September 7, 1962; Kazami, "Ozaki Hotsumi hyōden," *Kaizō,* August 1951, p. 78; Ryū Shintarō, "Shinjitsu no mutsukashisa" (The Difficulty of Truth), *Misuzu,* No. 49 (May 1963), pp. 4–5.

52. Harold S. Quigley, *Japanese Government and Politics* (New York and London, 1932), p. 283.

53. *Ibid.,* pp. 284–85.

54. *Gendai-shi shiryō geppō,* No. 1, p. 4.

55. *Gendai-shi shiryō,* I, 507.

56. Kazama, *Aru hangyaku,* pp. 240–41.

57. Matsumoto note, *Aijō wa furu hoshi no gotoku* (Sekai Hyōron Sha ed.), pp. 4–5.

58. Kazama, *Aru hangyaku,* p. 203.

59. *Gendai-shi shiryō,* II, 128–29.

60. *Ibid.,* p. 284.

61. *Ibid.,* p. 447.

62. Kazama claims that Ozaki's first counsel was selected by Matsumoto, on the advice of Miwa; but Matsumoto's own statement is probably more accurate, since he was the leading figure in planning Ozaki's defense. Matsumoto note, *Aijō wa furu hoshi no gotoku,* pp. 70–71; Kazama, pp. 209–10.

63. Letter of June 1, 1943; *Aijō wa furu hoshi no gotoku,* pp. 68–69.

64. There is no question but that this first statement was a *tenkōsho;* the Home Ministry clearly labeled it as such when it was published in the *Tokkō geppō* (Special Higher Police Monthly Journal) after Ozaki's execution. *Gendai-shi shiryō,* II, p. v.

65. *Ibid.,* p. 8.

66. *Tenkōsho,* I, *ibid.,* pp. 3–25.

67. *Ibid.,* pp. 21–22.

68. *Aijō wa furu hoshi no gotoku,* p. 93.

69. *Ibid.,* pp. 97–98.

70. *Ibid.,* p. 71; Ozaki Hotsuki, *Zoruge jiken,* pp. 143–44.

71. *Aijō wa furu hoshi no gotoku,* p. 119.

72. *Ibid.,* pp. 134, 148.

73. *Idai naru aijō* (The Great Love) (Tokyo, 1949), pp. 13–14; *Gendai-shi shiryō,* II, p. vii.

74. *Aijō wa furu hoshi no gotoku,* p. 125. The second *tenkōsho* is printed in *Gendai-shi shiryō,* II, 29–75.

75. *Gendai-shi shiryō,* II, p. ix. This letter is not included in the Sekai Hyōron Sha edition of *Aijō,* but it is printed along with a selection of Ozaki's letters concerning the problem of his *tenkō* in *Gendai-shi shiryō.*

76. *Gendai-shi shiryō,* II, 34.

77. *Ibid.,* pp. 483–85.

78. *Aijō wa furu hoshi no gotoku,* p. 171.

79. Ozaki Hotsuki, *Zoruge jiken,* p. 151.

80. Kazama, *Aru hangyaku,* pp. 253–54.

81. *Aijō wa furu hoshi no gotoku,* pp. 53–56.

82. Letter of May 3, 1944, *ibid.,* p. 195; Ozaki Yōko, "Chichi no koto" (My Father), *Idai naru aijō,* p. 23.

83. *Gendai-shi shiryō,* II, 50.

84. *Tenkō,* II, 91.

85. Letter of July 24, 1944; *Aijō wa furu hoshi no gotoku,* p. 231.

86. Ozaki Hotsuki, *Zoruge jiken,* pp. 147–48; *Shūkan Asahi,* September 7, 1962, pp. 19–20.

87. Maruyama Masao, *Thought and Behavior in Modern Japanese Politics,* I. Morris, ed. (London, 1963), p. 16.

88. *Aijō wa furu hoshi no gotoku,* p. 51.

89. Kazami, "Ozaki-kun no omoide" (Recollections of Ozaki), *Aijō wa furu hoshi no gotoku,* Mikasa Bunko ed., I, 247; Tsurumi, *Tenkō,* II, 85–86; *Shūkan Asahi,* September 7, 1962, p. 20.

CHAPTER NINE

1. Ozaki Hotsuki, *Zoruge jiken,* pp. 178–80.

2. Ozaki Eiko's introduction to *Aijō wa furu hoshi no gotoku,* Sekai Hyōron Sha ed., pp. 5–6; Kazama, *Aru hangyaku,* p. 264.

3. Miyamoto Yuriko (1899–1951) was the author of *Mazushiki hitobito no mure* (The Common Run of Poor People) and many other books; she was the wife of Miyamoto Kenji, one of the major figures of the postwar JCP. See *Gendai-shi shiryō,* III, 710. Her article, "A Life Sacrificed for the People," was included at Matsumoto Shin'ichi's insistence; it was cut from later Sekai Hyōron editions after Matsumoto's untimely death, but was restored in the 1951 Mikasa Bunko edition. In this study I have used a copy of the eighth printing of the Sekai Hyōron Sha edition (June 30, 1948) of *Aijō,* in addition to the two-volume Mikasa Bunko edition.

4. Ara Masato, *et al., Shōwa bungaku shi* (History of Shōwa Literature), II, 19.

5. These are, in order of publication: (1) *Jinmin hyōron,* February 1946; (2) Sekai Hyōron Sha, September 1946; (3) Mikasa Bunko, 2 volumes (all 238 letters), October and November 1951, with articles on Ozaki by Kazami Akira, Ozaki Eiko, Matsumoto Shin'ichi, Miyamoto Yuriko, and Tsuge Hideomi; (4) Aoki Bunko, 2 volumes, August and September 1953; (5) Supplement to *Kingu* (King Magazine), March 1956, "Bestseller Reprints"; (6) *Aijō no kiroku* (Record of Love), Chikuma Shobō, December 1958, "Collected Works of Modern Culture, Volume IV"; (7) Kōbunsha "Kappa Books," June 1960.

6. See Yamasaki Ken's article, *Idai naru aijō,* p. 69.

7. Matsumoto Shin'ichi, "Nihon teikokushugi to Ozaki Hotsumi" (Japa-

nese Imperialism and Ozaki Hotsumi), *Sekai,* December 1946, p. 84. Also see Matsumoto, "Ozaki Hotsumi no omoide" (Recollections of Ozaki Hotsumi), *Jinmin hyōron,* Vol. 2, No. 11 (December 1946), pp. 34–36.

8. *Nihon o ugokasu sambyaku nin* (The Three Hundred Men Who Move Japan), pp. 42–43; Evelyn S. Colbert, *The Left Wing in Japanese Politics* (New York, 1952), p. 313; Kōan Chōsa Chō, *Nihon kyōsantō daihakkai taikai ni tsuite* (Concerning the Eighth Congress of the Japanese Communist Party) (Tokyo, September 1961), pp. 259–60; and Koyama Hirotake, *Sengo no Nihon kyōsantō* (The Postwar Japanese Communist Party) (Tokyo, December 1962), pp. 160–63.

9. Kamiyama, "Shi mo mata suzushi" (Death Can Be a Relief), *Akahata,* No. 78 (November 9, 1946), p. 2.

10. Kamiyama, "Saigo no akushu," *Jinmin hyōron,* Vol. 3, no. 6 (November 1947), pp. 48–51.

11. Kazama, *Aru hangyaku,* p. 264.

12. Matsumoto, "Kaji-shi no 'Ozaki Hotsumi' ron" (Mr. Kaji's Essay on Ozaki Hotsumi), *Jinmin hyōron,* November 1947, pp. 45–47.

13. *Idai naru aijō* (Tokyo: Ikuseisha, 1949), p. 2.

14. *Ibid.,* p. 165.

15. *Ibid.,* pp. 169–70.

16. *Ibid.,* pp. 23–43.

17. Ozaki Hotsuki, *Ikite iru yuda* (The Living Judas) (Tokyo, 1959), pp. 36ff.

18. *Ibid.,* pp. 62–64.

19. *Ibid.,* p. 93.

20. *Ibid,* p. 111.

21. Kazama, *Aru hangyaku,* pp. 265–66.

22. Willoughby identifies Noble as a Professor of History at the University of Oregon and a writer for the *Saturday Evening Post.* U.S. Army, Far East Command, Military Intelligence Section, *A Partial Documentation of the Sorge Espionage Case* (Tokyo, 1950), p. 2.

23. U.S. Army Intelligence School, Fort Holabird, *The Sorge Spy Ring,* p. 85.

24. *Akahata,* February 11, 1949. Also see Matsumoto Seichō, "Kakumei o uru otoko, Itō Ritsu" (Itō Ritsu, The Man Who Sold Out the Revolution), *Bungei shunjū,* June 1960, p. 196; and Ozaki Hotsuki, *Zoruge jiken,* pp. 186–87.

25. Ozaki Hotsuki, *Ikite iru yuda,* p. 163; and Kazama, *Aru hangyaku,* p. 265.

26. Quoted in U.S. Army, *A Partial Documentation of the Sorge Espionage Case,* pp. 8–9.

27. Frontispiece letter to W. E. Woods, Chairman, House Committee on Un-American Activities, May 1, 1950, *ibid.*

28. *Ibid.*, Appendix, p. 23.

29. *Ibid.* (Punctuation slightly modified.)

30. Ozaki Hotsuki, *Zoruge jiken*, pp. 200–201; *Ikite iru yuda*, pp. 176–87; and Kazama, *Aru hangyaku*, pp. 266–67.

31. U.S. Army, *A Partial Documentation of the Sorge Espionage Case*, Appendix, p. 23.

32. Ozaki Hotsuki, *Zoruge jiken*, p. 200.

33. *Ronsō* (Disputation), March 1962, p. 181.

34. Neither SCAP's contention that Itō was an unwitting Judas nor Ozaki Hotsuki's belief that Itō knowingly betrayed the Sorge ring is fully accepted by any authority on the Sorge case. See, for example, Tsurumi, *Tenkō*, II, 113 (note 26); and Aochi Shin, *Gendai-shi no magarikado*, pp. 194–95.

35. For example: (1) motion pictures: *Inochi aru kagiri* (As Long As One Lives), 1948; and *Shinju-wan zen'ya* (The Eve of Pearl Harbor), French-Japanese production, 1961. (2) Play: Kinoshita Junji, *Otto to yobareru Nihonjin* (A Japanese Called Otto), 1962. (3) Novels and short stories: Tateno Nobuyuki, *Taiyō wa mata noboru, Kōshaku Konoye Fumimaro* (The Sun Also Rises, Prince Konoye Fumimaro) (2 volumes, 1953); Togawa Yukio, *Kasumi aru rakujitsu* (The Mist Over the Setting Sun) (1958); Kō Haruto, *Ushinawareta sokoku* (The Fatherland in Mourning) (1959); Gotō Nobuo, "Nagai yoru, supai Zoruge no koshū" (The Long Night, The Lonely Contemplations of the Spy Sorge), *Shōsetsu shinchō* (The New Tide of Fiction), January 1962 (special number), pp. 132–64. (4) Fictionalized accounts: Nagamatsu Asazō, *Zoruge jiken* (The Sorge Incident), "True Tales of Detection, II" (Tokyo, 1956). (5) Journalistic studies: Takezaki Yōnosuke, *Futatsu no sokoku* (Two Fatherlands) (Tokyo, 1949); Yamazaki Rintarō, *Sekishoku kakumei wa semaru* (The Red Revolution is Close at Hand) (Tokyo, 1949); Ohata Takemi, *Kakusaretaru rekishi* (Hidden History) (Tokyo, 1951); Ozaki Hotsuki, *Zoruge jiken* (Tokyo, 1963).

36. *Aru hangyaku, Ozaki Hotsumi no shōgai* (A Case of Treason, The Life of Ozaki Hotsumi) (Tokyo: Shiseidō, 1959).

37. The mistress-as-betrayer story is given in Meissner. For the "Ozaki-as-patriot" case, see Kazami Akira, "Ozaki Hotsumi hyōden—junkyōsha e no banka" (A Critical Biography of Ozaki Hotsumi: An Elegy to a Martyr), *Kaizō*, August 1951, pp. 72–83. For the "peace movement," see *Gendai-shi shiryō geppō*, No. 3 (December 1962), pp. 6–7; and note the epitaph inscribed on Sorge's tombstone in Tama cemetery: "Here lies a hero who sacrificed his life fighting against war and for world peace" (*Sensō ni hantaishi sekai heiwa no tame ni seimei o sasageta yūshi koko ni nemuru*). The new tombstone was erected in November 1956 by Ishii Hanako and "The Society to Aid the Victims of the Ozaki-Sorge Incident." See Ozaki Hotsuki, *Zoruge jiken*, p. 204.

APPENDIX

1. Ozaki Hotsuki, *Zoruge jiken,* p. 191.

2. Matsumoto Seichō, "Kakumei o uru otoko Itō Ritsu" (Itō Ritsu, The Man Who Sold Out the Revolution), *Bungei shunjū,* June 1960, p. 195.

3. Kamiyama Shigeo, "Saigo no akushu" (The Last Handshake), *Jinmin hyōron,* November 1947, pp. 49–50.

4. Interview with Shiga, *Akahata,* February 11, 1949.

5. Asahi Shimbun, ed., *Nihon o ugokasu sambyaku nin* (The Three Hundred Men Who Move Japan) (Tokyo, 1948), pp. 4–5, s.v. Itō Ritsu.

6. Shakai Keizai Rōdō Kenkyū Sho, *Sengo Nihon kyōsantō shi* (History of the Postwar Japanese Communist Party) (Tokyo, 1958), p. 18.

7. *Ibid.,* p. 38.

8. *Ibid.,* p. 50; Ozaki Hotsuki, *Ikite iru yuda,* pp. 62, 100, 266–71.

9. *Mainichi shimbun,* Osaka, English ed., August 13, 1955, p. 1.

10. *Ibid.,* August 14, 1955, p. 1.

11. *Ibid.,* July 17, 1955, p. 5.

12. *Ibid.,* July 31, 1955, p. 1, plus photograph of Tokuda. The exact date of Tokuda's death was first reported as October 24, 1953, but Party Headquarters later corrected this to October 14, 1953.

13. *Ibid.*

14. *Ibid.,* August 1, 1955, p. 5.

15. *Ibid.,* September 16, 1955, p. 1. (The JCP spokesman was Shida Shigeo.)

16. The most important sources are: Japanese Communist Party Central Committee, 1950 Problems Documents Compilation Committee (Nihon kyōsantō chūō iinkai gojūnen mondai bunken shiryō henshū iinkai), ed., *Nihon kyōsantō gojūnen mondai shiryōshū* (Tokyo: Shin Nihon Shuppan Sha, December 1957), 3 volumes (Documents from the period January 1950 to October 1951); Shakai keizai rōdō kenkyū sho (Society-Economy-Labor Research Institute), *Sengo Nihon kyōsantō shi, Tōnai tōsō no rekishi* (The Postwar Japanese Communist Party: A History of Inner Party Struggle), Koyama Hirotake, ed. (Tokyo: Sangatsu Shobō, July 1958); Koyama Hirotake, *Sengo no Nihon kyōsantō* (Tokyo: Aoki Shoten, December 1962); and the publications of the Kōan Chōsa Chō (Public Security Investigating Bureau).

17. *Mainichi shimbun,* Osaka, English ed., July 31, 1955, p. 2.

18. See Koyama Hirotake, *Sengo no Nihon kyōsantō, passim;* and *Junkan zembō,* January 15, 1959, in U.S. Embassy, Tokyo, *Summaries of Selected Japanese Magazines,* January 26, 1959, pp. 34–36.

19. Cf. *Jen-min jih-pao* (People's Daily), Peking, July 7, 1950; and September 3, 1950.

20. It is believed that Itō's self-critique is the one published in the May 31, 1951 *Naigai hyōron* (Foreign and Domestic Review) (Vol. II, No. 12), under

the name of "Mori Kōichirō." This self-critique is concerned with errors made in the Party's publishing activities during 1950, when Itō was editor of *Akahata* after Shiga and the other "internationalists" had broken away. The other piece of major self-criticism published during the underground period—that of Shiino Etsurō—was also signed with a pseudonym. *Sengo Nihon kyōsantō shi*, pp. 104–5; Ozaki Hotsuki, *Zoruge jiken*, p. 194.

21. *Sengo Nihon kyōsantō shi*, p. 147.

22. Japanese Communist Party Central Committee, "Itō Ritsu shobun ni kan suru seimei," *Akahata*, No. 1225, September 21, 1953, p. 1.

23. See Matsumoto Seichō, *Bungei shunjū*, June 1960, for complete details of Shida's September 14 press conference. Also note *Sengo Nihon kyōsantō shi*, p. 229.

24. Maruyama Masao, *Thought and Behavior in Modern Japanese Politics* (1963), p. 194.

25. Kōan Chōsa Chō, *Naigai jūyō shakai undō nenpu* (Chronology of Major Foreign and Domestic Social Movements) (January 1, 1957–December 31, 1958) (Tokyo: February 24, 1959), p. 120; Koyama Hirotake, *Sengo no Nihon kyōsantō*, pp. 153–60.

26. For a formal critique of the evil influence of Itō on the postwar Party—one published after the Sixth Zenkyō—see Inoguchi Masao, *Nihon kyōsantō ni kan suru shomondai* (Various Problems of the Japanese Communist Party) (Tokyo: Shinkō Shuppan Sha, May 1956), pp. 13–88.

27. Ozaki Hotsuki, *Zoruge jiken*, pp. 192–93, 195.

28. "Bunkajin kara tō e no kotoba" (Remarks from Intellectuals to the Party), *Akahata*, No. 1770, September 27, 1955, p. 4.

Glossary

All Japanese names in this book are given in the Japanese form: surname followed by given name. It should be noted that the reading "Hotsumi" for Ozaki's given name is extremely rare; the alternate readings "Hidemi" and "Shūjitsu" are used in many Japanese and foreign books. The spelling "Hotsumi" was used by Ozaki himself in his English-language articles, and I have checked its accuracy with a member of his family. The *nigori* form, "Hozumi," is incorrect.

Anzai Kuraji 安齊庫治
Aochi Shin 青地晨
Asameshi Kai 朝飯會
Ch'uang-tsao She 創造社
Daitōa Kyōei Ken 大東亞共榮圈
Funakoshi Hisao 船越壽雄
Furuta Hikaru 古田光
Fuyuno Takeo 冬野猛夫
Gisō tenkō 僞裝轉向
Gotō Fumio 後藤文夫
Gotō Shimpei 後藤新平
Higa Gichihō 比嘉義知方
Horie Yūichi 堀江邑一
Horikawa Yūhō 堀河祐鳳
Hosokawa Karoku 細川嘉六
Ikoma Yoshitoshi 生駒佳年
Inukai Ken 犬養健
Ishii Hanako 石井花子
Itō Ritsu 伊藤律
Itō Taketora 伊藤猛虎
Kaieda Hisataka 海江田久孝

Kaji Ryūichi 嘉治隆一
Kamiyama Shigeo 神山茂夫
Katō Eitarō 加藤榮太郎
Kawai Teikichi 川合貞吉
Kawamura Yoshio 河村好雄
Kazama Michitarō 風間道太郎
Kazami Akira 風見章
Kempeitai 憲兵隊
Kinoshita Junji 木下順二
Kishi Michizō 岸道三
Kitabayashi Tomo 北林とも
Kitō Gin'ichi 鬼頭銀一
Kobayashi Shunzō 小林俊三
Kodai Yoshinobu 小代好信
Konoye Fumimaro 近衞文麿
Kozai Yoshishige 古在由重
Kusano Genkichi 草野源吉
Matsumoto Seichō 松本清張
Matsumoto Shigeharu 松本重治
Matsumoto Shin'ichi 松本愼一
Miki Kiyoshi 三木清

Minami Ryūichi 南龍一

Miwa Jusō 三輪壽壯

Miyagi Yotoku 宮城與德

Miyake Hanako 三宅華子

Miyazaki Seiryū 宮崎世龍

Mizuno Shigeru 水野成

Morito Tatsuo 森戶辰男

Moriyama Takashi 森山喬

Nagahama Retsu 長濱列

Nakamura Mitsuzō 中村光三

Nakamura Tōneo 中村登音夫

Nakanishi Ko 中西功

Nants'aiyüan 南榮園

Nishizato Tatsuo 西里龍夫

Nomura Kita 野村きた

Ōhara Magosaburō 大原孫三郎

Ōhashi Hideo 大橋秀雄

Ou Tso-ch'i 欧佐起

Ōuchi Hyōe 大內兵衛

Ōyama Ikuo 大山郁夫

Ozaki Eiko (née Hirose) 尾崎英子 （廣瀬）

Ozaki Honami 尾崎秀波

Ozaki Hotsuki 尾崎秀樹

Ozaki Hotsuma 尾崎秀眞

OZAKI HOTSUMI 尾崎秀實

Ozaki Yōko 尾崎楊子

Rōyama Masamichi 蠟山政道

Ryū Shintarō 笠信太郎

Saionji Kinkazu 西園寺公一

Sassa Hiroo 佐佐弘雄

Shida Shigeo 志田重義

Shiga Yoshio 志賀義雄

Shin Taisei Undō 新體制運動

Shina Kenkyū Shitsu 支那研究室

Shinozuka Torao 篠塚虎雄

Shirakawa Jirō 白川次郎

Shōwa Juku 昭和塾

Shōwa Kenkyū Kai 昭和研究會

Shuki 手記

Tachibana Shiraki 橘樸

Taira Teizō 平貞藏

Taisei Yokusan Kai 大政翼賛會

Takada Tadashi 高田正

Takahashi Yosuke 高橋與助

Takane Yoshisaburō 高根義三郎

Takano Iwasaburō 高野岩三郎

Takeuchi Kintarō 竹內金太郎

Tamazawa Mitsusaburō 玉澤 光三郎

T'ao Ching-sun 陶晶孫

Tenkō 轉向

Tōa Dōbun Shoin Daigaku 東亞 同文書院大學

Tōa Kyōdō Tai 東亞協同体

Tōa Mondai Chōsa Kai 東亞問題 調査會

Tōa Shinchitsujo 東亞新秩序

Tokkō 特高

Tokuda Kyūichi 德田球一

Ushiba Tomohiko 牛場友彦

Wang Hsüeh-wen 王學文

Yabe Teiji 矢部貞治

Yamakami Masayoshi 山上正義

Yamana Masazane 山名正實

Yamasaki Ken 山崎謙

Yang Liu-ch'ing 楊柳青

Yoshikawa Mitsusada 吉河光貞

Bibliography

❦❦❦

Bibliographical information is supplied under the following headings, with the works of Ozaki and Sorge (Sections I and III) in chronological order:

   I. The Works of Ozaki Hotsumi (A. Books, B. Articles in Japanese, C. Articles in English)
  II. A Note on Sorge's *shuki* (memoirs)
 III. Sorge's Articles for Karl Haushofer
  IV. Sources on Ozaki and the Sorge Incident (A. Japanese works, B. Western works)

I. THE WORKS OF OZAKI HOTSUMI

This list of Ozaki's works has been compiled on the basis of the writer's investigations and the bibliography prepared by his brother, Ozaki Hotsuki, which was published in *Gendai-shi shiryō*, III, 705–11. The entries based on the writer's research are more complete than those derived from the Ozaki Hotsuki bibliography. Unfortunately, copies of some of Ozaki's works have not survived the war and could not be read by the author. Ozaki's newspaper articles and his introductions to books by other authors have not been included here. Works published in several editions are cited only in the first edition. Details on other editions are given in the Notes. Shirakawa Jirō and Ou Tso-ch'i are pseudonyms of Ozaki Hotsumi.

A. Books

A-Q seiden (The True Story of Ah Q), by Lu Hsün. Shen Tuan-hsien (pseud. for Hsia Yen), Lin Shou-jen (pseud. for Yamakami Masayoshi), Mizuki Ryōsaku, and Shirakawa Jirō, translators. Tokyo: International Proletarian Library, Shiroku Shoin, October 1931.

Hōki (Insurrection), by Yeh Ch'en. Ou Tso-ch'i and T'ao Ching-sun, translators. Tokyo: International Proletarian Library, Shiroku Shoin, October 1931.

Onna hitori daichi o yuku (A Woman Walks the Earth Alone), by Agnes Smedley. Shirakawa Jirō, translator. Tokyo: Kaizō Sha, August 1934.

Arashi ni tatsu Shina, tenkanki Shina no gaikō seiji keizai (China Facing the Storm; The Foreign Relations, Politics, and Economics of China at a Turning Point). Tokyo: Ari Shobō, September 1937.

Kokusai kankei kara mita Shina (China Seen From the Point of View of International Relations). Tokyo: Dainikokuminkai Shuppanbu, November 1937.

Gendai Shina hihan (Critical Studies of Modern China). Tokyo: Chūō Kōron Sha, November 1938. [Copyright page reads Shōwa 11, but this is an error.]

Ajia mondai kōza (Lectures on the Problems of Asia). Ozaki Hotsumi et al., eds. 12 volumes. Tokyo: Sōgen Sha, January 1939 – April 1940. [Ozaki's main contributions are: "Kokumin kakumei igo no rekkyō to Shina" (The Great Powers and China After the National Revolution), Vol. I, pp. 257–84; "Tōa ni okeru shin-heiwa taisei e no michi" (The Road to a New Peace System in East Asia), Vol. II, pp. 3–20; "Shina shihonshugi hattatsu ryakushi" (Brief History of the Development of Chinese Capitalism), Vol. V, pp. 23–54; and "Kokumintō no keizai kensetsu" (Economic Construction by the Kuomintang), Vol. V, pp. 297–316.]

Gendai Shina ron (On Modern China). Tokyo: Iwanami Shoten, May 1939.

Shina shakai keizai ron (On Chinese Society and Economy). Tokyo: Seikatsu Sha, June 1940. [Gendai Shina ron and Shina shakai keizai ron were reprinted as Chūgoku shakai no kihon mondai, Ozaki Hotsumi senshū (Basic Problems of Chinese Society, Selected Works of Ozaki Hotsumi), Hosokawa Karoku and Horie Yūichi, eds. Tokyo: Sekai Hyōron Sha, September 1949.]

Tōa shinchitsujo kensetsu no riron to hōsaku (The Theory and Method of Constructing a New Order in East Asia). Shōwa Kenkyū Kai, East Asia Political Research Subcommittee, ed. Tokyo: Seikatsu Sha, June 1940. [Contributors: Ozaki Hotsumi, Okazaki Saburō, Koizumi Yoshio, Wada Kōsaku, Tachibana Shiraki, and Taira Teizō.]

Aijō wa furu hoshi no gotoku (Love Is Like a Falling Star). Tokyo: Sekai Hyōron Sha, September 1946.

B. Articles in Japanese

"Rintenki o kiku" (Listening to the Rotary Press), Ichikō dōsōkai kaihō (Bulletin of the Ichikō Alumni Association), No. 5, June 15, 1927, pp. 24–27.

"Hoku-Shi jihen no ato ni kuru mono" (Things to Come After the North China Emergency), Chūō kōron, No. 573 (August 1935), pp. 97–108.

"Tai-Shi seisaku no suishinryoku to sono genkai" (The Force Behind Our China Policy and Its Limits), Chūō kōron, No. 574 (September 1935), pp. 64–70. [Reprinted in Arashi ni tatsu Shina.]

"Shina no kokusai bōeki ni kan suru ikkōsatsu" (An Inquiry Concerning the International Trade of China), Jiyū tsūshō (Free Trade), April 1936. [Reprinted in Arashi ni tatsu Shina.]

"Shina o meguru Nisso kankei" (Soviet-Japanese Relations Concerning China), *Kokusai hyōron* (International Review), April 1936.

"Shō Kai-seki seiken saikin no dōkō" (Latest Trends in the Chiang Kai-shek Regime), in Nihon kokusai nenkan (Japan International Yearbook), 1936 ed. Published by Nihon Kokusai Mondai Chōsa Kai. Kawade Shobō, June 1936.

"Santō" (Shantung) and "In Jo-kō shi to no kaiken no ki" (Record of an Interview with Mr. Yin Ju-keng), in Tokyo Asahi Shimbun, East Asia Problems Investigation Association, ed., Genchi ni Shina o miru (China Seen Firsthand). Tokyo: Asahi Shimbun Sha, June 1936.

"Shina ni okeru Nichi-Ei keizaisen" (Anglo-Japanese Economic Warfare in China), *Jiyū tsūshō,* July 1936.

"Taiheiyō kaigi no Shina mondai" (The China Problem at the Pacific Conference), *Chūō kōron,* November 1936.

"Bōkyō mondai no tamen sei" (The Many Facets of the Anti-Communism Problem), *Nihon hyōron,* December 1936. [Reprinted in Arashi ni tatsu Shina.]

"Chō Gaku-ryō kūdeta no igi, Shina shakai no naibu-teki mujun no bakuhatsu" (The Significance of Chang Hsüeh-liang's Coup d'état, the Explosion of the Internal Contradictions in Chinese Society), *Chūō kōron,* No. 590 (January 1937), pp. 406–14. [Reprinted in Arashi ni tatsu Shina.]

"Shina ni okeru rekkyō" (The Great Powers in China), in Tokyo Asahi Shimbun, East Asia Problems Investigation Association, ed., Utsuri-yuku Shina (Changing China). Tokyo: Asahi Shimbun Sha, February 1937, pp. 269–99. [Series: Asahi jikyoku tokuhon, I.]

"Igirisu tai-Shi seisaku no shindankai" (New Stage in England's China Policy), *Kokusai hyōron,* March 1937. [Reprinted in Arashi ni tatsu Shina.]

"Sensō no kiki to tōa" (The War Crisis and East Asia), *Chūō kōron,* No. 593 (April 1937), pp. 153–60. [Reprinted in Arashi ni tatsu Shina.]

"Nisshi keizai teikei hihan" (Critique of Sino-Japanese Economic Cooperation), *Kaizō,* XIX:5 (May 1937), pp. 53–64. [Reprinted in Arashi ni tatsu Shina.]

"Shina no keizai kensetsu hihan" (Critique of China's Economic Construction), in Japanese Council, Institute of Pacific Relations, *Taiheiyō mondai* (Problems of the Pacific), June 1937. [Report on the IPR's Sixth Conference, Yosemite, California, 1936.] [Reprinted in Gendai Shina hihan.]

"Tenkanki Shina no kihon mondai" (Basic Problems of China at a Turning Point), *Chūō kōron,* No. 596 (July 1937), pp. 69–79. [Reprinted in Arashi ni tatsu Shina.]

"Nihon no tairiku seisaku to Manshū-Shina mondai" (Japan's Continental Policy and the Manchurian and North China Problems), in Tokyo Asahi Shimbun, East Asia Problems Investigation Association, ed., Shokuminchi no bunkatsu (Dismemberment of the Colonies). Tokyo: Asahi Shimbun Sha, August 1937. [Jointly authored with Masuda Toyohiko. Series: Asahi jikyoku tokuhon, VII.]

"Chūgoku kokumintō kyōsantō kankei shi" (History of Relations Between the Chinese Kuomintang and the Communist Party), *Nihon hyōron*, XII:9 (August 1937), pp. 109–24. [Reprinted in Gendai Shina hihan.]

"Hoku-Shi mondai no shindankai" (New Phase in the North China Problem), *Kaizō*, XIX:8 (August 1937), pp. 94–101. [Reprinted in Gendai Shina hihan.]

"Nankin seifu ron" (On the Nanking Government), *Chūō kōron*, No. 598 (September 1937), pp. 23–36. [Reprinted in Gendai Shina hihan.]

"Shina ni okeru Eikoku no seiryoku" (The Influence of Great Britain in China), *Chūō kōron*, October 1937. [Reprinted in Gendai Shina hihan.]

"Jikyoku to tai-Shi ninshiki" (The Present Situation and Knowledge About China), *Kaizō*, XIX:11 (October 1937), pp. 43–50. [Reprinted in Gendai Shina hihan.]

"Makao—'Tōyō no shinju' " (Macao, "Pearl of the East") by Agnes Smedley, Shirakawa Jirō, trans., *Chūō kōron*, No. 600 (Special issue, October 1937), pp. 414–22.

"Shū On-rai no chii" (The Position of Chou En-lai), *Chūō kōron*, No. 601 (November 1937), pp. 97–105.

"Haiboku Shina no shinro" (The Road Ahead for Defeated China), *Kaizō*, XIX:13 (November 1937), pp. 42–52. [Reprinted in Gendai Shina hihan.]

"Shina jihen to kokusai shihon" (The China Incident and International Capital), in Tokyo Council of Commerce and Industry, Research Department, ed., *Shina keizai nenpō* (Chinese Economic Annual), 1938 edition. Tokyo: Kaizō Sha, December 1937. [Reprinted in Gendai Shina hihan.]

"Kokkyō gassaku no shōrai" (The Future of Kuomintang-Communist Collaboration), *Nihon hyōron*, December 1937. [Reprinted in Gendai Shina hihan.]

"Chōki kōsen no yukikata" (The Methods of Protracted Resistance), *Kaizō*, XX:5 (May 1938), pp. 80–91. [Reprinted in Gendai Shina hihan.]

"Chōkisenka no shomondai" (Problems of a Protracted War), *Chūō kōron*, No. 609 (June 1938), pp. 70–82. [Reprinted in Gendai Shina hihan.]

"Shiki no uta" (Songs of the Four Seasons), *Tairiku*, June 1938.

"Nisshi sensō dai-san-ki" (The Third Phase of the Sino-Japanese War), *Tairiku*, August 1938. [Reprinted in Gendai Shina hihan.]

"Chōkisen o tatakai-nuke" (The Ability to Fight a Protracted War to the Finish), *Tairiku*, August 1938. [A round-table discussion including Nakano Seigō, Taira Teizō, and Ozaki.]

"Jihen to Shina keizai" (The Incident and China's Economy), in Tokyo Asahi Shimbun, East Asia Problems Investigation Association, ed., *Asahi tōa mondai nenpō* (Asahi Far Eastern Problems Yearbook), 1938 edition. Tokyo: Asahi Shimbun Sha, October 1938.

" 'Tōa kyōdō tai' no rinen to sono seiritsu no kakkanteki kiso" (The Idea of an "East Asian Cooperative Body" and the Objective Basis for Its Realization), *Chūō kōron*, No. 616 (January 1939), pp. 4–18. [Reprinted in the 75th Anniversary Issue of *Chūō kōron*, November 1960, pp. 400–411.]

"Jikyoku shūshū to kokumin saihensei" (Saving the Situation and the Reorganization of the People), *Kaizō*, January 1939. [A round-table discussion including Arima Yoriyasu, Takahashi Kamekichi, and Ozaki.]

"Tōa ni semaru sekai no atsuryoku" (The Pressure of the World Closing In on East Asia), *Bungei shunjū*, February 1939. [A round-table discussion including Ashida Hitoshi, Itō Masanori, and Ozaki.]

"Tōa seikyoku ni okeru ichijiteki teitai no arata naru hatten no yosō" (The Temporary Stagnation in the East Asian Political Situation and a Forecast of Future Events), *Kaizō*, XXI:3 (March 1939), pp. 6–21.

"Tōa shinchitsujo-ron no genzai oyobi shōrai" (The Present and Future of the Theory of a New Order in East Asia), *Tōa mondai*, April 1939.

"Kokumin seifu no seiritsu to tōitsu seisaku" (The Establishment of the National Government [in China] and the Policy of Unity), in *Tōa no gensei* (East Asia Today). Tokyo: Seibundō Shinkōsha, May 1939. [Series: Tōyō bunka shi taikei (Outline of the History of the Culture of the Orient), Vol. VII.]

"Dai-ni-ji sekai taisen to kyokutō" (The Second World War and the Far East), *Chūō kōron*, No. 620 (May 1939), pp. 72–96. [A round-table discussion including Hosokawa Karoku, Horie Yūichi, Taira Teizō, and Ozaki.]

"Ō Chō-mei mondai no shintenkai" (New Developments in the Wang Ching-wei Problem), *Chūō kōron*, No. 620 (May 1939), pp. 98–108.

"Chin kan-shō sensei" (Mr. Ch'en Han-sheng), *Gurafuikku* (Graphic), May 30, 1939.

"Abe naikaku seiritsu dai-ni-ji Ōshū taisen no jomaku" (Establishment of the Abe Cabinet and Raising the Curtain on the Second European Great War), *Jiji shiryō geppō*, No. 2 (September 10, 1939) (Current Materials Monthly Report) [South Manchurian Railroad].

"Ō-ha no kaobure" (The Lineup of the Wang Ching-wei Faction), *Tōa kōron-sha tsūshin*, No. 1 (October 1939).

"Dōran Ōshū no zento" (The Future of the European Upheaval), *Chūō kōron*, No. 625 (October 1939), pp. 62–89. [Round-table discussion including Ashida Hitoshi, Masuda Toyohiko, and Ozaki.]

"Shin tōa tembō" (Prospects for a New East Asia), *Tairiku*, January 1940.

"Kaishin subeki naisei no chikan jōtai" (The Need for Vigilance in the Precarious Internal Situation), *Jiji shiryō geppō*, No. 9 (April 15, 1940).

Ōshū senkyoku no kyūtenkai to seikyoku" (The Sudden Change in the European War and the Political Situation), *Jiji shiryō geppō*, No. 10 (May 22, 1940).

"Shintō mondai to seikyoku" (The Problem of the New Party and the Political Situation), *Jiji shiryō geppō,* No. 11 (June 15, 1940).

"Tōyō no shakai kōsei to Nisshi no shōrai" (The Social Composition of the Orient and the Future of Japan and China), *Chūō kōron,* No. 635 (July 1940), pp. 48–69. [A round-table discussion including Tachibana Shiraki, Hosokawa Karoku, Hirano Yoshitarō, and Ozaki.]

"Dai-ni-ji Konoye naikaku no seiritsu to shin seiji soshiki" (The Establishment of the Second Konoye Cabinet and the New Organization of Politics), *Jiji shiryō geppō,* No. 12 (July 30, 1940).

"Shintō undō no kokumin-teki kiso" (The Mass Basis of the New Party Movement), *Tairiku,* August 1940. [A round-table discussion including Miki Kiyoshi, Suzuki Tōmin, and Ozaki.]

"Manshūkoku to kyōwakai" (Manchukuo and the Concordia Society [Hsieh Ho Hui]), *Chūō kōron,* No. 640 (December 1940), pp. 90–98.

"Nanpō mondai to Shina mondai" (The Southern Question and the China Question), *Shin Ajia* (New Asia), December 1940.

"Kokumin seifu no shinkadai" (New Problems of the [Chinese] National Government), *Tōa kaihō* (East Asian Liberation), December 1940.

"Genjō iji seiryoku no ichijiteki antei to saikin no seiji jōsei ippan ni tsuite" (Concerning the Temporary Stability in the Present Maintenance of Power and the Contemporary Political Situation), *Jiji shiryō geppō,* No. 18 (January 24, 1941).

"Fuan no kasumi o motsu seiji jōsei" (The Mist of Uncertainty in the Present Political Situation), *Jiji shiryō geppō,* No. 19 (February 25, 1941).

"Hokushi jin kishitsu" (The Temperament of the North Chinese), *Tōa kaihō,* March 1941.

"Tōa kyōeiken no kitei ni yokotawaru jūyō mondai" (Important Problems in Laying the Foundation for the East Asia Co-Prosperity Sphere), *Kaizō,* March 1941.

"Jikyoku taidan" (Conversation on the Present Situation), *Tairiku,* March 1941. [A discussion between Kazami Akira and Ozaki.]

"Tōa no genjitsu to shisō" (The Reality and Thought of East Asia), *Tōa kaihō,* April 1941.

"Genjitsu seiji no suii" (The Transition in Current Politics), *Tairiku,* June 1941.

"Tenki o haramu kokusai jōsei to tōa" (The Crisis-Laden International Situation and East Asia), *Chūō kōron,* No. 647 (July 1941), pp. 4–25.

"Sekai sensō ni okeru Jūkei no yakuwari" (Chungking's Role in the World War), *Tōa kaihō,* July 1941.

"Doku-so kaisen to Jūkei no tachiba" (The Outbreak of the German-Soviet War and the Position of Chungking), *Kaizō,* August 1941.

"Tai-Bei kōshō to nanpō mondai" (The Negotiations with America and the Southern Question), *Jiji shiryō geppō,* No. 26 (September 30, 1941).

"Taisen o saigo made tatakai-nuku tame ni" (In Order to Fight a Great War to the End), *Kaizō*, November 1941.

C. *Articles in English*

"Japan's Friends in China," *Contemporary Japan*, Vol. IV, No. 2 (September 1935), pp. 252–58.

Recent Developments in Sino-Japanese Relations. Tokyo: Japanese Council, Institute of Pacific Relations, Data Paper No. 14, June 28, 1936.

"New Far Eastern Diplomacy," *Contemporary Japan*, Vol. VII, No. 1 (June 1938), pp. 29–39.

"Activities of Wu P'ei-fu and Wang Ching-wei," *Contemporary Japan*, Vol. VIII, No. 2 (April 1939), pp. 245–55.

"The New National Structure," *Contemporary Japan*, Vol. IX, No. 10 (October 1940), pp. 1284–92.

II. A NOTE ON SORGE'S SHUKI (MEMOIRS)

The primary sources of information on Sorge's early life and position within the Comintern–Red Army organization are his *shuki* (memoirs). There are two *shuki,* and the second is in two parts.

The first is not technically a *shuki*. It was written by Japanese police officers and prosecutors as a summary of Sorge's answers to the first phase of questioning. It was then printed in Naimushō Keihokyoku (Home Ministry, Police Bureau), *Shōwa jūshichi-nen-chū ni okeru gaiji keisatsu gaikyō* (Summary of Police Work Connected with Foreign Affairs for 1942, known to SCAP as the "Foreign Affairs Yearbook") (Tokyo, 1943), pp. 513–35. It served as a supplement to a general analysis of the Sorge case, printed in *ibid.,* pp. 398–512. Both the analysis and Sorge's first *shuki* are reprinted in *Gendai-shi shiryō,* I, 3–110 (analysis) and 113–35 (*shuki*).

The second *shuki* was written by Sorge in German on a typewriter supplied to him by Yoshikawa Mitsusada. It was then translated into Japanese by Ikoma Yoshitoshi and published in two parts, as follows: (1) Shihōshō Keijikyoku (Justice Ministry, Bureau of Criminal Affairs), *Zoruge jiken shiryō, II, Rihiaruto Zoruge shuki yakubun dai-ichi-hen* (Materials on the Sorge Incident, II, First Part of the Translation of the Memoirs of Richard Sorge) (Tokyo, February 1942); and (2) same source and title except for numeral "III" and "Second Part" (Tokyo, April 1942). Each copy was numbered, and they were labeled "Handle with Caution" and "Secret" (*kimitsu*). Copies of the printed documents comprising the first and second *shuki* were discovered by SCAP after the war in storage outside of Tokyo.

The original German typescript of Sorge's second *shuki* was destroyed in the bombing of the Justice Ministry in the spring of 1945. However, 24 pages of it have survived. Yoshikawa Mitsusada removed 24 pages from Sorge's original draft in 1942—pages in which he dealt with his espionage activities in Shanghai, on which Yoshikawa asked him to elaborate. Yoshikawa kept these 24 pages in his private files and turned them over to General Willoughby in 1949. Yoshikawa also gave Willoughby an affidavit which reads in part: "That said document [the 24 pages] is a portion of a statement which Richard Sorge first prepared and corrected in my presence in the procurator's examination room within the Tokyo detention house during October and November 1941 and handed to me." House Committee on Un-American Activities, *American Aspects of the Richard Sorge Spy Case,* testimony of Yoshikawa, August 9, 1951, pp. 1148–49. These pages are the only parts of the German original still extant.

Willoughby returned his copies of the Justice Ministry publications and Yoshikawa's German draft to Japan in approximately 1952. The Foreign Ministry reprinted the original Ikoma translation of the second *shuki* plus the Yoshikawa supplement in October of 1953; and the Public Security Office (Kōan Jimushitsu) reprinted the same material in November 1953. In January 1957, these documents were reprinted a third time as Keisatsuchō Keibibu (Police Agency, Police Guard Division), "Zoruge o chūshin to suru kokusai chōhō-dan jiken" (The International Spy Ring Incident Centered Around Sorge), *Gaiji keisatsu shiryō* (Foreign Affairs Police Materials), Vol. III, No. 5. It is a copy of the latter edition that is printed in *Gendai-shi shiryō,* I, 139–222. Willoughby had these items translated into English by his staff prior to returning them to Japan, and he published certain parts of them in *Shanghai Conspiracy,* pp. 134–230. As we have noted in this book, Willoughby's version contains several mistranslations. All translations in the present volume were made independently by the author from the Japanese text in *Gendai-shi shiryō.*

For the history of Sorge's *shuki,* see *Gendai-shi shiryō,* I, pp. v–xv; Ikoma Yoshitoshi, "Zoruge kaisō" (Recollections of Sorge), *Misuzu,* IV:3 (March 1962), pp. 19–22; and "Zoruge jiken ni-jū-nen me no shinsō" (The Truth of the Sorge Incident After Twenty Years), *Shūkan asahi,* September 7, 1962, pp. 12–20.

III. SORGE'S ARTICLES FOR KARL HAUSHOFER

"Mandschukuo im Umbau," *Zeitschrift für Geopolitik,* Vol. XII, No. 6 (June 1935), pp. 342–50.
"Die Armeerevolte in Tokio," *ibid.,* Vol. XIII, No. 5 (May 1936), pp. 307–17.
"Japanische Agrarfragen," *ibid.,* Vol. XIV, No. 1 (January 1937), pp. 18–24; Vol. XIV, No. 2 (February 1937), pp. 132–38; and Vol. XIV, No. 3 (March 1937), pp. 211–21.
"Zur Lage in der Innerem Mongolie," *ibid.,* Vol. XIV, No. 5 (May 1937), pp. 361–73.
"Hongkong und Südwest-China im japanisch-chinesischen Konflikt I," *ibid.,* Vol. XV, No. 7 (July 1938), pp. 524–32.

"Kanton und Südwest-China im japanisch-chinesischen Konflikt II," *ibid.*, Vol. XV, No. 8 (August 1938), pp. 638–44.

"Die japanische Wirtschaft im Chinakriege," *ibid.*, Vol. XVI, No. 2 (February 1939), pp. 104–13; Vol. XVI, No. 3 (March 1939), pp. 173–84.

"Die japanische Expansion," *ibid.*, Vol. XVI, Nos. 8–9 (August – September 1939), pp. 617–22. ["Festschrift zum 70. Geburtstag ihres Herausgebers Karl Haushofer am 27 August 1939."]

IV. SOURCES ON OZAKI AND THE SORGE INCIDENT

A. Japanese Works

Aochi Shin. Gendai-shi no magarikado (Turning Points in Modern History). Tokyo: Kōbundō, 1959.

———. "Janarizumu to kyōfu" (Journalism and Terror), *Shisō*, No. 360 (June 1954), pp. 67–71.

Asahi Shimbun, Political and Economic Section Associates, eds. Nihon o ugokasu sambyaku nin (The Three Hundred Men Who Move Japan). Tokyo: Niyūsu Sha, 1948.

Furuta Hikaru. "Dai-ni-ji taisenka no shisō-teki jōkyō" (Ideological Conditions During World War II), in Kindai Nihon shisō shi (Intellectual History of Contemporary Japan), Vol. III. Tokyo: Aoki Shoten, 1956, pp. 679–733.

Horie Yūichi and Kozai Yoshishige, eds. Idai naru aijō (The Great Love). Tokyo: Ikuseisha, 1949.

Hosokawa Karoku. "Shosai no omoide" (Memories From My Study), *Shisō*, No. 357 (March 1954), pp. 105–14.

———. Shina kakumei to sekai no myōnichi (The Chinese Revolution and the World of Tomorrow). Tokyo: Dōjin Sha, 1928.

Ikoma Yoshitoshi. "Zoruge kaisō" (Recollections of Sorge), *Misuzu*, Vol. IV, No. 3 (March 1962), pp. 12–22.

Inukai Ken. "Yōsukō wa ima mo nagarete iru" (The Yangtze Still Flows), *Bungei shunjū,* June 1959, pp. 260–75.

Iwabuchi Tatsuo. "Kizoku to seiji to shi to" (Nobility, Politics, and Death), *Bungei shunjū,* June 1954 (extra issue), pp. 116–29.

Kainō Michitaka. "Dokuso kaisen no nazo" (The Puzzle of the Outbreak of the Russo-German War), *Asahi Journal,* Vol. V, No. 8 (February 24, 1963), pp. 56–57.

Kamiyama Shigeo. "Saigo no akushu" (The Last Handshake), *Jinmin hyōron,* Vol. III, No. 6 (November 1947), pp. 48–51.

———. "Shi mo mata suzushi" (Death Can Be a Relief), *Akahata,* No. 78 (November 9, 1946), p. 2.

Kawai Teikichi. Aru kakumeika no kaisō (Memoirs of a Revolutionary). Tokyo: Nihon Shuppan Kyōkai, 1953.

————. "Shuki o yonde" (On Reading [Sorge's] Memoirs), *Ronsō,* March 1962, pp. 179–81.

Kazama Michitarō. Aru hangyaku, Ozaki Hotsumi no shōgai (A Case of Treason, The Life of Ozaki Hotsumi). Tokyo: Shinseidō, 1959.

Kazami Akira. Konoye naikaku (The Konoye Cabinets). Tokyo: Nihon Shuppan Kyōdō K.K., 1951.

————. "Ozaki Hotsumi hyōden—junkyōsha e no banka" (A Critical Biography of Ozaki Hotsumi, An Elegy for a Martyr), *Kaizō,* August 1951, pp. 72–83.

Kinoshita Junji. Otto to yobareru Nihonjin (A Japanese Called "Otto"). Tokyo: Chikuma Shobō, 1963.

Kiya Ikusaburō. Konoye kō hibun (Private Conversations with Prince Konoye). Takano, Wakayama Prefecture: Takanoyama Shuppan Sha, 1950.

Kobayashi Gorō. Tokkō keisatsu hiroku (Secret Record of the Special Higher Police). Tokyo: Seikatsu Shinsha, 1952.

Koyūkai. Tōa dōbun shoin daigaku shi (History of the East Asia Common Script University). Tokyo: Koyūkai, 1955.

Matsumoto Seichō. "Kakumei o uru otoko Itō Ritsu" (Itō Ritsu, The Man Who Sold Out the Revolution), *Bungei shunjū,* June 1960, pp. 194–226.

Matsumoto Shin'ichi. "Kaji-shi no 'Ozaki Hotsumi ron' " (Mr. Kaji's "Essay on Ozaki Hotsumi"), *Jinmin hyōron,* Vol. III, No. 6 (November 1947), pp. 45–47.

————. "Nihon teikokushugi to Ozaki Hotsumi" (Japanese Imperialism and Ozaki Hotsumi), *Sekai,* December 1946, pp. 81–89.

————. "Ozaki Hotsumi no omoide" (Recollections of Ozaki Hotsumi), *Jinmin hyōron,* Vol. II, No. 11 (December 1946), pp. 34–36.

Misuzu Shobō, ed. Gendai-shi shiryō, Zoruge jiken (Materials on Modern History, The Sorge Incident). Tokyo: Misuzu Shobō, 1962. Three volumes.

————. Gendai-shi shiryō geppō (Materials on Modern History Monthly Report). Three numbers. Tokyo: Misuzu Shobō, August, October, December, 1962.

Mitamura Takeo. Sensō to kyōsanshugi, Shōwa seiji hiroku (War and Communism, Secret Records of Shōwa Politics). Tokyo: Minshu Seido Fukyū Kai, 1950.

Miyakawa Tōru. Miki Kiyoshi. Kindai Nihon no shisōka (Thinkers of Modern Japan), Vol. X. Tokyo: Daigaku Shuppan Kai, 1958.

Miyake Hanako [Ishii Hanako]. Ningen Zoruge, Aijin Miyake Hanako no shuki (The Man Sorge, Memoirs of His Mistress Miyake Hanako). Tokyo: Nisshin Shoten, 1949.

Moriyama Takashi. "Share-otoko Ozaki Hotsumi" (Ozaki Hotsumi, a Bel Esprit), *Bungei shunjū,* June 1955, pp. 122–26.

Oda Toshiyo. Konoye shintaisei no zenbō (A Full View of the Konoye New Structure). Tokyo: Kōkoku Nihon Shimbun Sha, 1940.

Ohata Takemi. Kakusaretaru rekishi (Hidden History). Tokyo: Hokushindō, 1951.

Ozaki Hotsuki. Ikite iru yuda (The Living Judas). Tokyo: Hachi-un Shoten, 1959.

―――. "Kakumei—densetsu, henkaku, to yutopia" (Revolution—Legend, Reform, and Utopia), Shisō no kagaku, No. 13 (April 1963), pp. 11–17.

―――. Zoruge jiken, Ozaki Hotsumi no risō to zasetsu (The Sorge Incident, The Ideals and Frustrations of Ozaki Hotsumi). Tokyo: Chūō Kōron Sha, 1963.

Ryū Shintarō. "Shinjitsu no mutsukashisa—Ozaki Hotsumi kun no koto" (The Difficulty of Truth: Notes on Ozaki Hotsumi), Misuzu, No. 49 (May 1963), pp. 2–8.

Saionji Kinkazu. Kizoku no taijō (Exit of the Nobility). Tokyo: Bungei Shunjū Shinsha, 1951.

Sassa Hiroo. Shōwa seiji hishi (The Tragic History of Shōwa Politics). Tokyo: Nihon Hōsō Shuppan Kyōkai, 1946.

Shigemitsu Mamoru. Shōwa no dōran (The Upheavals of the Shōwa Era). Tokyo: Chūō Kōron Sha, 1952. Two volumes.

Suda Teiichi. "Nitchū mondai ni shōgai o kakete, Kazami Akira no hito to shisō" (A Life Staked on the Sino-Japanese Problem; Kazami Akira, the Man and His Thought), Sekai, No. 207 (March 1963), pp. 264–72.

Takezaki Yōnosuke. Futatsu no sokoku (Two Fatherlands). Tokyo: Chūō Sha, 1949.

Tsurumi Shunsuke. "Yokusan undō no sekkei-sha" (The Planners of the Imperial Assistance Movement), in Tenkō (Conversion), Vol. II, pp. 53–120. Tokyo: Heibon Sha, 1960.

Uirobii, C. A. [Willoughby]. Sekishoku supai dan no zenbō, Zoruge jiken (Full Report on the Red Spy Ring, The Sorge Incident). Fukuda Tarō, trans. Tokyo: Tōsei Namboku Sha, 1953.

Yabe, Teiji, ed. Konoye Fumimaro. Tokyo: Kōbundō, 1952. Two volumes.

Yamada Munemutsu. "Miki Kiyoshi," Asahi Journal, Vol. V, No. 14 (April 7, 1963), pp. 88–93.

Yamazaki Rintarō. Sekishoku kakumei wa semaru (The Red Revolution Is Close at Hand). Tokyo: Jiyū Hyōron Sha, 1949.

B. Western Works

Dallin, David. Soviet Espionage. New Haven: Yale University Press, 1955.

Dirksen, Herbert von. Moskau, Tokio, London. Stuttgart: W. Kohlhammer Verlag, 1949.

Dōmei Tsūshin Sha, ed. Wartime Legislation in Japan. Tokyo: Nippon Shōgyō Tsūshin Sha, 1941.

Erickson, John. The Soviet High Command, A Military-Political History, 1918–1941. London: St. Martin's Press, 1962.

International Military Tribunal for the Far East. Proceedings. Tokyo: April 29, 1946 – November 12, 1948.

Lyushkoff, General G. S. "The Far Eastern Red Army," Contemporary Japan, Vol. VIII, No. 8 (October 1939), pp. 1022–25.

Maruyama Masao. Thought and Behavior in Modern Japanese Politics. I. Morris, ed. London: Oxford University Press, 1963.

Massing, Hede. This Deception. New York: Duell, Sloan and Pearce, 1951.

Meissner, Hans-Otto. The Man With Three Faces. New York: Rinehart, 1955.

Presseisen, Ernst L. Germany and Japan, A Study in Totalitarian Diplomacy. The Hague: Nijhoff, 1958.

Schellenberg, Walter. The Schellenberg Memoirs. Louis Hagen, ed. and trans. London: Andre Deutsch, 1956.

Smedley, Agnes. Daughter of Earth. New York: Coward-McCann, 1935.

———. "The Tokyo Martyrs," Far East Spotlight, Vol. V, No. 3 (March 1949), pp. 3–5.

Tolischus, Otto D. Tokyo Record. New York: Reynal and Hitchcock, 1943.

U.S. Army, Far East Command, Military Intelligence Section. A Partial Documentation of the Sorge Espionage Case. Tokyo: Toppan Printing Co., 1950.

———. "The Sorge Spy Ring—A Case Study in International Espionage in the Far East." U.S. 81st Congress, First Session, Congressional Record, Vol. 95, Part 12 (February 9, 1949), Appendix, pp. A705–A723.

U.S. House of Representatives, 82nd Congress, First Session, Committee on Un-American Activities. Hearings on American Aspects of the Richard Sorge Spy Case. Washington: Government Printing Office, 1951.

U.S. Senate, 82nd Congress, First Session, Committee on the Judiciary. Institute of Pacific Relations Hearings, Part 2. Washington: Government Printing Office, 1951.

Willoughby, Charles A. Shanghai Conspiracy, The Sorge Spy Ring. New York: Dutton, 1952. (The English edition is Sorge: Soviet Master Spy. London: William Kimber, 1952.)

Index

A Japanese Called "Otto," 2, 84–85, 237–38
A Woman Walks the Earth Alone, 62, 100. *See also Daughter of Earth*
Abwehr, 148f
Aijō wa furu hoshi no gotoku, see Love Is Like a Falling Star
Akahata (Red Flag), 200, 203, 210, 219, 221, 224, 226, 244, 256
Amakusa Masahiko, 29
Amemiya Yōzō, 135
Amsterdam Handelsblad, 16, 96
Anarchism, 29, 94
Anti-Comintern Pact, 154
Anzai Kuraji, 55–58 *passim*
Aochi Shin, 6, 8, 98, 116
Arashi ni tatsu Shina, 16, 123
Arima Yoriyasu, Count, 121, 130
Asahi shimbun, 18, 25, 121, 201; and Ozaki, 3, 10, 34, 40, 49, 88, 124, 138, 203; East Asia Problems Investigation Association (Tōa Mondai Chōsa Kai), 99–101, 239
Asameshi Kai, *see* Breakfast Society
Asanuma Sumitsugu, 187
"Asiatic mode of production" theory, 131, 197. *See also* Wittfogel, Karl
Axis Alliance, 155, 172

Baldwin Park, California, 92f
Bauer, Dr. Max, 77
Berliner Börsen Zeitung, 96
"Bernhardt," 91, 95, 97, 101, 164, 167
Berzin, General I. A., 68, 90–91, 95, 97, 101
Bickerton, William M., 134, 244–45
Blücher, V., *see* Blyukher, Vasili K.
Blyukher, Vasili K., 149
Boxer Rebellion, 22
Breakfast Society, 26, 50, 113, 125–27, 146, 155
Britain, *see* Imperialism, British
Bukharin, N., 32, 73

Canaris, Wilhelm, 148
Chang Hsüeh-liang, 64, 112

Chang Tzu-p'ing, 52
Chang-ku-feng Incident, 146–49
Chapei, 43, 80
Chattopadhyaya, Virendranath, 63
Ch'eng Fang-wu, 52
Chiang Kai-shek, 15f, 37, 42, 44–46, 49f, 64, 77, 131–32
China, 1ff, 222f, 226; revolution in, 5, 9, 17, 19, 33; thought reform in, 188–89. *See also* Nationalism, Chinese
China Facing the Storm, 16, 123
China Research Office (Shina Kenkyū Shitsu), 55, 133–35
Chinese Communist Army, 138
Chinese Communist Party, 3, 16, 20, 64, 101, 191, 197; and Shanghai, 42, 45–46, 55ff, 67; and Japanese Communist Party, 223
Chinese Revolution and the World of Tomorrow, The, 39
Chu Teh, 62
Ch'uang-tsao She (Creation Society), 9, 51–54
Chūbu mimpō, JCP organ, 207
Chūō kōron (Central Review), 38n, 101, 128–29, 135–36, 173
Clausen, Anna, 102–5, 163, 166, 168, 199f
Clausen, Max, 95, 101–6, 143, 156, 162–68, 178, 182, 199f
Codes, 95–96, 101, 106, 165
Cominform, 220
Comintern (Communist International), 1ff, 12, 20, 33, 61, 92; Sorge ring as directed by, 9–10, 87, 183, 206, 213; Third Congress, 63; Sixth Congress, 63, 73; Fourth Congress, 72n; Executive Committee (ECCI), 72–73; and Peace Preservation Law, 170, 184–86; Ozaki's attitude toward, 195–96
Communism, 1f, 6, 188–89
Communist International, *see* Comintern
Concordia Society (Hsieh Ho Hui), 121, 138
Confucianism, 24
Contemporary Japan, 134

Conversion, see *Tenkō*; *Tenkōsha*; *Gisō tenkō*; *Tenkōsho*
Council in the Imperial Presence (July 1941), 11, 154, 157–58, 162
Cox, James, 142, 184
Creation Society (Ch'uang-tsao She), 9, 51–54
Cunningham, Defense Counsel before IMTFE, 145
Current Materials Monthly Report, 137, 178. See also South Manchurian Railroad

Dai Tōa Kyōei Ken (Greater East Asia Co-Prosperity Sphere), see East Asian Cooperative Body
Dan Takuma, 87
Daughter of Earth, 10, 62, 66, 100
Davis, Lieutenant Colonel T. P., 209
Dennis, Eugene, alias "Paul Walsh," 82–83
Department Four (Intelligence), see Red Army, Soviet
Deutsches Nachrichten Büro (DNB), 140, 142
Dirksen, Ambassador Herbert von, 16, 123, 140ff, 156
Disguised conversion, see *Gisō tenkō*
Doihara Kenji, 197
Dōmei News Agency, 105, 107, 126, 143
Dutch community, Tokyo, 143

East Asia Problems Investigation Association (Tōa Mondai Chōsa Kai) 99–101, 239
East Asian Cooperative Body (Tōa Kyōdō Tai), 5–8, 15, 116, 119–20
Emperor system, 27, 117, 190, 192, 201
Erickson, John, 149, 159
Espionage, 72–73, 82, 90–91, 98, 106–7, 124; techniques of, 126–28, 140, 162–68, 178–79. See also Sorge spy ring, exposure of; Tokkō; Ozaki Hotsumi; Sorge, Richard; Radio
Everson, English police inspector, 44f

Farben, I. G., cartel, 100
February 26 Incident, 13, 109, 141–42
Feng Nai-ch'ao, 52
First International, 1, 12, 69
Fort Holabird, U.S. Army Intelligence School, 209n
Frankfurter Zeitung, 11, 16, 61, 63, 96, 100, 143f
French Communist Party, 92
Fujita Isamu, 109
Funakoshi Hisao, 58, 60, 81–82, 110, 138, 182
Funatsu Hiroshi, 172

Fundamental Japan Society (Genri Nihon Sha), 117
Furuta Hikaru, 116, 118
Fuyuno Takeo, 39

Genchi ni Shina o miru, 101
Gendai Shina ron, 3, 131–32
Gendai-shi shiryō, 2, 214
Genri Nihon Sha (Fundamental Japan Society), 117
German Communist Party, 12, 60, 71–72, 95, 145
German Embassy, Tokyo, 96, 101, 105, 140–46, 155–56, 161, 164, 171
German Social Democratic Party, 70–71
Germany, 69–70, 77, 89
Gestapo, 171–72
Gifu prefecture, 21, 24, 35, 174
Gisō tenkō (disguised conversion), 18f, 117f, 174
Gotō Fumio, 115
Gotō Ryūnosuke, 114, 133
Gotō Shimpei, 22ff, 32
Gozen kaigi, see Council in the Imperial Presence
Great Love, The, 205–6, 244–45
Greater East Asia Co-Prosperity Sphere (Dai Tōa Kyōei Ken), see East Asian Cooperative Body

Hakuun roku (Reflections on a White Cloud), 198
Hamburg, 12, 70f, 103
Han Fu-ch'ü, 101, 132
Hasegawa Hiroshi, 219, 223
Haushofer, Karl, 12, 96, 142, 144
Havas Agency, 91f, 150, 168
Heinkel Aircraft Company, 142
Heydrich, Reinhard, 171
Himmler, Heinrich, 12, 171, 180
Hirano Yoshitarō, 17
Hirata Atsutane, 24, 195
Hirose Eiko, see Ozaki Eiko
Hitler, Adolf, 141, 154f, 167, 180
Hongkew, 49, 80
Horie Yūichi, 2, 14f, 89, 134, 204f, 210
Horikawa Yūhō, 194
Hosokawa Karoku, 2, 17, 37–39, 89, 115, 134
House Committee on Un-American Activities, 65, 79, 182f, 211
Hsiao Hua, 62
Hsin Min Hui (New Citizen's Association), 121

Ichikō, 25f, 33, 38, 113, 174, 189, 244
Ichijima Seiichi, 198
Idai naru aijō, 205–6, 244–45
Ikite iru yuda, 25n, 208, 213–14
Ikoma Yoshitoshi, 160, 183, 188

Imperial Rule Assistance Association (Taisei Yokusan Kai), 6f, 121, 130, 138
Imperial University, *see* Teidai
Imperialism: Japanese, 2, 4f, 78–81, 111–13, 122–23, 192, 194; British, 7, 44–45, 86, 112, 191; in Shanghai, 9, 46–50 *passim*
Inomata Tsunao, 28
Inouye Junnosuke, 87
Institute of Pacific Relations, 87, 107, 111–13 ,121, 204n
International Military Tribunal for the Far East, 145
International Red Relief (MOPR), 55, 61, 88
International Settlement, Shanghai, 41, 54, 80
International Union of Revolutionary Writers, 60, 64
Inukai Ken, 2, 14, 50, 55, 126, 180, 204; and Wang Ching-wei, 133, 153
Inukai Ki, 50, 87, 141
Ishihara Kanji, 78
Ishii Hanako, *see* Miyake Hanako
Ishikawa Tatsuzō, 135–36
Itagaki Seishirō, 78, 128, 152
Itō Ken'ichi, 223
Itō Ritsu, 174–77; as betrayer of the Sorge ring, 14f, 25n, 210, 212–14, 217–18, 226; as leader of postwar JCP, 207–8, 219–25, 255–56
Itō Taketora, 176f, 218
Iwabuchi Tatsuo, 179
Iwamoto Iwao, 223
Iwanami Publishers, 38n, 131, 243–44
Iwasaki Gorō, 176

Japan, 26–29, 91; militarism in, 1, 5, 18, 86–89, 114–21, 192, 200, 204; police repression in, 38–40, 88–89; oil reserves, 158; prewar legal system, 186–89; occupation of, 200–201, 204. *See also* Imperialism, Japanese
Japan-China Struggle League (Nisshi Tōsō Dōmei), 55–58
Japanese Army, 3, 99, 105, 148, 152, 158, 173. *See also* February 26 Incident; Kempei; Kwantung Army; Tokumu Kikan
Japanese Communist Party, 2, 27, 55, 89, 118, 134; March 15, 1928, Incident, 39–40; prewar rebuilding of, 110, 174f, 203; and expulsion of Itō, 176, 213–14, 217, 223–25; postwar activities, 200–207, 218–22; and Sorge case, 210, 212
Japanese Communist Youth League, 174f
Japanese government: Communications Ministry, 164–65, 169; Justice Ministry, 181–85, 190, 206; Home Ministry,

182; War Ministry, 182, 185; Foreign Ministry, 184–85; Supreme Court, 184, 187–88, 192, 195f
Japanese Navy, 58, 80–81, 87, 99, 169, 174
Jiji shiryō geppō,137,178. *See also* South Manchurian Railroad
Jinmin hyōron, 201ff, 205

KPD, *see* German Communist Party
Kaieda Hisataka, 137
Kaizō, 38n, 173
Kaji Ryūichi, 18, 99, 205
Kamiyama Shigeo, 174f, 203–6, 218
Kanokogi Kazunobu, 119
Kantō Earthquake, 28–29
Kantō Publishing Workers Union, 34
Kao-sha, Taiwanese minority group, 24
Kapp Putsch, 71
Kasuga Shōichi, 223
Kasuga Shōjirō, 219
Katō Eitarō, 55–56
Kawai Teikichi, 6, 58, 60, 66, 80, 85, 163, 199f; espionage work of, 79, 90, 109–10; postwar activities of, 201, 206–8, 210–14, 220
Kawai Yoshitora, 29
Kawakami Hajime, 52, 57, 88
Kawamura Yoshio, 55–56, 182
Kazahaya Yasoji, 134
Kazama Michitarō, 89, 98, 175, 194, 201, 204, 208, 211–12, 214
Kazami Akira, 15, 114, 121–24, 126, 130, 133, 153; and Sorge case, 2, 179–80, 214
Kempei, 8, 74, 172–74, 184, 190, 210
Kensetsusha Dōmei, at Waseda University, 29
Ketsumeidan (The Blood Brotherhood), 87
Khabarovsk, 14, 106
Khalkhin-gol, 149
Kiangnan Student News (*Kōnan gakuhō*), 56
Kiel Mutiny, 71
Kinoshita Junji, 84–85
Kishi Michizō, 125–26, 160, 189
Kishi Yamaji, 226
Kita Ikki, 141
Kitabayashi Tomo, 94, 107, 177–78, 217, 226
Kitabayashi Yoshisaburō, 94, 177–78
Kitō Gin'ichi, 67
Kiyonoya Toshisumi, 34
Kobayashi Shunzō, 192–95 *passim*
Kobayashi Takiji, 11, 88, 244
Kodai Yoshinobu, 151
Kodama Gentarō, General, 22
Kokutai (national polity), 18, 117, 170, 185, 188–89, 195
Komatsu Yūichirō, 218

Konno Yojirō, 223, 225
Konoye Atsumaro, 17n, 24
Konoye Fumimaro, Prince, 6ff, 14, 114ff,
  126, 128–29, 150, 153, 179f; first cab-
  inet, 1f, 16, 26, 85, 105, 113, 120, 130–
  31; second cabinet, 2, 158, 161; third
  cabinet, 14, 158–59, 161, 179
Korea, 5, 28f, 214, 221
Kozai Yoshishige, 194, 205
Kretschmer, Colonel, 145, 155–56
Kriebel, Lieutenant Colonel Hermann
  von, 68n, 77f
Kronstadt Mutiny, 101
Ku Cheng-hung, 43
Kuo Mo-jo, 52
Kuomintang, 16, 54, 129, 131–32
Kuusinen, O., 68, 72, 95
Kwantung Army, 49, 78, 137, 139, 145,
  147–52, 157–58, 196–97
Kyoto University, 27, 88, 118

Labor unions: in Japan, 27ff, 34, 38f; in
  China, 42–46
Lake Khasan Operation, 146
Lao She, 62
League of Left-Wing Writers, 53–54
League of Nations, 88, 113
League to Struggle Against Imperialism
  and Colonial Oppression, 60, 63
Li Tsung-jen, 132
Lin Piao, 64
Litvinov, Maxim, 147
Liu Hsiang, 132
Living Judas, The, 25n, 208, 213–14
Losovskii, S. A., 72
Love Is Like a Falling Star, 36, 135, 189–
  90, 202–3, 206, 214
Lu Hsün, 9, 53–54, 62, 234
Lukouch'iao, *see* Marco Polo Bridge
Lytton Commission, 113
Lyushkov, General G. S., 148–49, 247

MacArthur, General Douglas, 200f, 221
Makino Takeo, 135
Manchester Guardian, 65, 245
Manchukuo, 100, 137, 146, 149–52
Manchurian Incident (1931), 49, 59, 78–
  80, 86, 112–13, 152
Mantetsu Chōsa-bu (South Manchurian
  Railroad Investigation Department),
  see South Manchurian Railroad
Manuilskii, D. Z., 68, 72, 95
Mao Tse-tung, 37, 46, 218
Mao Tun, 62
Marco Polo Bridge (Lukouch'iao), 16,
  122
Maruyama Masao, 155, 198, 225
Mass Literature (Ta-chung wen-i), 52–
  53

Massing, Hede, 108–9
*Materials on Modern History (Gendai-
  shi shiryō)*, 2, 214
Matsukata Gisaburō, 126
Matsumoto Saneki, 223
Matsumoto Seichō, 174, 176, 218
Matsumoto Shigeharu, 11, 18, 115, 124,
  126, 160
Matsumoto Shin'ichi, 26, 31, 36, 134–35,
  189–90, 192, 194–97, 244; postwar ac-
  tivities, 201–7
Matsumoto Toshiko, 205
Matsuoka Yōsuke, 152–55, 157–58
Matzki, Colonel, 145, 155
May 30 Movement, 33, 42–46
McCarran Committee, IPR investiga-
  tion, 108, 183
Meisinger, Colonel Joseph, 171–72
Meissner, Hans-Otto, 144, 214n
Miki Kiyoshi, 19, 115, 118–19, 128
"Minami Ryūichi," *see* Miyagi Yotoku
Minobe Tatsukichi, 27, 117
Mitsubishi combine, 99
Mitsui combine, 87, 99, 137
Miwa Jusō, 115, 189, 192
Miyagi Yosei, 92–93
Miyagi Yotoku, 90–95, 97, 105, 110, 144f,
  168, 178, 182f; espionage by, 137, 141,
  147, 151, 154, 217
Miyakawa Tōru, 118
Miyake Hanako, 14, 173, 229
Miyamoto Kenji, 134, 203, 219ff, 225
Miyamoto Yuriko, 202
Miyashita Hiroshi, 176, 218
Miyazaki Seiryū, 51, 85n
Miyazaki Torazō, 40
Mizuno Shigeo, 30n, 110
Mizuno Shigeru, 55–56, 85, 89, 110–11,
  134, 150, 178, 182
Molotov-Ribbentrop Pact, 150, 154
Mongolian People's Republic, 150
Morin, Relman, 142
Morito Tatsuo, 31–32, 38, 40
Moriyama Takashi, 25, 100
Motoori Norinaga, 195
Münzenberg, Willi, 60

Nabeyama Sadachika, 189, 197
Nagahama Retsu, 208
Naigai Wata Kaisha (Foreign and Do-
  mestic Cotton Company), 42–43
Nakamura Mitsuzō, 183, 187–88, 190, 192
Nakamura Tōneo, 183, 190
Nakanishi Ko, 17, 55–58, 82, 138, 202;
  and postwar JCP, 2, 205f, 210, 218
Nankatsu Labor Union, 29
Nanking government: Chiang Kai-shek,
  46, 77, 112, 123, 131–32; Wang Ching-
  wei, 133, 153

Nants'aiyüan, 23
Nappu (Nippon Proleta Federatio), 53
Nara park, 11, 90, 97, 99
Nashiki Sajirō, 175
National Defense Security Law, 74, 170–71, 184–88, 192
Nationalism, 193; Chinese, 3, 33, 36–39, 40ff, 42–49, 112, 131–32
Nazi Party, 60, 96, 120f, 171; in Japan, 11, 140, 143, 161
Nehru, Jawaharlal, 60, 63
New Man's Association (*Shinjinkai*), 9, 29–32
New Order in East Asia (Tōa Shinchitsujo), *see* East Asian Cooperative Body
New Structure Movement (Shin Taisei Undō), 6f, 116, 120–21
Niedermayer, Colonel Oskar Ritter von, 156
Nineteenth Route Army, Chinese, 10, 81
Nishida Kitarō, 27, 118
Nishizato Tatsuo, 57–58
Nishizawa Ryūji, 223ff
Noble, Dr. H. T., 209, 253
Nomon-Han Incident, 105, 149–52
Nomura Kita, *see* Ozaki Kita
Noro Eitarō, 88, 134
Northern Expedition, 45
Nosaka Sanzō, 15, 204, 218f, 221–26 *passim*
Noulens Incident, 61, 64, 134

Ogata Taketora, 99
Ōhara Social Problems Research Institute, 37–38, 89, 232
Ōhashi Hideo, 108, 181–82, 184
Okada Bunkichi, 223
Okinawa, 92–93
Ōmori Yoshitarō, 32
On Chinese Society and Economy, 3f, 131f, 197
On Modern China, 3, 131–32
Ōnishi Itsuki, 99f
Onna hitori daichi o yuku, 62, 100. *See also Daughter of Earth*
"Oriental despotism," 131, 197
Ōsugi Sakae, 29
Ōtsuka Kinnosuke, 88
Ott, General Eugen, 16, 123, 140–45, 148, 161, 163–64, 180f
Ōuchi Hyōe, 31–32, 38
Ōyama Ikuo, 31
Ozaki Eiko, 2, 25, 35–37, 66, 86–87, 131; during Ozaki's trial, 135, 189–90, 194–99; postwar activities, 201, 204–7
Ozaki Honami, 21, 35
Ozaki Hotsuki, 25n, 98, 207–8, 210–14, 220, 223, 225

Ozaki Hotsuma, 21–25
Ozaki Hotsumi: prison letters, 2, 25, 131, 189–90, 193–98, 201–3; and the New Structure Movement, 6, 120–21, 125, 129–31, 192; and the East Asian Co-operative Body, 7–8, 118–20, 128–29, 191; as a *gisō tenkōsha*, 18–19, 215; childhood and education, 23–33; and Marxism, 30–32, 34, 38–39, 193; influenced by Chinese revolution, 33, 36–42 *passim*, 49, 51, 84–87; as a news-paperman, 33–35; marriage, 35–37; in Shanghai, 40–41, 46, 81–83; and Chinese left-wing writers, 51–54; and Smedley, 61–63; and Sorge in Shanghai, 67, 77–81; and Kawai Teikichi, 79–80, 90, 109–10, 212; writings on China, 101, 131–32, 173–74; espionage work of, 105, 126–28, 141, 147, 150, 152–59; and Konoye cabinet, 124–25; and South Manchurian Railroad, 136–39, 145, 157–58, 218; advocates "Southern Advance," 160–62; prosecution of, 188–96. *See also Asahi shimbun*; Sorge, Richard; *Tenkōsho*; Tokkō
———, aliases: Otto, 2, 84, 101; Shirakawa Jirō, 21, 53f, 62, 100; Kusano Genkichi, 34; Ou Tso-ch'i, 53f
Ozaki Hotsumi Biography Compilation Committee, 205–8, 210, 213f
Ozaki Kita, 21, 24–25
Ozaki-Matsumoto Anti-Fascist Memorial Meeting, 205–6
Ozaki Matsutarō, 24
Ozaki Shōtarō, 82
Ozaki Yōko, 10, 66, 86–87, 175, 190, 198, 204ff

Pacific War, *see* World War II
Pai Chung-hsi, 132
Peace Preservation Law, 110f, 134, 170, 173, 189, 194, 203, 218, 244; and the Sorge case, 74, 184ff, 192
P'eng K'ang, 52
P'eng Te-huai, 64
Petersdorf, Lieutenant Colonel Fritz von, 145
Photography, 92, 149, 162f, 169. *See also* Espionage, techniques of
Piatnitskii, O. A., 68, 72, 95
Pravda, 142
Proletarian Youth News (Musan seinen shimbun), 58

Quigley, Harold, 186–87

Radek, Karl, 95, 142
Radio, 106, 162, 164–67. *See also* "Wiesbaden"; Espionage, techniques of

Red Army, Soviet, 161; Department Four (Intelligence), 3, 10, 12, 68, 74–75, 87, 92, 95–97, 182–85, 213; Moscow Radio School, 95, 103f

Red Flag, see Akahata

Rengō Tsūshin, news agency, 51, 81

Rickert, Heinrich, 26, 118

Ritgen, Wilhelm von, 171

Rōdō Hyōgikai, labor federation, 34, 39

Roosevelt, Franklin D., 158

Rote Kapelle, 159

Roy, M. N., 95n

Rōyama Masamichi, 18, 114–15, 118, 126

Russo-German War, 152, 154–62, 167

Russo-Japanese Non-Aggression Pact, 11, 139, 154–55, 159, 185

Ryū Shintarō, 18, 38, 115, 126, 214

Saionji Kinkazu, 2, 14f, 132f, 138, 154, 204n; and Breakfast Society, 113, 125f; and Sorge case, 153, 157–58, 180, 185, 194, 197, 199

Sano Manabu, 28, 189, 197

Sansom, Sir George, 107

Sassa Hiroo, 115, 121, 126

Satō Tsuji, 193

Schellenberg, Walter, 12, 14, 171–72, 179f

Schol, Lieutenant Colonel, 148, 156

Sekai Hyōron (World Review) Publishers, 202, 208

Sekiguchi Kihachirō, 175

Shakee-Shameen Massacre, 44

Shanghai, 9ff, 16f, 25, 40–61, 103–5, 163; Incident (1932), 10, 49, 80–81, 84–86, 112; Municipal Council, 44–45, 80

Shanghai Weekly News (Shanghai shū-hō), 58, 79

Shen Tuan-hsien, 52

Shida Shigeo, 176, 223–25

Shiga Yoshio, 29, 176, 204f, 210, 218–22, 256

Shigemitsu Mamoru, 14, 116, 147

Shiino Etsurō, 223, 256

Shin Taisei Undō (New Structure Movement), 6f, 116, 120–21

Shina shakai keizai ron, 3f, 131f, 197

Shinjinkai (New Man's Association), 9, 29–32

Shinoda Hideo, 194

Shinozuka Torao, 110

Shintō, 24, 195

Shirai Yukikara, 235

Shōwa Academy (Shōwa Juku), 132–33, 174

Shōwa Research Association (Shōwa Kenkyū Kai), 7, 18, 50, 114–22, 173f, 189

Sian Incident, 15f, 64, 121

Siberia, 11, 26, 64, 103, 159ff

Skidmore College, 65

Smedley, Agnes, 54, 63–65, 208; and Ozaki, 10, 36, 61–63, 84–85, 100, 193, 236; and Sorge ring, 64–67, 80, 89–90, 211–12. *See also Daughter of Earth*; Willoughby, General Charles A.

Sōda Kiichirō, 26

Sorge, Christiane, 75–76

Sorge, Friedrich Albert, 12, 69

Sorge, Richard, 1, 4, 11–13, 69–72, 76; as a German spy, 12, 146, 171–73; and Smedley, 60, 64, 66–67; and Ozaki in Shanghai, 67, 78–82, 85–86, 193; and Department Four, 68, 74–75, 101–2, 161, 184–86; and Comintern, 72–74; and Ozaki in Japan, 87, 90–91, 97–99, 123; as leader of ring, 105–6; espionage work in Japan, 140–43, 145–52, 154–59; political influence of, 141–45, 160–62; private research of, 144–45, 246; prosecution of, 181–88; last words of, 214n

———, aliases: Johnson, 9, 66–67, 87; R. Sonter, 76

Sorge spy ring, 1, 11, 65–66, 81–83, 196–97, 201; prosecution of, 74–75; exposure of, 94, 169–79, 207; organization of, 105–7; couriers of, 107–8; communications of, 162–68; documents concerning, 152, 205, 209, 212; fictionalized accounts of, 214, 254

South Manchurian Railroad, 51, 105, 112, 185; Investigation Department, 1, 17, 56, 136–39, 169, 173–77 *passim*. *See also* Kwantung Army; Ozaki Hotsumi, and South Manchurian Railroad

"Southern Advance," 6, 154, 157–62, 179. *See also* Russo-German War; World War II

Soviet Communist Party, 72

Soziologische Magazin, 66

Spain, 10, 68n

Spartacus League, 71

Stalin, Joseph, 75, 91, 149, 160, 220f

Stein, Günther, 107–9, 163f

Sun Society (T'ai-yang She), 53

Sun Yat-sen, 42, 50, 55, 132ff

Sung Che-yüan, 101

SCAP (Supreme Commander for the Allied Powers), 200f, 207, 212, 218, 221, 225f; report on Sorge case, 3, 15, 65, 108, 182, 209–11, 213

Suzuki Bunshirō, 34

Tachibana Shiraki, 17, 115

Tägliche Rundschau, 96

Taihoku Middle School, 23, 25

Taira Teizō, 18, 115, 126, 133, 197
Taisei Yokusan Kai, *see* Imperial Rule Assistance Association
Taiwan, 21–25, 93, 203, 207
Taiwan nichi-nichi shimpō, 22f
Takada Tadashi, 179, 188, 192ff
Takagi Yasaka, 99
Takahashi Yosuke, 190
Takakura Teru, 119, 223
Takane Yoshisaburō, 189–90
Takano Iwasaburō, 37–38, 89
Takenaka Tsunesaburō, 223
Takeuchi Kintarō, 6, 194, 198, 204n
Takikawa Incident, 88, 117
Tama Cemetery, 14, 113, 204f
Tamazawa Mitsusaburō, 190
T'ao Ching-sun, 52–54
Teidai (Tokyo Imperial University), 9, 23, 26–32, 38, 131
Tenkō (conversion), 40, 170, 187–90, 203–4
Tenkōsha (converts), 18, 117
Tenkōsho (documents of conversion), Ozaki's, 86–87, 98–99, 188–89, 192–96, 203–4
Textile mills, Shanghai, 42–47
Third International, *see* Comintern
Ting Ling, 62
Tōa Dōbun Shoin Daigaku (East Asia Common Script University), 17, 51, 55–58, 67, 234–35
Tōa Mondai Chōsa Kai, *see Asahi shimbun*
Tōjō Hideki, 159, 179
Tokkō (Special Higher Police), 8, 18, 89, 106, 110, 210, 212, 230, 244; and investigation of Sorge ring, 14, 136, 165–67, 169, 174–79; rivalry with Kempei, 74, 172–73
Tokuda Kyūichi, 27, 200, 204, 210, 218–26, 255
Tokumu Kikan (Special Affairs Departments), Japanese Army, 82, 109n
Tokyo Dai-Ichi Kōtō Gakkō, *see* Ichikō
Tokyo District Criminal Court, 182–83, 187–88, 192
Tokyo Metropolitan Police Agency, 175
Tolischus, Otto, 182, 230
Transocean News Agency, 140
Treason, 88, 162, 169
True Story of Ah Q, The, 9, 54, 234
Tsuge Hideomi, 204
Tsurumi Shunsuke, 198, 215
Twenty-One Demands, 43

Uesugi Shinkichi, 27, 32
Union of Free Jurists (Jiyū Hōsō Dan), 175–76

U.S.S.R., 1, 4ff, 86, 91, 152f, 191, 196, 222
United States Communist Party, 60, 90, 94, 177f
United States–Japanese negotiations (1941), 126, 152, 158, 179
United States War Department, Military Intelligence Division, 209ff
Uritskii, General M. S., 68n, 90–91, 101–2
Ushiba Tomohiko, 18, 26, 113, 123–26, 160f, 180
Utsuri-yuku Shina (Changing China), 101

Vasiliev, General, 145
Vladivostok, 14, 106, 146, 165
Volga-German Autonomous Soviet Socialist Republic, 104–5, 166
Voroshilov, K., 91, 105, 149
Voukelitch, Branko de, 91–92, 95, 97, 163, 168, 181ff, 199, 248; espionage by, 105, 143, 150–51, 165
Voukelitch, Edith de, 92, 163, 165f, 168
Vowinckel, Kurt, 96

Wallenius, Anna, *see* Clausen, Anna
Wallenius, General Kurt, 103
Wang Ching-wei, 129, 133–34, 138, 152–53. *See also under* Nanking government
Wang Hsüeh-wen, 57
Waseda University, 28f, 31, 35, 81
Watanabe Sahei, 126
Weimar Republic, 141
Wenneker, Captain Paul W., 142
White Terror, 10, 45–46, 54, 61
Wiedemeyer, Irene, 60–61, 85
"Wiesbaden," 11, 13, 106, 139, 148, 159, 165
Willoughby, General Charles A., 3, 17, 19, 108, 181; research of, 61n, 68n, 95n, 102n, 151n, 238–39; and Agnes Smedley, 65–66, 100, 211–12; and Kawai Teikichi, 79, 211–13
Windelband, Wilhelm, 26
Wittfogel, Karl A., 33n
World War I, 4, 25, 69–70, 103, 140, 191; social unrest following, 26–28
World War II, 5, 11, 149, 191. *See also* Russo-German War; "Southern Advance"
Wu Shao-kuo, 60
Wuch'ang Rebellion, 24

Yabe Teiji, 115f
Yamakami Masayoshi, 51, 58, 81, 234
Yamana Masazane, 147
Yamasaki Ken, 30–31, 85n, 204f
Yang Liu-ch'ing, 57, 79

Yangtzepoo, 49
Yen Hsi-shan, 132
Yin Ju-keng, 101
Yomiuri shimbun, 118, 201
Yosemite Conference, *see* Institute of Pacific Relations
Yoshikawa Mitsusada, 149, 173, 181ff, 187–88, 214n

Yoshin (preliminary trial), 186–87, 189–90
Yü Ta-fu, 52, 54

Zeitgeist Bookstore, 9, 60–61, 66, 235
Zeitschrift für Geopolitik, 12f, 96, 142
Zen Buddhism, 190, 195, 198
Zhukov, Marshal G. K., 149f